Pitirim A. Sorokin

Pitirim Sorokin in 1917 as secretary to Prime Minister Kerensky.

Pitirim A. Sorokin

AN INTELLECTUAL BIOGRAPHY

Barry V. Johnston

University Press of Kansas

Documents cited are by permission of the Harvard University Archives; Dr. Sergei P. Sorokin; the Vassar Archives; Library of Congress; and the Lilly Endowment Archives.

Portions of text from "Sorokin and Parsons at Harvard: Institutional Conflict and the Rise of a Hegemonic Tradition" (22:107–127) and "Pitirim Sorokin and the American Sociological Association: The Politics of a Professional Society" (23:103–122) are reprinted here by permission of the *Journal of the History of the Behavioral Sciences.*

Photographs were provided courtesy of Dr. Sergei P. Sorokin and are reproduced here with his permission.

Published by the University Press of Kansas (Lawrence, Kansas 66049), which was organized by the Kansas Board of Regents and is operated and funded by Emporia State University, Fort Hays State University, Kansas State University, Pittsburg State University, the University of Kansas, and Wichita State University

Library of Congress Cataloging-in-Publication Data

Johnston, Barry V.
    Pitirim A. Sorokin : an intellectual biography / Barry V. Johnston.
      p. cm.
    Includes bibliographical references and index.
    ISBN 0-7006-0736-6 (alk. paper)
    1. Sorokin, Pitirim Aleksandrovich, 1889–1968. 2. Sociologists–United States–Biography. 3. Sociology–United States–History. I. Title.
HM22.U6S638 1996
301'.092–dc20
[B]

95-43645

British Library Cataloguing in Publication Data is available.

Printed in the United States of America

10 9 8 7 6 5 4 3 2 1

The paper used in this publication meets the minimum requirements of the American National Standard for Permanence of Paper for Printed Library Materials Z39.48-1984.

To Blake, Ian, and Caitlin
with boundless love

Contents

Preface

This work originates from a casual conversation at Duke University between Edward A. Tiryakian and members of his 1983 National Endowment for the Humanities Seminar, "Great Schools and the Development of Modern Sociology." In passing, Tiryakian observed that Pitirim Sorokin and Talcott Parsons were men of equal brilliance but Parsons founded a major sociological tradition while Sorokin left no school or intellectual stamp on the discipline. Although not anticipated then, this comment prompted the long process of research, reading, and interviews that resulted in this book.

My interest in Sorokin grew slowly, haunted by a shard of conversation from graduate school, where my classmates rejected any significant position for him in the lineage of important contributors to the rise of American sociology. Undeterred, but cautious, I completed the seminar paper that eventually led to "Sorokin and Parsons at Harvard: Institutional Conflict and the Rise of a Hegemonic Tradition," published in 1986. By then I had done my first deep search into the archives at the University of Saskatchewan and Harvard, interviewed several of Sorokin's former students and colleagues, and developed a synoptic table of contents for the manuscript *Pitirim A. Sorokin*.

Looking at the manuscript's penultimate incarnation last night, I asked myself what makes it distinctive and timely. The distinctive features are tied to three qualities: the powerful persona of Pitirim A. Sorokin; the quality of evidence used to tell the story; and its significance for history and theory in sociology.

Sorokin was one of sociology's most stimulating and controversial statesmen. In a six-decade career his works opened new fields and broadened traditional sociological concerns. Sorokin crafted major contributions to the study of social mobility, war and revolution, altruism, social change, rural sociology, the sociology of science and knowledge, and sociological theory.

Don Martindale (1972) wrote that by 1963 Sorokin was the most widely published and translated sociologist in history. More importantly, the case for Sorokin is made not by the number of his publications but by their significance. *Social Mobility, Contemporary Sociological Theories, Principles of Rural-Urban Sociology*, and *A Systematic Source Book in Rural Sociology* all defined their fields at the time. On the basis of these books and Sorokin's scientific promise, Abbott Lawrence Lowell named him the founding chairman of Harvard's Department of Sociology.

Once Sorokin was settled in Cambridge, his concerns led him to distant intellectual frontiers. His major Harvard works broke with standard American sociology, explored questionable fields (e.g., altruism and the philosophy of history), and bitingly criticized the canon of sociological scientism. For this heresy Sorokin saw his books condemned and his works pushed to the periphery of a discipline hungry for legitimacy and acceptance as a science.

Sorokin's ostracism resulted not so much from what he said but from how he delivered the message. With great energy and Russian fervor he ridiculed, taunted, or angered at least two generations of American sociologists. Many retaliated with a silence in their classrooms and scholarship that removed him from serious consideration by their generation and the succeeding one. This volume breaks that silence and invites today's sociologists and their students to judge Sorokin's work unbiased by the politics, prejudice, and resentments of the past.

A scholar's work must stand on its merits, and reading Sorokin is often surprising! He has imaginative and creative ways of testing hypotheses. He provides useful insights into key sociological concerns. He develops a body of sociological concepts that are clear and helpful tools for thinking about social structure and change. His work reflects a surprisingly organized, though prolix, approach to social order, change, modernity, and social improvement. He also had a fundamentally sound understanding of what sociology is about, one which today's students and faculty will find helpful in a period of theoretical eclecticism. Lewis Coser observed (1977:508) that Sorokin paid the price for his intellectual arrogance, eccentricities, and self-righteousness. This volume makes possible a balanced reconsideration, in which his work can be judged for its contributions rather than ignored for the imperfections of his personality or the politics of his time.

Access to archival documents at Harvard, Sorokin's papers at the University of Saskatchewan, the Records of the American Sociological Association at the Library of Congress, and the Eli Lilly–Harvard Center for Creative Altruism material at the Lilly Endowment make possible the accounts of significant events heretofore known only to a few. Among them are the following:

The origin and development of the Harvard Department of Sociology, 1930–44

The rise of the Department of Social Relations at Harvard, 1944–46

New insights into the conflict between Parsons and Sorokin

The account of Sorokin's election to the presidency of the American Sociological Association, the first successful write-in campaign for that office

A detailed history of the Harvard Center for Creative Altruism, a chapter missing in our study of altruism, emotions, and prosocial behaviors

These records also give new insights into Sorokin and his career, and balance his autobiographies *Leaves from a Russian Diary* (1924) and *A Long Journey* (1963), where the reader is dependent on Sorokin to present Sorokin. This intellectual biography offers new information, benefits from more psychological and sociological distance, and is, I believe, free from hagiography.

Throughout the book I rely on three sources of information: the public records of scholarship and publication, interviews with informed observers and participants in the Sorokinian journey, and archival documents. These form the basis for my narrative on Sorokin as sociologist. I depart from that format once, in the first chapter, to tell the story of Sorokin's early life through a flashback technique. I did this for two reasons. First, I worried that those familiar with Sorokin would lose enthusiasm for reading further upon encountering once again the widely known and often mechanically told events of his youth. Second, I could engage the seasoned, as well as the new, reader with Sorokin's early journey through a more creatively told yet factually driven account of a truly engaging period in his life. Thus I ask for a small indulgence in the retelling of this often-told tale.

Finally, the distinctive character of the volume is also reflected in the intertwining of history and theory. As Robert Merton (1980:xi) has noted, a substantial amount of knowledge in any scientific field is transmitted from its past and becomes, in diverse ways, the cognitive basis for new departures of thought. The reconsideration of Sorokin adds a valuable source of ideas for new approaches to current sociological concerns such as problems in the sociology of knowledge and science, social change, altruism, the sociology of emotions, and sociological theory. Critical exploration of Sorokin's work will help others to see with new eyes issues with which they presently wrestle. His work provides both stimulus and irritant, provoking new directions of thought and research. This is clearly the contribution of a cacophonic pioneer.

I have been tempted at times to describe my engagement with this book by using a line from A. E. Housman: "Out of a stem that scored the hand I wrung it in a weary land." I do so now because I know that this is only part of the story and not the most meaningful part. Along the way there were key experiences with wonderful people: A snowy day spent in Denver with Wilbert Moore. Days, weeks, and months of sorting letters, memoranda, notes, lectures, and drafts of articles carefully stored under the stewardship of Clark Elliott at Harvard, Shirley Martin in Saskatoon, and other archivists from Indiana to New York and Washington, D.C. The openness and hospitality of Dr. Sergei Sorokin at the family home in Winchester, along with the wonderful music and memories that he shared. Long conversations and correspondence with Robert Bierstedt, O. D. Duncan, George Homans, Robin Williams, Edgar Schuler, C. A. Anderson, Lawrence T. Nichols, and Palmer Talbutt added depth and energy to the book. For the kindness, consideration, and scholarship of these and many others I will remain long indebted. My final and deepest acknowledgement of scholarly debt is due Robert K. Merton. As I move through the Symplegades of the Mathew Effect on one side and honest debt on the other, I acknowledge my gratitude and appreciation.

I am also grateful for the support of many institutions and their leaders: the National Endowment for the Humanities, Indiana University Northwest, the Institute for Advanced Study and University Research Operations Committee at Bloomington, Kenneth Gros Louis, Lloyd Rowe, and Peggy Gordon Elliott have been particularly helpful. The patience and encouragement of Michael Briggs of the University Press of Kansas saw me through many trying times. I am grateful to him for his faith in this book and its author. Great patience also characterizes Barbara Bradfield and Leona M. Lashenik, whose typing skills and good humor carried me through a mountain of drafts and rewrites. I will long appreciate and remember their kindness, grace, and helpfulness.

To my intimate companions on this journey, Paula, Blake, Ian, and Caitlin, I am forever grateful.

1

The Journey

THE YOUNG MAN STANDING at the rail of the *Martha Washington* looked intently through the thin mist of the Adriatic. His mind was traveling past the Yugoslavian coastline, through Hungary, Czechoslovakia, and Poland. He visualized the vast expanse of Russia, the cities of Petrograd and Moscow, and his mind's eye came to rest on the homelands of the Komi. It was a searching look over a war-torn land and the vicissitudes of his early life. Turning, Sorokin moved to a more comfortable vantage point on a small deck bench. Drawing his wool coat across his shoulders, he thought of Prague and Elena. They had been married six and a half years earlier, in the middle of the revolution's agony. The crosscurrents of events in Petrograd had the city in disorder, and their wedding celebration became a hasty half-hour lunch. These musings, the water, and the sky brought back the turbulence and anxieties of Petrograd in 1917. It was a city just past the first blushes of revolutionary success. The tyranny of the czarist regime was waning, and the fearsome turmoil of the future had yet to appear. The city and country were divided by political factions struggling for supremacy. The former leaders of the Duma, who then acted as a temporary government, were being challenged by growing soviets of workmen and soldiers. Citizens walked the streets with banners declaring "Long Life to the Revolution!" "The Peasants to the Plow, the Workers to the Looms and Presses, the Soldiers to the Trenches! We, the Free People of Russia, Will Defend the Country and the Revolution."[1] Crowds glorifying the rebellion and chanting slogans of freedom were everywhere. An enterprising lady of the evening put new meaning to the dictum "Let the proletarians of all countries unite. . . . Come home with me."[2]

However, the peasants were not in the fields, workers spent their days in political meetings, and regiments refused to report to the front. The euphoric period of revolutionary triumph was giving way to turmoil and mob rule. These had been trying times for Sorokin, who was a leader of the Social Revolutionary Party. The Social Revolutionists in Petrograd were divided. He had led the right-wing faithful and edited their newspaper, *The Will of the People*. As party fought against party and member against member, the uncertainties over Russia's fate increased among the intelligentsia. With

1

Lenin's arrival from Germany a new and potent strain was placed on the tenuous order in Petrograd.

As the silent figure continued gazing toward his lost homeland, the confrontations between the forces of the Right, the Bolsheviks, the Internationalists, and the leftist Social Revolutionaries reverberated through his mind. In great sweeps from June through December of 1917, power ebbed and flowed among these camps. Winning then losing, fearful and hungry, confrontation built on confrontation. Finally, on 25 October, Lenin carried out his coup.[3] With bold strokes he took control of Petrograd's major transportation and communication networks, arrested a majority of the officials in Kerensky's provisional government, and seized the banks. Having accomplished this, he declared a Bolshevik victory for the people.

The rapidity of change was staggering. Possessing power, the Bolsheviks shook Russia like an angry dog. Private lands were seized from the church and aristocracy, and given to peasant soviets for administration or redistribution. Industrial workers took control of the manufacturing, financial, and commercial enterprises. A state monopoly on banking followed the nationalization of industry. Codes limiting work to eight hours a day and protecting the rights of workers were passed. The church's authority was undermined in marriage, divorce, and education. As in the French Revolution, class distinctions were abolished and a strict separation of church and state imposed. In order to prevent a German invasion, the Bolsheviks also pushed for peace. Though not without difficulties, they negotiated with Germany and reluctantly accepted the Treaty of Brest Litovsk. These changes whipped over Russia like a tornado. The old institutions had crumbled, and new ones were not yet strong enough to support order. The disarray set the stage for civil war, brutality, and wide-scale starvation. As Sorokin sat on the bench, the winds from the Adriatic brought memories of the hunger etched on Elena's face, of angry mobs looking for bread where there was none. The taste of cakes made from potato skins and dinners of half a sausage, preserved peaches, and tea with sugar filled his mouth, and he recalled how revolution "makes people more modest in their appetites and desires."[4]

Shortly after the October Revolution, elections were held for the Constituent Assembly.[5] Though opposed, the Bolsheviks were not able to stop them. The people would now speak. Would they support Lenin's new direction or seek more moderate mechanisms of bringing Russia out of traditionalism? Sorokin recalled how his heart had soared at the results. The Bolsheviks were defeated, and the Constituent Assembly was largely made up of Kerensky's Constitutional Democrats, Social Revolutionaries, and Mensheviks. Sorokin had been elected to membership by over 90 percent of the voters from the Vologda Province. Yet he knew that Lenin, Trotsky, and the others would not accept the election. As a new deputy he was now legally free from arrest. He could stop the cat-and-mouse game he had been playing with Lenin's police force, the "Chekha." However, the law was one thing, the power of the Bolsheviks another. Therefore, he was not surprised when he was arrested on 2 January 1918. They had charged him with attempting to assassinate Lenin and ordered his execution.

Childhood's Trials

Pitirim Alexandrovich Sorokin was born on 21 January 1889 in the small village of Turya. Located in the Vologda Province of northern Russia, it was part of the Komi homelands. His Russian father, Alexander Prokopievitch Sorokin, had met and married his Komi mother while working in her village. Alexander was a craftsman, a maker of icons and master of ornamental works in gold and silver. His work kept him moving as he repaired and restored the small Orthodox churches in one village, then another. Pitirim recalled him as a loving and tender man who occasionally was transformed by bouts of alcoholism. His father was also a proud man, proud of his skills and of his three sons: Vassiliy, Pitirim, and Prokopiy.

In the winter of 1892, while his father was away looking for work, Pitirim's mother died. Her death was the first image etched on his memory. A smell of birch had filled the room as Vassiliy and a woman whispered over his mother's still figure. Something in their posture alarmed the three-year-old, and a feeling of irreparable loss gripped him. The cold of the room, the shadows moving across the floor, and the withdrawn, shocked look on his brother's face reinforced his feeling of catastrophe. He knew his life had changed but was at a loss to explain how. Sitting there, hugging his knees to his chest, he had started to cry.

The funeral marked the first change in a life that would be shaped by sudden changes. It was the end of the family's unity. In a few days Prokopiy, the youngest, would go to live with Aunt Annisya and Uncle Vassiliy. The rest of the Sorokins would leave the village of Kokvitzy and begin their search for work. The Orthodox funeral ritual had signaled an end and a beginning.

The Komi region was a rich, beautiful land.[6] In the eyes of a boy the vast expanses of magnificent forests stretched to the ends of Russia. Clear, crisp rivers were full of the finest salmon, and animals of all kinds moved through the pine forests. With the snows a magnificent winterland was created that captured the mind with its beauty and could terrify the soul with its openness. Komi folklore was rich with spirits of the forest, lakes, skies, winds, and night. A people close to nature, they were steeped in a naturalistic knowledge of the woods and its creatures. Layered on top was the transcendent mythology of the supernatural. Not only the elusive spirits of mountain and forest but the deeply moving rituals of the of the Orthodox Church filled their lives.

For the Sorokins, the life of itinerant artisans was one of beauty and hardships. They were often cold and hungry as they traveled in search of work. A week in one village, two months in the next, then on again to still another hamlet. If times were good, they rented a peasant's cart and labor to move them. When things were hard, they packed their tools and, with a handful or more of bread, set out on the quest. Nights were spent in the forest or fields, huddled together around fires to keep off the cold and fears that came with the night.

Pitirim, barely five, and Vassiliy, almost nine, often lived with hunger and the anxieties of unemployment. Alexander carried fatherhood's burden squarely and looked long and hard for their next job and roof. But for him life possessed a loneliness that had deepened with the death of his wife. There were times when it combined with the poverty and uncertainty to produce a depression from which his only escape was alcohol. Then, dominated by vodka, Alexander became delusional and had fits of delirium tremens.[7] Ghosts and devils would leap at him from the fires, and he would cry in loneliness and pain over the loss of his wife. His children watched with fear and compassion. When he became angry and violent, they fled or cowered and would rest easier when he lapsed into unconsciousness. In time intoxication gave way to periods of violent psychosis. On one occasion a delusional Alexander hit Vassiliy in the shoulder with a hammer, then struck Pitirim in the mouth. For Vassiliy the pain and numbness passed in a few days, but Pitirim's upper lip for years remained slightly misshapen. The hammer produced more than pain; it shattered the family. The next day the boys left their father. While they worked in one part of the region, Alexander roamed another. Their paths never again crossed. A year or so later they learned of Alexander's death. Because news traveled slowly, the boys heard only after the funeral. Pitirim was then ten, Vassiliy fourteen.

The *Martha Washington* left the Adriatic, moved to the Ionian, and then into the Mediterranean Sea. During the past few days she had steered steadily from Pátrai to Tunis toward Spain and the Strait of Gibraltar. The journey marked another beginning and end. As Sorokin moved about the ship, his mind kept returning to the world he was leaving behind.

While difficult, his boyhood had not been filled only with friendless misfortune. There were delightful periods spent with Aunt Anissya and her husband, the redheaded Vassiliy. This man of the forest was both trapper and peasant. Pitirim spent many happy days working on their farm and learning the ways of the forest from his uncle. Vassiliy had a vast knowledge of nature, magic, and folklore. Many people considered him tun or shaman because of his osteopathic gifts.[8] He enjoyed teaching the boys about nature and the mysterious forces of the supernatural that were intertwined with the natural rhythms of the earth.

There were also other types of learning stimulated by the village clergy, medical practitioners, teachers, and nimble-minded peers. Pitirim could not recall how he had learned the three Rs. Perhaps it was from his father, who had also taught them his craft and the basic outlines of the Orthodox faith, or perhaps from the priests for whom they worked and in whose company they spent hours and days, or perhaps from other children or the old woman in Rymia who taught children in her home. The life of the mind was an integral element of the villages. The Komi were bilingual and highly literate. Having learned to read, Pitirim expanded his knowledge through a voracious study of the Russian classics. Turgenev, Gogol, Tolstoy, Pushkin, and Dostoevski were augmented with translations of Twain and Dickens. Lessons and ideas from these books were debated and discussed with the literati of the towns and villages.

While working in Gam, Pitirim and Vassiliy learned that entrance examinations were being given for the new advanced grade school. On listening to the public examinations, Pitirim decided to compete. He did well, and won a full scholarship for the academic year. Later, after proving himself the best student in the school, his scholarship was extended for a three-year period. In Gam, Sorokin started on the path toward scholarly distinction. There he was stimulated by teachers, priests, and fellow students to master broader bases of literature, feel comfortable with conflicting ideas, and integrate his own view of the world.

Religion was an important element in this emerging worldview. All his life Pitirim had earned a living around churches and priests. His hands had formed icons and rizas, and there were daily dialogues with clergy. However, religion was not just Orthodox doctrine, it included the pagan Komi mythology. Pitirim's aesthetic sense and spirituality were formed by these influences. Orthodox ceremonies stimulated his love of music and gave him profound insights into the emotional and social power of ritual. As an acolyte and later a teacher for other peasants, he held values that were strongly influenced by the message and rites of the church. The spirits of nature came together with those of the Deity and the saints to forge a sensitivity to phenomena that transcended science and the senses. For this young man, knowing was not only an empirically conscious process but one of superconsciousness as well. Human reality was not confined to the material senses. There were deeper, more mysterious, truths, and they were found in the realm of spiritual life.[9]

Pitirim probed the world from many perspectives, searching for the mystical and material ties that made life a unity. While secular studies trained his mind, the drama of the Mass, Crucifixion, Resurrection, and Redemption disciplined his spirit. These mysteries, along with the Sermon on the Mount and the Christian Beatitudes, were moral guides for the rest of his life.[10] Religion and education integrated and crystallized his philosophy deeper than he could then know. They were among the potent forces that shaped his personality. But this ordered and harmonious picture of the world would be shaken by his later experiences, the eruption of the Russo-Japanese War, and the 1905 Revolution.[11]

Political Awakening and Intellectual Growth

Graduation from the Gam school was followed by a scholarship to the Khrenovo Teachers' Seminary in the Kostroma Province. This Russian Orthodox institution trained teachers for the synod's elementary schools. Pitirim arrived there in homespun clothes, rough mannered and politically childlike—a country bumpkin. However, the town had its effects, and a callow teenager was transformed into a fiery revolutionary. At Khrenovo Pitirim increasingly questioned czarist rule and learned alternatives to monarchy. He became aware of new places, different social conditions, and new ideas. Observing the autocracy's failures in the towns was followed by dialogues with townspeople seeking change. He became conscious of political parties, learned their ideologies, and came to identify with the Social Revolutionaries.[12] His waning support for the monarchy was replaced by democratic and socialistic ideologies. Soon he became a loud voice for the anticzarist revolution and a leader of the Social Revolutionary Party at school and in the surrounding areas. Pitirim was now sixteen years old. After two years of deepening political activism he would celebrate his eighteenth birthday in a czarist jail. He was arrested in December 1906 and spent four months as a political prisoner. To his surprise, he was given many freedoms and was in constant dialogue with other political prisoners. Having access to books, he read the political works of Mikhailovsky, Lavrov, Marx, Engels, Bakunin, Kropotkin, Plekhanov, and Lenin, along with the evolutionary writings of Darwin and Spencer. He discussed their ideas with fellow prisoners in a common search for an ideological foundation for the revolution. Pitirim was released in early 1907. Having been expelled from school and with no possibilities for work, he became an itinerant revolutionary organizer.

Leaving Kostroma Province, Pitirim moved to the Volga region and, under the code name Comrade Ivan, continued his revolutionary work. He was a passionate and moving speaker who quickly drew a following and the vigilant awareness of the local police. Here the cat-and-mouse game began in earnest as he brought to others the message of revolution and a better world. For three months he evaded the Cossacks and built support for his party. A close call along the Volga convinced him that his situation was too dangerous, and he reluctantly returned to his aunt's farm in Rymia. After two months with Annisya and Prokopiy he left the Komi region for St. Petersburg.[13]

Pitirim began life in St. Petersburg the way immigrants often do: he located friends from home. Arriving "rabbit class" (ticketless) from Vologda, he sought out Pavel Kohovkin, who gave him a place to stay until he found work. Within days Pitirim had a tutoring job and made arrangements for his own education. Lacking a high school (gymnasium) degree, he had to pass an "examination of maturity" to enter the university. The exam required good facility with Latin or Greek, French or German, and mathematics. Most of those without the eight years of gymnasium went to night school. Unfortunately, such schools were expensive, and his earnings from tutoring provided only room and two meals a day. Undeterred, he located Professor K. F. Jakov, "the first Komi man to achieve the distinction of university professor" and a sympathizer with the Social Revolutionary Party.[14] Jakov taught at the Tscherniayevskye Kursy, one of the best night schools in St. Petersburg. This philosopher and novelist was impressed by his Komi kinsman and arranged free admission to the Kursy. A warm friendship developed that lasted until Jakov's death in the 1920s. They worked together on field studies of the Komi, and both would be known for a bullheadedness that led others to undervalue their contributions. In Jakov, Pitirim found a friend, mentor, and perhaps an early role model.

During the first year in St. Petersburg Pitirim walked six miles to and from night school six times a week. These walks gave him a look at the shady side of nightlife in a large city and removed some of his country innocence. His tutoring situation was comfortable enough, and he read widely, thought carefully, and debated his new ideas at the Jakovs' monthly literary soirees. At one of these gatherings he met a beautiful young student from Bestudjeff Women's University. Nine years later she became his wife.

From 1907 until he passed his exams in May 1909, Sorokin grew in depth and breadth. Because he valued intellectual organization and integration, he strove to incorporate his experiences into a coherent worldview. Like a sponge he absorbed philosophy, art, science, politics, economics, ethics, and law. Reading was enriched by visits to museums, galleries, theaters, and symphonies. He met important leaders in science, the arts, critical thought, and politics. Spurning the disorganized mind in which ideas simply "squat side by side," he drove toward consistency and integration of his experiences. After the disintegration of his earlier views at the Teachers' Seminary, he wanted to restore unity to his mental life. But his new system was only half built. The remainder of the scaffolding would be constructed at the Psycho-Neurological Institute and University of St. Petersburg.

With diploma in hand, Sorokin became a student at the Psycho-Neurological Institute. Having decided to study sociology, he chose the institute because the University of St. Petersburg did not offer a sociology program. Furthermore, the institute was livelier, with many students from the peasantry and major scholars teaching the discipline. Particularly distinguished were M. M. Kovalevsky and E. V. de Roberty. Sorokin's year at the institute was intense. Attendance at lectures was not required, so he spent his time reading and thinking about the assigned works. He attended classes only if a professor offered something original and important that had not been published.[15]

His method worked. It allowed him to concentrate on original works and organize a system of notes. When exams came, he did well. Lost time with professors was made up through office discussions. From these talks he became known as a capable and promising scholar. But by the end of the year he left the institute for the university to avoid the czar's military draft.[16] University students were exempted, but not those at the institute. Pitirim entered the university in the spring of 1910. Based on his maturity exam and record at the institute, he was given a full scholarship that paid tuition, fees, and part of his living expenses. He was now free to concentrate on his work and to participate in the political transformations that were shaping Russia.

Sociology was not yet part of the program at the University of St. Petersburg, so Sorokin studied under the Faculty of Law and Economics, which offered several courses that dealt with sociological problems and topics. Continuing to avoid lectures, he began to master the literatures of sociology and law. He focused on Roman, European, Western, and Russian theories of law and read the Russian works in sociology. He later studied Weber, Durkheim, Simmel, Tarde, and Pareto. With these ideas resonating in his mind, it was not surprising that Pitirim started to publish as an undergraduate. He had earlier written for newspapers and popular magazines, but from 1910 to 1914 he published ten scholarly articles and one book.[17] The book brought together his interest in law and sociology under the title *Crime and Punishment, Service and Reward*, published in 1913.

As a student he was strongly influenced by M. M. Kovalevsky, E. V. de Roberty, and V. M. Bekhterev at the institute; and by Leon Petrazhitsky, M. I. Rostovtzeff, Ivan P. Pavlov, and N. O. Lossky at the university. Many of these scholars became lifelong friends who stimulated and supported his drive toward an integrated worldview. Philosophically he was becoming an empirical neopositivist and politically a socialist. His sociology was moving toward a synthesis of Comtean and Spencerian evolutionism modified by Mikhailovsky, Kropotkin, and a few Western sociologists.

It was through de Roberty that Pitirim began to form his sociological perspective. His teacher argued for interaction as the foundation of social behavior and the absolute dependence of psychological facts on social facts. For de Roberty the world was defined in the process of interaction, and through it the characteristics of individuals were shaped. The similarity to Durkheim is obvious. On this Sorokin would observe that, while de Roberty's theories were not as well known as Durkheim's or Simmel's, he had laid out the same ideas earlier and in a more consistent way.[18] De Roberty's insistence on the priority of society led him to focus on the transformation of human animals into civilized beings. Following Aristotle, we were social animals and "without law and justice (and society) would be the worst of all animals." There was no doubt society was logically prior to humanization and should be the fundamental object for understanding humans as social creatures.

De Roberty advocated an evolutionism similar to Comte's. Beginning with analytical thought, his system moved to religion and philosophy, and then on to the higher realm of aesthetic and artistic thought. While all were present in each historical period, one was dominant. For de Roberty, each stage influenced the characteristics of the next. However, because knowledge developed unevenly, he postulated a law of lagging analogous to that of William F. Ogburn. While de Roberty and Comte gave thought the central role in the development of society, they differed on which form was most important. Comte, in Sorokin's view, emphasized the philosophical and religious, while de Roberty emphasized analytical and scientific processes.[19]

Another of Pitirim's teachers, Leon Petrazhitsky, held similar ideas but believed that the basic moral and emotional forces that humanized us were reflected in laws. Unlike mores, laws institutionalized emotions and specified rights and duties. The subject of a duty was *obligated* to perform it, and the subject of a right could *demand* satisfaction. Laws were thus imperative and attributive. They were the foundation of social order, embodied primal human emotions, and when tied to rights and obligations demanded particular forms of behavior. If not followed, they were coercive and forced compliance. If the violator persisted, law removed him from "the field of social life." In this way it was an agent of social control that eliminated the socially unfit.[20]

Petrazhitsky was keenly interested in the social-psychological foundations of law and attempted to ground it in the basic fabric of human nature. In his work Pitirim found an elegant and provocative statement on order and power. Along with his quest for a phenomenology of law, Petrazhitsky also sensitized Sorokin to the role of collective mentalities as forces in civilizational change and alerted him to the theoretical and practical significance of altruism in human behavior.[21]

Maksim M. Kovalevsky, who had trained in law at the University of Kharkov, also influenced Sorokin. He taught law at the University of St. Petersburg and was the founding chairman of sociology at the Psycho-Neurological Institute. As an undergraduate, Pitirim was Kovalevsky's research assistant and secretary. Kovalevsky was a Comtean positivist who believed in progress and evolution. Sociology should be a policy science guiding the orderly implementation of change. In Kovalevsky, Pitirim saw how the disciplined mind moved from the study of ethnographic data to the genesis of institutions, and on to broad patterns of historical change.[22] From him he also learned to eschew theories based on single-variable interpretations of history or other social phenomena. Here, Kovalevsky argued, "Sociology will gain measurably if the effort to find a first cause is eliminated from its immediate problems and if it limits itself . . . to showing the simultaneous and parallel actions and reactions of many causes."[23]

Though the professor and the student differed in their politics, they saw a vital role for sociology in times of revolution and rapid change. Kovalevsky supported Sorokin's skepticism about historical Marxism, and both favored a more complex theory of history, with ideas playing the central role. The scholar showed the neophyte how to deal with complexity, avoid oversimplification, and approach the relationship between people's cultural mentalities and their social structures. Pitirim learned to recognize the dependence of sociology on history; to overcome timidity in searching for large-scale historical generalizations; to utilize ethnographic materials and the comparative historical method;

to seek a role for sociology in the politics of society; and to maintain a sensitivity to the relationship between knowledge, worldview, and social organization.[24]

Sorokin did not escape the influences of the Russian behaviorists, particularly Vladimir Bekhterev at the Psycho-Neurological Institute and Ivan Pavlov at the institute and the University of St. Petersburg. These two great scholars were colleagues and competitors over the concept of the conditioned or associative reflex. For Sorokin, both were on to something fundamental about human behavior. Indeed, their ideas were extensively used in his early study entitled *Hunger as a Factor in Human Affairs*.[25] Judging from his later assessment in *Contemporary Sociological Theories*, he came to find Pavlov's works more fruitful. While acknowledging Bekhterev's early works as significant, he found Bekhterev's *Collective Reflexology* a major disappointment. His "laws are nothing but a caricature of scientific law, in which the meanings of the laws of physics and chemistry, as well as of social facts, are disfigured."[26] For behaviorism on the whole, however, Sorokin saw a better future. "The prospect is rather bright, but in order that it may be realized, it is necessary to forsake existing 'flapping around instincts'; or the metaphysical intrusion into the field of inner experiences; . . . it is necessary that we get busy with a careful objective study of the unconditioned and the conditioned responses."[27]

Looking back on those days, Pitirim was moved by the tremendous excitement of it all. From these and other scholars an edifice of ideas had taken shape. There was not only the excitement of his scholarly explorations but the high drama of the revolution as well. He recalled how through Kovalevsky, Petrazhitsky, and de Roberty he had become entrenched in the political life of St. Petersburg. Kovalevsky was prominent in the State Council and, with Petrazhitsky, was a member of the Duma. These men introduced him to many important political figures, and through his connections, critical writings, and ongoing activities with the Social Revolutionaries he came to Kerensky's attention. Through seminars and study groups at the university he met other political leaders. These anticzarist intellectuals differed in their strategies and philosophies but were united in resistance to autocracy. Many of these friendships later proved important to Pitirim, particularly those with the Bolshevik strategists Piatakov and Karakhan.

A growing reputation among fellow radicals also brought attention from czarist's spies. Arrests, followed shortly by release, were a common part of his student experience. However, when the heat became intense in 1911, he went to Italy. On return he resumed leadership in the revolt and stayed ahead of the police until 1913. He was arrested in March for writing an inflammatory political pamphlet and was jailed for three weeks. Again he was well treated and read, among other things, Twain's *Life on the Mississippi.* On release he went back to school to finish his degree.

The year 1914 brought graduation from the university, and Pitirim was selected to prepare for a career in scholarship. Selection came with a four-year stipend to study for the master's degree and privatdocentship. He now intensely pursued sociology along with his major fields of criminal law, penology, and constitutional law. The requirements for a master's degree in Russian universities were stiff. Successful examinations and public defense of the master's dissertation often led to the position of university lecturer (privatdocent). Because of the rigorous master's requirements, the doctorate was given only to scholars whose work went well beyond the achievements of their peers. Both doctoral and master's dissertations were printed, but only the master's required an oral defense.

Advanced students were given extensive reading lists (in Pitirim's case, over nine hundred titles) and told to master them. How to do so was up to them. They could study abroad, or do it on their own or through private conferences with their professors and mentors. Regardless, it was the students' responsibility to pass the examinations and submit their work for public defense. Preparation usually took four years, but a determined, enthusiastic Sorokin completed it in two. From October through November 1916 he passed three oral examinations and a written exercise. He was then examined by the faculty on criminal law, criminal procedure, and constitutional law. On passing the exams he obtained the degree magistrant of criminal law and became a lecturer on the juridical faculty at the university.

Oral defense of his *Crime and Punishment, Service and Reward* was set for March 1917. Because of the revolution, however, he had to wait until 22 April 1922 to complete the defense requirements. He did this by defending his *System of Sociology* (1920) for the degree of doctor of sociology.[28] In the interim, Russia had passed through the violent revolutionary period and was reorganizing. In the universities degrees were abolished, but by 1921 they were reinstated and Pitirim continued toward the doctorate. The revolutionary interval had seen the introduction of sociology into the university's curriculum, and Pitirim served as chairman of the new department from 1919 to 1922. His oral defense lasted approximately six hours and ended with success and a "thunderous ovation."[29]

Life had indeed been torn asunder by the revolution. The intense academic preparations of 1914–16 were conducted in the turmoil of World War I and the looming revolution. While supporting the domestic war effort, Pitirim was busy mapping new paths should the czar be overthrown. Failure at war, rising unrest in the cities and villages, hunger, inflation, and poverty strengthened the idea of revolt. With the war going badly and the autocracy falling apart, a new design for Russia's survival was needed. Sorokin dedicated himself to this with the same intensity that he had applied to his studies. Politics and academic life blended together. However, the difficulty of the times intensified when, from 1914 to 1917, his three great teachers died: E. V. de Roberty was murdered in Tverskaia Province in 1915, M. M. Kovalevsky died in Petrograd in April 1916, and L. I. Petrazhitsky committed suicide in Poland in 1917. These were trying years for Sorokin. Death, uncertainty, threat of capture and execution, and building a political state and a personal future were all being carried on the narrow yet incredibly strong shoulders of a man in his midtwenties.

Jail, Execution, or Exile

As these thoughts faded, Sorokin's mind returned to the helplessness he had felt in the Bolsheviks' jail. It was then 1918, and his hopes for Russia had failed. Lenin was triumphant, and Sorokin was a prisoner in Petrograd. While he was thinking back on this, the *Martha Washington* had cleared the Strait of Gibraltar and entered the Atlantic. A new beginning awaited, but he was still coming to grips with the past. The fortress of Peter and Paul had been a human stratigraphy of the revolution. Officers of the czar were followed by leaders of the provisional government, members of soviets, the Constituent Assembly, and a variety of political parties. They all were losers in the struggle for power. For some the fight would continue, but for many their fates were sealed. Death or exile would be the only way out of the fortress. The Bolsheviks' jail lacked nearly all the amenities of the czar's. Quarters were dirty and poorly furnished. Books were rare, and prisoners were kept in their cells. Anxiety was high. Rumors circulated that a proclamation had been issued to execute all those involved in the plot to kill Lenin. Sickness, particularly tuberculosis, was rampant. There was no outside word about families and friends. For the first ten days or so, no visitors were permitted, and after that only on a weekly basis. Pitirim worried over Elena. The dangers of the city, the rumors of executions, the hunger, her fears for him, all fueled his worry. Also, she was now tied to him and hence was more vulnerable. This was a terrible, frightening time for the newlyweds. Surely word had reached Elena of the murders of former members of Kerensky's government, particularly Professor Kokoshkin and Dr. Shingoreff. With them dead, what could she expect for her husband?

It took Elena fifty-seven days to manage his release. One day guards simply told him to get his things and go to the warden's office. There, in front of Elena and his benefactor, Kramaroff, he was officially released. Kramaroff was an old revolutionary who now walked a thin line between the Bolsheviks and the resistance. His intervention had saved Pitirim. It was a stroke of good fortune brought about by the persistence and intelligence of Elena.

A week later, in early March 1918, they left Petrograd for Moscow. There Pitirim met with Kerensky and returned to the mainstream of the resistance. By May he was again involved in plans to liberate Russia from the Bolsheviks and Germans. Members of the Constituent Assembly combined with provisional government activists, Social Revolutionaries, Social Patriots, and other dissidents formed a League for the Regeneration of Russia. Sorokin was sent to Veliki Ustyug, Vologda, and Arkhangelsk to help organize a move against Lenin. The idea was to liberate northern Russia and eventually surround the capital cities controlled by the Bolsheviks.[30]

The initial phases of the assault went well, and Nicholas Tschaikovsky ousted the Bolsheviks from Arkhangelsk. Unfortunately, strategic complications gave the Communists a chance to bring in reinforcements and turn the tide. As Bolshevik forces regained lost ground, they put out rewards for rebel leaders; the bounties could be collected either dead or alive. To escape, the rebels divided into small groups and headed for the villages and forest. Pitirim and his band took to the forest. For five weeks they roamed through the massive woodlands. For food they hunted and foraged. Clothing soon turned to rags, and shoes were fashioned out of bark. At night the insurgents slept under leaves and moss, constantly vigilant. The climate, fear, hunger, and deprivation at times produced a deep despair. They had lost all hope for a successful counterrevolt, and each day was a gut-wrenching ordeal of survival.

After more than two months Pitirim walked to Ustyug. There with his wife, his brother Prokopiy, and close friends, he turned himself over to the Chekha. He could still feel the intense emotion as he prepared to leave his loved ones. All were sure he was going to die. Holding Elena for what he believed to be the last time, he looked at Prokopiy and realized that while brothers, most of their lives had been spent apart. Now the time for a relationship was gone. There was only the tearful sadness of great loss and fear of impending death. One choked on the emotion. It was the most intense and fearful event of his life, the first time he had to prepare himself to die early.

After his good-byes Pitirim walked to the Chekha, announced his identity, and was taken to the field commander for interrogation. Questioning was brief, and with blunt candor the officer informed him he would be shot. However, given Pitirim's position in the counterrevolution, the commander had to first get instructions from the central Chekha. With the execution temporarily postponed, Pitirim was jailed.

This jail was also unsavory. Thirty men occupied a single cell with no bedding and a bare minimum of furniture. A scattering of books and some writing materials were available. The diet was bread and water, with a few beans and vegetables in the water, making it a thin soup. Meals came twice a day and left the men hungry. At one corner of the cell three prisoners huddled together in almost unbroken sleep. They had typhus. With little else to do, the men passed time talking and exchanging information with newcomers. At eight o'clock all stretched out on the floor and tried to sleep. Pitirim laid quietly for several hours, his mind occupied with his life and impending death. The commander was unequivocal, but when would he die? What would he feel in front of the firing squad? Would he have courage and not give in to the finality and fearful uncertainty of life's last minutes? His thoughts were shattered as the door of the cell suddenly opened. Ten guards entered, and among them was the chief executioner, Petersen. Immediately the names of six prisoners were called, and they were commanded to put on their coats and go with the guards. One, a student named Popoff, said his good-byes, then called out, "Long life to Russia and death to the Communist hangmen of the Russian people!"[31] In response, Petersen struck Popoff in the face with his revolver, and a cut was opened. Popoff again confronted Petersen, who then aimed the gun at the student. At the end of Popoff's next sentence three shots were fired, and he fell dead. Shoving the prisoners and carrying Popoff's body, the guards forced the others from the cell and closed the door. There was stunned silence as the living looked into each other's pale faces. Shortly conversation followed as they again took their places on the floor. But sleep would not come; death was too close. For the next few days the ritual continued, as sometime between six and midnight the guards called prisoners for execution.

A few days after the Popoff incident, Pitirim was moved to a private cell. Feeling that his end was near, he wrote letters to his wife, his brother, and many of his friends. The cell had a small window that allowed him to look out at an open field. There, one morning, he saw Elena. Shouting and waving, he attracted her attention. They were only able to exchange gazes, but it was so much more than he had hoped for. Shortly after this he was returned to the common cell.

The routine of prison life was rarely broken, although 7 November, the first anniversary of the revolution, was an exception; as a celebration, executions were halted. Nonetheless, on 6 November twelve were killed, and on 8 November sixteen more went up "execution hill." Day in and day out, the deaths continued. As weeks gave way to months, the pressure of impending death began to crush the spirit. One simply wanted to walk out and face the firing squad, rather than to die by pieces day to day. It was at this point that Pitirim came to fully understand and participate in one of the prisoners' strange rituals. Shortly after his arrival, he noticed that his cellmates crowded around those with typhus. Later he saw them take lice off the unconscious men and put them on their own bodies. It was some time before he understood the rationality of this act: typhus brought delirium and long periods of unconsciousness. If one was sure of death, then a coma reduced the daily terror of execution. After several weeks of waiting for the call, Pitirim found himself trying to catch a cold and starting to compete with others to get near the typhus patients. But life at prison continued, and each day ended with new deaths. One horrible evening almost sixty people were executed, among them women and children. This was the crucible that forged Pitirim's hatred for the butchery and waste of Communism and revolutions. On 12 December 1918 he was again taken to the commander's office. Elena greeted him, and there was a tone of servility in his jailer's voice. Pitirim was being sent to the Central Chekha in Moscow. Once there, he was told that he would be released as a result of a direct order from Lenin.

Remarkable circumstances had led to this surprising event. Shortly after being moved to a private cell in the fortress, Pitirim had been visited by a local commissar.[32] The official informed him that while they were now enemics, he felt Sorokin was a valuable scientist who should be saved for the good of the country. Although he was not optimistic, he would do what he could to effect Pitirim's release. In the following weeks two important events transpired: Pitirim had a letter published in *Pravda* (20 November 1918) in which he completely withdrew from all political activities and memberships;[33] and the commissar prevailed on two of Pitirim's old friends, Piatakov and Karakhan, to intercede with Lenin. As students Pitirim and these men had been friends, and they were now members of the cabinet. In turn, they went to Lenin to seek Sorokin's release. Lenin granted the pardon but not before writing and publishing in *Pravda* his article "The Valuable Admissions of Pitirim Sorokin."[34] In this piece Lenin took Sorokin's withdrawal as evidence of the bankruptcy of his politics. Like many intellectuals of the middle ground, Sorokin was misdirected and falsely conscious. Lenin used Pitirim's letter to argue that moderates should either quit or become Bolsheviks. To stay in the middle on critical issues was historically stupid. It slowed the transition to the Soviet form of government and postponed the good of the people.

Regardless of the politics, on 16 December 1918 Pitirim was freed. Being on the streets of Moscow without money or a place to stay, he sought his old friend Professor Kondratieff. The famous economist was shocked by Pitirim's condition. The months in prison showed their toll, and Kondratieff judged Pitirim to have aged twenty years. After his initial shock, he gave his friend the comforts of his household and a safe place to regain his composure. Pitirim returned to Petrograd a few days later. His old apartment was now occupied, and almost all of his possessions were either lost, stolen, or destroyed. Homeless again, he rented a room from some old neighbors and set about preparing for Elena's arrival. At the university he was restored to professional status and told to begin his classes after the Christmas break. He then contacted his publishers to see about the condition of some of his unfinished works. In a short time he arranged for the publication of one volume on sociology and another on law. An independent publisher, F. Sedenka, also agreed to publish his *System of Sociology*. After Elena arrived from Moscow, they settled into a new routine in a familiar setting. On New Year's Eve each said a prayer of thanksgiving that they were reunited and the terrible year was over. Now they were no longer hunted. The apprehensions and fears for each other's well-being were passing, and they looked forward to a time of comparative normalcy. Holding hands, laughing with their friends, and enjoying tea and potato cakes, they brought 1918 to a close.

The year 1919 began well but was not without hardships. Shortages marked every aspect of life. The Communist society was based on sharing scarcity: not enough food, fuel, building supplies, paper, clothing, shoes, medicine, or soap. Even water was a problem. Typhus was rampant, and all water had to be boiled before drinking. But what if one could not get the fuel to boil the water? Without heat, pipes broke, and the stench of raw sewage was detectable in almost all dwellings. Diseases abounded in places with no pure water, fuel, soap, baths, or clean clothes. Electricity was in short supply, and the city spent most nights without lights. A few days a week the lights burned for two or three hours; then the power was shut off. These hardships took their toll. Several of Pitirim's friends and acquaintances committed suicide: one jumped from the fifth floor of a building, another swallowed cyanide, and still another hanged himself. Typhus, influenza, pneumonia, starvation, exposure, and cholera raised the death rates. While dying was easy in Petrograd, being buried was another matter. Permits for burial were needed and often took several days. There was a coffin shortage, and burial plots were difficult to locate. The Communists did move on this problem by building a large crematorium in the city.

In spite of such difficulties, Pitirim and Elena survived. In 1920 they found jobs at the Agricultural Academy of Czarskoe Selo and relocated to the former city of the czars. Shortly after their arrival, *The System of Sociology* was published. This book and some of Pitirim's lectures, articles, and public addresses were again bringing him to the attention of Lenin's secret police. But life here was much more civil than in Petrograd. With both of them working, things improved, and the city itself was still capable of inspiring some awe.

By 1921, however, the situation became more desperate. Peasants had no seeds to plant, factories had no fuel, the railway system broke down, schools closed, and buildings fell into ruins. Communism was in a crisis, and order was maintained only through the bloody practices of the army. Revolts, demonstrations, and protests were everywhere. Major confrontations in February 1922 forced the government to introduce economic reforms and announce a New Economic Policy (NEP). These changes came about only after massive famine and violent rebellions. The NEP was a change bought with the lives of a great number of Russians.

Pitirim would see the starvation of 1921 close-up. He decided to postpone a third volume of his *System of Sociology* in order to study the impact of hunger on human behavior and social life. Famines had been constants in human history and were particularly common in times of war and revolution. In cooperation with Pavlov, Bekhterev, and several others, he began his study in the laboratory provided by the Bolsheviks. In the winter of 1921 Pitirim set out for the areas hit hardest by the famine: Somara and Saratov Provinces. The shock of what he saw there precluded any type of scientific research. He "broke down completely before the spectacle of the actual starvation of millions."[35] Having grown jaded to urban hunger, he was unprepared for the living skeletons he saw in these areas. There was simply nothing left for people to eat. The straw thatch from roofs, all livestock, and even dogs, cats, and crows had been eaten. Constables had to lock away corpses and guard graves because people were stealing the bodies for food. Murders were even occurring for that desperate purpose. One woman "had killed her child, cut off his legs, cooked and ate them." The twenty days that Pitirim spent in the districts made him fearless in his attacks on the revolution. In May 1922 his book on hunger and human behavior was being circulated. Though cut by censors, it was still a moving firsthand account of the devastation and ruin of the peoples in these districts. As an intellectual and emotional testimony to their sufferings, it guaranteed that this lesson of revolution would not be forgotten.

By the time of the book's publication, things were improving in Russia. Existence was still hand-to-mouth, but unmistakable signs of improvement were visible. People were repairing their homes, the churches were restored and services regularized, the universities were again functioning. The NEP was beginning to show results, and Russia was reviving from the bleak postrevolutionary period. Unfortunately, the executions of the regime's critics continued, and for most life was still a struggle.

In August 1922, while in Moscow, Pitirim also learned of a nationwide assault by the Chekha on scholars, scientists, and writers. These intellectuals were rounded up, processed, and then ordered to leave the country. Several of Pitirim's friends and colleagues (e.g., N. Kondratieff, N. O. Lossky, and I. I. Lapshin) were among them. Realizing that his life in Russia was over, Pitirim decided to turn himself over to the secret police and prepare for voluntary exile. Surrendering in Moscow, he was given ten days to prepare for departure. Elena sold their unwanted goods, then went to meet him. On 22 September 1922 they left Moscow for Germany. The trip was uneventful, and a week later Pitirim was lecturing in Berlin on the current conditions in Russia. From letters and newspapers he learned that his banishment had been a mistake and those responsible for it were being censured. Additionally, the government was now destroying his book on the famine. However, for the first time in five years, he and Elena could sleep without wondering if this would be the night that the police would again come for him.

The Sorokins were not in Berlin long before Pitirim received an invitation from the president of Czechoslovakia, Thomas G. Masaryk, to teach at Charles University. Pitirim accepted and asked for a brief leave to rest and prepare himself for the classroom. President Masaryk agreed and offered a special scholarship to provide for his needs during that period.[36] A few days later he and Elena rented a small house near Prague. For the first time since their marriage they lived a normal life. Most days they would shop, read, walk, or garden in the early hours and go to the city in the afternoon to pursue their different interests. Elena was doing graduate work in cytology, and Pitirim would either read or lecture at the university. Evenings were spent with friends. There was a large community of Russian scholars living in Prague who gathered for a variety of reasons;[37] several talked politics, while others were concerned with science, the arts, or just enjoyed the familiar company.

Many exiles, believing that the Communist government would be short-lived, spent their days planning a return to Russia. Pitirim disagreed. Viewing the Soviet system as more stable, he sought his opportunities in Prague and elsewhere. He and Elena were happy in Czechoslovakia and would likely have stayed had he not received an invitation from Edward C. Hayes and Edward A. Ross to come to America and present a series of lectures on the Russian Revolution. He accepted the offer because he valued his independence and realized that in Prague he was benefiting from the friendliness of the government rather than making a place for himself. Furthermore, he was curious and favorably impressed by America.

These forces contributed to Sorokin's being on board the *Martha Washington* as it approached Boston and his first sight of the new land. After staying at the Boston Custom House for a few hours, the ship moved on to New York. The next morning, after sixteen days at sea, it arrived, and Pitirim walked out into the country that would now be his home.

Beginning

If the concept of socialization tells us anything of human behavior, it reinforces the poetic maxim that "the child is the father of the man." This chronicle of Sorokin's early years tempts one to focus on the improbability of his experiences and the hardships and loneliness he endured. To do so, however, would obfuscate significant insights, because his early life was much more than that. Komi culture, Russian society, and the academic milieu were important forces that shaped Sorokin's fundamental character. From the Komi he learned a love of ideas and debate, a facility for language, a commitment to hard work, and a deep involvement with religion and spiritual life. For the young Sorokin, reality was multidimensional. The Komi lived as one with nature, and from his uncle Vassiliy he had learned about spirits of the forest, winds, and plains. Komi folklore was rich in such beliefs. His naturalistic knowledge of the woods and its creatures became infused with this transcendent pagan mythology and was intensely felt by the young Sorokin.

The forces of nature and Komi myths intertwined with Russian Orthodoxy to shape Pitirim's aesthetic sense, spirituality, and worldview.

A pious youth, committed to prayer and meditation, he had spent his childhood around churches and priests. His early experiences brought together the spirits of nature and those of the Deity and saints to forge a sensitivity to life that transcended the senses. For this young man, knowing was more than an empirical process; it was one of super-consciousness. Human reality was not to be confined to the material. There were the deeper, more mysterious, truths of spiritual life. Religion and Komi culture integrated and crystallized his philosophy deeper than he could then know. They were among the important forces that shaped his personality and would drive his scholarship toward Integralism.

However, the world of man was not to be ignored, and the Komi love of knowledge and argument engaged Sorokin in other forms of learning. He took to scholarship with a rare intensity. Early on he became engaged with questions of human nature and humanity. Who were we? What was the best way for humans to live? How could society and human nature be most fruitfully reconciled? As a voracious reader, and one gifted in languages, he sought the answers in ever-widening bodies of scholarship—first in his native languages of Komi and Russian, then later in Latin, French, English, German, and some of the Slavic languages. Little in the environment of his interests escaped disciplined attention. From the Gam school through the University of St. Petersburg, the Komi love of ideas and debate became embedded in his personality. Reading was essential, but controversy was the sieve that clarified thought. Argument was a learning mechanism and had to be pursued with ingenuity, a fierce commitment to truth, and a firm grasp of facts.

The Komi love of debate was joined in Sorokin by a lawyer's passion for argument, a skill the young scholar had acquired while earning his magistrant of criminal law degree at St. Petersburg. Argument, while heated and occasionally fierce, was not personal, but a means toward truth. Scholars in conflict were simply honest people whose disagreements served the higher purpose of eliminating the false in quest of the true. Such a task demanded that truth claims be vigorously dissected and evaluated; anything less would undermine the scholar's search and was unacceptable.

Independence and hard work were also important parts of Sorokin's character. His mother's death when he was three years old set him on the road with his father and brother. By ten he and Vassiliy had left their father, and Pitirim was on his own by fourteen. For this youth, life meant work, and a stern discipline was required to survive. Coping with life's realities compelled him to be strong and self-reliant. He learned to deal with his anxieties, to plan, and meet life's challenges head-on. Sorokin's situation demanded that he learn these lessons at an age when most children were still in grammar school. If he weakened, then life would break him. To live required courage, continuous work, and a strong belief in himself. This fierce independence applied not only to the fight for survival but to scholarship as well. Sorokin felt that the scholar must be unswerving in the commitment "to find and tell the truth." He must not rely on the authority of others but independently test ideas by all available evidence. Sorokin's deep belief in his ability to recognize truth often isolated him from other intellectuals and made him appear stubborn and arrogant. However, isolation and independence had shaped his personality and relations to others.

While comfortable with loneliness, Sorokin was also strongly committed to the common good. As a politician and teacher he worked to improve the lives of others. He took great personal risks to spread the truth as he knew it and to bring Russia out of parochialism and tyranny. Upon Lenin's victory, however, he withdrew from politics and focused on the life of the mind. The young man who left the *Martha Washington* in 1922 would never again return to the political stage. Instead, he would direct his energy toward understanding the complex social dynamics that shaped human history. In this search he would draw heavily from the sociology and social philosophy of his teachers: the behaviorism of Bekhterev and Pavlov; the concern with cultural mentalities and social structure expressed by Petrazhitsky, Kovalevsky, and de Roberty; Petrazhitsky's study of law and altruism; Kovalevsky's work on contemporary theory and the use of the comparative historical method; and de Roberty's evolutionism would all infuse his inquiry. But in the end what emerged was distinctly Sorokin's, and it would leave its mark on the work of others.

2

Emigré Scholar

Riding the Circuit

NEW YORK IN 1923 was truly a door to the promised land. From 1890 to the mid-1920s, millions of new immigrants arrived from southern and eastern Europe. To generations of WASPs were added new generations of PIGS, Michael Novak's acronym for the Polish, Italian, Greek, and Slavic arrivals.[1] From the late 1880s to shortly after Sorokin's entry, almost 3.2 million people immigrated from Russia.[2] Approximately 44 percent were Jews escaping the pogroms that had ripped through the pale. They were businessmen, merchants, skilled workers, artisans, intellectuals, and professionals. Most settled in major East Coast cities. Non-Jewish immigrants were also occupationally diverse, but were more concentrated in the laboring classes and tied to basic industries (coal, iron, textiles, and agriculture).[3] Both groups contributed to the professional, scientific, and intellectual strata of American society. Arriving at approximately the same time as Sorokin were Igor Sikorsky, the aviation expert whose ideas led to the development of modern helicopters; Vladimir Zworykin, inventor of the cathode-ray tube and one of several responsible for the electron microscope; the mathematician Oscar Zariski; and the composer Igor Stravinsky.[4]

While the twenties were a period of isolationism, traditionalism, and xenophobia, Sorokin received a warm welcome to the United States. The Russian Student Relief Organization found him a room at 145 West Eighty-fourth Street and helped him make new friends. B. A. Bakhemetiev, Kerensky's ambassador to the United States, introduced him to Franklin Giddings and other prominent intellectuals interested in the revolution. Pitirim came to the United States early to work on his English before giving lectures at the Universities of Illinois and Wisconsin.[5] After a few days in New York he renewed his acquaintance with Henry Noble MacCracken and sought the Vassar president's advice on finding a job. MacCracken had met Sorokin in Prague and later reviewed his *Contemporary State of Russia: Essays in Pedagogy and Politics* for the *Yale Review*.[6] MacCracken invited Sorokin to his home for a long Sunday chat. The reunion resulted in Pitirim being asked to stay at Vassar while he prepared for his speaking tour.

Sorokin moved to Poughkeepsie in late November and took a room near the campus. MacCracken opened Vassar's lecture halls to Pitirim to help with his English. With customary energy and enthusiasm, Sorokin attended several lectures during the day, ate his meals in the dining halls, and spent afternoons and evenings with students or listening to public lectures. He was struck by the differences between this American university and those in Europe. The open attitudes and friendliness of the students impressed him, and he particularly enjoyed attending the speech and journalism classes. Students and faculty found him to be frank, direct, and charming. Professors welcomed him for his grasp of European politics and because he often contributed questions and insights to their classes.[7]

Before leaving Vassar, Sorokin delivered a lecture series entitled "The Sociology of Revolution." The specific topics were behavior in a revolutionary society, the effects of revolution on conduct, modifications of the biological composition of society, and deformation of the social structure. At the lectures the press questioned him on events in the Soviet Union and the likelihood of the Communist government staying in power. Pitirim was direct, speaking critically of the revolution and its ruinous effects on Russian society. Indeed, the revolution was so destructive that the government would not survive another three years. Despite Sorokin's views, the Soviet government invited him to return. The request was made informally by a government representative. Pitirim declined. He believed the government was failing. If critics returned, it might suggest they supported the regime. For Pitirim there was nothing to be gained in Russia. Only a major political change would tempt him to return.[8]

The time in Poughkeepsie was well spent. Sorokin's English improved, and his reading and writing skills developed as his note-taking, scholarly writing, and correspondence grew. By mid-January 1924 he was ready to leave Vassar and begin his tour. Leaving was hard. He had made many friends among students, staff, and faculty. He and the MacCrackens had also established the foundations of a friendship that would continue for over forty years. The times spent at the MacCrackens' retreat at Yelping Hill, the long conversations, and the probing insights into each other would be missed. The Vassar president would maintain an open door for the Sorokins, who often sought his advice and fellowship.[9]

Leaving Poughkeepsie, Pitirim stopped at the University of Chicago to visit Samuel Harper. Later, on arriving at the University of Illinois, he was hosted by Edwin Sutherland, who was then sitting in for Edward C. Hayes.[10] In the Midwest Sorokin's message met with resistance. Many intellectuals and activists viewed the Communists' overthrow of the czar as a move toward human rights and democracy. The revolution promised a better Russia, and they disliked the picture Sorokin presented. However, as he so clearly stated, the war and the revolution had changed his views of the world:

Already World War I had made some fissures in the positivistic, "scientific," and humanistic Weltanschauung I had held before the War. The Revolution of 1917 enormously enlarged these fissures and eventually shattered this world-outlook with its positivistic philosophy and sociology, its utilitarian system of values, and its conception of historical process as a progressive evolution toward an ever better man, society, and culture. Instead of increasingly enlightened, morally ennobled, aesthetically refined, and creatively developed humanity, these events unleashed in man "the worst of the beast" and displayed on the historical stage—side by side with the noble, wise, and creative minority—a gigantic world of irrational human animals blindly murdering each other, indiscriminately destroying the great values, overthrowing the immortal achievements of genius, and glorifying vulgarity in its worst form. This unexpected world-wide explosion of the forces of death, bestiality, and ignorance in the supposedly civilized humanity of the twentieth century categorically contradicted all "sweet" theories of progressive evolution of man from ignorance to science and wisdom, from bestiality to noble morality . . . from tyranny to freedom . . . from the man-beast to the superman-god.[11]

His denunciations of Lenin and the Communists were often hostilely received. He was viewed as an ignorant, naive antirevolutionist who refused to see the benefits of the new regime. Although he had his defenders (Charles Ellwood, Charles H. Cooley, Edward A. Ross, Franklin Giddings, and others), a current of resentment was being formed against the outspoken émigré.

After the few nurturant weeks at Vassar, Sorokin was again immersed in conflict. He was lonely. Months had passed since leaving Elena in Prague. During the mornings and afternoons he worked on the manuscripts of *The Sociology of Revolution* and *Leaves from a Russian Diary.* Professor Hayes had arranged to translate and edit *The Sociology of Revolution* for publication. While busy, Sorokin missed the friendships of Poughkeepsie and eagerly looked toward Elena's arrival. Before she could come, however, he must have a job. The series of lectures were vital. Scholars and potential employers could hear his ideas, quiz him on a range of subjects, and see how he handled himself and how well he could use English. He was constantly aware of their scrutiny and of the importance of his lectures for finding an academic position in America.

From Illinois Sorokin went to the University of Wisconsin at Madison. Again he was challenged but was supported by his old friend and teacher Michael I. Rostovtzeff. It was from this great historian of the ancient world that Sorokin had learned the important uses of history. Rostovtzeff often drew on his knowledge of the past to interpret the present and future. He did not argue that history repeated itself but believed its careful study gave important insights into human beings and their social institutions. Knowledge of the past provided a special understanding of the present and a vantage point for looking to the future. This orientation would inform many of Pitirim's works. Rostovtzeff was also an anti-Communist émigré. He left Russia in June 1918 for Sweden and then Norway. From late 1918 until early 1920 he lectured at major universities in England and France. In 1920 he accepted a chair of ancient history at the University of Wisconsin. He later became Sterling Professor of Ancient History at Yale and remained there until retirement.

Pitirim had met Rostovtzeff in 1910. Through classes and conversations the two became friends. The historian carefully molded the younger scholar's basic orientations to historical materials. Rostovtzeff, even at that time, had a wide international reputation. From 1903 to 1911 he had published five major works dealing with the history of early Rome. In America his list of publications grew to dozens of books and over five hundred articles on history and archaeology. Among the more famous were *The Social and Economic History of the Roman Empire* (1926); the two-volume *History of the Ancient World* (1926, 1927); and the three-volume *Social and Economic History of the Hellenistic World* (1941). Rostovtzeff was president of the American Historical Association in 1935 and received many honorary degrees and awards over his long career.[12] Michael and Sophie Rostovtzeff would be lifelong friends of the Sorokins and godparents for both the Sorokin boys.

During the month spent with Rostovtzeff and Ross at Madison, Pitirim received other speaking invitations. Albion Small encouraged him to come to Chicago, and C. H. Cooley invited him to Ann Arbor. More importantly, through Ross, F. Stuart Chapin offered him a summer teaching job at the University of Minnesota. No doubt Sorokin found comfort in the stalwart company of his old teacher and E. A. Ross. They were kindred spirits—Rostovtzeff an anti-Communist, and Ross a man who stood up for his beliefs. Indeed, the latter's politics had cost him his job at Stanford and possibly the presidency of the University of Washington.[13] Even with the controversy Sorokin's lectures provoked, the trip was a success. He was meeting important people, renewing friendships, and finding enough work to save for Elena's trip to the United States.

In March 1924 he returned to New York. Disliking city living, he moved to Laurelton, Long Island. Prospects for the future were looking brighter. The books were nearly done, and he was writing journal articles and reviews. The lecture circuit was steady and paid well enough to save a nest egg. With optimism he sent for Elena. Shortly she arrived in New York, and his loneliness was over. He had now made his commitment to a future in the United States.

Elena settled into Laurelton and commuted to Columbia University to work in the plant cytology laboratory. Pitirim continued writing and preparing his courses for Minnesota. Together they enjoyed the pleasures of New York. Pitirim made occasional trips to speak at colleges and universities. More regularly, he spoke at social clubs around the city, receiving small stipends for his efforts. The time passed happily and quickly. In early July he and Elena went to Vassar. Hearing of her arrival, the MacCrackens extended their welcome and offered the hospitality that Pitirim had earlier enjoyed. Later, at Yelping Hill, long talks, exercise, and a bit of hard physical work kept Noble and Pitirim busy during the day; evenings were spent with friends of the MacCrackens. Over dinner and drinks, lively conversation yielded laughter, stimulation, and good fellowship.[14]

Finding a Home

Shortly after returning to Long Island, Pitirim left for Minneapolis. In terms of size and enrollments, the University of Minnesota was one of the largest in the United States. The campus was bordered by the Mississippi River and surrounded by bookstores, restaurants, and shops. While known for the severity of its winters many were unaware that the summer could be equally uncomfortable. Arriving on campus, Pitirim secured a room, moved in, and prepared for the semester's work.

The Department of Sociology was then led by F. Stuart Chapin, who had come to the university in 1922. Under his leadership the program had received national recognition and attracted strong faculty and promising graduate students. Indeed, the 1920s were a golden decade for the department. Chapin had studied at Columbia under Franklin Giddings. When he came to Minnesota, at the age of thirty-three, he was the youngest head of a major sociology department in the United States. A neat, slender, impeccably mannered person, Chapin had an aura of formality that kept most people at a distance. He was a widely published, well-respected scholar who held a variety of important editorships and appointments.

Chapin was surrounded by colleagues who would become leaders in the discipline. Among the talented was L. L. Bernard, who stayed on the faculty until 1925. Students enjoyed Bernard's lectures and appreciated his antiestablishment style. His most important book at Minnesota was *Instincts: A Study in Social Psychology,* published in 1924. Later in his career Bernard became a major force in challenging the University of Chicago's control of the American Sociological Society. He was pivotal in the drive to replace the *American Journal of Sociology,* as the official journal of the society, with the *American Sociological Review.*[15] Ross Finney, another member of the department, wrote a major text, *Elementary Sociology* and was a pioneer in educational sociology. His *Principles of Education* and *Introduction to Educational Sociology* (with L. D. Zeleny) were important contributions to the field. The family sociologist and social researcher Manuel C. Elmer was on the faculty until 1927. Edwin H. Sutherland, the acclaimed criminologist, served in the department from 1926 to 1929.

Along with quality faculty, Chapin attracted a generation of high-quality graduate students, many of whom became important sociologists. Among those present during the Sorokin period, Carle C. Zimmerman would go on to a position at Harvard; Paul Landis became famous as a family sociologist and demographer; Elio D. Monachesi followed Chapin as department head in the early 1950s; George Vold established himself as a criminologist; and Conrad Taeuber became a distinguished demographer and director of the Bureau of the Census.

Pitirim correctly perceived that his invitation to teach summer school at Minnesota was, in fact, an audition. It gave Chapin and the others an opportunity to assess his abilities and facility with the language. During the summer he taught two courses: the sociology of revolution, and social morphology. Students liked him, and his work met the standards of the department. Thus he was offered a visiting professorship to replace L. L. Bernard, who was going on sabbatical leave.

The graduate department at Minnesota was then ranked fourth in the nation (only Chicago, Columbia, and Wisconsin were ranked higher), and Sorokin's selection added more luster to Minnesota's rising star. Shortly after his appointment, he published *Leaves from a Russian Diary* (1924) and followed with *The Sociology of Revolution* (1925). In addition he published two articles in *Social Forces* and another in the *Michigan Law Review.*[16] Sorokin was also well received by students, and students from his summer classes even wrote him a poem of appreciation.[17] Similarly, he established a number of warm relationships with the graduate students. As a visiting full professor of sociology (half-time), he was expected to teach three undergraduate courses (rural sociology, history of social theory, and modern social problems) and two seminars. The rural sociology and theory courses were upgraded and later offered as seminars. This was quite a load for a half-time appointment; however, half-time referred to the level of pay, not teaching load. Sorokin observed: "The . . . half-time economic contributions are comparatively modest but they give me the possibility to live on, and that is all I want in this respect."[18] Commenting further on salary, Sorokin noted:

This offer established my title as full professor with a salary of $2,000 for the academic year (instead of the regular $4,000 salary of full professors of the University at that time). Like many other American universities, the University of Minnesota followed a bargaining policy of hiring its professors at as low salaries as possible. The administration of the University well realized my urgent need to secure an academic position in the United States and took this into consideration in making its offer.[19]

Nevertheless, he was glad for the opportunity, which allowed him to send for Elena, who arrived in Minneapolis shortly before the new academic year.

Settling into the modest comforts of their apartment, the Sorokins continued their respective research. In late 1924 Pitirim launched his inquiries into social stratification and completed some early pieces on elites. These studies led him to focus on social mobility and the dynamics of success and failure in modern societies. Elena enrolled in botany courses and continued her work for her doctorate. Life was enjoyable and more secure, and their days were full and endowed with purpose. They became pleasantly involved with their neighbors and with the tradesmen and shopkeepers in the area. The people of the Twin Cities made the Sorokins feel like they belonged. Elena made friends with other graduate students, spending so much time with her research that Pitirim kidded her about giving him dinners made from chromosomes and about his having to fix his own lunches.[20]

As the semester got under way, they learned that their old friend Nikolai Kondratieff would be visiting in early November. Kondratieff was widely known in Russia as a theorist of economic cycles, a statistician, and an agricultural economist. Pitirim had not seen Kondratieff since staying with him in Moscow after being released by the Chekha. They had first met as boys at the Khrenovo Teachers' Seminary when Pitirim was fourteen and Nikolai almost eleven. Kondratieff, like Sorokin, was expelled for revolutionary activities. When he learned that Pitirim was in night school at the Tscherniayevskye Kursy, he went to St. Petersburg, where the two were roommates for several years. They completed night school together and went on to the University of St. Petersburg. Nikolai had met Elena shortly after she became acquainted with Pitirim, and all had endured the trials of the revolution. Kondratieff had also served in the Kerensky government as the deputy minister for food.

Kondratieff's visit lasted for nearly a month, and the Sorokins delighted in showing him the Twin Cities. Pitirim also introduced Nikolai to some of his colleagues in the department and to others in agricultural economics. As Kondratieff's work had not yet been translated into English, American scholars were largely unaware of his ideas, although some knew of him as a Soviet economic planner and farm expert. Sorokin kept Kondratieff's visit quiet because he feared that their association might create problems when his friend returned to Russia. Pitirim's concern actually foreshadowed his friend's ultimate fate. Five years later, Kondratieff's economic ideas brought him into conflict with Soviet policies. He was jailed in 1930 and appeared in the mock trials of 1931–32 in which Stalin purged so-called enemies of the state. However, Pitirim did not sense that when Nikolai left for Washington in early December 1924 it would be the last time he would see his boyhood friend. Kondratieff would die in prison; the date of his death is unknown.[21] Although Kondratieff's fate was not sealed by his association with Sorokin, Pitirim's concern was not far-fetched. His younger brother, Prokopiy, had been killed by the Communists because of their blood ties and suspected political associations.[22]

December 1924 was a very busy month in the Sorokin household. Elena was writing candidacy examinations, and Pitirim cared for himself as the holidays approached. The new year saw Elena working on her thesis and Pitirim's second book coming out; the year also witnessed the first reactions to *Leaves from a Russian Diary*. This highly personalized account of the revolution was greeted with praise and criticism. Colonel A. N. Nikolaieff wrote:

This is an important book. . . . it should be considered as a human document of great historical interest. . . . Professor Sorokin's narrative is so far the only book written in English by a Russian eye-witness which covers the whole period . . . from the beginning of the revolution up to the famine of 1922. . . .

Undoubtedly . . . the future historian of the Russian revolution . . . will find in the "Leaves from a Russian Diary" a corroboration of Tocqueville's fundamental idea . . . that: The revolution, having destroyed what it wanted to destroy and what no doubt would have fallen to pieces by itself, built nothing new; on the contrary, methods which had been in use under the monarchial regime were taken up again, only they were made more oppressive.[23]

Others believed the work was an important political statement. Louis Wetmore argued that Sorokin's book cut through much of America's romanticism about Russian character and the revolution. It was a necessary palliative for those poorly informed writers who saw Russia as an extension of Western civilization and drew inexact parallels between their revolution and that of the United States. He supported Sorokin's analysis of the Bolshevik's rise and the foundation of their power:

Professor Sorokin, as a Russian, gives in this book some interesting sidelights on the revolution and the Russian character. He shows us the contradictions and the hopeless chaos of the early revolutionary days, when every political party, with the exception of the Bolsheviks, wasted precious hours in interminable talk—a constant Russian failing. The Bolsheviks acted and acted on the simple theory that the easiest way to secure power was to kill everyone who stood in the way. They remain in power today through a rigid application of this program.[24]

Others, however, were critical and saw Sorokin as a naive sentimentalist. Johan J. Smertenko described him as a parlor revolutionary without the guts to see through the revolution he had advocated. Sorokin, he felt, quickly reversed himself when he saw what had to be done to overthrow the monarchy. Smertenko found the book to be "a biased and sorrowful exposition of the events which culminated in the Bolshevik coup d'état".[25] Sorokin was also criticized at Minnesota, where some faculty members found him biased and historically shortsighted.[26]

As the reviews of *Leaves*[27] were coming out, Sorokin was putting the final touches on *The Sociology of Revolution*. His writing program was going well, and he was deepening his friendships with graduate students. The nature of his appointment created less social distance between Sorokin and students than was typical for other department members. He often found himself stopping off at the graduate students' basement office, a large bull pen of a room with the desks arranged along the walls. Frequently, informal talks were going on, and Pitirim contributed to the topic of the hour. These visits led to other activities. Pitirim was an athlete and enjoyed handball, swimming, and running. Often he alternated his two-mile-a-day runs with an hour in the pool or on the handball court. From these friendly competitions T. Lynn Smith, Nathan Whetten, Fred Frey, Carle Zimmerman, and Otis Durant Duncan came to know Sorokin more casually. Along with sports there were fishing trips, picnics, hiking, and camping. On these outings Pitirim and Elena became better acquainted with other graduate students like Conrad Taeuber, Irene Barnes, Arnold Anderson, and Edgar Schuler. These activities blended life and work into an undifferentiated whole.

The Minnesota graduate students were diverse and spent much of their time together. Carle C. Zimmerman had come to the university from

Chicago and was known among students as "nature boy." A man of boundless energy, Zimmerman had a casual, open style. He enjoyed informality, the outdoors, and the free expression of his feelings. While at Minnesota he married the daughter of a French professor and established himself as a force in rural sociology. Madeline Zimmerman recognized her husband's talents and was, from the beginning, a strong advocate for his career.[28] T. Lynn Smith, Nate Whetten, and Fred Frey were all Mormons. Whetten and Smith were not very religious, and many recall them as renegades of a sort. Smith was ambitious and competitive, whether on the handball court or in the classroom. The relationships between these men spanned their careers. Each was tied to the others and to Sorokin. Edgar Schuler, C. Arnold Anderson, and Otis Durant Duncan would also maintain warm lifelong friendships with the Sorokins.

Under Chapin the methodological and theoretical thrust of the department was toward a scientific sociology. He recruited faculty and graduate students who were positivists. The faculty, in turn, deepened students' grasp of statistical methods and appreciation of empirical research. Chapin believed that the way to build a quality department "was to get strong men in fields which needed to be covered and to give them the freedom to develop, instruct and research as they saw fit."[29] Minnesota, like other successful departments, was not without cliques, conflicts, and troubles. Chapin's recruitment policy led to a faculty of strong, ambitious personalities who often found each other to be difficult colleagues. When Pitirim was given a permanent position, he too entered the fray.[30]

Chapin, a strong and very organized person, had a "passion for order." Students quipped that "when Chapin goes to bed at night he files himself under 'C'."[31] However, he was often away from the department, and at such times conflicts could get out of hand. Typically, faculty competed for research funding, salary increases, released time, graduate assistants, and a share of departmental assets. Rivalries frequently emerged between programs that at times resulted in great acrimony among faculty and between them and each other's graduate students.[32] One such instance occurred in the late 1920s as Minnesota sought to develop the fields of both rural and urban sociology. There was often tension and heated competition between the two, which intensified as Sorokin and Zimmerman developed an international reputation for rural sociology at Minnesota. Lowry Nelson recalled, "There was bad blood between rural, represented by Sorokin and Zimmerman, and the anti-ruralites, represented by Willey and others. . . . I was told how rural candidates were humiliated in the orals, and all that."[33] In light of such events, it's not surprising that strong bonds developed among like-minded faculty and between faculty and their graduate students.

However, this competitive atmosphere did not deter Sorokin, and after his appointment was made permanent he entered the most productive period of his life. In addition to *Leaves* (1924) and *The Sociology of Revolution* (1925), he published *Social Mobility* (1927), *Contemporary Sociological Theories* (1928), *Principles of Rural-Urban Sociology* (1929) with Carle C. Zimmerman, and the first volume of *A Systematic Source-Book in Rural Sociology* (1930) with Zimmerman and Charles J. Galpin. To these he added a long list of articles and presentations at professional meetings. By the end of six years at Minnesota, Sorokin believed he had established himself "as a better-than-average sociologist." Elena also completed her doctorate in botany and took a teaching position at Hamline University in St. Paul. She had been promised a position in the labs at Minnesota, but a nepotism rule prohibited her hiring. The rule, however, did not stop her from doing her research work there.[34]

Sorokin's *Sociology of Revolution*, unlike *Leaves*, is not a personal account but analyzes revolution as a social phenomenon. The work describes the common denominators of the process and attempts to remove the ideological and romanticized elements attached to them. Sorokin's approach to the problem was largely biological and behavioristic. Human actions were driven in part by the forces of heredity, biochemistry, and the endocrine system. Humans were, first and foremost, biological organisms. They possessed drives, instincts, and reflexes coupled with subconscious impulses and were strongly influenced by suggestion and imitation. Unlike the eighteenth-century or modern rationalist's conceptions, humanity is thought of as a bomb loaded with contradictory inborn reflexes:

His instincts force him to desire not only peace, but warfare; not only self-sacrifice, but murder; not only justice, but the satisfaction of his necessities, though at the cost of his fellow-men; not only work, but idleness. They spur him to independence, at the same time, make him seek . . . domination over others; they teach him not only to love, but to hate.[35]

Sorokin used the terms impulse, instinct, heredity, inborn, or unconditioned reflex synonymously. When the bomb bursts, humanity's basic unconditioned reflexes are set free. If the social forces that channel peoples' behavior are weak, then disorder and debasement result. The unconditioned reflexes are basic drives (e.g., food, protection, sex). The conditioned reflexes are learned, socially standardized, and acceptable means of satisfying the drives. Revolutions and wars attack people's basic adaptation to the environment and frustrate their unconditioned reflexes (the first stage of revolution). These upheavals simultaneously undermine the efficacy of the conditioned reflexes to channel drives and meet needs. The social "brakes" that stop humans from encroaching on each other are weakened, and the socially desirable patterns of behavior are no longer effective in meeting needs. When conditioned reflexes lose their ability to restrain and direct actions, unconditioned drives are unchecked. Conflicts between peoples' basic needs then erupt, causing social disorder and violence. This is the second stage of revolution. This process was described by Sorokin earlier in *Leaves:*

If future historians look for the group that began the Russian Revolution, let them not create any involved theory. The Russian Revolution was begun by hungry women and children demanding bread and herrings. They started by wrecking tram cars and looting a few small shops. Only later did they, together with workmen and politicians, become ambitious to wreck that mighty edifice the Russian Autocracy.[36]

In the second stage, revolutionaries begin to fight among themselves for the necessities of survival. The conflict escalates from individuals to groups, to organized political parties, and becomes so extensive that collective survival is threatened. At this point people are being brutalized by the very process that was supposed to free them, and restraint is needed if culture is to survive. Restraint usually comes in the form of terror. Society is bound and put in irons. Anarchy is replaced by coercion. But, gradually, new "brakes" (conditioned reflexes) evolve to restore order. These new reflexes grow stronger with time and begin to replace the mechanical checks of terror and compulsion. If suppression ends before new socially regulated behavior patterns are in place, then revolutionary activity flares up again. The new violence produces more oppression, which lasts until the new conditioned reflexes are strong enough to maintain order. At this stage society has reached a plateau, and a new period of normalcy is established.

Sorokin examined the revolutionary process in many spheres of personal life and society. He described changes in the patterns of speech and writing, in relationships of property and labor, in sexual behavior, and in patterns of authority and subordination. As society's "brakes" slipped, Sorokin examined the changes in structure and functions of major institutions affected by the revolution. His analysis used the Russian, French, German, English, Egyptian, and Persian revolutions as data. Most reviewers were impressed by the quality of the work. Harry Elmer Barnes praised the theoretical arguments as "the most important and original"; as "much the most up-to-date effort at a psychology of revolution available, it renders the old study of Le Bon thoroughly anachronistic."[37] Wilbur C. Abbott found the book scholarly and creative: "Since the publication of the work of Le Bon there has been no such remarkable and interesting . . . study of this great sociological subject written."[38] The review in the *American Journal of Sociology*, however, was less favorable. The reviewer concluded that the work was emotional, lacked objectivity, and was more ideological than scientific.[39] In another review Robert Park observed: "Even as a work of science the best and perhaps the worst that can be said of it, is that it is suggestive."[40] I. M. Rubinow, while not addressing the assertions of Grierson and Park directly, made the following observation:

I believe Professor Sorokin has done a signal service . . . first in furnishing a scholarly description of the symptoms, processes and course of development of revolutionary appeals. The value of that scientific contribution remains even after the subjective bias caused by Professor Sorokin's experience in the Russian revolution is entirely discounted.[41]

While Park and Grierson correctly noted that the book was not without affect, they overlook much of its comparative historical value and theoretical creativity.[42]

Breaking New Ground

The next four works by Sorokin defined their fields at the time. *Social Mobility*, published in 1927, was a pioneer study of the historical and contemporary dynamics of inequality. As Ellsworth Huntington observed in his review, "Most sociological writers speak as if every institution and individual were glued into place. Professor Sorokin goes to the opposite extreme . . . proving that everything is in a state of flux."[43] Sorokin began *Mobility* with a discussion of the movements of actors in social space. In social stratification, space is pyramidal. Depending on the dimension of stratification (economic, political, or occupational) and its organization, the pyramids take distinct forms. Consider, for example, countries with different occupational structures. Country A has little occupational diversity. Most of the workers are in agriculture and extractive work; there are few skilled workers and tradesmen, and a smaller number of professionals. This pyramid would have a very broad base and be relatively flat. Country B has a smaller agricultural base, more diversity in semiskilled and skilled workers, a variety of people in commerce, clerical, sales, and service occupations, and specialized strata of managers and professionals. The pyramid thus becomes narrower and taller. Within stratification pyramids, actors move from one position to another. When the movement is in the same plane, horizontal mobility has occurred. If actors move between two or more planes, then there has been vertical mobility. It is this form of movement that was of most concern to Sorokin, who was deeply interested in the rates of movement in each sphere of stratification and in how these rates were influenced by a society's stage of development.

On a broader level the book addressed the essence and forms of social stratification in different historical periods; the relationship between social status and psychophysical characteristics; the channels and screening mechanisms of social mobility; and the social and psychological consequences of mobility and stability for individuals and social life. Carlsson[44] observed that this study also anticipated some of the arguments raised by Kingsley Davis and Wilbert E. Moore twenty years later in their important and controversial article "Some Principles of Stratification." Specifically, some jobs are more important for group survival than others, and demand that incumbents be more skilled and intelligent. Society, in turn, develops testing mechanisms to ensure that the best-qualified come to fill these important positions. If the mechanisms work, most people will fill jobs appropriate to their talents.[45]

The methodology employed in *Social Mobility* differed from that in Sorokin's earlier works. While keeping an interest in historical trends, Sorokin had shifted toward a more quantitative approach. He states early on that the period of speculative or armchair sociology was ending. Moving into its place was a more objective, factual, and quantitative sociology. Speculation and the "illustrative method," using one or two facts to confirm a general statement, were to be abandoned. They were "a plague of sociology" on which he declared war.[46] The data in *Social Mobility* are remarkable. They reflect an exhaustive search of the literature combined with the more time-consuming task of gathering one's own information. Data are presented for ancient and modern civilizations. Geographically, many of the world's major regions and countries are represented, and often comparative information on a specific topic (e.g., divorce) is analyzed and discussed. The work is a cornucopia of social data. Sorokin was perfectly aware that even these data allowed only preliminary and circumscribed conclusions. The more complete information necessary for testing some of his hypotheses would not be available for decades. The United States, for example, would not begin to systematically collect the basic items for mobility analysis until the 1950s. Cross-cultural mobility analysis is still hindered by the lack of systematically collected and reliable data.[47]

The pioneering character of *Social Mobility* was grasped by Franklin Giddings in his review:

In three respects this book is a work of first rate importance. First, it is a study of an important process in human society which has never before been examined in a thorough-going way; second, its method is scientific, and third, the material brought to light and presented in orderly arrangement is surprisingly extensive and valuable. . . . An astonishingly large part of it is quantitative.[48]

E. A. Ross, who commented favorably on the book to Harper and Brothers, wrote Sorokin:

Your book *Social Mobility* has just come to hand and I hasten to congratulate you upon it. It is wonderful that you are able to put out such a volume of very high class work so completely documented by works in all languages. . . . I feel that you have really subjugated this field and made it henceforth a province of Sociology. From now on every general treatise in Sociology will contain a chapter or chapters on social mobility. I foresee that you are destined to become a very large figure among American sociologists.[49]

Clearly this work opened a new field of sociological study.[50]

Sorokin's next work, *Contemporary Sociological Theories,* further broadened the horizons of American sociology and established him as a force to be dealt with. The book originated from his desire for a basic text summarizing the previous sixty or so years of developments in theory. No such work existed, and he needed one to use in his graduate theory course. He further realized that the recent growth of theory had isolated both sociological specialists and novices. Criminologists, demographers, and statisticians rarely had the time to read the hundreds of sources addressing theoretical issues. The novice had the more complicated problem of discriminating between existing theories and sorting the valid from the false. Unless these problems were addressed, students and researchers would waste valuable time going down theoretical dead ends or reinventing the wheel. Thus a carefully done, critical analysis of contemporary theory would be "a real service to the science of sociology."[51]

The book focused on schools of sociological theory. A school is a system of sociological ideas with a common definition of reality that stresses the same variables in the explanation of social phenomena. The school may include a variety of perspectives that share a common set of domain assumptions. On these criteria Sorokin defined nine major schools and discussed the principal works that defined each. The schools' important generalizations and principles were evaluated with a critical eye toward how well they accounted for the facts they purported to explain. In this way Sorokin provided readers with a sense of each theory's validity.

Critics could take issue not only with the analysis but with the evaluations and the accuracy or objectivity of the classification scheme. Sorokin acknowledged that all contained subjective elements. Readers should not take the classification as a dogmatic statement of the structure of theory and quibble over its precision and completeness. Instead, they should see it as a technical device for presentation of material. As to analysis and evaluation, he had focused mainly on those theories that addressed facts and, he believed, assessed them accurately. If others found his analysis too critical, they should recall that science lives and grows through criticism; his and theirs in tandem would move sociology toward a better understanding of the social world.

In the eyes of many of America's sociologists, Sorokin achieved the goals of his book. He also correctly anticipated several lines of opposition. As Harry Elmer Barnes wrote Harper and Brothers:

It is a monumental volume showing remarkably wide acquaintance with the field of sociology. I know of very few other men who could have written such a book. It will be of untold value to all serious students of sociology in this country. While I believe that the classification of the writers studied could have been more logical and illuminating, nevertheless there is no other book in the English language which in any way compares with Sorokin's as a summary of the achievements of contemporary sociology.[52]

E. A. Ross stated: "To the sociologist or the graduate student of sociology, this book is invaluable. It will save him from getting lost in the jungle of theories. . . . Every sociologist in the world will keep this book not far from his elbow in the next five years."[53] Floyd N. House, while cautious of Sorokin's evaluations, observed: "Naturally, one does not agree with all of the criticisms . . . but I must agree that in most cases they are very intelligent. The mass of material brought together in this volume is remarkable. . . . this will make a very useful text for use in graduate courses, as well as a good handbook of reference for the instructor or research worker."[54]

Professional journal reviewers voiced similar assessments of the book's strengths and limitations. Robert MacIver, writing in the *Annals of the American Academy of Arts and Sciences*, commented:

"In the opinion of the writer," says Professor Sorokin, "the primary task of the scholar is to deal with facts rather than theories." [This is] the popular pragmatic notion that there is something almost illicit about theorizing . . . that there is in short some deep opposition between facts and theories. It implies a weakness in the fundamental logic of the author. . . . There is a peculiar lack of balance and proportion in his treatment. His want of sympathy for theory leads him to omit all consideration of sociological thinkers like Oppenheimer or Muller-Lyer. There is no reference to the more important works of Hobhouse, which he would probably dismiss as a kind of metaphysics, while he devotes many pages to trumpery writers like Winiarsky. At the same time his work is critical as well as descriptive of the various sociological schools of the present and the near past, and often his criticisms are trenchant and effective. His knowledge of European as well as American sociology is exhaustively drawn upon.[55]

Another future president of the American Sociological Society, Edward B. Reuter, reviewed the book for the *American Journal of Sociology* and concluded: "The book is very valuable. It is by no means a great book. Its style is rough, its organization mechanical, its tone dogmatic, and its bias pronounced. Nevertheless it attempts a much needed survey. Its harsh criticism of much current theory is stimulating. . . . The sociologists should read it; graduate students should be required to read it."[56] The book's value for students and researchers was also appreciated by A. B. Wolfe in his piece for the *American Economic Review:* "Not only sociologists but social scientists in other fields will find the book informing and valuable. Students of population and social selection, in particular, will find it worth while to consult. It cannot fail to remain for a long time a valuable reference work."[57]

In fourteen chapters Sorokin takes a panoramic walk through what he described as the forest of sociological theory. As in any forest, one finds sterile flowers, weeds, strong trees, healthy plants, and beautiful flowers. The wily sociologist should seek and use the beautiful, healthy, and strong forms while avoiding their barren or uncultivated counterparts. Sterile flowers are theories that exhaust themselves on questions such as these: What is sociology? What should it be? What is progress? What is the relationship between society and the individual? What are the differences between cultural, social, and psychological phenomena? Many scholars spend entire careers in these "antechambers of sociology" and mistake them for the whole building. They pile words upon words without producing any genuine understanding of the social world. In Sorokin's mind these theorists were partly responsible for the anti-sociological sentiments of many intellectuals. Critics of sociology right-fully said, "Instead of a long and tedious reasoning of what sociology is, show it in fact. Instead of a discussion of how sociology ought to be built, build it. Instead of 'flapping' around the introductory problems of a science . . . give us a single real analysis of the phenomena."[58] To coun-ter this unfortunate tendency, Sorokin offered an operational approach to the discipline. He argued that what sociologists are doing clearly reveals the subject matter of the discipline. Sociology is

a study, first, of the relationship and correlations between various classes of social phenomena, (correlations between economic and religious; family and moral; juridical and economic; mobility and political phenomena and so on); second, that between the social and the nonsocial (geographic, biological, etc.,) phenomena; third, the study of the general characteristics common to all classes of social phenomena.[59]

All of the general schools concern themselves with different aspects of this definition. Whether sociologists like it or not, such seems to be the real subject matter of their discipline.

The sociological forest also abounds with weeds. The most trouble-some and damaging among them is the "sociological preacher," who is concerned with what is good or bad, how to save the world from evil, and how humans should best progress in the modern age. Practitioners of this style

have pretended to be omniscient doctors who know how the world is to be saved and give their "prescriptions" about war eradication, birth-control, labor organiza-tion, . . . and so forth. In this way, all kinds of nonsense have been styled, published, circulated and taught as "sociology." Every idler has pretended to be a sociologist. Shall we wonder that this again has discredited sociology greatly.[60]

Other weeds in the forest are those who overgeneralize from their find-ings, insufficiently study existing facts, are ignorant of past knowledge, and use sloppy logic combined with carelessness in testing and verifying hypotheses. These practices and the scholars who use them create major problems for the acceptance of sociology by serious scientists. Such underbrush must be cleared away so the strong plants and beautiful flowers of scientific sociology can bloom and replace the forest with a well-tended garden.

Sorokin followed *Contemporary Sociological Theories* with his studies of rural and urban sociology. He wrote *Principles of Rural-Urban Sociology* with Carle Zimmerman and the three-volume *Systematic Source-Book in Rural Sociology* with Zimmerman and Charles J. Galpin. Zimmerman, who had completed his doctorate in 1925, was given a professional appointment upon graduation. His principal interests were statistics and rural life. Zimmerman had come to Minnesota to study empirical methods with Chapin and the agricultural economist John D. Black. There he learned to apply cross-tabulation analysis, partial and multiple correlation techniques, and a variety of other statistical measures to large data sets. At the time there were few places in the country that provided such training. He joined his statistical skills to rural sociology and distinguished himself as a student.

Shortly after commencement, Chapin suggested that he and Sorokin teach a seminar in rural sociology. The course was successful, and they decided to continue their collaboration by publishing a volume containing all available materials on the moral, psychological, and environmental differences between populations in urban and rural areas. Sorokin was then busy on *Contemporary Sociological Theories,* so Zimmerman began the work with the understanding that Sorokin would catch up later. Indeed he did. As Zimmerman notes, the story of these volumes is an interesting one:

To make a long story short, by 1927 we had written not one but *three* volumes covering every field we could visualize about rural-urban differences and made our interpretations.

Since that was too much for one work I agreed to try and find subsidy money for publishing our venture. Hence I wrote Dr. C. J. Galpin, then director of studies of Rural Society in the Department of Agriculture at Washington D.C. and asked him to subsidize our work from funds available in his budget. He agreed to meet me at a conference . . . in Michigan State University the summer of 1927. I went there hoping for a positive answer but he refused to grant any. . . .

Fortunately an hour or so later I met Eduard C. Lindeman, a sociologist and free-lance writer, who took an interest in my grief. He noticed my extreme depression. There were tears in my eyes. He took me to dinner and said that he would get a grant of five hundred dollars for us if we would agree to cut our three volumes down to one and publish it as a text book in rural sociology. . . . So I took the money . . . and purchased two typewriters and some other equipment. Within a year we cut down the three-volume results into a one-volume work, and published it early in 1929 with Henry Holt and Co. as *Principles of Rural-Urban Sociology.* When Dr. Galpin saw this work, he apparently regretted his earlier rejection and came to the University of Minnesota and offered to finance the preparation and elaboration of the original three volumes with pertinent readings. He agreed to pay for the expense of making the manuscript ready if the University would publish it. This was done gradually over the next several years.[61]

And so the first volume of *A Source-Book in Rural Sociology* was published in 1930, and the others came out in 1931 and 1932.

Principles was published as a single volume for two additional reasons. First, and most important, there was nothing like it among existing rural textbooks. Its character, scope of materials, and method of analysis were unique. Second, it provided students and the public with a text of manageable size at a reasonable cost. *Principles* was not simply a collection of information on rural living but a sociology of rural life. As such it formulated the important and persistent differences between rural and urban life and explained their distinctive characteristics through social structural analysis. Sorokin and Zimmerman refused to oversimplify their analysis and quickly introduced readers to sociology as a generalizing science. The discipline was not concerned with the unique or idiosyncratic but with the patterned, repetitive, and recurrent aspects of social life. The focus of sociology was described in the same general way as at the conclusion of *Contemporary Sociological Theories*. As a generalizing science it differed from the individualized social sciences. Sociology incorporated the specialized sciences and accounted for their uniformities and differences in findings with a more general theory that did not ignore the complexities of the phenomena. Such was the distinctive task of the discipline:

It does not postulate any one-sided and simplified homo-economicus or homo-politicus. It deals with men and their relationships in all their real complexity. Homo-sociologicus is a composite homo who in part is homo-economicus, in part homo-politicus, in part homo-religiocus, in part homo-aestheticus, and so on. . . . The social relationships of such sociological men are far more complex than those postulated by the above special sciences.[62]

The database of *Principles* further distinguished it from existing texts that dealt only with the United States. This book marshaled data from an impressive number of foreign countries. The broader base avoided culture-bound generalizations and presented more accurate, reliable, and valid statements about the differences between rural and urban life. Cross-national information further allowed the authors to clarify or correct faulty generalizations made by previous researchers. Comparative data on rural and urban differences in physical characteristics, health, patterns of morbidity and mortality, rates of suicide, fertility, longevity, marriage, IQ, and mental illness were presented and analyzed. To these characteristics was added a comparative analysis of institutions that included family, stratification, religion, deviance, art, and politics. *Principles* did not re-cover old ground but was devoted to unanswered questions about rural life.

Sorokin and Zimmerman avoided other common textbook pitfalls. The level of discussion was not diluted for the sake of "entertaining simplicity." Issues were presented in all their complexity and the gaps in understanding made clear. Furthermore, the sterile flower of "sociological preaching" was strictly avoided. Excluded were the common value-laden discussions of the good and bad in rural and urban life. Each author supressed any "sympathetic attitudes" toward rural life in favor of objective discussion.

Reviews were again mixed. Writers in technical publications and the popular press were more positive than those in the sociological journals. R. D. McKenzie, in the *American Journal of Sociology*, found the book full of important imperfections. Unclear, imprecise, and poorly formed definitions marred the work with major conceptual ambiguities, particularly the questionable distinction drawn between the fundamental ideas of rural and urban. Divergent data sets often yielded unconvincing conclusions followed by inadequate explanations. Usually these were either commonsensical or something less noble. For McKenzie the book promised more than it delivered. While a superficial examination suggested a work of great erudition, closer study showed it was "far from being a work of science." While it contained much useful information, it failed as a systematic analysis.[63] Floyd N. House was similarly unimpressed. To him, readers were bombarded with data and a pretentious scientific analysis that provided little beyond commonsense understanding.[64]

Nels Anderson, a sociologist who reviewed the book for the *New Republic*, found it a superior text: "Rural American sociology, basking in provincialism, needs just such a stimulus as this. Sorokin and Zimmerman show that these rural problems are not only world-wide but often ages old, and Old World scholars have been facing them and studying them for years. Such a larger perspective is just what rural sociology needs if it is to rise to the dignity of a natural science."[65] An unsigned review in *Information Service* found that the book broke new ground and did "much to bring American rural sociology out of the provincialism from which it has admittedly suffered."[66] A reviewer in *Commonweal* stated, "With the publication of this volume, rural sociology has become of age both chronologically and psychologically."[67]

In 1930 the first volume of the *Source Book* came out, followed by the others over the next two years. The book was intended to be a complete compendium of theory and research in rural sociology. A complex set of chapter introductions, interstitial materials, and excerpts from over 150 articles were the means used to tie the materials together. Discussion began with a theoretical account of rural life from ancient times to the nineteenth century. The second part focused on rural social organization, particularly the distribution of property, social mobility, and stratification of the populations. Sources and data were global and established a foundation for generalizations that was not bound in narrow corridors of space and time. The second volume, organized similarly, was an institutional analysis of rural life. The family was focal, but discussion included the economy, education, crime, morality and deviance, religion, art, and politics. The third volume covered physical, demographic, and psychosocial characteristics of rural populations. The final section dealt with the dynamics of rural-urban relationships. Almost sixty readings were used to integrate the materials in this volume.

These two works laid the foundation for the rural sociology program at Minnesota. However, the program was only a part of the broader tradition of scholarship begun there by Sorokin and Zimmerman. "The Sorokin-Zimmerman Sociological School"[68] emphasized the study of social change as fundamental. Their approach differed from that of the social evolutionist in that it recognized no patterns or ultimate goals for change. While they did not ignore social structure, it was not given the same priority later assigned it by the structural functionalist. A knowledge of structure was important only as an aid to understanding change. Their approach further emphasized a lineage of sociological thought grounded in the great European traditions of the nineteenth and early twentieth centuries. Using *Contemporary Sociological Theories* as a hub, they stressed the continuity of Western social thought. The third major element of their approach was method and application. Sociology should be both scientific and useful. While value neutrality was essential for logical judgments, it was a fiction in terms of the application of knowledge. The goal of sociology was "to understand mankind and to be guided by these conclusions."[69] Sorokin and Zimmerman set these goals for rural sociology, and they were plainly reflected in their coauthored works.

Both books did much to dispel the theoretical provincialism of the subfield. The scope of their data produced more scientifically useful generalizations than were typical for the time. Additionally, these volumes cleared away many conventional, almost stereotypical, beliefs about people in rural areas. For example, the genuine class position of farmers was shown to be intermediate to that of owners and workers. By working the land they owned, farmers shared interests with both capital and labor. As such, they were a distinctive stratum and opposed to those who hoped to build a Farmer-Labor Party. It was unlikely, in Sorokin and Zimmerman's analysis, that farmers would ever join with the urban proletariat to oppose the capitalist. Indeed, farmers were largely unmoved by the problems of urban labor. They were radicalized only when their possessions and control of land were jeopardized.[70] Sorokin and Zimmerman's work also provided new insights into arguments over the physical differences between urban and rural dwellers. They provided novel ideas on the social-psychological makeup of the two groups, how each relied on different types of experience (direct and indirect) for learning, and the stability and fluctuating nature of their attitudes. Variances in criminality were explained as a result of population density, family stability, psychosocial heterogeneity, and mobility. The authors documented the city as a source of cultural innovation and the countryside as a stabilizing preserver of culture. The dynamics of this relationship illustrated their fundamental sensitivity to social change.

Sorokin's and Zimmerman's impact on rural sociology was strongly felt in and outside of Minnesota. Through their teachings they developed a crop of disciples whose work also influenced the field. Among their prominent students were T. Lynn Smith, who wrote *Sociology of Rural Life;* Charles Price Loomis, who with J. Allen Beegle published *Rural Social Systems* and *Rural Sociology— The Strategy of Change;* Paul H. Landis, author of *Rural Life in Process;* and Edgar A. Schuler, Nathan Whetten, C. Arnold Anderson, Otis Durant Duncan, and Fred Frey, who also published widely in the field. Sorokin and Zimmerman were the teachers of teachers who went out and spread the word. Their students did pioneering studies in foreign lands, occupied important research positions in government agencies, were instrumental in establishing a separate society and journal for rural sociologists, and later filled leadership positions in that society.[71]

Charles J. Galpin, who joined the team on the *Source Book,* was also a major force in rural sociology. He had been educated at Colgate, Harvard, and Clark University. For all his life he was an enthusiastic student of rural America. At the age of forty-one he went to Madison, Wisconsin, as a student pastor in a local church. There he met Henry C. Taylor, who later organized the Bureau of Agricultural Economics in the Department of Agriculture. Galpin's research impressed Taylor, then chairman of the economics department at the university. Taylor invited Galpin to join the faculty. Galpin accepted and stayed with the university until 1919, when Taylor called him to Washington as head of the Division of Farm Life Studies, a position he kept until retiring in 1934. During his career he would not only publish important books, and develop seminal ideas and methodologies, but would also become a prime source of funding for research projects in rural sociology. It was these credentials that brought him onto the *Source Book*.[72]

Relationships among these three scholars were not without strains, as became apparent years later when Galpin published an abbreviated statement of his memoirs, *My Drift into Rural Sociology*, in the December 1937 issue of *Rural Sociology*.[73] In this piece Galpin draws on the preface to the first volume of the *Source Book* and gives Sorokin the lion's share of the credit for the production and the analysis of the work. Sorokin had written in the preface:

> It should be stated also that most of the introductions, selections, and systematization of the material and, in general, the greater part of the work of the *Source Book* were done by Professor Pitirim Sorokin. Without the encyclopedic knowledge of the literature of rural thought and of sociological theory that he brought to this task and his indefatigable attention to the details of arrangement and interpretation, the *Source Book* would not have been thought possible at this time.[74]

Zimmerman wrote Galpin, objecting to his comments based on Sorokin's claim. Zimmerman began by restating the history of the *Source Book*, leading up to their first meeting in East Lansing. After *Principles* came out, they met again in Minneapolis, and Galpin agreed to finance the *Source Book*. Zimmerman wrote:

> At that time, as I gathered the proposal, it was to be an arrangement whereby the *Source Book* was to be published jointly by Sorokin and yourself. I felt considerably cut-up about the matter then, but finally agreed to give up any right to a thing which I felt I had fathered. . . . Dean Coffey, who knew the work I had been doing on the *Source Book* since 1925, objected to that proposition . . . and as a result my name was still carried as a partner in the *Source Book*. After that time until I wrote the Preface to the third volume and finished the Index in '32, I was busy all the time on this *Source Book*, except the year I was in Siam. When I left for Siam practically all of the details were completed because Sorokin left Minnesota the same year to begin his new work at Harvard. *You wrote the Preface to Volume I, but Sorokin rewrote it (contrary to my feelings on the matter) and made it appear as if the work were practically all his* [emphasis added].
>
> Without minimizing the contributions of any one to the *Source Book*, the point I want to make is that I think I played a greater role in the whole matter than you indicate in the first line of page 428 in *Rural Sociology*. This was my first great plan for a life work, and . . . I think I really contributed something of importance. I suffered exceedingly in trying to balance and hold forth my views and contributions. . . .

I write this letter merely to establish my viewpoints on three problems. First, I hope I do not or have not ridden Sorokin's shoulders to any reputation; second, I am not a "yes" man but, I hope, a plodding scholar in my own right; and third, I conceived and made original contributions to these four volumes in about the same proportions as the allocation of chapters is made in the Preface to *Principles of Rural-Urban Sociology*.[75]

Galpin replied to Zimmerman on 19 January 1938 that "it was a gross oversight of mine not to have written you and Dr. Sorokin before completing my statement about the *Source Book*." He blamed memory and his own narrow point of view for the oversight and encouraged Zimmerman and Sorokin to draw up an appropriate statement giving the division of labor so he could include it in his book.[76] Zimmerman's reply shows that he held no malice toward Galpin, but he clearly stated he was not in a position to get any clarifying statements from Sorokin:

Unfortunately, however, I am not in a position nor do I wish anyone else to ask Sorokin to make any statements. Sorokin has had a change of personality since he came to Harvard, and I do not plan to ask him for any favors of any kind whatsoever. He has indicated to me that he is very tickled by your statements, and I can see that he is pleased because they give him all of the credit and in addition help to bolster up his ego. I felt this development when he rewrote the Preface to Volume I of the *Source Book*. I could not at that time protest. I dropped the whole matter and was not reminded of it again until your *Memoirs* came out repeating for permanent record overstatements which Sorokin made at that time.[77]

Regardless of their differences, these men did forge an important part of the history of rural sociology in America. Sorokin and Zimmerman, through their scholarship and teaching, occupy a significant position in the lineage of that discipline.

Reviewers received the *Source Book* favorably. Carl C. Taylor pointed out certain minor flaws but concluded that "it will be instantly recognized . . . that the *Source Book in Rural Sociology* is by long odds the greatest contribution yet made to the field."[78] Carl Rosenquist, in the *American Economic Review*, felt the book was unusually scientific for a work in sociology: "To one who has felt a lack of solidity in much of the literature of sociology, the reading of this volume gives genuine pleasure. It exhibits the qualities of objectivity in its approach, freedom from notions of social reform, and the application of thorough-going scholarship—qualities not yet as common in sociological writing as might be desired."[79] Dwight Sanderson credited the interpretation and systematic analysis to Sorokin and observed: "It is an American product of European scholarship, and should stimulate and aid sociological analysis of rural life throughout the world, by giving a new perspective and a more adequate background of the best thought and research in this field. It will be indispensable to the library of every college where rural sociology is taught, and to every serious student of the subject."[80]

The *Source Book* was widely read by rural sociologists. Those in Japan were impressed by the work and by Sorokin as a scholar. Eitaro Suzuki wrote that "both the system of the book and greater part of the contents is the work of Professor Sorokin [whose name] is too well known in our academic circles of sociologists, and so are his works, e.g., *Social Mobility* and *Contemporary Sociological Theories*. . . . He has appeared among the circle of American sociologists just like a comet and has been shining so brilliantly." Suzuki concluded that the *Source Book* and *Principles* had substantially raised the level of scholarship in American rural sociology.[81]

Enemies and Opportunities

These four works put Sorokin on the sociological map. The books simultaneously stimulated and irritated American sociologists. All were primary works. Each was scientific in approach, cross-cultural in scope, and employed a historical perspective. Individually and collectively, they broadened the horizons of American sociology. The books had an enduring quality and were widely read by sociologists. *Social Mobility* was republished in 1959 as *Social and Cultural Mobility;* there were also Chinese and Spanish translations of *Social Mobility* in 1933 and 1956, respectively. In 1963 an Italian translation of *Social and Cultural Mobility* appeared. *Principles of Rural-Urban Sociology* and the *Source Book* also lived long: *Principles* was reissued in 1959 and again in 1969; an abbreviated Japanese edition appeared in 1931–32. The *Source Book* was reissued in 1965, and *Contemporary Sociological Theories* was reissued in 1964. The earlier edition of *Contemporary Sociological Theories* was translated into nine languages: German (1931), French (1938), Serbian (1933), Czechoslovakian (1936), Chinese (1932 and 1936), Turkish (1949 and 1950), Portuguese (1951), Hindi (1963), and Japanese (1930). Even a cursory glance through the more contemporary literature in these subfields will show that the books still regularly appear.

Sorokin's works challenged and alienated important advocates of major theoretical perspectives in the discipline. As he notes, "A small minority of American sociologists have tried to undervalue my works as much as they could. . . . a part of this minority even started a deliberate campaign to 'discredit Sorokin.' " Sorokin attributed this action mostly to genuine disagreements over ideas, his anticommunist position, and the mistaken belief that he played a role in L. L. Bernard's "resignation." He further believed his detractors saw him as a Russian émigré whose writings had little scholarly value and who, as such, should be put in his place.[82] Sorokin's ideas and style gored many a sacred ox of early American sociologists. His approach to sociology showed little patience for social reformers or "sociological preachers." Both of these traditions, however, were deeply embedded in the discipline. The content of early American sociology was shaped by the effects of industrialization, urbanization, and immigration on post–Civil War society. Each process had transformed the nation. Urbanization had reconstructed the eastern states and spread to the Midwest. The material quality of life was changing. New technology transformed daily life: incandescent lightbulbs, telephones, mass transportation, department stores, skyscrapers, and automobiles brought change into all but the most remote hamlets. In the wake of each process came new social problems: unemployment, poverty, racial issues, crime, juvenile delinquency, alcoholism, and mental illness all increased. These problems and processes became the content of sociological teaching, writing, and research. The concern had two foci: the systematic explanation of these changes, and amelioration. Sorokin felt sociology should be useful but was more inclined toward a science of society as the basic business of the discipline. In his enthusiasm he often depreciated others' concerns with practical problems and social improvements. He was far removed from the social Darwinists and Spencerians who stressed survival of the fittest and noninterference. However, it was useless to concern oneself with unanswerable questions such as What is the good society and how do we bring it into being? Is progress good or bad? What form of social organization would minimize current social problems? These were philosophical, ethical issues and not amenable to scientific study. The goal of sociologists should be a science of society.

Sorokin was further separated from the mainstream by his denunciation of "sociological preachers." Early practitioners came largely from rural and religious backgrounds, and many such men had powerful positions in the discipline. Of the nineteen presidents of the American Sociological Society born prior to 1880, only one had an urban upbringing. Furthermore, almost all were fundamentally concerned with the ethical dimensions of social issues and sociology.

This concern can be understood when it is realized that these men grew to maturity at a time when the religious and ethical traditions of Protestantism still dominated the nation. Often their reformism was a secular version of the Christian concern with salvation and redemption and was a direct outgrowth of religious antecedents in their personal lives. Lester F. Ward's maternal grandfather, and Franklin H. Giddings' and William I. Thomas' fathers had been ministers; William G. Sumner, Albion W. Small, George E. Vincent, Edward C. Hayes, James P. Lichtenberger, Ulysses G. Weatherly, and John L. Gillian had themselves had earlier ministerial careers. This recurrent combination of rural background with inculcation of religious ideals was an important part of the experiential framework within which so many early sociologists interpreted and evaluated the conditions and problems of urban, industrial life.[83]

Furthermore, there were twenty-one ministers among the founding members of the American Economic Association, and five influential clergymen were prominent in the founding of the American Sociological Society, an offspring of the AEA.[84] Sorokin's focus on "preachers" was unfortunate because it offended many social reformers and others who were tied to the ministry. Taken together, this was a sizable and important group to alienate.

Sorokin was also critical of those who viewed sociology as a speculative form of philosophy; who were concerned with developing a philosophy of history; or who valued case approaches to the study of society over statistical, cross-national methods. Discussing these as weeds and sterile flowers in the sociological forest did not endear him to such sociologists. Many found his criticisms unpalatable and would have supported, if not joined, a movement to discredit his position.

Sorokin also lost support among many members and participants in the Chicago School of Sociology. The Chicago scholars exerted great control over the discipline and a hegemonic influence over sociological ideas. While Sorokin knew their works, he did not give them the salience and paeans to which they were accustomed. In *Mobility* he hardly acknowledged Chicago. The works of Park and Burgess are mentioned mainly in footnotes or in long listings of theorists concerned with a particular problem. Such is also the fate of Ellsworth Faris, W. I. Thomas, and William F. Ogburn.[85]

The Chicago scholars got more attention in *Contemporary Sociological Theories,* but not all of it was flattering. Sorokin placed Park and Burgess among the prominent members of the formal school and found their classifications of social phenomena problematic. Their definitions lacked clarity, and many of their concepts, such as attitude, were "logical monsters." These problems were a product of their reliance on Simmel's method, which itself lacked logic, a scientific foundation, or a "systematic factual study of the phenomena discussed."[86] Sorokin's trenchant criticisms of Simmel extended to the whole formal school. While not explicitly calling formalism a weed or sterile flower, he does say that this view of sociology made the discipline "represent something so insignificant that it scarcely would deserve the name of a sociology or any other science."[87]

Sorokin also criticized Albion Small and William Ogburn. He found Small's thinking on Gumplovitz "loose and misleading" and could not understand how Small and Ward reconciled Gumplovitz's theory with their own. To Sorokin they were contradictory. The sharpest barb was reserved for Small's analysis of Marx. He found Small's prediction that in "the ultimate judgement of history Marx will have a place in social science analogous with that of Galileo in the physical sciences" to be poorly informed and naive.[88] Also, Small blundered in ascribing to Marx the discovery of the idea of class struggle.[89] Sorokin saw some value in Ogburn's work on culture change but did not accept Ogburn's thesis that in the modern era changes in material culture preceded changes in nonmaterial culture. Ogburn's thesis of culture lag was flawed. He correctly perceived that material inventions were the motor force of technological change. But inventions were the results of the application of ideas (nonmaterial culture) to a problem, and thus precede the appearance of the physical invention. Therefore, Ogburn's dynamics of culture change was at the very least questionable and most likely incorrect.[90] The works of Ellsworth Faris and W. I. Thomas were discussed mainly in footnotes, while G. H. Mead and Louis Wirth were not discussed at all. Wirth had just been published, and Sorokin may not have seen his work. Mead had written little; his major works would not be compiled by his students until after 1931.

The Chicago sociologists were also ignored in the *Source Book* and *Principles.* As Nels Anderson observed in his review of *Principles:* "I feel that the authors did not strengthen their case by failing to recognize the so-called 'Chicago group' of sociologists. None of them are mentioned but some of them made contributions to this field."[91] The exclusion of the Chicago scholars from the limelight was particularly notable in *Contemporary Sociological Theories,* where Sorokin almost totally ignored the most important body of American theory and gave short, and at times caustic, attention to its progenitors.[92]

Sorokin's works, in turn, were given critical and often bruising treatment by the Chicago scholars. The review by Andrew Lind of *Social Mobility* in the *American Journal of Sociology* followed in the footsteps of Grierson's and Park's earlier treatment of *Revolution.* Lind disposed of the entire 559-page book in a fifteen-line review.[93] His treatment of Sorokin led C. H. Cooley to write the then editor of the journal, E. W. Burgess:

that the review of Sorokin's *Social Mobility* in the March number is deplorable. . . . . perhaps you have been unable to get a more competent or less indolent reviewer. Wouldn't it have been better to have had no review at all of *Social Mobility* than to inflict upon it so perfunctory, and hence so contemptuous, a notice? Surely the book is . . . *comparable to the best work produced in this country or anywhere else.* How must the author feel when such a work is received in such a manner by the leading review in his field?[94]

Burgess agreed, and the book was reviewed by Rudolf Heberle later that year.[95] Other Chicago men had also been critical of Sorokin's books—for example, E. B. Reuter's review of *Contemporary Sociological Theories* and R. D. McKenzie's and Floyd House's respective reviews of *Principles.* A line had indeed been drawn in the sand, and the breech between Sorokin and the Chicago scholars was growing. Some believe that a person's importance is indicated by the stature of his enemies. If true, then Sorokin was emerging as a major figure in American sociology.

The pioneering nature of Sorokin's books, combined with changes in the discipline, contributed substantially to his ascent. World War I raised several important issues for social scientists. The war challenged the social evolutionary views that humankind had advanced from its primitive origins to a rational and civilized state; war was irrational and clearly demonstrated a lack of human progress. Furthermore, it shifted attention from domestic social problems and their amelioration. Social scientists now wanted a body of theory capable of explaining human actions in the same way that physical scientists accounted for natural order. Before humankind could be changed or improved, it must first be understood. This was best accomplished when concrete phenomena were dealt with empirically. Explanations using a philosophy of history, a social evolutionary, or a speculative framework were eschewed. These basically deductive approaches were replaced by an inductive preference for theory building. In this new approach objective concepts and data replaced a traditional reliance on more subjective indicators. Sociologists became concerned with things that were observable, quantifiable, and verifiable. They avoided concepts such as mind, wishes, motives, subconsciousness, and self, which were nonobservable and hence nonverifiable. Older particularistic (single-factor) explanations were shunned in favor of more adequate multicausal explanations, and statistical methods and data became the preferable forms of analysis and information. If sociology was to become a science, then it must use "the common credential of scientific respectability—quantification."[96] This emerging reorientation of the discipline was highly congruent with the form of sociology advocated by Sorokin. He was thus in an admirable, strong, and conspicuous position at the cutting edge of the discipline.

Along with these theoretical changes, the postwar period was one of great growth for the discipline. College enrollments doubled between 1920 and 1930, and sociology was popular with the new students. Undergraduate majors increased substantially, and the number of graduate students and doctoral degrees multiplied three- and fourfold, respectively, between 1920 and 1930. This growth was also reflected in the American Sociological Society, whose membership increased by 113 percent in the same period. The society was transformed by its growth, becoming dominated by younger midwestern sociologists looking for change and committed to a scientific sociology. The older founding members were now outnumbered, and the society's politics reflected the change. Topical areas for the meetings and formats of discussion changed as the midwesterners came to control the society.[97] Such changes meant opportunity for Sorokin. Many of his books became required reading in graduate and undergraduate courses. Minnesota was a force within the discipline, giving him visibility and prestige, and putting him on the crest of a wave that would reorient the discipline and alter its politics. His works were innovative at a time when sociologists were seeking new approaches and answers. Sorokin's books had clearly defined and contributed to important sociological subfields. As a result of intellect, hard work, and vision, in seven years he went from émigré scholar to a power to be dealt with in American sociology.

3

Golden Opportunities

A Visit to Boston

SOROKIN'S RISING STAR did not go unnoticed by academic institutions wanting to make or improve their reputations in sociology. After the publication of the first volume of the *Source Book*, he received offers of full professorships from two major state universities. Feeling at home in Minnesota, he turned them down. In the spring of 1929 the Department of Economics and the Committee on Sociology and Social Ethics at Harvard invited Sorokin to give a short series of lectures and seminars. Although Harvard had no sociology program, the school's reputation convinced him to accept. As Sorokin noted, he was surprised by the invitation because he "had never visited Harvard and knew hardly any of its eminent scholars personally. Up to the time of this invitation my contacts with Harvard had been limited to receiving complimentary letters about my work from professors F. Taussig, T. Carver and J. D. Black and to reading quite favorable review articles about my volumes in the *Harvard* [*sic*] *Quarterly Journal of Economics.*"[1]

Sorokin suspected there was more to the invitation than a simple desire to hear his ideas. He felt like a "bridegroom" as he moved between the speaking engagements and the more informal meetings with many of Harvard's notables. Most of his visit was spent with economists Charles J. Bullock, Edwin F. Gay, Frank W. Taussig, Thomas N. Carver and their junior colleagues Karl Bigelow, Carl Joslyn, and Talcott Parsons. During this time, however, there was no discussion of a possible position, and Sorokin left Harvard with a large check in his pocket and feeling his lectures had been successful.

On returning to Minnesota, Pitirim and Elena prepared for a vacation in Colorado. They would spend a month camping, fishing, and enjoying the grandeur of the mountains. After a few changes to the *Source Book*, they left for a well-deserved rest. As their Model T Ford moved west, Pitirim thought about his next major effort. He was becoming increasingly preoccupied with the idea of a major study of social change. When the thought took shape, the enormity of it produced a deep apprehension. As envisioned, the study

54

would demand all of his energies and the work of a great number of other scholars. Years of his life and substantial support would be required to complete the task. This last item was worrisome because, besides Galpin's contribution for the *Source Book,* Minnesota in six years had given him only $12.45 in research support.[2]

Except for an occasional flash, these thoughts were put aside as the Sorokins became engulfed in the beauty of Trail Ridge, Never-No-Summer, Mount Elbert, Monarch Pass, Pike's Peak, and other Colorado wonders. On this trip all of their nights were spent in the open. Though the old Ford was often "disorderly," they moved over the narrow dirt roads and high, hairpin turns with happy hearts. No schedules had to be followed. They were free to eat and sleep when and where they chose; dress as they liked; take their baths in rivers and hot springs; and stay up to count the stars during the clear and chilly mountain nights. Days were full of fishing, canoeing, climbing, and long, aimless walks through the forests of the great mountain state. There was plenty of time to think, talk, plan, and hope, and most of all to relax and enjoy each other in the serenity of their mountain campsites. Small wonder that they returned rested and full of optimism.

Back at the university, Pitirim again pondered his next great challenge and the coming semester's work. But his world changed when the following letter arrived from Harvard's president, Abbott Lawrence Lowell:

SEPTEMBER 25, 1929

Dear Professor Sorokin:

I write to ask whether you would consider a professorship of Sociology at Harvard University. We have no such chair but are thinking of establishing it and there is no one whom I should like to have in it as much as yourself. Perhaps you would not mind letting me know what the scale of your salary is now to guide me in making a recommendation to the Corporation.

The Economists would like the chair of Sociology within their Department, but I think there are others with which it is quite as much, if not more closely related, but I think we can leave that to your own choice if you come here.

Hoping very much that you will do so, I am

Yours very sincerely,[3]

At the time of this offer, Harvard lagged behind other distinguished universities in establishing a sociology program. A partial explanation is suggested in a December 1929 conversation between Lowell and Sorokin: "Among other things, at this meeting President Lowell told me that Harvard had already decided to establish a chair of sociology some twenty-five years before. They had not done so until then because there was no sociologist worthy to fill the chair. Now, in their opinion, such a sociologist had appeared, and they had promptly made the decision."[4] One may be tempted to view this statement as pure self-serving hyperbole, but an examination of the facts suggests otherwise. Harvard had indeed had several opportunities to appoint distinguished scholars to such a position.

The university's interest in sociology originated from earlier programs in the Divinity School and Department of Economics. Initially, sociology was tied to the field of social ethics and taught in the Divinity School. Francis Greenwood Peabody, the first U.S. professor of social ethics, gave a course in Practical Ethics in 1881. In 1883 he introduced a second course, Ethical Theories and Moral Reform, into the program. Both were popular and soon were incorporated into the undergraduate program of the college.[5] Peabody's sociology was heavily influenced by Unitarianism and the Social Gospel. He sought the foundations for a Christian society consistent with emerging modernity and constructed ethical bridges between older religious values and the newer secular scientific practices of society. Moral responsibility for Peabody began with individuals, and moral communities included the just and the sinful. The latter he divided into the redeemable and the damned. The redeemable merited charity, compassion, and assistance from the just. They were the worthy poor. Their disreputable brethren were beyond salvation and deserved miserable fates. An important task for Puritan authority was to distinguish between the two categories and establish the conditions for redemption. Sociology, as the new science of society, would provide a rational means to make these judgments and to work out a moral calculus for redemption.[6] Peabody's sociology sought the secular scientific understanding for the reconstruction of sinners and establishment of a moral community founded on the values of the just.

In 1906 his mission became institutionalized in an independent Department of Social Ethics. This entity resulted from Peabody's and Alfred Treadway White's concern for the moral education of young Harvard men. They believed in the importance of preparing students for social responsibility. White donated a quarter of a million dollars to ensure that Peabody's work became a permanent part of the university's course of instruction.[7] Peabody's program reached maturity under Richard Clarke Cabot, chairman from 1920 until the absorption of the department into sociology in 1931. In 1926, besides Cabot and Ford there were five tutors and fifty-six concentrators (majors) in the Department of Social Ethics.[8]

Sociology, as taught in economics, was formed by different goals and values. It sought a theory of social order. Although more theoretically oriented than Social Ethics, there was also a practical desire to apply sociology to the problems of poverty, immigration, and urbanization. This was particularly true for Edward Cummings. Cummings, who was strongly influenced by Le Bon and Tarde, became Harvard's first appointee in sociology.[9] Unlike Peabody, under whom he had studied, Cummings saw collective action as the way to effect social reform. He supported the settlement movement, workingmen's universities, and cooperatives. He firmly believed that the collection and analysis of sociological data were essential for intelligent public policies. Cummings's sociology was committed to inductive investigations directed at social reconstruction, although he never worked out the mechanism to accomplish this. He wrote no books and established no tradition of teaching or research. In 1900 Cummings was discharged from Harvard and replaced by Thomas Nixon Carver.[10] Carver represented sociology until the arrival of Sorokin.[11]

At the time of Carver's appointment, the Department of Economics had cast its lot with the Graduate School of Business. The department's scholars focused on economic ideology and policy, seeking to provide scientific guidance and vision aimed at the maximization of profit with the minimization of social disorder. Carver's sociology was evolutionary and ideological. He used a framework that simultaneously provided moral principles for economic development and rationales for the existence of morally inferior economic actors, races, and ethnic groups.[12] His sociology valued American superiority, Puritanism, and eugenics. The good society would result when immigrants, the poor, and the descendants of slaves accepted these values. IQ batteries, personal screening, and gene manipulation would constitute a "genetic means test" for entrance into society. Scientific sociologists should work with biologists and other scientists to establish a calculus for assimilation into the moral, materialistic order of American society.[13]

By 1927 changes at and outside of Harvard had led to a restructuring of sociological studies. Most important was the merging of students interested in sociology and concentrators in Social Ethics under the authority of the Committee on Sociology and Social Ethics, chaired by the eminent philosopher Ralph Barton Perry. On 4 October 1927 the faculty approved Abbott Lawrence Lowell's appointments of Professors Richard C. Cabot, William Y. Elliott, Edwin F. Gay, Earnest A. Hooton, Arthur M. Schlesinger, and Edward A. Whitney to serve under the direction of Professor Perry.[14] The new field superseded the concentration in Social Ethics. The concerns of this new program were clearly stated by Perry:

The new field of concentration is designed especially to unite the study of social facts with an examination of the standards and ideals by which these facts are to be judged. It is assumed that there are two equally legitimate questions which may be asked about society. First, what is society? and second, what ought society to be? . . . It is not intended that either of these inquiries shall be slighted. It is believed that their union will be fruitful, and that it will conduce to sound judgment on the concrete problems of contemporary civilization.[15]

It was clear, from the committee's title and Perry's statement, that the intent was to combine the most promising aspects of sociology and social ethics. The disciplines would become a single unit of study. The committee's work continued for three years, the final effort being completed under Sorokin.

Varied forces produced this transition. The Social Gospel had declined in influence as American society became more heterogeneous and pluralistic. There was increasing disenchantment with social Darwinism and evolutionary theory. Sociology, as the scientific study of human society, had been incorporated into the academic programs of many major universities, and Harvard was still behind in this major innovation. President Lowell was also uncomfortable with social ethics as a field for concentration. In February 1926 Cabot wrote Lowell requesting additional funds for his program. He pointed out that growing enrollments (from fourteen to fifty-eight concentrators over the last four years) had not been accompanied by an increase in the university's allowance for the program. Consequently, his department needed an additional $830 to meet the new demands. Lowell replied on 9 February:

I have not yet presented your letter to the Corporation, but will do so if you want me to. In the meanwhile, I write to say how the matter lies in my own mind. As you know, I do not think that Social Ethics is by itself a good subject for concentration; and therefore it seems to me that it is a mistake to offer as many courses in the subject as are now given. Personally, I think it would be better to have no courses except those offered by Professor Ford and yourself. If so, the difficulties of cost which you describe would disappear. The courses you offered would be taken by men concentrating in other subjects, and this, it seems to me, ought to be the case. Feeling as I do I cannot advise that the appropriation for the Department should be increased.[16]

Lowell disapproved because he believed that social ethics attracted lazy students looking for an easy way through college. The department was becoming a "refuge for students who do not care to work hard." Students did not see the program as a "severe discipline," and Lowell viewed Cabot as ineffective in maintaining the academic integrity of the program. So Lowell withheld support and did not appoint Cabot chairman of the Committee on Sociology and Social Ethics. He felt the chairmanship had to be in "the hands of a man belonging to one of the older and more severe subjects of education" and therefore appointed Perry.[17] The committee, with aid from Karl Bigelow, Carl Joslyn, and Talcott Parsons, completed its task at the end of 1930 and submitted its recommendations to the faculty. The new program called for the creation of an independent Division and Department of Sociology.

The new department would absorb the Department of Social Ethics and be staffed by two types of members: those with full-time commitments to the department and those dividing their teaching between sociology and their original departments. The "interdepartmental professors" were to be few in number but with full voting and participatory rights in sociology. The new program required students to complete prerequisites in other social sciences as a condition for concentration in sociology. Sociology was to be, in Lowell's words, a "severe discipline."

Had Harvard chosen to move earlier, the administration could have appointed Carver or Cabot to head sociology. Even before Sorokin's appointment, the social ethicists had nominated Leonard T. Hobhouse for the intended chair. No doubt there were other opportunities to call prominent scholars to Harvard, but the administration had decided not to do so. Now, with the offer to Sorokin, a decisive step had been taken and the gap filled.

While Sorokin's statement gives some insight into how he came to Harvard, it does not explain how he came to Lowell's attention or how the president was persuaded to make him an offer. Two other accounts shed light on these events and suggest Thomas Nixon Carver as the pivotal figure. Carver taught other courses in economics besides sociology. His offerings in agricultural economics were important because many graduate students attended Harvard to specialize in the subject. These obligations and those for courses in social reform and the distribution of wealth were spreading him thin. He would either have to drop a class or find a capable agricultural economist to carry the subfield. He had been unsuccessfully looking for some time when he was asked to review the manuscript of the Minnesota economist John D. Black. Carver was impressed:

As soon as I read Black's manuscript I not only advised Ginn and Company to publish it but made up my mind that Black was worth considering for a position at Harvard. After making numerous inquiries I decided to bring him to the attention of the department. On my recommendation he was invited to give a course of three lectures at Harvard. This gave other members of the department a chance to look him over. The upshot was that the department voted to recommend to the

Corporation that Black be offered an assistant professorship at Harvard. The offer was made, he accepted, and our offering in agricultural economics was notably strengthened.[18]

Black came to Harvard in 1927. He knew Sorokin and thought well of his works, particularly those in rural sociology. But Carver again took the initiative in bringing Sorokin to the university:[19]

At one of the meetings of the American Sociological Society I heard Sorokin of the University of Minnesota read a paper. I was impressed by his prodigious learning and general sanity. I began to cultivate his acquaintance and finally was instrumental in bringing him to Harvard. The procedure was the same as in the Black case. The Department of Economics, on my motion, invited him to give a course of three lectures at Harvard. While he was in Cambridge, I introduced him to President Lowell. Later, on my motion, the department voted to recommend to the Corporation that Sorokin be offered a professorship in the Department of Economics to give courses in sociology at Harvard. The offer was made, he accepted, and a beginning was made toward starting a department of sociology.[20]

Black encouraged Carver in his move to get Sorokin, and they both gently advocated his candidacy with colleagues and administrators.[21]

Sorokin replied to Lowell on 28 September 1929, saying it was a great honor to be offered such a position and that he would give it his most serious consideration.[22] While reflecting on these new possibilities, he wrote Henry Noble MacCracken, asking for advice. His friend replied that it was a great opportunity to "found a school of thought" and that most viewed a Harvard appointment as a great promotion. However, "It is a cold austere sort of place, full of jealousies and prejudices." Regardless, MacCracken suggested that Pitirim accept the offer. "You are still young and terribly bedeviled with energy. . . . you have done great things for Minnesota, but sociology would gain more from a Harvard chair, in aligning itself with sciences than from the Northwest. After all, perhaps your best work lies in that direction." Additionally, he cautioned Pitirim to "make your treaty in advance I beg. Don't trust to generosity and magnanimity there—there is not enough of it—sad, but true."[23]

Following MacCracken's advice, Pitirim queried Lowell on the following points: Would the teaching load allow enough time for research and organizational activities? Were research funds available? Was there the possibility of a departmental journal? When could he expect a sabbatical? Did Harvard want to be a national and international center of sociological thought, or did the offer merely mean teaching some undergraduate sociology courses?[24] Lowell replied that the teaching load would be two courses per semester; that reasonable funding was available for research; that the journal depended on the feelings of Pitirim's departmental colleagues, but editing often drained energy away from writing books; and that Sorokin would be credited with three years toward a sabbatical. Lowell also expressed interest in eventually having sociology as an independent department.[25] Based on these conditions, Pitirim accepted the call and placed his chair in economics. He then asked Lowell's help in locating an appropriate position for Elena. He noted that he would be attending the American Sociological Society meetings in Washington, D.C., in early December and, if convenient, would come to Harvard to finish their discussions. He thanked Lowell for time toward the sabbatical, explaining that "I am not petitioning for sabbatical leave for rest, but in order to complete a work more important than my previous publications, the work which I hope to make worthy of the high standard of the works of the Harvard scholars."[26] He was, of course, referring to his planned *Social and Cultural Dynamics.*

Once the Harvard offer became known, Sorokin received a flood of congratulatory letters. Howard Odum wrote that the move was good for Sorokin and American sociology.[27] E. A. Ross was "immensely pleased at the good news. . . . I am all the more glad in your case that within six years after your arriving in this country you have attained probably the most desirable chair of sociology that there is anywhere. You have attained it by the hardest of hard work and you richly deserve it."[28] E. H. Sutherland regretted Sorokin's departure from Minnesota because "I don't know how we can get a controversy started if you are not there, and what is life without a controversy. . . . At any rate Harvard is generally regarded as the academic Heaven . . . and you have my best wishes."[29] Henry Noble MacCracken congratulated him over the successful negotiations with Lowell: "For one who cannot bargain the Harvard offer would be satisfactory. One could hardly imagine better conditions and now for the magnum opus which shall finally outline the techniques of sociology as a study among the other disciplines and free it from the suspicion and averted eyes of its fellows in the curriculum."[30]

However, Sorokin's appointment was not without controversy. Joseph Lee, a prominent Bostonian and chairman of the Visiting Committee on Philosophy, wrote the Harvard Corporation that his feelings on Sorokin were "unfavorable to his confirmation." While admitting that his reaction was based on others' opinions and an incomplete study of Sorokin's work, he was inclined to be negative. He found Sorokin "interesting and stimulating, but careless in some of his statements and, I think, unsound in his methods, specifically in claiming at times a physically scientific accuracy for his methods and conclusions which they do not and could not possibly possess."[31] Lee eventually changed his mind on Sorokin's appointment but not on his method. He came to see Sorokin as a stimulating teacher and knowledgeable on a wide variety of subjects. However, he was also a clear example of a prevalent and unfortunate trend among some scholars in the social disciplines: "What I am objecting to is not that Sorokin applies scientific and concrete reasoning, but that he says and doubtless thinks he does when he doesn't, and to that extent is talking bunk." To corroborate his statements, Lee used various arguments and themes from *The Sociology of Revolution,* specifically, the sections dealing with stimuli-reflexes, the canons of reform, certain analogies, and the exclusion of major positive functions of specific revolutions. For Lee, what was valuable in the study of rebellions was that Sorokin was mad about the Russian Revolution:

I think his way of feeling about revolution . . . especially his conclusions that it should never be resorted to, is chiefly the result of a very disagreeable experience in Russia and is practically independent of his study of the subject. I believe that such prejudices are the best sort of ground for his conclusions, but they had nothing to do with science.

Furthermore, "there is a definite evil in the use of quasi-scientific words for describing human situations." For instance, Sorokin claims, "If the desire for food (or alimentary reflex) of a considerable part of the population is 'repressed' by famine, we have one cause of riots and revolution."[32] Lee argues that "calling hunger 'the repression of the alimentary reflex' not only adds nothing to our knowledge of what Sorokin is talking about, but tends to prevent our seeing the thing he is trying to describe in its reality." Why not simply state, "When people are hungry they get mad"? Sorokin is at his best, in Lee's mind, "when he forgets his theory altogether and talks like other people." Lee concludes that, while a certain amount of bunk may be forgiven in a great teacher, it would be disastrous to employ a great many of them in any particular department. Furthermore, "in making future appointments to teaching positions in the university this particular sort of bunk needs watching."[33]

The surprising nature of Sorokin's appointment to the Harvard chair was later commented on by Robert K. Merton when he observed that it was "a quite implausible event which had a Lowell, then President of Harvard, actually displacing a Cabot with a Russian émigré, Pitirim Sorokin—all this in the course of transforming a venerable Department of Social Ethics into a newfangled Department of Sociology."[34] Merton further shows the improbability of this event by recalling "the old and popular jingle about the Boston Brahmin elite:

> And this is good old Boston
> The home of the bean and cod,
> Where the Lowells talk to the Cabots
> And the Cabots talk only to God.[35]

While Sorokin's arrival at Harvard was in many ways an improbable event, it was also a major move by the university to establish itself in sociology. Lowell was plainly looking to resolve his problems with the Department of Social Ethics. With Sorokin he was replacing a marginal discipline with a more "severe" field of study. Sociology specifically dealt with the world as it was. Sorokin, whose orientation was explicitly directed toward the scientific study of social facts, was concerned with a comparative and exhaustive study of world societies intended to move sociology toward a nomothetic theory of social organization and change. Under Sorokin both social ethics, and sociology as taught in economics, would move away from the unanswerable questions of what ought to be. For Lowell this change of direction would put social ethics in a proper context and establish sociology as a rigorous discipline for undergraduate study. Lowell also saw Sorokin as a prominent representative of the discipline.[36] As a scholar, Sorokin had opened new directions in the fields of stratification and social mobility; rural sociology had been moved from a culture-bound, value-laden field toward a true sociology of rural life; and the provincialism of the American discipline had been breached by this émigré's panoramic introduction of European thinking. Lowell felt that in Sorokin he had found what Harvard sought in permanent staff members: the best and most qualified man in the field.

Making the Transition

In December 1929 Sorokin stopped in Cambridge to meet with Lowell and members of the Committee on Sociology and Social Ethics.[37] On this visit he worked closely with Taussig, Gay, and the younger economists, Joslyn, Bigelow, and Parsons. He learned from them that sociology's fate was not clear. It presently existed under the committee's umbrella, but its future was yet to be determined. The concentration in social ethics had been eliminated shortly after Perry's committee was appointed. Former concentrators could complete their degrees or switch majors. New students were required to take eight courses from an approved list. These included Cabot's "Introduction to Social Ethics," Carver's "Principles of Sociology," and other appropriate courses in four specializations including the structure and development of society; social history; social standards and values; and social problems. A student's work was directed by members of the committee, with tutorial guidance provided by Joslyn, Bigelow, and Parsons. At the beginning of the 1929–30 academic year there were over thirty concentrators in the new field.[38]

Among the important issues Sorokin would face were developing and organizing the contents of the program; staffing; setting the standards for undergraduate and graduate students; determining with which department the program would align or whether it would be independent; working out an acceptable relationship with the Department of Social Ethics; and getting the department ready, in all other ways, to open in the 1931–32 academic year. Pitirim left the December meeting feeling a heavy responsibility on his shoulders. So much must be done for this to be the first-rate department he envisaged.

Returning to Minnesota, he continued working on the outline for *Dynamics*. Though the research held his attention, the Harvard situation was never far from him. Important and irreversible decisions must be made in an entirely new context. With Harvard came great prestige and pressure. Excellence was expected, and little else would be tolerated. He would have ultimate responsibility for the program's success or failure. In June 1930 he became chair of the Committee on Sociology and Social Ethics. He now had the opportunity to lead a great institution to a position of prominence in American sociology. History would judge his success or failure.

While these things pressed on him, he and Elena continued making their arrangements. There were things to be packed and sent on to Cambridge or sold. Academic and social obligations had to be met and farewells said to the friends who had filled their lives for seven years. It was hard to leave. Elena said her good-byes to colleagues, friends, neighbors, and acquaintances. While Pitirim took his leave from some graduate students, he also laid the foundation for bringing others to Harvard. Karl Bigelow, chairman of the board of tutors, had written him that an increase in concentrators required a new tutor to be added for the following year. Bigelow and Gay felt the new addition should be someone who had studied with Sorokin and in whom he had confidence; they suggested Conrad Taeuber.[39] Sorokin replied that Taeuber had taken an offer from Wisconsin and recommended Edgar Schuler, a young and promising scholar who had recently completed his master's degree and was currently in the doctoral program. A hard worker who would soon publish his first article in the *American Journal of Sociology*, Schuler was also interested in studying at Harvard and would be a good choice for the tutor's job.[40] In due time the appointment was approved, and Schuler arrived at Harvard shortly after the Sorokins. After completing their last-minute business, the Sorokins set out for Massachusetts in early August. The trip was indirect. They first drove to Canada for a vacation at Lake of the Woods. This venture almost ended in disaster when they were caught in a violent storm on the lake. Fortunately, they weathered the turbulence and arrived safely on shore—wet, pale, and totally shaken by the experience. After a day to recuperate, they started toward the East Coast. They would spend a day in one spot fishing, then move on to another for a couple of days of camping and hiking. At the end of August 1930 they arrived in Cambridge and found a comfortable duplex on Washington Avenue.

Shortly after the Sorokins arrived, Pitirim's work at the university began in earnest. His days were spent learning his way about the university. At night he and Elena "ate their way throughout Cambridge and Boston" as colleagues gave dinners for the new arrivals. Social activities, preparation of lectures, committee meetings, and directing the organization of the department filled his days. Free nights were spent together solving the problems of making a new home.

While Pitirim had worked with the committee before arriving, responsibility for its direction was now squarely his. The present committee consisted of himself, Carver, Gay, Perry, Hooton, Schlesinger, Elliott, Allport, Joslyn, and Parsons.[41] They immediately set out to complete the work for the department's opening. Where the department would be placed was the first important issue. There was talk of staying in economics and forming a new Division of Economics and Sociology.[42] For this, economics would have to withdraw from the Division of History, Government and Economics. Because this was the most powerful division in the university, most members of its faculty were opposed. Lowell considered aligning sociology with his former department, government, but did not pursue this alternative. Because Sorokin's chair was in economics, the decision on sociology's place in the college would be made by the committee, the Department of Economics, President Lowell, and the dean of arts and sciences, Clifford Moore. Interestingly, five of the committee's ten members came from economics. After much thought, the committee unanimously recommended that an independent Department of Sociology be organized and begin to function in the

academic year 1931–32. The new department would constitute a separate division and not be tied to any existing division or department.[43]
This was, of course, a major victory for Sorokin, who had parlayed
his chair into a separate and independent department.[44] While such was
not Lowell's first choice, he had long considered it a possibility. The
decision created the least organizational disruption to the College of Arts
and Sciences.

The problem of what to do with the Department of Social Ethics
remained a point of contention for the entire history of the committee.
Richard Clarke Cabot wanted to retain the department's independence;
in his mind it had a unique mission and a record of distinction and
accomplishment. Cabot was a distinguished physician who had been tied
to Harvard since his undergraduate years. For most of his early career he
studied diseases of the blood and problems of accurate diagnosis. As a
hematologist, he discovered "Cabot's ring bodies," which appear in
certain types of anemia. His skill in diagnostics led to his appointment as
chief of the Medical Staff at Massachusetts General Hospital (1912–21)
and professor of Clinical Medicine at Harvard Medical School (1919–31).
He had long been interested in the relationship between social service
and medicine, and his books *Social Service and the Art of Healing* (1909) and
Social Work (1919) were pioneering efforts in the case study approach to
social service. He was also an early advocate of the case approach in
medical education. His work in social ethics creatively blended these
interests into courses that sought the ethical principles which should
underlie professional services. His department was a major innovator in
the field. Cabot's seminars were well attended by members of the Harvard faculty and professional practitioners. He not only changed the way
many social services were delivered in the Boston area but contributed to
a major reorganization of the requirements for the bachelor of social
services degree at Harvard.[45]

Cabot had resisted Lowell's cutbacks and often clashed with Dean
Moore and the president over their desire to reduce the department's
offerings. Cabot objected by noting that the cutbacks resulted in the
absurd situation of reducing supply in the face of increasing demand.[46]
However, Cabot did not prevail. The committee unanimously recommended "that the present Department of Social Ethics be unified with
the new Department of Sociology to form a single department which
shall be called the Department of Sociology."[47]

The staffing of the new department was also a problem. Sorokin
commented that the administration insisted on having "a first-class department in regard to teaching staff, instruction, and research but it

prescribed to recruit the staff exclusively from the faculty at Harvard, without any outside sociologists added to it. Since Harvard had almost no ex-officio sociologists, one could easily understand the difficulties of building a first-class Department of Sociology without sociologists."[48] However, the administration's response provided sociology with a stellar staff. The committee endorsed the administration's position and voted that the department's staff would consist of full-time members and those dividing their time between sociology and their original departments. The latter provision brought some of Harvard's most notable scholars to the new department.

The part-time members of the sociology faculty were taken from a variety of departments. Among them was Edwin F. Gay, a renowned economic historian of Europe and America who had distinguished himself as a past editor of the *New York Evening Post*, the *Quarterly Journal of Economics*, and *Business History*. He had also occupied the unique position of first dean of Harvard's Graduate School of Business Administration. Later the Department of Economics would contribute the services of the great, demanding, and erudite Joseph A. Schumpeter. Lawrence J. Henderson, a biochemist and world authority on the blood, also came to the department. Though a physician, he never practiced but spent his life among many of Harvard's great departments. At the time of his appointment he had responsibilities in chemistry, the history of science, and the Fatigue Laboratory of the Harvard Business School.

Henderson was a man of great intellect, power, and experience. He was a close personal friend of Lowell's and made distinguished contributions to a wide variety of disciplines from physiology to sociology. Henderson enlivened the early department through his Pareto Circle, a selective discussion and study group, and left his mark on the university as a founder of the Society of Fellows.[49] The latter resulted from the creative vision of Lowell and Henderson, both of whom were alarmed by the increasingly mediocre products coming off the treadmill of American graduate education. Even Harvard was not immune to this decline of creativity and independence in scholarship. Their concern led Lowell to send Henderson in 1925 to England to study the Prize Fellows of Trinity College. There he was joined by Alfred North Whitehead, Charles Pelham Curtis, and John Livingston Lowes. Based on their observation of the Cambridge scholars, the Foundation Thiers in France, and their intuitive feelings of what was required to further the cause of "the rare and independent genius," they returned to Harvard with a plan for the Society of Fellows. The group would be small, no more than twenty-four Junior Fellows whose studies would be generally supervised by the Senior

Fellows of the society. To this group all libraries, laboratories, and classrooms of the university would be open. They would be completely subsidized for three years of independent study with the possibility of renewal for another three. Initially they were not allowed to work toward a doctorate, but this provision was later changed. The unmarried members of the group would be given free board and lodgings in one of the houses of the university. They were encouraged, when possible, to take their meals together, and met weekly for dinner and discussion of their work among themselves and invited outsiders. Junior Fellows would be selected on promise of originality and past record of excellence. When Lowell found no patron to support the society, he established it with two million dollars from his own funds.

Lowell further shaped the group's ethics by composing the charge that has been given to each incoming cohort during its first formal function:

You will practice the virtues, and avoid the snares, of the scholar. You will be courteous to your elders who have explored to the point from which you may advance; and helpful to your juniors who will progress farther by reason of your labors. Your aim will be knowledge and wisdom, not the reflected glamour of fame. You will not accept credit that is due to another, or harbor jealousy of an explorer who is more fortunate.

You will seek not a near but a distant objective, and you will not be satisfied with what you may have done. All that you may achieve or discover you will regard as a fragment of a larger pattern of the truth which from his separate approach every true scholar is striving to descry.[50]

Henderson led the founding committee, authored its report, and was elected chairman of the Senior Fellows. His presence in the department gave sociology visibility and luster.[51]

The polymathic mathematician-physicist-statistician E. B. Wilson came into the department from his post as professor of vital statistics in the Harvard School of Public Health. Prior to returning to his alma mater in 1922, Wilson had been professor of mathematics and physics at the Massachusetts Institute of Technology and head of its Department of Physics. In 1922 he was president of the American Statistical Association. The same year he was elected to a two-year presidency of the Social Science Research Council.

Along with Wilson, the venerable mathematician-philosopher Alfred North Whitehead joined the department. Whitehead was a graduate and Prize Fellow at Cambridge, where he also had started his teaching career. It was there that he collaborated with his former student Bertrand Russell on the logical foundation of mathematics that soon led to their publication of the *Principia Mathematica*. Whitehead spent most of his early career at the University of London, where he held the chair of applied mathematics at the Imperial College of Science until retirement in 1924. He was then appointed to a professorship of philosophy at Harvard and began the second period of his distinguished career. Though he came to Harvard late in life, "through his originality and fecundity as well as his great personal distinction Whitehead had come to exert a notable influence" at the university.[52]

William Morton Wheeler, the noted entomologist and principal American authority on ants, was also added to the faculty. Wheeler came to Harvard in 1908 from his post as curator of invertebrate zoology at the American Museum of Natural History. He also served Harvard as dean of the Bussey Institute for Research in Applied Biology from 1915 to 1929. His work on the social behavior of ants and other insects had achieved for him a national and international reputation as an original scholar. His books *Social Life Among the Insects* (1923), *Emergent Evolution and the Development of Societies* (1928), *Foibles of Insects and Men* (1928), and *Demons of the Dust: A Study in Insect Behavior* (1930) all contributed to the lectures he gave for the department in his memorable course on animal sociology. Wheeler's interest in the social worlds of insects carried over into human societies. It was he who suggested that L. J. Henderson read Pareto's *Sociologie Generale*.[53]

The Department of Anthropology was represented by two senior scholars: Earnest A. Hooton and Alfred M. Tozzer. Hooton had come to Harvard in 1913 with an anthropology degree from Oxford, where he had been a Rhodes scholar. His British education provided new ideas of great value to the Harvard anthropologists. Among his contributions to the department was his work in criminal anthropology. Tozzer had been at Harvard since his undergraduate days and for all of his graduate training. He joined the faculty in 1905 and reached the rank of professor in 1921. The Mayans and other South American Indians were his specialities.

The Department of History was represented by Arthur M. Schlesinger, who had been educated at Columbia by Herbert Levi Osgood and Charles A. Beard. Under these scholars he produced *The Colonial Merchants and the American Revolution*, which Sir Dennis Brogen considered "perhaps the most remarkable Ph.D. dissertation in modern American historiography."[54] Schlesinger came to Harvard in 1924 while working with Dixon Ryan Fox on the first volume of the thirteen-volume series *History of American Life*. Schlesinger, a prolific writer and a major voice of the "New History," would follow E. B. Wilson as president of the Social

Science Research Council and become president of the American Historical Association in 1942.

Along with these prominent Harvard scholars, Sorokin obtained the services of Carle C. Zimmerman. Despite the administration's desire to restrict outside recruiting, Sorokin moved early on to bring Zimmerman to Harvard. He communicated this interest to John D. Black shortly after accepting his appointment. Black replied, "The best strategy so far as Zimmerman is concerned is not to push his case at Harvard yourself but to so manage that presently someone else does it. . . . Zimmerman has already been brought to the attention of some of the members of our department. About all he needs to do now is to turn out only very high grade work."[55] Black and Sorokin wanted Zimmerman because he would contribute substantially to the agricultural and rural programs in sociology and economics. Sorokin originally approached Zimmerman with the idea of a one-year appointment as an assistant professor; if Zimmerman did well, Sorokin and the others would push for a permanent appointment and an increase in rank. This strategy was best because the administration would be less resistant and critical of a temporary appointment. Furthermore, with a permanent appointment, there would be additional complications related to rank and salary. It would be easier to bring Zimmerman in on a temporary status so he could prove his worth. If he failed, he would still have his position at Minnesota.[56] But Sorokin felt that with Zimmerman, himself, Black, Gay, Gras, and Carver, "Harvard will be unquestionably the strongest fortress of agricultural and sociological sciences in the world." It was based on this expected rise to prominence that Zimmerman's permanent appointment would be argued.[57]

However, Sorokin and his supporters underestimated their influence. In February 1931 Sorokin wrote Zimmerman that he would be appointed associate professor for a period of three years, at a salary of fifty-five hundred dollars. "Three years means if you fail—what is improbable—your contract will not be renewed. If you make good—you will be permanently appointed and promoted in salary (what is certain) and eventually in rank."[58] The formal offer was made by Dean Moore on 10 March 1931 and approved by the board of overseers on 11 May 1931. Zimmerman accepted and resigned from Minnesota.[59] He joined the faculty for the academic year 1931–32.

Sorokin's last staffing problem was the administration's reluctance to appoint Talcott Parsons as a faculty instructor. Sorokin was impressed by Parsons and puzzled by the administration's resistance. He took the matter up with Harold H. Burbank, the chairman of economics, who believed that because Parsons's interests were in sociology his work in economics had not been of the highest quality. Sorokin, who felt that Parsons had great promise, asked Taussig, Gay, Carver, and Perry to support Parsons's candidacy with President Lowell.[60] Sorokin also discussed Parsons with Lowell on several occasions, and with the others finally convinced the president to support the appointment.[61] Correspondence between Clifford Moore and Lowell shows they had some concern about Parsons.

Dear Lawrence:

On the basis of new evidence that has appeared since I recommended that Dr. Talcott Parsons be appointed Instructor in Sociology and Tutor in the Division of Sociology for one year from the first of next September, I beg to recommend that the appointment be changed to one as Instructor in Sociology and Tutor in the Division of Sociology for three years from September 1, 1931 at . . . the same salary which was originally recommended. The new evidence consists chiefly of a substantial article which Mr. Parsons has written, which has been read by Professor Gay and others. In this he shows unusual knowledge and acumen.[62]

With these additions, the sociology faculty was now complete. Full-time members were Sorokin and Richard C. Cabot as full professors, James Ford and Carle C. Zimmerman as associate professors, Carl Joslyn and Talcott Parsons as instructors, and Paul Pigors, W. Lloyd Warner, and Edgar Schuler as tutors. Part-time members were Gordon W. Allport, John D. Black, Thomas N. Carver, William Y. Elliott, Edwin F. Gay, Sheldon Glueck, Lawrence J. Henderson, Earnest A. Hooton, Ralph B. Perry, Arthur M. Schlesinger, William M. Wheeler, Edwin B. Wilson, Alfred North Whitehead, Edward A. Whitney, and Alfred M. Tozzer. This distinguished faculty brought the program to the attention of the profession and talented students at the university.

With staffing completed, Sorokin and the committee turned to the curriculum. Lowell wanted sociology to be academically rigorous. In response, Sorokin suggested that entrance be restricted to graduate students. The administration and committee did not support this but passed the provision that only honor students could major in sociology. Concentration was also restricted to those of sophomore rank or higher. Undergraduates were required to take eight full courses. They should begin with four preparatory courses chosen from anthropology, biology, economics, government, psychology, philosophy, or history. This would be followed by a year-long course, "Contemporary Sociological Theories," with Sorokin, Joslyn, and Parsons. Afterward, students took another five full courses[63] in sociology and a year of study in a related

discipline. Then, during their candidacy year, they faced a general examination in sociology that tested their mastery of the entire field. Students,
regardless of their course performance, could not graduate without passing the exam. Students in fields with general examinations were required
to begin work with a tutor at the start of the sophomore year, meeting
regularly to discuss material, correlate their studies, and work on problems. Tutors helped students develop "habits of profitable reading, independent thinking and scholarly methods." They also guided their tutees'
independent studies and provided general academic direction.[64]

Graduate students were selected on their proven quality and potential. Sorokin had written Zimmerman that an advantage of teaching at
Harvard was working with extremely bright and promising graduate
students.[65] Once selected, students were required to perform in six fields
of study. Satisfactory performance in two fields could be demonstrated by
an honors pass of two full courses approved by the department. There
were many courses from which to select, including economic or political
institutions, the family, the sociology of religion, population, or experimental sociology. The core of the program required candidates to pass a
general written examination over four comprehensive areas of sociology,
one in sociological theory and the others chosen from social science
methodology, social organization, social psychology, social evolution and
dynamics, social standards and values, or comparative social institutions.
Once the general doctoral examination was passed, the candidate was
given a master of arts degree. Completion of the doctor's degree required
that students write an acceptable thesis. This done, they must pass an
oral examination on the thesis and their special field.[66] On completion
the doctorate would be awarded.

These issues having been decided, the program was ready to function. The department opened its doors in September 1931 to 29 concentrators, 4 graduate students, and 330 students enrolled in various
courses. The first of Sorokin's administrative tasks were now complete.
He turned his attention to research and settled into Mr. Lowell's Harvard.

Scholarly and Administrative Pressures

For Sorokin 1930–31 was so busy administratively that he had been
pressed to find writing time. The vitality of the university kept him
constantly moving as he tried to integrate the department into the
system. His publications drew on the intellectual capital of previous
work. As a result, his earlier studies in experimental sociology were

beginning to appear. In March 1930 "An Experimental Study of Efficiency of Work Under Various Specified Conditions" appeared in the *American Journal of Sociology*. Sorokin had long been curious as to which organization of labor and reward was most efficient, capitalism or communism. He had planned to study this in Russia but was banished before beginning. At Minnesota between 1926 and 1928 he had designed an experiment to explore the question. Using three groups of children, ages three to fourteen, he tested the effects of different reward systems on their work efficiency. Subjects worked independently or in groups and were rewarded equally or unequally for work completed. Sorokin found that the children worked more effectively for themselves than for the good of the group. Unequal compensation also stimulated greater output. Indeed, competition itself was a stimulant, and the children often performed in order to win regardless of other rewards. Because the experimental groups consisted of younger children, Sorokin saw the results as due to differences in the organization and rewards of labor rather than to the stimulation of a value system (e.g., socialism versus capitalism). While individualized, competitive, and differentially rewarded work was more productive, it was also subject to more "strikes" than its cooperative counterpart.[67]

Sorokin's first professional presentation as a new Harvard scholar was on 25 April 1931. At the invitation of the president of the Eastern Sociological Society, he spoke on "Sociology as a Science"; the text of this address was later published in *Social Forces*.[68] In March 1932 his second experimental study appeared. Here Sorokin reported the effects of dogmatic and persuasive suggestions on the perceptions of 1,484 high school and college students. These students were dogmatically told that they would hear two different variations on the same piece of music, one of which had been judged by experts to be far superior to the other. In fact, the pieces were identical, but only 4 percent of the participants recognized them as such. Additionally, 60 percent of the sample agreed with the experts' judgments on quality. Based on these and other findings, Sorokin showed that dogmatic claims had a greater effect on peoples' perceptions than simple persuasive statements. But both tactics were used by political and religious figures wishing to convince people that things were different than they in fact were. Furthermore, once people became committed to false perceptions they often defended their blunders through elaborate processes of justification.[69] This study of suggestion anticipated the later findings of Soloman Asch on perception and conformity. These and other cases were also used by Sorokin in his course on experimental sociology.

While these works were coming out, Pitirim returned his attention to *Dynamics*. As Lowell had agreed, money was available for his research. To proceed he must now recruit experts to gather the specialized data required for analysis. For this Sorokin hired primarily Russian scholars in exile, including N. S. Timasheff, N. O. Lossky, I. I. Lapshin, N. L. Okuneff, P. B. Struve, N. N. Golovine, A. A. Zaitzoff, P. N. Savitsky, S. G. Pushkareff, E. F. Maximovitch, S. S. Oldenburg, P. A. Ostrovchov, and G. Michwitz. At Harvard he employed John W. Boldyreff and Robert K. Merton.

These scholars were paid through a grant by the Harvard Committee for Research in the Social Sciences. The committee, established in 1932, monitored and distributed a five-year, $250,000 award from the Rockefeller Foundation. The funds were provided to the university at the rate of $50,000 a year. However, a matching arrangement plus careful management yielded enough money for a decade. Beginning in 1932, Sorokin received more than $10,000 from the committee for his work on *Dynamics*.[70] Besides research assistants, most of this money was spent on statistical work done by the committee's staff in its laboratory.

By early 1932 Sorokin had put the research team together. In order to minimize bias, he kept the others in the dark as to the nature and scope of the overall project:

None of the experts was told for what purposes I needed the statistical tables and other materials he agreed to prepare for me. Nor was any one of them informed of what sort of hypothesis or theory had to be tested by the systematic, largely quantitative data he was to compile according to my outline. I used this procedure of keeping them completely uninformed about my tentative hypothesis quite deliberately: I wanted from them a competent and complete series of relevant facts entirely uninfluenced by any sort of tentative theories I had in my own mind.[71]

Under this provision Sorokin put Professors Lapshin and Lossky to work demonstrating historical changes in systems of ethics and knowledge (e.g., idealism, materialism, determinism). Timasheff worked on the historical forms of agreement, contract, and law. He also studied changing patterns of internal disturbances in European countries and determined the periods and places that were the most turbulent or orderly. Merton and Boldyreff worked on fluctuations in scientific discovery, technology, and invention, while Merton alone studied changes in the forms of scientific theorizing. The Russian generals, Golovine and Zaitzoff, gathered data on the frequency of war from ancient to modern times. Struve and Timasheff reported on the theoretical and practical importance of singularism and universalism in social ethics and social affairs. Michwitz, Savitsky, Pushkareff, and Maximovitch studied changing economic conditions using a Kondratieff-like long-waves approach; the observed changes were examined for any relationships to shifting patterns of culture. Sorokin's arrangements with these scholars led to the sociology department becoming known as "the White Russian WPA."[72]

With the research on *Dynamics* now under way, Sorokin turned to demands in the department. As chairman he taught two classes and directed many individualized readings courses and dissertations. He was responsible for the routine activities and daily problems of the department. As chairman and full professor he sat on special committees and read all dissertations and theses. He was a reader for all general examinations, was chairman of the board of tutors, and oversaw graduate student advising.[73] Given these demands, the pressures of his scholarly work, and changes in his personal life, there was little time for close relationships with graduate students.

In 1931 the Sorokins' home life dramatically changed. After more than fourteen years of marriage, they had their first child. Peter was born while they were living at 88 Washington Street in Cambridge. His arrival led them to look for a new home—something away from the city, with space where a young, growing, and curious child could explore the world in safety and tranquillity. Their search brought them to Winchester, Massachusetts. They had been there before and enjoyed the serenity and pace of life. Fortunately, a house that held some promise was available on a short, one-block street. The large two-story house was well built but a bit run-down; it could accommodate new additions to the family and was adjacent to the Middlesex reservation, a wooded area filled with lakes and other attractions "in which one could walk for hours undisturbed by automobiles or crowds." The Sorokin's bought the house at 8 Cliff Street in February 1932. In 1933 their second son, Sergei, was born.

By the end of the academic year the department had made a fine start. The rule restricting concentrators to honor students had yielded a body of Harvard's best undergraduates. The graduate students were also first-rate. Among those to come in the first five years were Robert K. Merton, Kingsley Davis, John W. (Jack) Riley, Charles P. Loomis, John W. Boldyreff, Edgar A. Schuler, Nathan L. Whetten, Emile B. Smullyan, Neil B. DeNood, Leo A. T. Haak, Clarence Q. Berger, and Walter Lunden. In all, there were forty-six graduate students during this interval, most of whom became career sociologists. Many made substantial contributions to specific areas of research, and a few became great leaders in the field.[74] Several of these students were in residence when Robert Park observed the following:

I was very much impressed with the quality of your graduate students. The undergraduates who took my course were not very high grade. They, I suppose, were students who had been compelled to do time in the summer school because of their deficiencies. But the graduate students, a very considerable number of them at any rate, I was very glad to meet. I think you are probably getting a higher grade of graduate student at Harvard than we are getting in Chicago, from my judge of the samples.[75]

Park's observation on undergraduates was also accurate. As early as 17 May 1932, Dean Kenneth B. Murdock had written Sorokin expressing concern about the overall performance of sociology students and the quality of incoming majors. The dean's data showed that freshman and sophomore sociology majors came from the lowest academic ranks. Projections for 1935 indicated that 25 percent were either unsatisfactory or class VI students (the lowest level of passing students). For 1936 things were worse. Almost 45 percent of the students would be either class VI or unsatisfactory. Only 15 percent were now passing courses with good marks, and none were of high or highest distinction.[76] This created two departmental problems: students of such poor quality were not likely to graduate, and how could sociology attract better students?

Sorokin explained the problems as a result of the change in rules:

Formerly, as you know, there was a rule that only honor students could be admitted to concentration in the field of Sociology and Social Ethics. As long as this rule existed, it resulted in an extraordinarily high level of concentrators. When, under pressure from other departments and the Administration, it had to be abolished, we naturally expected the standing of our students to fall and come nearer the general level of the college. The class of 1934, however, was still slightly above the general college level; that of 1935 fell slightly below it; and the concentrators in Sociology from 1936 happen to be of very low grade. The facts which you and Dean Hanford mention are quite correct, although the situation did not become quite clear until recently; and we therefore had not sounded an official alarm.[77]

Sorokin observed that poor students might be attracted to sociology because they thought it an easy subject with lenient grading. However, data on sociology's grading patterns showed them to be a bit more demanding than those of other social science departments.[78] This was true for course work and for the general examinations, which received very critical readings from outside members of the department.

The courses were demanding. "Contemporary Sociological Theories," using Sorokin's book, served as the introductory course; students read deeply in the classical traditions of Comte, Spencer, and Durkheim. Equally stiff standards prevailed in all courses. Reading lists avoided popular sources in favor of original works, and there were no "snap courses." Sorokin concluded that the best way to deal with these problems was to reintroduce the rule restricting concentration in sociology. If this were done for two or three years, the problem would be resolved.[79]

Murdock would not reintroduce the rule but forwarded a suggestion from Lowell. The president was concerned about this nascent trend because of the previous difficulties with the Department of Social Ethics. It was important to nip it in the bud. While denying Sorokin's request for the rule change, Murdock stated:

President Lowell in talking to me the other day about the matter made what seems to me a still better suggestion to this effect. Would it not be possible for each man who has indicated his desire to concentrate in Sociology to be assigned to a tutor this spring and to be told that during the summer he must read some important book thoroughly and pass an examination on it in the fall, this examination to be used as a qualifying examination so that men who fail it will not be allowed to go on? This would, I think, at least weed out the weak men. Moreover, it does not represent any new precedent since in many fields some reading is required in the summer before the Sophomore year and this reading is often tested by the tutors in the fall. If you approve, I suggest that you try this plan and that each one of your concentrators know what he should read during the summer and that he will be required to pass an examination on it when College opens.[80]

The department implemented Lowell's suggestion, and reading lists were assigned to incoming students. Even with such changes, however, maintaining high-quality concentrators would be a struggle for the department throughout its history.

The department was also critically understaffed. Interdepartmental professors did not do any of the routine work or counsel students. They mostly taught courses that were tangential to mainstream sociology. Professors Cabot and Ford taught primarily in social ethics and professional social work, which were not areas of student concentration, nor were many students interested in them. Thus the majority of the sociological work was done by Sorokin and Zimmerman. Both were stretched thin by trying to cover the undergraduate and graduate programs. Many of the core courses and thesis and dissertation work could not be assigned to the junior faculty. Joslyn, Parsons, and Pigors were not general sociologists, and Warner was an anthropologist. It was unfair to them and to students to assign them the more important courses. Sorokin had tried once, and the move met a wave of student complaints. Sorokin and Zimmerman had had to sacrifice research time to meet obligations, leaving little time for the important, but informal, discussions and friendships with graduate students.

This situation could not continue, and as early as December 1931 Sorokin wrote Lowell and Murdock asking for a new, senior member of the department.[81] Sorokin also recalled that Dean Moore had earlier promised that more senior staff would be available for the department within two or three years.[82] The time had now come for a new staff in order to balance the workload, and to provide for the continued vitality and growth of the department. In his annual report Sorokin observed:

It is also my belief that it is very stimulating for the faculty themselves as well as for the younger scholars in a Department when there are two or three equally strong professors with considerable differences in theories, viewpoints, and methods. Such a situation hardly exists at the present moment. All this makes the training and guidance of the graduate students, especially, somewhat one-sided. It would be a great help, therefore, to the Department if it were possible to add to its staff one big man—an accomplished scholar with real scientific prestige and real achievements.[83]

The wake of the depression was not a propitious time for this request. Changes in the dean of Arts and Sciences in 1931 also slowed a response. However, at the beginning of 1934 Sorokin was asked to recommend a senior scholar. Based on department discussions Sorokin wrote Murdock:

Following your suggestion that I should present the name of the person considered the best choice for a professorial position in the Department of Sociology, . . . I have consulted my colleagues in the Division, J. D. Black, R. C. Cabot, E. F. Gay, Sheldon Glueck, L. J. Henderson, A. M. Tozzer, Edwin B. Wilson, and W. M. Wheeler. It is our unanimous opinion that Professor Robert Morrison MacIver of Columbia University is the best man for the appointment. . . . taking everything into consideration, Professor MacIver seems to be more desirable than any other sociologist in the United States.[84]

MacIver's candidacy was forwarded to President Conant in October of that year.[85]

The department had discussed getting MacIver, Gorrado Gini, and Rene Maunier to each come for one semester as a way of testing them. When this proved impractical, they decided to recruit MacIver.[86] After much consideration, however, Conant declined to recommend the appointment to the corporation.[87] This decision left Sorokin and Zimmerman in one of the largest and most understaffed departments in the Division of Arts and Sciences.

Even with these strictures, sociology was off to a good beginning. In its first five years the number of graduate students increased from four to twenty-two, and concentrators from twenty-nine to seventy-seven. The quality of concentrators, though a problem area, stayed at or slightly above the college average. In the same period graduates were placed in the federal government, several private agencies, and with such colleges and universities as Cornell, Clark, Columbia, Smith, Mount Holyoke, Minnesota, Wisconsin, Louisiana, and Connecticut. Undergraduate enrollments were increasing in spite of strict standards of grading. This led Sorokin to state that

> the Department has grown possibly more rapidly than any other department in the University during these years and this growth has not been at the cost of the quality of the students—undergraduates as well as graduates. This fact is a convincing evidence of the invalidity of the irresponsible rumors that the Department is an easy one and has students poorer than most of the departments of Harvard.[88]

The staff of the department had changed with the retirements of Carver and Cabot and the addition of several junior people. The core faculty had been joined by C. A. Anderson, E. P. Hutchinson, J. W. Boldyreff, R. K. Merton, C. Q. Berger, N. L. Whetten, and H. D. Lampson, who not only helped with instructional obligations but were productive young professionals busily writing books and journal articles. For Sorokin, *Dynamics* was now under way, and he had been elected to the presidency of the International Institute of Sociology. He thus felt that the department had made a good beginning and had come to occupy an important place on "the sociological map." The next few years would determine its overall position in the discipline.[89]

New Challenges: *Recent Social Trends* and the Emergence of *Social and Cultural Dynamics*

Sorokin had come to Harvard with great hopes for building on his reputation from Minnesota and becoming a theoretical force in sociology. *Social and Cultural Dynamics*, his magnum opus on social change, would be his theoretical exemplar. The sociological importance that Sorokin placed on this work was adumbrated in a highly visible polemic between him and William F. Ogburn over the two-volume report of the President's Research Committee on Recent Social Trends, *Recent Social Trends in the United States.*[90] This project, which began in September 1929, assembled a prominent group of American scholars to do a social survey for President Hoover on developments in American society. Hoover wanted a complete and impartial examination of all the facts to help the nation "see where social stresses are occurring and where major efforts should be undertaken to deal with them constructively."[91] *Trends* was to be an impartial and factual examination of major social processes and institutions. Hoover desired a "strict scientific determination" of these facts and one in which researchers' opinions were held to a minimum. The chairman of the committee was Wesley C. Mitchell of the Social Science Research Council (SSRC), and the vice chairman was Charles E. Merriam of the University of Chicago. Responsibility for research was given to William F. Ogburn of the University of Chicago, who was then president of the American Sociological Society. His assistant director of research was Howard W. Odum of North Carolina. Among the twenty-nine major contributors were seven faculty from Chicago and eleven Ph.D.s in sociology, most of them tied to Columbia and all but one with connections to the SSRC.[92] Indeed, *Trends* was led by a group of significant social scientists and contained the works of prominent and well-placed academics. It brought social science to bear on issues of importance in the public sphere.

Trends also raised key methodological questions on how to best study social phenomena. Ogburn pursued Hoover's directive for an impartial examination of the facts by relying on a descriptive statistical presentation of information in which interpretations and recommendations were kept to a minimum. Some sociologists, like Sorokin, would object to the reliance on statistical description, while others were put off by the theoretical timidity of not pushing toward a deeper analysis and more satisfying projections of social change.[93]

Among the first responses to *Trends* were Sorokin's criticisms in the *Journal of Political Economy*.[94] Sorokin praised the committee for a thorough and professional job of quantitatively describing major social trends and on its prognostications of future changes in the United States. In his mind, however, *Trends* was methodologically flawed. Ogburn's insistence on quantification committed the study to a shallow level of understanding and resulted in the substitution of the measurable for the meaningful. Consequently, many key issues were missed in the discussion of social institutions. Sorokin made this point in his analysis of the committee's report on the arts, which he viewed as typical of the other reports. That is, it missed art's essential properties. Instead, the reader was swamped with superficial facts on the dollar value of art objects, the number of museums, a count of symphony orchestras, and the number of novels published. One learned nothing of literary currents or preferences in music and literature. Indeed, "One can but marvel at how an investigator could make such a long and laborious research on the contemporary American arts and succeed in saying nothing about them!"[95] This continued dependence on quantification yielded a uniformly thin understanding of the trends studied and told the reader almost nothing new. That is, the committee did little fact-finding but substantial fact-transcribing, often simply restating what was known and could be easily found in basic textbooks. Also, the data were too gross and one-sided to sustain the "inductive conclusions" that the authors offered as the forms of future changes.[96]

Trends also failed to holistically integrate the changes discussed in American society. As stated by Wesley C. Mitchell in his introduction to the committee's findings, "The primary value of this report is to be found not merely in the analyses of separate trends . . . but in their interrelation—in the effort to look at America as a whole, as a national union."[97] To this claim Sorokin responds: "If such is the main objective of this entire study, I can but welcome it. Is the work, however, a realization of this aim? I am afraid it is not. The twenty-nine studies . . . remain *membra disjecta*. There is no organic connection between them. . . . Apart from the common trends-topic, they scarcely have any other organic bond but the bindings of the volumes."[98] This failure was the clear result of too much dependence on Ogburn's culture lag model. Sorokin asserts that while Ogburn can talk about the speed of change he cannot, and *Trends* does not, measure it. To do so requires a unit that standardizes the rate of change in an institution and makes it comparable to others. *Trends* fails to do this because "most social changes are not as much quantitative as qualitative . . . and are quite heterogeneous and irreducible to any common quantitative denominator."[99] Consequently, the theory, data, and method lack the necessary precision for the posited scientific understanding of interrelated institutional change in America.

Sorokin ends his review by charging that *Trends* puts old wine in new bottles and reports little that is new. Even more regrettable was the committee's failure to move beyond the facts and report something theoretically imaginative about current conditions and future prospects. Instead of a "pathfinding epoch-making contribution," they have recast existing information to produce a reiteration of the known. While "we should be grateful to the Committee for what it has given, . . . in all sincerity, . . . it has not given us all that it could."[100]

Ogburn's reply had a similar but less colorful tone, and he accused Sorokin of having a "complex" about numbers, claiming Sorokin, like the victim of hallucination, sees what is not there."[101] Sorokin had his facts wrong, cited data and examples not reported in the book, and missed the point of quantification and the nature of the study. In defense of his method, Ogburn argues for different ways of answering the question How do we know it? Scholars and intellectuals cite authorities, but scientists are more skeptical and prefer to use data. Sorokin is uncomfortable with this approach because it does not grasp the inner meaning of things. Clearly, it does not, because scientists have only partial data and to go further is to substitute opinion and lose the scientific edge. In the chapters that Sorokin criticized the authors restricted their scope to their data and their charge, which was to study changes in American society, not to discover the essence of art, religion, or philosophy. Certainly a study should not be faulted for what it never intended to do.[102]

Sorokin's methodological naïveté, in Ogburn's view, also permeates his theoretical criticisms. The demand for a "unit of change" asks too much of a young discipline. Though he has previously rejected the quantitative method Sorokin now demands refinements beyond what is realistically possible.[103] The best that can be done is to determine the general pattern of social transformation, and this *Trends* does.

Ogburn ends his response by addressing the charge of little new information in the volumes. Specifically, the committee was to study changes in American life over the last thirty-years. One would suppose that much of this information would necessarily be available and known. Again, Sorokin does not grasp the difficulty of gathering objective descriptions of social facts. Unlike speculation, it is not easy to obtain, and there is a sizable proportion of new information in each chapter. Given the standards of science compared with those of other ways of knowing, how much discovery did Sorokin expect?[104]

Sorokin fired the final volley in the exchange in June 1933,[105] asserting that Ogburn has avoided the serious charges that the data in *Trends* are misleading or meaningless, and the methods inappropriate for proving the hypotheses considered in the work: "The issue . . . is not that Professor Ogburn wants to be a scientist and Professor Sorokin wants to be a 'poet,' but that the scientific work in question is not properly done."[106] Sorokin then states that Professor Ogburn's deep belief in quantification is even more disturbing. Granted, it tells us a lot about some social phenomena but frequently tells nothing about what is important in social life. The history of ideas shows that early factual studies have been dwarfed by the great social philosophies of Aristotle, Aquinas, Plato, and others. It is these that "have been preserved by mankind as the jewels of its treasury of knowledge."[107]

Sorokin was also dissatisfied with Ogburn's avoidance of his concerns about scientism. However, Ogburn put a fair challenge to him by pointing out that it is easier to criticize another's work than to do a better job oneself. Specifically, Ogburn asserts: "I should like to see an account of trends in these various subjects (art, philosophy, religion, etc.) written by Professor Sorokin in the short space of two chapters . . . and then I should like to apply the test of the question: How do you know it? I dare say he would have his answers, but I suspect I could find dozens of others who would disagree."[108] Sorokin brushed aside the space limitation and stated that the challenge could not be met on a comparable basis because he could not direct a large, well-funded research group.

However, within a few years, Professor Ogburn may have a chance to criticize my work in a somewhat related field, if he wishes. For several years . . . I have been trying as a mere ordinary craftsman in science—or is it "social philosophy?"—to understand a little . . . of the great mystery of social life and its processes, including long-time and short-time trends, the hows and whys of their movement and relationships. Without a corporation, almost without making use of public funds . . . I have been musing, meditating and (not to be classified simply as a "poet") . . . "collecting" and "analyzing" some data ("researching"!). Within a few years something will result from this. . . . Then Professor Ogburn is welcome to mobilize all his quantitative guns, and all his "scientific research methods" to tear it to pieces. This, it seems to me, is a square acceptance of his fair challenge.[109]

In one paragraph Sorokin cast down his gauntlet and challenged not only Ogburn but major scholars at Chicago, Columbia, the Social Science Research Council, and other prominent institutions to a joust. The engagement would be fought at Harvard, and the battlefield would be *Social and Cultural Dynamics*.

4

Professional Politics and Prophetic Sociology

THE CONTENT OF *Social and Cultural Dynamics* was coming together. The mail regularly brought packets of data from the European scholars working for Sorokin. On returning from the university, Pitirim would take the bundles to his study and work into the night. The study was not large, but the built-in bookcases and fireplace made it comfortable. Pitirim's desk faced Cliff Street and part of his garden. During the winters, with a fire burning and snapping, he watched the snow swirl and fall around the windows. Spring and summer brought the pleasures of longer days and slowly setting suns. After each delivery, hours were spent scrutinizing the reports and studying their impact on his hypotheses. There was an enormous amount of material, and only the most significant could be used. Often the information was restructured and new tables built by the statistical staff of the Committee for Research in the Social Sciences.

Starting this work in the second semester of his first Harvard year, he completed a draft of the manuscript by early 1936, working evenings and early mornings before leaving for the office:

Working steadily, I typed a first draft of each chapter and, after many corrections, retyped it two or three times until I was more or less satisfied with it. When a chapter reached this stage, with its tables checked and its diagrams drawn satisfactorily for printing purposes, the complete manuscript of each chapter was added to those of other chapters to be given eventually to a professional typist who would prepare the final version for the printer. Toward the end of 1935, the total manuscript with its tables and diagrams grew to the bulky extent of filling several cartons in my study. Glancing at these boxes now and then, I anxiously wondered whether I would find a publisher for this mass of "scrap-paper" which promised no particular profit and no large sales. "Who nowadays—when most people read only newspapers and popular magazines—would be interested in buying and reading several volumes of fairly dry stuff"? I thought. From time to time this anxiety somewhat troubled me but it did not impede my labors over the *Dynamics* because at the back of my mind persisted a firm belief that somehow the work would be published. This belief proved to be correct.

84

Even before the manuscript of all four volumes of the *Dynamics* was finished, a representative of the American Book Company came to my house and offered me a contract for my work which his firm wanted to publish not so much for the sake of profit as for "prestige."[1]

By 1936 it was clear that the first three volumes were a unit and should be published before the fourth. This was done in 1937.

For most men an effort like *Dynamics* is enough, but not for Sorokin. In 1935 and 1936 he published an article with Robert K. Merton on Arabian intellectual development; a study of fluctuations in idealism and materialism over a period of twenty-five-hundred years; and a paper on cultural integration.[2] In the year of *Dynamics'* release he also published an article on social equilibrium and a study, with Merton, of social time.[3]

The article on Arabian intellectual development focused on method. There Sorokin and Merton wrestled with creating quantitative indices of scientific achievements as judged by historians of science. When the evaluations of historians like George Sarton were quantified, one more clearly saw the fluctuations in patterns of knowledge. By quantifying Sarton's data on growth and change in science, Sorokin and Merton provided a compact summary of achievements and facilitated easy comparisons between disciplines and periods. Their scales accurately reflected the intellectual movements described by the historians. Consequently, quantification did not distort qualitative assessments but clarified them. The indices also provided a barometer for measuring scientific growth and decline that Sorokin, Merton, and Boldyreff would use to study the fluctuation of scientific activity in *Dynamics*.[4]

The work for this piece was done in 1934. Merton, then a third-year graduate student, was Sorokin's teaching and research assistant. Destined to become the brightest star among a host of luminaries, Merton had come to Harvard in 1931. He and Sorokin shared similar backgrounds. Both were from impoverished eastern European origins that would have determined the lives of lesser men. The young Merton was from the slums of South Philadelphia. His father, an immigrant, worked as a truck driver and carpenter. For Merton South Philadelphia was not a slum but "a friendly, noisy, and continuously interesting place to live." Like Sorokin, he was infused with "an almost obsessive hunger for learning." By eight he was a regular at the local library, reading extensively and particularly enjoying biographies. At twelve Merton was established as the neighborhood's magician and made up to ten dollars a show.[5] Being nimble with his hands and language, he quickly grabbed and held the interest of his audiences. Later at Harvard he entertained friends with magic and combined the talents of showman and scholar to keep the rapt attention of his classes.

Merton's intellectual abilities earned him a scholarship to Temple University, where he studied sociology under George E. Simpson. Through Simpson he learned "that it was possible to examine human behavior objectively and without using loaded moral preconceptions."[6] The value of an objective social science was reinforced by his early reading of Sorokin's *Contemporary Sociological Theories.* While the book was his intellectual introduction to Sorokin, it was at a meeting of the American Sociological Association in Washington, D.C., that Merton first saw him in action. There Sorokin "was his dramaturgic and dramatic self as he repeatedly reiterated his attack on Hornell Hart for an unacceptable formulation, and then proceeded to his own alternative."[7] While Merton found the presentation a bit dramatic, it was still "the occasion which led me to decide that I wanted to do my graduate work with Sorokin, wherever he might be."[8]

Like Sorokin, Merton possessed a driving energy and often worked very long hours. As a graduate student he lived on five hundred dollars a year, subsisting mostly on sandwiches, milkshakes, and his own home-made whiskey. Student poverty did not prevent him, however, from enjoying classical music, fox-trotting with the ladies, and developing a competitive tennis game. Merton was charming and at ease with people, so many found him good and stimulating company.

The article on Arabian intellectual life was also a product of Merton's association with George Sarton, "the acknowledged world dean among historians of science."[9] Sarton had fled Belgium during the Great War and came to the United States. After short-term appointments at the University of Illinois and George Washington University, he was brought to Harvard by L. J. Henderson. There Sarton won support from the Carnegie Foundation for his history of science project and his journal *ISIS.* At Harvard he wrote his magnum opus, the three-volume, five-part *Introduction to the History of Science.*[10] It was while he labored on this work that Merton first approached him about a dissertation focused on seventeenth-century English science. Sarton also knew Sorokin, and both men shared a deep interest in the sociology of knowledge, invention, and science.[11] Indeed, Merton was working in these areas as Sorokin's assistant on *Dynamics.* The 1935 article resulted from their methodological efforts to develop quantitative indicators of scientific growth and decline.[12]

Sorokin and Merton also published a perceptive essay in which they questioned the suitability of calendrical time for the study of social change.[13] They observed that astronomical or Newtonian time is only one manifestation of the concept; philosophers, psychologists, and economists all treat time and its measurement differently. Sorokin and Merton argued that social groups also reckon time to suit the rhythms and patterns of their activities, and that it is rarely desirable to confine time measured by behavior into solar equivalents of days, weeks, and so forth. Time thus varies with social structure. Even in calendrical time, different groups trace their beginnings from different, socially important, events. Christians started with the birth of Christ, Muslims with the Hegira, and the Japanese with the founding of the empire by Jinny Tenno. Weeks of different lengths—three, four, six, seven, or ten days—have more to do with marketing patterns than with the moon. Nor are months determined astronomically. The Roman calendar system had months of varying lengths irrespective of the lunar cycles. Hours, too, change. Witness the conventional practice of daylight saving time, when hours are renumbered to maximize recreation and leisure time.

Time is thus a social fact and is measured in many ways. Sorokin and Merton introduced "social time" as a concept to foster discovery of patterned social phenomena. Moving from calendrical to social time more clearly demonstrated relationships and possible causative associations between events. Therefore, "If we are to enhance our knowledge of the temporal aspects of social change and process, we must enlarge our category of time to include the concept of social time."[14]

George Devereux responded to the article, asserting that while social and physical time were not synchronic, this did not mean that they differed in nature.[15] Following Leibnitz, time was defined as the order of succession among events and did not exist apart from those events. Newtonian time is an ideal possibility, but it is only by "definition that two seconds, two days or two years have equal duration. . . . The choice of units for measuring time is a matter of pure convenience."[16] Thus if time is fundamentally a phenomenon found in the sequence of events, then there is no basic difference between social and physical time. Only the yardstick changes.

Sorokin saw no conflict between Devereux's observations and his own. All times are but a variety of social time, constructs, and social facts.[17] However, the sociologist's concern with time differed from that of other scientists. Why does one society reckon time one way and another differently? Why are metaphysical conceptions prevalent in some cultures and sensate in others? Could a system of social time be constructed to include all social events, even those believed to be timeless and eternal? The concept of social time was essential because of the issues it raised and its special utility for social scientists.[18]

Between these two articles Merton completed his graduate studies, and wrote and defended his dissertation. Sorokin sponsored and chaired the dissertation and the examining committees, which included Sarton, Zimmerman, and Parsons.

Merton later acknowledged his debt to Sorokin and Sarton in *Social Theory and Social Structure:*

No man knows fully what shaped his thinking. . . . But among these are six to whom I owe a special debt, though of varying degree and kind, and to them I want to pay tribute. . . .

Before he became absorbed in the study of historical movements on the grand scale as represented in his *Social and Cultural Dynamics,* Pitirim A. Sorokin helped me to escape from the provincialism of thinking that effective studies of society were confined within American borders and from the slum-encouraged provincialism of thinking that the primary subject-matter of sociology was centered in such peripheral problems of social life as divorce and juvenile delinquency. I gladly acknowledge this honest debt, still not discharged.

To George Sarton, most esteemed among historians of science, I am thankful for friendship as well as guidance, and for the privilege of having been allowed to work the greater part of two years in his famed workshop at Harvard Library 189. Some small sign of his stimulus will be found in Chapter 1 of this book devoted to the requirements for a history of sociological theory and in Part IV devoted to studies in the sociology of science.[19]

As these publications were coming out, *Dynamics* was also in preparation for print. However, changes in the department were now requiring substantial attention from Sorokin. As ever, staffing was one of the central problems.

Turnover and Instability

The administration's reluctance to appoint more full-time members to the department meant that Sorokin was constantly recruiting sociologists for short-term service. In 1935–36 four such sociologists were brought on board. Gorrado Gini, the statistician from the University of Rome, taught in the department during the second semester and summer session. He offered courses on self-regulation in the social organism and the demography of isolated groups. Along with Gini came E. Wright Bakke from the Yale Institute of Human Relations. Bakke, though relatively unknown, was invited for a variety of reasons. He had recently written *The Unemployed Man,* which was considered important by several English and American scholars. He was also appealing because Sorokin felt obliged to carry on the work of social ethics, and Bakke's concern with unemployment and race fit this objective.[20] Bakke's appearance was also timely, as Zimmerman and Sorokin were doing a major study of unemployment for the federal government. The project, which included the publication of eleven separate monographs, was directed by Zimmerman, who was responsible for two of the studies ("Rural Rehabilitation" and "The Never Employed"), and was a contributor to a third ("Boston High School Graduates and the Depression"). Sorokin, along with Clarence Q. Berger, a graduate student, did a study of time that was published in 1939 as *Time-Budgets of Human Behavior.*[21]

James Ford, the sole remaining full-time member from Social Ethics, was still teaching in the department. Ford, a career-long Harvard scholar, had studied under Francis Greenwood Peabody. Ford's career in Social Ethics began in 1907, and he became an associate professor in 1921. He wrote on a variety of topics, but his main works were on housing and social problems. In 1933 he completed editing the twelve-volume *White House Conference on Home Building and Home Ownership.* His major two-volume work, *Slums and Housing,* was published in 1936. This was followed by the *Abolition of Poverty* in 1937 and *Social Deviation* in 1939. Ford was a quiet, sensitive man with a lifelong sympathy for the poor and the oppressed. Students found him warm, kindly, and more than willing to help in the development of their ideas. However, his commitment was to ethical concerns, and he represented that viewpoint in the department until his death in May 1944.[22]

A third visitor, Howard Becker of Smith College, came to the department in 1935–36. He had taught in the summer of 1933, and Sorokin was interested in having him return to do a course entitled "Social Thought Before Comte." Becker and Bakke were competitors for a three-year assistant professorship. Being unable to hire a senior man with permanency, Sorokin and Zimmerman needed help. Actually, in the spring of 1936 Sorokin was on sabbatical; however, his need for faculty was so great that he participated in the recruitment process. While Zimmerman was acting chairman, Sorokin negotiated with the administration. Both candidates were promising, but the recommendation went to Becker, who could offer a greater variety of courses and was more broadly educated. However, Becker declined and Sorokin continued his search.[23]

The opening was eventually filled by the prominent Russian criminologist and pioneer in the sociology of law, Nicholas S. Timasheff. Formerly at the University of St. Petersburg and the Polytechnic Institute, Timasheff had emigrated to Germany in 1921, where he worked as a journalist and teacher. In 1923 he became professor of sociology and jurisprudence at the

University of Prague. He next moved to Paris in 1928 and became assistant editor-in-chief of the Russian newspaper *Vozrozhdemic*. He also taught in the Institute of Slavic Studies at the Sorbonne and lectured at several important western European universities.

Nicholas Timasheff descended from ancient Russian nobility. A man of vast learning and careful scholarship, he would fill an important need in the department. Sheldon Glueck, of the Law School, regularly offered a criminology course for sociology students. His interests, however, were becoming more specialized, and he decided to teach only law students. Consequently, Sorokin needed a criminologist. He had known Timasheff since the revolution, and they had worked together in the Kerensky government. Timasheff, with others, had drafted the code of law for the provisional government. At the time Sorokin considered him "if not the most prominent, then certainly one of the three most prominent criminologists in Russia."[24] Timasheff would be an ideal replacement for Glueck. He had published important works on parole and criminal law, and was a founding figure in the sociology of law. Furthermore, Timasheff was superior to most American criminologists "because the weakest point of all American criminologists has been their lack of training in law. Timasheff happily unites in himself a rather exceptional knowledge in this field and all the related fields; comparative history of law, general and criminal law, and sociology."[25]

Timasheff's nomination was well received. Sorokin wrote him in France, offering a one-year lecturer appointment for 1936–37. His teaching load would be two full courses or four half courses, and he could repeat one course at Radcliffe for extra income. Sorokin specified that one course be in the sociology of law and not duplicate Glueck's offerings in criminology or penology. He advised Timasheff to send his vita and a list of courses he could offer. Sorokin suggested that he review the major American criminology texts to acquaint himself with standard expectations. Timasheff should also begin to work on English because it was crucial to his success.[26]

Sorokin was also motivated by friendship. He was aware of Timasheff's modest circumstances in France and that there might be first-class academic opportunities for him in America. He concluded his letter by writing:

Now, as Mr. Sorokin, and not as the chairman of this Department, I would like to say quite frankly that if you can accept this proposition and during the first year you have a certain amount of success, there is some chance of the continuation of your position, either at this University, or at some other. This is not a promise, you will understand, but I suggest this that you may take the task seriously and do your best along this line.[27]

Timasheff had financial problems and difficulties getting the necessary travel clearances. Sorokin helped with both money and documents,[28] allowing Timasheff to come to Harvard in mid-September 1936.[29]

In 1935–36 C. Arnold Anderson, despite his promotion to faculty instructor, resigned for a position in Iowa. Carl S. Joslyn was in his final year as department statistician and demographer, and would be replaced by Edward P. Hutchinson. Robert Merton, who received his doctorate in February 1936, continued on as a newly advanced instructor. Other positions at the lower ranks were filled by a new group of graduate students, among them Edward C. Devereux Jr., Edward Y. Hartshorne Jr., Walter C. McKain Jr., and Theodore W. Sprague.

Two years later the *Harvard Communist* and the Cambridge Teachers' Union, in its pamphlet "Alleged Liberal Myth of Harvard," would charge that these new appointments were necessary because four graduate assistants had been discharged for political reasons by a reactionary sociology chairman. The Teachers' Union alleged that Sorokin had fired J. B. Knox, C. E. Hopkins, L. M. Blumberg, and E. B. Smullyan for their politics and had driven away a Mr. Lester for similar reasons. These charges were likely leveled because of Sorokin's staunch anticommunist stand and cool attitude toward the union and plights of professors Walsh and Sweezy. Regardless, the facts show that when a graduate fellowship could not be provided for Lester, Sorokin obtained a scholarship for him at Duke University and later a fellowship at the University of Minnesota. The four teaching assistants were all discharged because they had reached the limits of support granted by the department and beyond which no continuation could be expected. In the case of Blumberg, the only one who might remotely be considered radical, student complaints were so numerous that he was discharged. Emile Smullyan and John B. Knox continued in the program and received their doctorates in 1938 and 1939, respectively.[30] Thus, for a variety of reasons, staffing was one of the chairman's consuming responsibilities, often loaded with special difficulties.

Promotion and Dismissals:
The Consequences of "Up or Out"

Among Sorokin's more important and difficult staffing decisions were the promotions of Talcott Parsons in 1936 and 1939. A major problem faced by Harvard's new president, James B. Conant, in 1933 was the reappointment and promotion policy for junior faculty. He and the then dean of arts and sciences, Kenneth B. Murdock, had met in December to formulate a general statement. The problem was a difficult one. Harvard's faculty and students had grown substantially under Lowell. The tutorial system required a large number of junior positions, and these additions changed the balance between permanent and untenured faculty. In the mid-1920s the number of permanent faculty (professors and associates) and nonpermanent faculty (assistant professors, faculty instructors, and instructors) was about equal. By 1933 the proportion had shifted to twice as many nonpermanent staff as permanent professors. Clearly, the old promotion policies would mean a substantial increase in permanent faculty. The depression had reduced income from contributions, and projected enrollment declines discouraged a larger permanent faculty. Increasing permanent appointments might also result in a loss of quality and flexibility at those ranks in years to come.

Conant and Murdock responded with new reappointment and promotion policies that had grave consequences for the sociology department. Under the new rules, no annually appointed faculty would be recommended for a fifth year. This meant that Timasheff, among others, must either be advanced to faculty instructor by 1940 or be terminated. In his case it led to termination despite the publication of his *Introduction to the Sociology of Law* in 1939. This book was well received and became a classic in the field.[31] According to Robert Bierstedt, Timasheff's dismissal was unfortunate because

he was one of the most underrated of contemporary sociologists. The reasons for this relative lack of recognition are several. In the first place, the range of his sociological attention was unusually comprehensive, moving easily from the sociology of law to the sociology of war and revolution in one dimension, from the history of sociological theory to the methodology of the discipline in another, and from voluminous papers on post-revolutionary Russia to particular pieces on particular men—Tocqueville, Comte, Petrajitsky, Kovalevsky, Ehrlich, Gumplowicz, Pareto, and Sorokin, among others—in still another.

In the second place, Timasheff wrote and published in many different countries and in several languages, with the result that the corpus of his work does not appear as an entity.[32]

Perhaps for similar reasons, the administration failed to see his promise and the contribution he could make to American scholarship and Harvard.

Conant and Murdock also agreed that a second three-year appointment for faculty instructors should not be made unless the department planned a recommendation for promotion. This rule had special significance for Talcott Parsons because he had been recommended for his third such appointment in November 1933. His reappointment preceded Conant's decision to implement what would become known as "the up-or-out policy" in 1936–37. However, Parsons was subject to the policy prior to the end of his appointment.[33] Robert Merton was also affected. His first appointment, as a faculty instructor, would end in 1939. Thus Conant's rule forced up-or-out decisions on two scholars soon to be among America's leading sociologists.[34]

Parsons had come to Harvard, as an instructor in the Department of Economics, in the fall of 1927. An Amherst graduate, he had studied biology but changed to the social sciences in his junior year. As Amherst had no sociology department, Parsons was primarily influenced by the economists Walter Hamilton and Clarence Ayers. Intrigued by institutional economics and attracted by sociology, Parsons followed Amherst with a year at the London School of Economics, where he began to perceive an intriguing border between sociology and economics. He explored this and other facets of social science with Leonard T. Hobhouse, Harold J. Laski, and Bronislaw K. Malinowski.[35]

In 1925 Parsons left London for Heidelberg. There, in the city of Max Weber, he focused on the works of this great sociologist. He worked under Karl Mannheim, Alfred Weber, and, most importantly, Karl Jaspers. Through Jaspers he received a proper introduction to Durkheim and did important work on Immanuel Kant. With Edgar Salin, "an iconoclastic economist close to both Weber brothers," Parsons pursued the study of capitalism in recent German literature. For that work, he received the Dr. Phil, degree in 1929.[36]

In the fall of 1926 Parsons returned to Amherst as a temporary instructor in economics. There he worked on his dissertation and became committed to a thorough study of the relationship between sociological and economic theory. Richard Meriam, the new chairman of the Department of Economics, convinced Parsons that the task required him to become better schooled in economics. Meriam suggested Harvard and arranged an instructor's appointment. As an instructor, Parsons could teach and take courses. The first two years the bulk of his time was spent in studying and seminars.

Allyn Young, the Harvard economist closest to Parsons's interest, was in England. However, Harvard was a fertile garden, and Parsons quickly discovered Joseph A. Schumpeter and Frank W. Taussig. From Schumpeter's course in general economics he glimpsed the necessary elements of a theoretical system. This conception was deepened by Alfred North

Whitehead, whose *Science and the Modern World* affected his thinking about theory and theoretical systems. From Frank W. Taussig came a masterly introduction to the theories of Alfred Marshall, the then-dominant figure in neoclassical economics whose *Principles of Economics* had replaced John Stuart Mill's *Principles* as the authoritative work defining the field.[37]

Parsons's concern with the junctures of economic and sociological theory found its first expression in his studies of Marshall. At the beginning of his second three-year appointment, he published "Wants and Activities in Marshall" and "Economics and Sociology: Marshall in Relation to the Thought of His Time" in the *Quarterly Journal of Economics*.[38] Further work on the common theoretical concerns of sociology and economics was published later in his two essays on "Sociological Elements in Economic Thought."[39] Along with Marshall, Parsons discovered Vilfredo Pareto, a technical and theoretical economist of considerable reputation. Through Pareto he came under the influence of L. J. Henderson.

Early on, Parsons found it necessary to restudy Durkheim. His introduction came in Clarence Ayers's class at Amherst on "The Moral Order." There he had read *The Elementary Forms of Religious Life,* but its significance and value did not register. In London he reencountered Durkheim, under the tutelage of Morris Ginsberg and Bronislaw Malinowski. Unfortunately, Durkheim was "dismissed by Ginsberg . . . for allegedly having a mystical 'group-mind' concept, and by Malinowski for more ambivalent reasons."[40] The great Polish anthropologist found much of the analysis in *Elementary Forms* to be "simply unscientific." It was at Heidelberg that Parsons later received a more sympathetic introduction to Durkheim from the eminent philosopher Karl Jaspers.[41] For one interested in the connections between economics and sociology, a title like *Division of Labor* could also not be ignored. As Parsons observed, "I finally got around to reading it during my second or third year at Harvard. I was simply astounded at the relevance of it and the extraordinary depth of Durkheim's analysis."[42] This led to a more intensive study of the French master and the incorporation of his works into Parsons's ideas. With his study of Durkheim the elements for his first major book in sociology were in place.

The year 1935 was to be a pivotal one in Parsons's career. By then he had been an instructor for eight years. Most of his original cohort from economics had been promoted or gone elsewhere. He too had left economics because, after three years, it was clear that his future there was not promising. The field and the department had shifted toward technical issues not of interest to Parsons, and his work in these areas was less than competitive. Consequently, the opportunity to participate on the Committee on Sociology and Social Ethics was attractive, particularly when it became clear that a new and independent sociology department would result. However, by 1935 Parsons felt it was his unlucky fate to be subject to two "unsympathetic chairmen: H. H. Burbank in economics and later P. A. Sorokin in sociology."[43] Thus his advancement was slow and difficult.

In 1935 Parsons published his first important sociological article, "The Place of Ultimate Values in Sociological Theory."[44] He then petitioned Sorokin for an assistant professorship. Parsons argued that he was in his ninth year (eight at Harvard) as an instructor and Sorokin had earlier agreed that he merited promotion. Sorokin had not pursued his case because it was not then in the department's interest to do so. For Parsons the time had now come. If not promoted, he would leave. Parsons sought promotion on the basis of his research, teaching, and departmental service. In research his publications had brought him to the attention of significant scholars in- and outside of Harvard.[45] While he had not written a major theoretical or empirical study, one was in progress. He submitted to Sorokin the manuscript of *Sociology and the Elements of Human Action*. This was the first statement of what became *The Structure of Social Action*.

Parsons also felt that his teaching and service were significant. He was the only member of the department on the tutorial staff of a house. He was properly proud of his Adams House discussion group, which was then three years old and had contributed substantially to the development of graduate students. Similarly, as only an instructor, he had done an inordinate amount of graduate teaching and taken on many other assignments. His Sociology 6 course on institutions and Sociology 21, his basic course on sociological theory were good examples. While some students believed he lectured over their heads, the success of the Adams House group and of his other classes clearly showed substantial student enthusiasm for his teaching.[46]

There is much to support Parsons's claims as a force in the education of graduate students. Indeed, his openness and receptivity to the ideas of others were among the factors that made him popular. This is particularly clear when one contrasts his teaching style with Sorokin's. Students were impressed by the power and scope of Sorokin's intellect but often found him distant, demanding, and too critical of their scholarship. As one student observed: "You couldn't be first rate with Sorokin. If you agreed with him, you were not original, if you disagreed with him, you were wrong. So you were kind of in a tight box with Sorokin. . . . He was not generous to his students."[47] Parsons was different. As one student noted: "We all studied under Parsons. And, in those days you could study under Parsons without having to agree with him. . . . He didn't like disciples."[48] Because some students found Sorokin difficult and not particularly helpful, they turned to Parsons. On Sorokin one student recalls:

If you had something you wanted to discuss with Sorokin, the strategy . . . was to go in there and pose it. For about ten minutes you got the most brilliant (analysis) you could imagine. And then he started off on, "Have you heard about the latest foreign language into which my books have been translated?" Then, you could forget it. You then spent another hour and a half, you know, but that was a complete waste of time.[49]

While for Parsons a student writes:

There was a sense that he (Parsons) gave people that they could acquire from him a style of analysis—functional institutional analysis—that could be applied to a whole variety of fields. I can remember people saying, "Well, look, Kingsley is doing 'the family,' I'll do . . ." I remember Wilbert Moore saying, I'll do "Labor," somebody will do this and that. In a sense, you know, we divide up the universe and did it all with the capacity for the analysis that Parsons (offered) institutional, structural functional analysis.[50]

Students were also attracted by the originality of Parsons's theory, its promise, and his willingness to include their ideas in his work. As one student observed,

One of the reasons why there was this confluence of people who really went out into the world and did something and had a big influence on the evolution of sociology and the social sciences was that we were all quite persuaded that we had hold of something that other people didn't. We had that wonderful, exciting sense that, you know, the rest of those people out there haven't got it right. We've got it right. We can do things others can't. And all sorts of people—I won't name names—but I know some people with quite mediocre intellect who have done quite good things, because we had a sense that we knew how to go at it . . . in a way that even the other [social sciences were not]. We were sure we were better than political scientists and we thought the economists were too policy-oriented and that the science of society was around the . . . bend of the next decade. And we really had something. There's no question about it. There was something in this.[51]

Similar feelings were expressed by members of the "Parsons Sociological Group." This group, later called the Adams House Group, started around 1932 and lasted until the end of the decade.[52] During its history many of the older and brighter graduate students became involved, among them Robert K. Merton, Kingsley Davis, Wilbert Moore, Robin Williams, Robert Bierstedt, Logan Wilson, and Edward Devereux. Even though the group was informal, minutes were kept, typed, and circulated. Meetings were held in Parsons's tutorial quarters in Adams House, "which invariably became tagged as the Parsonage."[53] Parsons's openness to students implied that, even as subordinates in the teacher-student relationship, their ideas counted for something. Merton recalls that many students came to Harvard to study with Sorokin but that

once there many of us "discovered" Parsons. This was especially the result of his first course simply entitled "The Sociological Theories of Hobhouse, Durkheim, Simmel, Tönnies, and Max Weber." Hobhouse, Simmel and much of Tönnies soon dropped from sight as Parsons made this course the source of his magisterial *Structure of Social Action*, six years later. We having discovered him, he in turn proceeded to discover us. He was both the cause and occasion for our taking sociological theory seriously. Because he, as a reference figure, accorded us intellectual respect, because he took us seriously, we, in strict accord with George Meadian theory, came to take ourselves seriously. We had work to do. Soon, some of us were less students than junior colleagues—fledgling colleagues, to be sure, but colleagues for all that.[54]

Merton also notes that few of Parsons's students became disciples. He instilled in them the sense that their "worth and promise were not being gauged by the extent to which we echoed his ideas." Indeed criticism, dialogue, and exchange were welcomed by the "not yet venerable" Parsons.[55]

To demonstrate his mastery of sociological theory, Parsons submitted to Sorokin a draft of *The Structure of Social Action*. Based on the manuscript and his other contributions, he sought promotion. If he was not promotable, he would go elsewhere. All he asked for "was a fair trial and a decision."[56]

Sorokin's response to the manuscript either marks the beginnings of difficulties between these two scholars or contributed to it. After reading and rereading the text for four full evenings, Sorokin reported to Parsons:

Your work is to be commended and heartily congratulated. If it is not too pretentious, I would say your work has many good tokens. But so far, in all sincerity and frankness—good tokens, not a fruitful harvest, as yet; and not a very large scientific building, as yet, in which one can live and work. This means, it has several weak points. . . . I am sure you would accept some of my critical remarks in the same friendly spirit in which they are written.

Sorokin saw two types of problems in the manuscript. These he called essential and technical. On the technical side, Parsons's writing was too long and slow. The style was difficult, and the main points were hard to follow. Indeed, the more important the point, the more difficult the reading. Sorokin believed that the style of the manuscript was more burdensome than Kant's *Critique of Pure Reason* or Edmund Husserl's phenomenology:

I may be wrong but I feel that your work would be "unreadable" for say, ninety per cent of the sociologists of the USA. Perhaps it is a plus, *un*understandable work creates a myth of being particularly great . . . but you hardly want such kind of prestige, not to mention that it is usually shortliving. The reason of such a "difficultness" may be in the manner of your exposition of your ideas; but it may be due also to the unclearness of the ideas in your own mind. Which of these reasons is real, I do not know positively. I am inclined, however, to think that the second reason is not totally absent. This leads to an enumeration of the *essential* shortcomings.[57]

Sorokin found the first three chapters difficult and unclear. Most of the trouble was due to terminology. Parsons gave meanings to key terms that differed from those of the original thinkers and often from contemporary understanding. ("One does not know what you mean by these terms and what currents of thought you have in mind.") The subsequent analysis was unclear because redefining established terms created confusion.

Also problematic was Parsons's habit of not defining key terms when he introduced them. To these he added more undefined concepts, producing a "manysided ambiguity." One could not follow, in Sorokin's estimation, "many of the subsequent reasonings tied up with the basic concepts." This conceptual difficulty resulted from using two modes of definition: mosaic and analytical. Although Sorokin had previously tried (fruitlessly) to point out the difficulty with mosaic definitions, Parsons persisted in using these unscientific "logical monsters." Because of the lack of conceptual precision and the misuse of established propositions, derivations and conclusions often "jump out in an unwarranted and unexpected way." Furthermore, the analysis became so fine, detailed, and finicky that Sorokin believed that Parsons "misses the elephant in your hunt for the mosquito."

Sorokin concluded the letter by noting that there was plenty of good in Parsons's work:

But in your work one finds not only this "gold" but plenty of "pseudo gold" and something even less noble. If I were you I would rewrite the first three chapters entirely, perhaps reducing them to one introductory chapter. [This] would somewhat make more concise and vigorous most of the other chapters, clarifying the main categories and throwing out many which are in no way necessary for the development of your main arguments. The book would gain a great deal from such a revision.

Such, Parsons, are my impressions in all their sincerity and frankness. The practical conclusion of that, so far as I am concerned, is a wish that you would further cultivate a very good analytical ability to your thinking. If it is freed from the shortcomings I mentioned, it promises to give us a "gold" which cannot be dug by the majority of your colleagues, sociologists and social scientists. Most heartily I wish you a complete success along this line.[58]

Sorokin's difficulty with this manuscript may have colored his assessment of Parsons's suitability for promotion. In reply to a letter from Conant in which Sorokin was asked to state the department's criteria for promotion, he wrote:

So far as promotion of a younger member is concerned, here I see only one criterion, mainly the total achievement of a young man and his potential possibilities as far as they can be judged. . . . By the totality of achievement I mean first of all whether the man is original and brilliant, a competent scholar or researcher; second, how good a teacher he is; third, how great are his potentialities along both lines. The last is mentioned last but in some cases it has the greatest importance.[59]

Judging from this letter, Sorokin may have found Parsons's achievements inadequate for advancement. The difficulties he observed were fundamental and serious. They were matters that a chairman was required to reflect on and assess in making a promotion decision.

Approximately a year later, four members of the Harvard Committee for Research in the Social Sciences (J. A. Schumpeter, J. D. Black, L. J. Henderson, and O. H. Taylor) reviewed a revised copy of Parsons's manuscript. Schumpeter shared some of Sorokin's concerns but praised Parsons's scholarship. He also provided a novel insight into the problem of language. While agreeing that the work was too long and that "much space seems to be needlessly lost in getting to the point," Schumpeter wrote:

The scholarly care with which the main elements of Max Weber's thoughts are analyzed and followed to their sources and displayed in their significance cannot be too highly commended. The author has in fact so deeply penetrated into the German thicket as to lose in some places the faculty of writing in English about it and some turns of phrase become fully understandable only if translated into German.

On the whole my opinion is definitely favorable to publication of this work that not everyone will appreciate, but which everyone must recognize as a very serious piece of research.[60]

Henderson, though positive and supportive, observed:

On the other hand there are in the work a large number of details that I regard as erroneous or inadequately analyzed or irrelevant or in a few instances as extraneous. Concerning not a few of these it is my impression that I have convinced Parsons that I am right. At any rate it is my view that the book, while very important as a whole, is much in need of modification at many points in detail. . . . Because the work is potentially so good I strongly urge that it should be once more revised.[61]

J. D. Black, the chairman of the committee, responded to Henderson six weeks later. He reported that Parsons had taken Henderson's comments to heart and "is now in the process of a very considerable revision of which he himself believes will improve it significantly. You may be interested to know that now the manuscript is taking a much more acceptable form than in its earlier stage."[62]

The draft was extensively revised. Parsons regularly went to Henderson's home for long sessions devoted to rewriting the manuscript.[63] He also acknowledged that "two other critics have been particularly helpful through the suggestions and criticisms they have given after reading the manuscript, Professor A. D. Nock, especially in the parts dealing with religion, and Dr. Robert K. Merton."[64]

The reinforcement for some of Sorokin's concerns found in the reviews of Parsons's supporters demonstrates that his objections had a credible basis. Indeed, it confirms that Sorokin's lack of support derived some momentum from sound scholarly observations and was not purely a product of pique or personality. Many students of the period, however, report that there was quite a "power struggle" between the two and "that Sorokin and Zimmerman were 'out to get' Parsons." Others report frequent "fights" between the two and that many students came to view Parsons as an "embattled young man."[65] While it is clear that they had problems with each other, the source of the difficulty is unknown.[66] However, it is not clear that Sorokin resisted Parsons's promotion for reasons other than strong scholarly reservations about the younger sociologist's work. In light of Harvard's new promotion policies and Conant's insistence that only the very best men be given permanencies, Sorokin was required by his position to be careful. Parsons notes that his promotion in 1936 was "pushed not by Sorokin but, notably by E. F. Gay, E. B. Wilson and L. J. Henderson, all of whom were 'outside members' of the department."[67]

The outcome of Parsons's struggles for advancement and permanency reveals the tension between him and Sorokin on scholarly and career issues. These episodes also show that Parsons had a power base, independent of Sorokin and the other sociologists, that included the support and esteem of many of the "interdepartmental professors." These outside members voted on departmental questions, and many were quite influential with President Conant. This was especially true of Lawrence J. Henderson, who was Mrs. Conant's uncle by marriage[68] and from whom the president often sought advice on the social sciences. Conant was an innocent in these areas, so he leaned on those who had a similar vision of Harvard.[69] This certainly included his fellow scientist L. J. Henderson, whom Conant trusted and who had played a role in his appointment to the presidency.[70]

Henderson's support of Parsons was again important in 1937. Parsons notes:

Even with the assistant professorship, however, I was by no means certain that I wanted to stay at Harvard. In the (to me) critical year of 1937 I received a very good offer. . . . I went to Henderson—not Sorokin. Henderson took the matter directly to President Conant who, with Sorokin's consent to be sure, offered to advance me immediately to then extant "second term" assistant professorship with a definite promise of permanency as associate professor two years later. On these terms I decided to stay at Harvard.[71]

On learning of the offer from Wisconsin, Sorokin and eight members of the department wrote Conant that they had unanimously "Resolved: That the Department hopes Professor Parsons will stay at Harvard and, if he continues to develop as he has been developing, has in mind recommending that he be promoted in somewhat less than the usual period."[72] With Henderson's support and Sorokin's consent Conant was convinced to promote Parsons to the associate rank and permanency in 1939.[73]

With Parsons's permanency Sorokin had three tenured sociologists in the department. He would also gain that year the services of George C. Homans as a faculty instructor in a five-year appointment. Homans came to the department as a replacement for Robert K. Merton, who had left to take an appointment at Tulane.[74] It is interesting to note that the department's inability to hire full-time permanent faculty and the up-or-out policy likely cost it an early position of leadership in American sociology. Had Merton been promoted and given an opportunity for permanency, he might have stayed at Harvard. Similarly, Kingsley Davis and Wilbert Moore also slipped through Sorokin's fingers and left to make their contributions elsewhere.[75] Had they and Timasheff stayed, the potential for the department's success would have been greatly increased. Clearly, this was not Sorokin's fault. He never had the necessary resources with which to build the department and recruit or retain people of talent.

Reputation and Respect

Harvard had been slow to develop a sociology program, and by the late 1930s the department's prestige in the university was not high. This resulted from several problems. Although Conant wished to recruit top-quality sociologists for the department, he received the strong impression from many Harvard notables of sociologists as men of mediocre intellect and ability. L. J. Henderson "was pretty contemptuous of sociology, with one major and one minor exception." The major exception was Pareto; the minor one was Robert Park, a classmate at Strasbourg around 1900.[76] The biochemist felt sociology misled students and the public by claiming it could produce a science of society. Sociologists did not teach the discipline and rigor essential for scientific work because of their intellectual inferiority and the low scientific standards they set and accepted.[77] Crane Brinton expressed similar sentiments, arguing that "sociology was committed . . . to bringing forth the kind of cumulative and systematic knowledge achieved by sciences like zoology and geology. This it has certainly not yet done." Additionally, the discipline lacked a core of basic concepts for teaching and research. "Sociologists can't agree on anything. . . . there just isn't any central core as yet in sociology." In turn, "Its practitioners are to an overwhelming extent partisans, improvers, preachers."[78]

E. B. Wilson echoed kindred concerns to Conant. Wilson felt that the field had not defined itself and that there was "no real subject as Sociology." Wilson also saw a shortage of high-grade personnel and believed that the United States had produced only three great sociologists: Lester F. Ward, William G. Sumner, and W. I. Thomas. These men, he noted, came to sociology late in life and after establishing themselves in other disciplines. Ward had been a geologist, Sumner an economist, and Thomas a professor of English. Wilson felt that the significant contributions to sociology were made by persons who had done something else very well. He cited Pareto as another example and noted that sociology shared this trait with philosophy, which was another discipline of wide interest to "persons of maturity." Wilson endorsed W. I. Thomas's idea that "sociologists are a lot of 'busted' ministers or would-be ministers of low intellectual standards." He concluded by observing, "Even though it might have been desirable to get rid of Social Ethics, why set up something more pretentious and more expensive but of no greater real substance? May we not have jumped from the frying pan into the fire?"[79]

On another level, an alumnus and important member of the Department of the Interior wrote President Conant:

I have a son in the freshman class. He desired to choose sociology as his subject for concentration, but came to the conclusion that the Department of Sociology at Harvard was so poor that it would be inadvisable for him to major in that subject. When he told me this, I made inquiry among some of the social scientists here in Washington whose opinion I value, and was interested to learn that their informed and mature judgment confirmed his. I feel that I should call this to your attention for whatever it may be worth.[80]

The president wrote in response:

I am very much interested in what you say about the Department of Sociology. I should be very much indebted to you if, in strict confidence, you could let me know from those whose opinion you value, what universities have better departments of Sociology; and, particularly, what men in those departments make them so outstanding. Within a year we have scoured both America and Europe in connection with making a new appointment in sociology, and I came to the conclusion that there were no first-rate sociologists in existence. I also came to the conclusion that our department, though small, was as good as any in the country. The department should be judged by comparing the quality of Professors Sorokin, Zimmerman, and Ford with similar men in other universities. I should greatly appreciate receiving as much detailed information along this line as you could send me.[81]

The alumnus took the request to heart and polled his Washington colleagues. The opinions of these "sociologists of repute" were not favorable to Sorokin or the department. By and large they judged the department to be inferior and viewed its faculty as "not first rate." Sharp criticisms of Sorokin were offered by anonymous "experts." According to one, "The existing department would fight against any first rate man, particularly Sorokin, who is to my mind the hollowest pretense to be found anywhere, even among sociologists. It is shocking to me that a university of Harvard's standing should be so lame in a field of first importance." Another believed that "Sorokin is a man of considerable learning but very little wisdom and no common sense. I have read many of his books and save for one on social mobility I think they are either second rate or third rate. Why they ever took him at Harvard I have no idea." The "experts" also believed that the best sociologists and programs were at the University of Chicago, and that Ellsworth Faris, Robert Park, William Ogburn, and Ernest Burgess were stronger scholars than any in the Harvard department. Ogburn was singled out as the best possible chair for the department. The program was also criticized as one-sided and conservative. New people with different outlooks had to be recruited if it was to become first-rate. Men of talent were available for a call to Harvard. Besides the Chicago scholars there were Karl Mannheim and several others in Alvin Johnson's "University in Exile."[82]

Conant also heard criticisms from the department. Parsons, after his promotion and tenure, had written him about administrative practices that were a cause for concern. These practices were adversely affecting his work, and he wanted to discuss them with the president. He hoped that Conant would agree with him and undertake to change some of the more objectionable aspects of the situation.[83] There is no record of what Parsons discussed with Conant at their meeting. However, Parsons was not alone in expressing dissatisfaction with internal affairs. Edward Y. Hartshorne, who had served as an assistant in Sorokin's Principles of Sociology course for two years and was the assistant-in-charge-of-the-course for another year, was another critic. He sent a report and letter to Parsons in which he states:

These are a few random ideas I have set down as they occurred to me. . . . I thought I would first send them to you for your comments and then possibly do the thing over. Are there any aspects which I have left out which occur to you? Does the present form fit your immediate purposes? What other suggestions do you have? I am somewhat tempted to send this to Conant personally in case you cannot bring it up. I suggest therefore that you return the present form to me with your comments.[84]

Hartshorne's "Report on Sociology A" contained a long list of criticisms about the course content, grading policies, admission of students, and, most of all, Sorokin. Hartshorne noted that Sorokin frequently admitted marginal freshman whom the assistants refused because of their low levels of academic performance. Sorokin took the view: "Well, I take a rather different approach. When a man comes to me I tell him that Sociology A is not an easy course but that every man has the privilege of hanging himself in any way he wants. Consequently I let them in if, after that warning, they still want to take it."[85] Hartshorne specified his objections to this approach:

The effect of this procedure is, however, a lowering of the quality of student in the course, since these poor men who are let in are, when the final grades are made out, not "hanged" as a matter of fact, since by that time their role has shifted. Now they are regarded by Professor Sorokin as potential concentrators whose affections for the department must not be slighted.

On the matter of grading Hartshorne's accusations are more piercing:

When the Instructors bring their grades to Professor Sorokin for approval something like the following scene takes place. (The present writer has only experienced it approximately ten times.) In the first place Professor Sorokin asks to see the distribution. If there is more than one "E" he immediately puts his foot down, citing certain other introductory courses with three or four times the enrolment [*sic*] of Soc. A which, he declares, have only one "E." Consequently one "E" out of 150 men is "very severe comparatively." Anyone who knows Professor Sorokin will recognize the difficulty of arguing with him under such circumstances. The result is that in the course of Sociology A a group of perhaps half a dozen or more flunks, admitted under threat of flunking them, have been saved. Naturally, therefore, word spreads that if one can't pass anything else "Try Sociology."

Next Professor Sorokin takes the actual grade sheets in hand. After the "E" problem is settled he takes up the "D's." "Cannot any of these be raised?" he asks. "Here is a D + ; let us make it a C − ," etc. I have been present on some occasions when he consistently went through my entire list for Radcliffe and erased all minus signs. This led to such monstrosities as the following: November Hour "C + ," Midyear "B − ," Final grade for course . . . B. He is likely to accompany these alterations in grades with such remarks as the following: "Townsend−that is a good name; let us raise grade." Or, "Perhaps he will concentrate," or "Perhaps he will leave some money." It should be understood that Professor Sorokin neither makes out the exam nor reads any of them. . . . It is my impression that anyone who has been associated with Professor Sorokin for any length of time could adduce numerous similar instances. This fact is supported by the informal title among the junior staff for the Chief Section Man in Sociology A: "Chief Scapegoat."[86]

Hartshorne further observed that the course content was too narrow to be an adequate introduction to the field. The required readings were largely Sorokin's published works, and Sorokin argued his own views in the course. While other men and ideas were mentioned, these were vigorously, and frequently unfairly, dismissed. This method often left students confused and "wavering between two points of view: either that Sorokin is right, in which case Sociology over the rest of the country, which is not Sorokinian, must be a lot of tommy-rot; or, Sorokin is wrong, in which case it would scarcely seem worthwhile to listen to him during a whole year." The lectures also frequently oversimplified complex topics. They did not deal with methodological issues or the strengths and weaknesses of various forms of statistical analysis. Students were given conclusions with no deep understanding of the evidence or adequacy of methodological investigations on which these claims were based.

Furthermore, the introductory course did not prepare students for other courses in the department. Concentrators' interests were in four fields: the courses given by Parsons and Merton, population (Hutchinson), rural sociology (Zimmerman), and practical sociology or social work (Ford). Sociology A did not lead into any of these. The only course to which it related was dynamics, which had been dropped because its content was absorbed by Sociology A. The course, therefore, had little utility as an introduction to sociology in general or sociology at Harvard. The lack of fit between Sociology A and other parts of the program also reflected "the strained personal relations existing between the members of the department and its chairman. In the last analysis it is difficult to see how the problem of Sociology A can be solved until it is taken from Professor Sorokin's hands."[87]

Based on such information, Conant no doubt had some important questions about the department. These concerns contributed to his reluctance to make permanent appointments or keep the department's more promising members. Furthermore, the criticisms of Sorokin raised serious questions about his effectiveness as the torchbearer for sociology at Harvard.

Social and Cultural Dynamics

While internal problems and struggles demanded much of Sorokin's attention, 1937 still witnessed publication of the first three volumes of *Dynamics*. Sorokin's magnum opus began with an analysis of cultural integration. Is human culture an organized whole? Or is it a congeries of values, objects, and traits bound only by proximity in time and space? Sorokin envisioned four relationships between cultural elements: mechanical or spatial adjacency, in which they are related only by proximity: integration of elements as a result of a common association with some external factor; unity as a result of causal functional integration; and the supreme and final form of cultural bonding, logico-meaningful integration. Sorokin observed that culture consists of millions of individuals, objects, and events with an infinite number of possible relationships. Logico-meaningful integration orders these elements into a comprehensible system and specifies the principle that gives the system logical consistency and meaning.[88] In this form, a culture is integrated around a central idea that gives it unity.

Different principles underlie causal and logico-meaningful integration. In causal analysis, complex entities are reduced to simpler ones until an ultimate simplicity or basic unit is reached. Studying relationships between basic units results in discovering the nature of their bonding into a more complex structure. Causal functional integration is a continuum. At one end, elements are so closely bound that when one is eliminated the system ceases to exist or undergoes a profound modification. At the other extreme, a change in one element has no discernible impact on the others, because not all cultural traits are causally linked. In the logico-meaningful method, reduction to basic units is impossible because no simple social atoms have been found. Instead, one seeks the central meaning that permeates cultural phenomena and brings them together into a unity. Causal analysis often describes uniformities without telling us why they exist. But we get a different insight from perceiving a logical unity. The properly trained mind automatically and apodictically grasps the unity in Euclid's geometry, a Bach concerto, a Shakespearean sonnet, or the architecture of the Parthenon. We clearly see the relationships and understand why they are as they are. In contrast, items may covary without any logical connection between them. For example, chocolate ice cream consumption may go up as juvenile crime increases. While associated, these facts have no logical relationship and give us no insight into the dynamics of juvenile crime.[89]

Logico-meaningful relationships vary in intensity. Some bind cultural elements into a sublime unity. Others simply merge them into low grades of unity. The integration of major cultural values is the most important form of logico-meaningful synthesis. Finding the principle maintaining this unity allows the scholar to grasp a culture's essence, meaning and integrity. Sorokin notes that "The essence of the logico-meaningful method is . . . finding the central principle ('the reason') which permeates all components [of a culture], gives sense and significance to each of them, and in this way makes cosmos of a chaos of unintegrated fragments."[90]

If the value of the method relies on finding such a principle we must ask How can it be discovered? How do we know the discovery is valid? How can we resolve different claims by investigators that they have found the organizing principle? The answer to the first question is straightforward. We discover the principle as any scientist would: by observation, statistical study, logical analysis, intuition, and deep thought. All of these are part of the first stage of scientific discovery. In turn, validity is decided by the logical purity of the principle. Is it free of contradiction and consistent with the rules of proper reasoning? Will it stand the test of the facts it proports to account for? If so, we can have faith in its claim to truth. The validity of competing truth claims is decided in the same ways: logical purity and explanatory power. Sorokin states: "Of the several rival theories, that theory is best which describes the field of the phenomena in question most accurately and embraces in its description the largest number of phenomena."[91]

Sorokin proposed that we seek principles that grasp the ultimate reality of different types of cultural systems. The most important principle is the one on which the culture itself depends for its perception of ultimate reality. What source of information is given supreme validity by a culture for judging what is real? Sorokin argued that some cultures accept the foundation of truth or ultimate reality as supersensory and agree that the truths detected by our senses are illusionary. Others are the opposite: ultimate reality is revealed by our senses, and other forms of perception mislead and misdirect us. Different perceptions of ultimate reality shape a culture's institutions and form its essential character, meaning, and personality.

Along with viewing cultural systems as logical unities, Sorokin suggested they possess degrees of autonomy and self-regulation. Furthermore, the most important determinants of the character and direction of change in a system are found within the system. Hence, cultural systems contain immanent mechanisms of self-regulation and self-direction. The history of a culture is determined by its internal properties—that is, "Its life course is set down in its essentials when the system is born."[92] Therefore, to understand sociocultural change, we should not rely on theories that emphasize external factors or on those that view change as driven by one element of a social system, such as economics, population, or religion. Change, instead, is the result of a system expressing its internal proclivities for development and maturation. Thus, our emphasis must be on internal unity and logico-meaningful organization.

With this in mind, Sorokin classified the forms of integrated culture. There are two main types, the Ideational and the Sensate, and a third, the Idealistic, which is formed from their mixture. Sorokin describes Sensate and Ideational cultures:

Each has its own mentality; its own system of truth and knowledge; its own philosophy and *Weltanschauung;* its own type of religion and standards of "holiness"; its own system of right and wrong; its own forms of art and literature; its own mores, laws, code of conduct; its own predominant forms of social relationships; its own economic and political organization; and, finally, its own type of *human personality,* with a peculiar mentality and conduct.[93]

In Ideational cultures, reality is perceived as nonmaterial, everlasting Being. The needs and ends of individuals are spiritual and are realized through pursuits of supersensory truths. There are two subclasses of the

Ideational mentality: Ascetic Ideationalism and Active Ideationalism. The ascetic form seeks spiritual ends through a denial of material appetites and a detachment from the world. In its extreme expression, the individual completely loses "self" in the quest for oneness with the deity or ultimate value. Active Ideationalism seeks to reform the sociocultural world along the lines of increasing spirituality and toward the ends specified by its main value. Its bearers strive to bring others closer to God and their vision of ultimate reality.

Sensate cultures are dominated by a mentality that views reality as that detected by our senses. The supersensory does not exist, and agnosticism shapes attitudes about the world beyond the senses. Human needs are met by modifying and exploiting the external world. Sensate culture is the opposite of Ideational in values and institutions. There are three forms of Sensate culture. The first is the Active Sensate, in which needs are satisfied by transforming the physical and sociocultural worlds. The great conquerors and merchants of history are examples of this mentality at work. The second is the Passive Sensate mentality, which meets needs by a parasitic exploitation of the physical and cultural world. The world exists simply to meet wants; therefore, eat, drink, and be merry. The Cynical Sensate will use all mechanisms to meet its wants. This mentality lacks strong values and follows any instrumental route to satisfaction.

Many cultures fall between these extremes, and Sorokin judges them to be poorly integrated. An exception is the Idealistic culture. It is a synthesis in which reality is many-sided and needs are both spiritual and material, with the former dominating. An unintegrated form of this type is the Pseudo-Idealistic culture, in which reality is mostly sensate and needs predominantly physical. Unhappily, needs are not well met, and privations are regularly endured. A group of primitive people are an example of this type.

Sorokin described in detail the ideal traits of each type. He discussed their social and practical values, aesthetic and moral values, system of truth and knowledge, social power and ideology, and the influences on development of the social self. However, he noted that no pure types exist. In some cultures one form predominates but simultaneously coexists with characteristics of the other types.

Sorokin wanted to find actual cases of the forms of integrated culture. His quest spanned twenty-five hundred years. While concentrating on Greco-Roman and Western civilizations, Sorokin occasionally studied the Middle East, India, China, and Japan. He described in great detail trends and fluctuations in their art, scientific discoveries, wars, revolutions, truth systems, and other social phenomena. While avoiding a cyclical theory of change, Sorokin observed that cultural institutions move through Ideational, Sensate, and Idealistic periods, often separated by times of crisis in the transition from one to another.

Sorokin explained these changes as the result of the operation of Immanent Determinism and the Principle of Limits. By Immanent Determinism he meant that social systems, like biological ones, change according to their inherent potentialities. That is, the functioning dynamic organization of the system establishes the boundaries and potentialities of change. Systems, however, have limits. For example, as they become more and more Sensate, moving toward the Cynical Sensate, they reach the border, or *limits*, of their potential for expansion. In a dialectical fashion, the move toward the Sensate extreme produces Ideational countertrends that grow stronger as the system polarizes. These countertrends cause discord and disorganization and move the system toward a more Idealistic form. As dialectical changes reverberate through the culture, violence, revolutions, and wars increase as the culture attempts to adjust to a new configuration or structure. Consequently, the study of change should focus on internal organization (Immanent Determinism) and the realization that a system can go only so far in any particular direction (the Principle of Limits) before it starts to transform.

Dynamics is filled with data testing Sorokin's hypotheses in a variety of contexts and periods. Patterns of change in art, philosophy, science, and ethics were scrutinized in search of the principles that explained their transformations. In each case Sorokin found support for his theory. For example, his analysis of Greco-Roman and Western philosophical systems showed that up until 500 B.C. these systems were substantially Ideational. By the fourth century B.C. they were Idealistic, and from 300 to 100 B.C. they moved toward a period of Sensate domination. From the first century A.D. to A.D. 400 was a period of transition and crisis followed by a reemergence of Ideational philosophy from the fifth to the twelfth century. This was followed by an Idealistic period and another transition, which brings us to the domination of Sensate philosophy beginning in the sixteenth century and continuing to the present. The analysis proceeds in a similar manner for other social phenomena.

Patterns of war, revolution, criminality, violence, and legal systems are also analyzed. These, however, are mainly studied as phenomena of transitional periods. Sorokin resisted the temptation to tie wars and revolutions to either Sensate or Ideational cultures. Instead, his analysis shows that revolutions result from the loss of compatibility between basic values in a culture. The better integrated a culture, the greater the probability of peace. As value integration diminishes, unrest, violence, and criminality increase. Similarly, war demonstrates a breakdown of crystallized social relationships between nations. In his analysis of 967 conflicts, Sorokin showed that wars increase during periods of transition. These changes often make the value systems of affected societies incompatible. War results from the malintegration of these intercultural relationships.

Sorokin's analysis of Western societies concluded with some bold prognostications for the future:

The organism of the Western society and culture seems to . . . be undergoing one of the deepest crises of its life. . . . its depth is unfathomable, its end not yet in sight. . . . It is the crisis of a Sensate culture, now in its overripe state. . . . we are experiencing one of the sharpest turns in the historical road, a turn as great as any . . . made by the Greco-Roman and Western cultures in passing from Ideational to Sensate, and from Sensate to Ideational, phases.

We have seen during the course of the present work quite definite signs of such a turn. Not a single compartment of our culture, or of the mind of contemporary man, shows itself to be free from the unmistakable symptoms. . . . The curves of painting, sculpture, music, literature; of movement of discoveries and inventions; of the "First Principles" of science, philosophy, religion, ethics, and law; up to those wars and revolutions—all make a violent turn as we approach our time.

Shall we wonder, also, at the endless multitude of incessant minor crises that have been rolling over us, like ocean waves, during the last two decades? . . . Crises political, agricultural, commercial, and industrial! Crises of production and distribution. Crises moral, juridical, religious, scientific, and artistic. Crises of property, of the State, of the family, of industrial enterprise. . . . Each of the crises has battered our nerves and minds, each has shaken the very foundations of our culture and society, and each has left behind a legion of derelicts and victims. And alas! The end is not yet in view. Each of these crises has been, as it were, a movement in a great terrifying symphony, and each has been remarkable for its magnitude and intensity. Each movement has been played, during the last three decades, by enormous human orchestras, with millions of choruses, stage performers, and actors. In 1911 the four-hundred-million-piece Chinese orchestra began one of its first festivals. . . .

In 1914 a new brass band of many nations with hundreds of participants started its deadening "*March Militaire:* 1914–1918." The effects of this performance were appalling. The stage—the soil of this planet—was soaked with blood. Most of our values were poisoned by gas; others were blown to pieces by artillery. The very foundations of our society and culture cracked. . . .

Before this festival had ended, the Russian orchestra of some 160,000,000 virtuosi set forth its own variation entitled "Communist Revolution.". . . Dozens of other companies—Turkey and Hungary, Austria and Germany, Bulgaria and Rumania, Spain and Portugal, Italy and Poland, Japan and Arabia, Palestine and Egypt, Syria and Afghanistan—have also been giving their crisis festivals. . . . If we turn our ears to Europe, we can hear, without the need of any short-wave radio, as many crisis festivals as we like. One day various fascists occupy the stage; another, communists, then the Hitlerites; then the Popular Front—red shirts and black shirts and brown shirts and silver shirts, and blue shirts and green shirts.[94]

Sorokin ends his description of the Western crisis by observing:

We are seemingly between two epochs: the dying Sensate culture of our magnificent yesterday and the coming Ideational culture of the creative tomorrow. We are living, thinking, and acting at the end of a brilliant six-hundred-year-long Sensate day. The oblique rays of the sun still illumine the glory of the passing epoch. But the light is fading, and in the deepening shadows it becomes more and more difficult to see clearly and to orient ourselves safely in the confusions of the twilight. The night of the transitory period begins to loom before us and the coming generations. . . . Beyond it, however, the dawn of a new great Ideational culture is probably waiting to greet the men of the future.

Such, it seems to me, is the position we are at on the road of history. The evidence of all the preceding chapters points in this direction. And we find our conclusion in an irreconcilable contradiction with the other current diagnoses.[95]

Sorokin argued that the more optimistic scholars and politicians were misleading; so were those who argued, like Oswald Spengler, for cyclical theories of change:

Finally, *my thesis has little in common with the age-old theories of the life cycle of cultures and societies with its stages of childhood, maturity, senility, and decay.* These conceptions have recently emerged once again in the works of Spengler and others. We have seen that in their cyclical form such theories are untenable. We can leave them to the ancient sages and their modern epigoni. Neither the decay of the Western society and culture, nor their death, is predicted by my thesis. What it does assert—let me repeat—is simply that one of the most important phases of their life history, the Sensate, is now ending and that we are turning toward its opposite through a period of transition. Such a period is always disquieting, grim, cruel, bloody, and painful. In its turbulence it is always marked by revival of the regressive tendencies of the unintegrated and disintegrated mentality. Many great values are usually thrown to the winds and trodden upon at such a time. Hence its qualification now as the great crisis.

Crisis, however, is not equivalent to either decay or death, as the Spenglerites and cyclicists are prone to infer. It merely means a sharp painful turn in the life process of society. It does not signify the end of the traveled road or of the traveling itself. Western culture did not end after the end of its Ideational phase. Likewise, now when its Sensate phase seems to be ending, its road stretches far beyond the "turn" into the infinity of the future.[96]

Sorokin concluded *Dynamics* with the following injunction:

In the light of these considerations, my theory and diagnosis are truly optimistic. Le roi est mort, vive le roi! "In my Father's house are many mansions. . . . Verily, verily, I say unto you. . . . ye shall be sorrowful, but your sorrow shall be turned into joy. . . . A woman when she is in travail hath sorrow, because her hour is come: But as soon as she is delivered of the child, she remembereth no more the anguish, for joy that a man is born into the world."[97]

Here we see captured not only Sorokin's sense of the crises and the future but his preference for the Ideational phases of civilization over the Sensate, particularly in its passive and cynical forms. This preference often clouds Sorokin's assessment of change in art, philosophy, science, and other institutions of society. It also raised in the minds of many scholars serious criticisms of his work.

The publication of the first three volumes of *Dynamics* would embroil Sorokin in a series of heated arguments with many leaders of American social science. Before that, however, came happier events. In 1937 Sorokin had an opportunity to teach a summer session at UCLA. The Sorokin children were now six and four, and their parents were anxious to show them the splendors of the West. Having shipped the family car to Salt Lake City, the Sorokins traveled there by train. On arrival they packed up and started the trek toward Los Angeles. In a leisurely fashion, they drove through the western desert to the Grand Canyon and spent days in exploration, picture taking, and admiration. From there they moved on to Bryce Canyon, Zion National Park, and other wonders of the West. Finally the nomads reached Los Angeles, took a house in Pacific Palisades, and settled in for a stay at the beach. Pitirim commuted daily to the university, taught his classes, and enjoyed the attention that the publicity surrounding *Dynamics* gave him. At the end of the term the Sorokins drove north to San Francisco and from there kept going north into the giant redwood country and on to Yosemite. Regretfully, the time came to turn south, cross the desert, and leave their car by the Great Salt Lake for shipment home. Boarding the train, the happy band of nomads returned to Massachusetts refreshed and eager to enjoy the rest of the summer.

On return Pitirim made his final preparation for Paris, where he would preside as president at the meetings of the International Institute of Sociology. Once at sea there was more time to reflect on Harvard and the evolving reception of *Dynamics*. But it was also a time for rest and putting the final touches on his presidential address. Arriving in Paris early, he took the opportunity to enjoy the city, work on his rusty French, and visit with colleagues. The busyness of Paris offered a crisp change from

California. The Louvre, Notre Dame, Versailles, the Rodin Gallery, and other centers of art, music, and history revived sensitivities and memories that had lost their vividness during the toil on *Dynamics*. It was good to be back in Europe. The change produced a deep relaxation.

At the end of the Congress Sorokin returned to America through Germany. During a short stay in Berlin he saw firsthand the prewar activities of the rising Nazi regime. Exposure to the Hitlerites and discussions with anti-Nazi scholars dramatically brought back the predictions in the third volume of *Dynamics*. The crisis was indeed intensifying. However, the trip home provided not only reflection but rest, and Sorokin returned prepared to meet the challenges of the new academic year.

Reception of *Dynamics*

The appearance of *Dynamics* was a major publication event of 1937. The book was widely hailed in public and academic circles. The *New York Times* and the *New York Herald Tribune* gave it lead coverage in their book review sections and printed large pictures of Sorokin. The Book-of-the-Month Club chose it as a July selection. *Dynamics* was also the most widely reviewed sociological work from 1937 to 1942.[98] The impact of these reviews is best considered in two categories: those by members of the academic community, particularly sociologists, and those by Harvard scholars.

The Paretian scholar and professor of romance languages at Columbia, Arthur Livingston, reviewed the book for the *New York Times*. Observing Sorokin's strong preference for the Ideational and Idealistic mentalities, he cast him as "a Tartar who has struck an alliance with neo Thomism." This preference and Sorokin's prediction of a new Ideational era concerned Livingston because he viewed such periods as "shabby, low-grade affairs." However, he found the work of this "Pareto for the pious" to "be clearly, simply and beautiful written" and was convinced enough by Sorokin's assurance of a new and magnificent Ideational period to feel it quite worthwhile having gone through "these three large volumes."[99]

Ernest Sutherland Bates, in the *New York Herald Tribune,* found Sorokin's "philosophy of fluctuations" to be the most devastating attack yet put forth against the idea of progress. Sorokin's dramatic representation of social changes in art, philosophy, science, invention, and war clearly demonstrated the absence of either unilinear or multilinear trends. Instead, we have fluctuations between expressions of the different cultural mentalities. Like Livingston, Bates noted that Sorokin was unable to be impartial about Sensate and Ideational culture. His prejudice for Ideational and Idealistic modes strongly limited the value of his analysis. The prejudice was so strong that Bates wondered if Sorokin might not have reached the same conclusions with little or no data. Bates also noted several errors in the chronology of events but attributed these to Sorokin's bias rather than naïveté. He concluded that the data and theory of fluctuations were the major merits of the work and reduced Sorokin's prophecy of a coming magnificent Ideational period to simply wishful thinking.[100]

Sidney Hook, one of America's leading analysts of social affairs, reviewed *Dynamics* for *The Nation*. Hook saw Sorokin's work as an extension of the philosophy of history tradition—an unfortunate extension that claimed to be scientific when in fact it was not. Hook observed that Sorokin's conclusions were metaphysical and unscientific. The statistical information presented in the tables was no more than "lattice work" for weak and unreliable interpretations. This was particularly evident in Sorokin's discussion of nudity in art. He took nudity as an index of the intensity of Ideational and Sensate mentalities but presented no evidence that the meanings associated with nudity are the same in the cultures and periods he was discussing. This left a study that purported to be historical in a disturbingly ahistorical light.

Hook was unmoved by Sorokin's principles of limits and immanence. To his mind they were tautological and simply asserted that it is the nature of culture to move from the Ideational to the Sensate pole and back again. Having no explanatory power, the principles beg the significant scientific question of why these changes are so. Sorokin's analysis was also biased. He was viscerally rather than objectively against empiricism, the value of the Sensate mentality, and the strengths of the modern age. This and other problems led Hook to state that *Dynamics* was "altogether without wisdom."[101]

The anthropologist Alexander Goldenweiser staged a dialogue between Socrates, Comte, Rembrandt, Quetelet, Spencer, da Vinci, Weber, Einstein, and others as his mechanism for reviewing *Dynamics*.[102] All these celebrated figures found fault with the work. Quetelet is guided by Socrates to conclude that Sorokin's work is a hollow reflection of his teachings and misses their spirit. Spencer finds Sorokin's antievolutionism mystically rather than scientifically grounded. Da Vinci, Rembrandt, and other artists question the conceptual and statistical approach to the arts. Rembrandt states, "Only a fellow wholly insensitive to what art really is can believe that our art (or for that matter any art) is limited to the sensory sphere."[103] Leonardo finds "this devise of counting pictures by the hundreds and thousands . . . to be applicable to a scrap yard of art, not to the throbbing art of living mankind."[104] Weber questions Sorokin's use of ideal types. After each historical figure had objected to *Dynamics,* Auguste Comte charged them with the following task:

As the founder of sociology, friends, and inventor of the very term, I feel very keenly about all this. Let me propose, now that we have had our say, that we constitute ourselves a jury and as such sit in judgment over our colleague Sorokin on the following counts: Do we or do we not find him guilty of imposing a logical scheme upon historic reality, of abusing statistical method to the obfuscation of qualitative entities, of ignoring and misrepresenting his forerunners and contemporaries, of murdering numerous straw-men, and—last but not least—of corrupting the King's English by the wholesale use of unidiomatic and manufactured terms? And let Socrates be our judge.[105]

Accepting the judicial mantle, Socrates received the "guilty on all counts" verdict of the jury and imposed the following sentence.

My task, as judge, is not a pleasant one. . . . But justice must be done. Had the defendant perpetrated all the aforementioned crimes within the covers of one volume, I should have deemed this an extenuating circumstance and imposed life-imprisonment. But he has written three volumes (with a fourth one to come). I have no choice. I hereby condemn the defendant to death by taking hemlock.[106]

The troublesome tone of the Goldenweiser review was not lost on Moses Aronson, the editor of the journal. On receiving it, he wrote to Sorokin for a response. Sorokin replied:

Here is the rejoinder to Goldenweiser's paper. I wrote it immediately after reading his paper. Last night, in a company of some six professors, including the editor of the American Sociological Review and the assistant editor of another journal, the paper of Goldenweiser was read. The reaction to it was unanimous. It was unanimously condemned—not for attacking me: none of the professors are my followers—but for its cheap, vulgar, and exceedingly poor character. Even its English was jeered strongly. They all advised me either not to answer anything or just to say that "it is so self-condemning that it makes any rejoinder unnecessary."[107]

Ignoring the advice, Sorokin responded and parried Goldenweiser's satire by asking:

Why ascribe shallow prattle to great thinkers? Had Socrates, Spencer, Comte or any of the other great thinkers mentioned ever discussed important problems so incoherently and carelessly as they are made to do, they never would have become anything more than friend Goldenweiser. Hence, let us leave them in peace and deal directly with the accusations.[108]

Sorokin then launched a counterattack. Goldenweiser's criticisms were contradictory and self-defeating. As such they indicated "no logical flaw or factual error in my statements." Furthermore, Goldenweiser's Weber overlooks the fact that Sorokin was using the Aristotelian, not Weberian, ideal types. Spencer's criticisms were groundless, as Sorokin's conclusions of trendless fluctuations were not the product of speculation but stem from a series of cultural data that were about as complete as possible. As to the verdict, Sorokin spurns the hemlock. The review is not a death stroke to *Dynamics* but simply a mudding of the waters and as such perfectly harmless and poorly formulated. "In all the review . . . besmears nobody and nothing but the critic himself."[109]

The pansophic Lewis Mumford found *Dynamics* logically flawed, prejudiced, and superficial. While Sorokin was wise to avoid the errors of unilinear evolution and the gospel of progress, he committed equally serious blunders. The most important was reification. Sensate, Ideational, and Idealistic cultures are treated as if they were concrete historical entities. Sorokin attempted to objectify them with elaborate statistical demonstrations. To Mumford these statistical proofs "are like an earnest attempt to count the number of feathers on an angel's wing. The feathers may be real and the counting may be done in good faith: it is the angel who is in question."[110] Sorokin's lack of objectivity and *static* doctrine of change also troubled Mumford and compromised the value of the book. These limitations led him to conclude that *Dynamics* had only limited value as a serious work of social science.[111]

The University of Chicago economist Frank H. Knight analyzed the book for the *Saturday Review*.[112] Although Knight admitted to an ignorance of the field, he saw several imperfections in the work. Important concepts were poorly defined, and the data presented on key theoretical issues were often unconvincing. The key point of interest for him was the relationship, if any, between social dynamics and physical dynamics as studied in mechanics. Here Sorokin was disappointing, and Knight hoped that more on this topic would be forthcoming in volume 4. Lacking social scientific insights, the book ended with a sermonizing prophecy of decline and rebirth—a vision based only on faith and intellectually unsatisfying.

Knight was not happy with his review. In a letter to Sorokin he stated that he was not qualified for the job, had hurried the essay, and had been too constrained by space limitations to do an adequate job. Consequently, the review had a certain flippancy that he did not intend. He ended the letter by acknowledging the failure of the review "to do any sort of justice to the book."[113] Sorokin replied that the review was poorly informed and careless. If, on reflection, he gleaned any meaningful criticism of his ideas in Knight's piece, they would be dealt with "without any diplomacy" in volume 4.[114]

Dynamics was also widely discussed in the sociological journals. In a very balanced review Robert Park wrote "that *Social and Cultural Dynamics* is a great intellectual achievement, a *magnum opus* in precisely the same sense as is true of Spencer's *Sociology,* Spengler's *Decline of the West,* and Marx's *Capital.*"[115] Park also realized that Sorokin's volumes would not be well received by hard-core empiricists. What they wanted was "a knowledge that is instrumental and empirical, if not experimental; a knowledge that justifies itself by its ability to bring about the effects it predicts." This type of understanding was not likely to result from a philosophy of history.[116] As a work in this tradition Park found the theoretical framework and the comments on change acceptable, but not very useful. The statistics, however, were "unquestionably, the most dubious and least thrilling part of the treatise. . . . Furthermore, the insistence on accuracy in fields of knowledge where any real accuracy is not possible, is itself a kind of *ism.* It is statisticism."[117] The statistics should thus be taken as tangential to the work and "as a concession to the prevailing mentality and the contemporary system of truth. . . . One suspects that at some time in the inception and planning of this project he [Sorokin] must have said to himself, 'Well, if they want'em, let's let'em have'em.' "[118] Park's observation reflected Sorokin's present and earlier concern that in their push for scientific status the social disciplines have attempted to measure many things, including some that cannot be measured. This had been carried to the point of technique becoming more important than thought in the research process. Certain techniques must be present if a study is to be taken seriously. The scientism of the modern age may have demanded in Sorokin's mind the statisticism that Park observed.[119] In closing Park stated that *Dynamics* was as credible as any work of its type, but he did not see much hope in this empirical age for a philosophy of history.

The December 1937 issue of the *American Sociological Review* contained four discussions of *Dynamics.* The lead article was Robert Bierstedt's essay on the logico-meaningful method; there also were three reviews, one for each volume. M. R. Rogers of the City Art Museum of St. Louis reviewed volume 1, *Fluctuations of Forms of Art.* Volume 2,

Fluctuations of Systems of Truth, Ethics and Law," was reviewed by the Columbia University philosopher John H. Randall Jr. Hans Speier wrote on volume 3 *Fluctuations of Social Relationships, War and Revolutions.*

Rogers observed that most of the ideas presented by Sorokin were not novel, but "they have never before been welded into such a completely coherent system or supported by such an awe-inspiring body of factual evidence. . . . On the whole Professor Sorokin makes an excellent case for his Ideational-Sensate analysis of Western art and sculpture."[120] Satisfied with the analysis, Rogers was unhappy with the tone and style of the book. He "would have found it much more effective had the author evidenced less personal bias for one side of his dualism. There is more than a touch of the propagandist and . . . the style, too is rather annoyingly prolix and repetitious. . . . the meat of the matter could have been set forth with great clarity in one-half the space."[121]

John Randall found "this rather pretentious volume" on philosophy and law much less satisfying. He argued that Sorokin's criticisms of science and method so well described his own work "that it is difficult to believe that he is not writing with his tongue in his cheek. Indeed, it is much easier to take his whole elaborate work as a parody of American social science, and it does vastly more credit to his intelligence, than to treat it seriously as a contribution to the theory of history."[122] Randall also said the work was arbitrary, filled with misconceptions, and prejudiced. The only chapters showing any genuine, firsthand knowledge of the subject matter were those written with N. S. Timasheff—"who really knows something about his subject."[123]

Hans Speier, of the New School for Social Research, in a very careful review found value in the work as a historical treatise on secularization. While troubled by the imprecise definition of key terms, concerned about reification, and challenging particular statistical usages, he still linked the work with "its great predecessors, Comte and Spencer." Speier thought the section on war was the book's most valuable contribution to sociology but was less satisfied with Sorokin's prediction of a new Ideational era. This appeared to him consistent with Sorokin's theory of limits and immanent change but was without any historical precedent. Indeed, it flew in the face of much of the best work of Toennies, Weber, and Sombart. As to the style, Speier disagreed with many reviewers when he stated, "One can only wonder at the literary achievement; the reader never gets lost in the welter of details, erudite references and polemical remarks. The clarity and simplicity of the fundamental conception of history which buttresses the structure of the book and which is impressed upon the reader's mind by each chapter anew is of inestimable didactic value."[124]

Robert Bierstedt's lead article originated from a term paper written in one of Sorokin's courses. As a participant in Sorokin's seminars, he had seen firsthand the "almost ritual hostility" with which Sorokin treated student papers.

The seminar would convene, with Sorokin in the chair. During the first hour one of the students would present a paper. During the second hour Sorokin, in full panoply, would tear it apart, paragraph by paragraph—almost, as it then seemed, syllable by syllable—until at the end of the period, vituperation unexhausted, he would conclude, "And so you see, gentlemen, this paper, it is worth nothing!" We were hardy souls in those days, and most of us wore our scar tissue with pride. [I decided] . . . with the impudence of youth, that I would turn his tactics against him—indeed try to emulate them—and accordingly wrote, as a term paper "The Logico-Meaningful Method of P. A. Sorokin." He was not amused. Indeed, as I should have predicted, he subjected me to an excoriation most colorful. W. I. Thomas, who took a benevolent interest in the fracas, suggested that I send the paper to the *American Sociological Review* where, to my surprise, it was accepted for publication.[125]

In his essay Bierstedt challenged the value of the logico-meaningful method as a contribution to sociological methodology. He asserted that Sorokin erred when discussing logical relationships between objects. Logic applies not to things but to what is said about them. Therefore, cultures cannot be logically integrated; only a system of analysis can. Sorokin's reification was also based on intuition, not logic. Consequently, the method was mystical. Logico-meaningful unities are, in Sorokin's own words, "sensed" and "felt by competent persons as certainly as if they could be analyzed with mathematical or logical exactness."[126] Thus, to follow Sorokin's method leaves one committed to an approach, the essence of which is subjective. The results of analytically applying the method, therefore, could change with each researcher. In the end Bierstedt concluded that Sorokin's approach "was neither logical nor meaningful, nor indeed a method."[127]

Sorokin briefly responded by arguing that culture and the organization of the life world are symbolic, that is, composed largely of words, propositions, and judgments. Logic, according to Bierstedt, applies to words; therefore, logical categories and relationships are applicable to large parts of culture. Bierstedt's argument was elementary, immature, and invalid. Sorokin's tone in the rejoinder was one of the patient teacher lecturing an unruly student, and he did away with Bierstedt's ten-page essay in a short rejoinder.[128]

Sorokin and Hornell Hart exchanged criticisms in later issues of the *American Sociological Review*. Hart, after a reorganization of Sorokin's data, questioned several major points. Hart wrote that Sorokin may have been correct in describing two great Sensate periods in his twenty-five-hundred year analysis, but these periods were in fact quite different. Such was also the case for each of the two epochs of Ideational and Idealistic culture. Consequently, the typology was flawed. Equally problematic was that Sorokin's data on art, philosophy, and cultural achievements were both inconsistent and unreliable. The poor database raised serious concerns about the validity of Sorokin's conclusions and predictions. Hart also questioned the belief that we were in the dying stage of a Sensate culture and facing a long, frightening period of turmoil before the dawn of an Ideational era. Hart, like Arthur Livingston, held Ideational periods in low regard.[129] Using Sorokin's data, he showed that these periods are the nadir of civilization; *Dynamics* itself shows that they have produced little growth in art, philosophy, invention, discovery, or material standard of living. While we may be at the end of a dying Sensate period, we also have unprecedented resources for an integrated approach to reality. Our science has demonstrated the importance of rationalistic constructs for understanding the physical world and has discovered the reality of intuition. Hence we are ripe for an Idealistic synthesis of cognitive forms rather than a period of decline. Hart concluded that "Sorokin's data offer no adequate justification for accepting his prognosis, or for resigning ourselves to a nine-hundred-year-long retreat into the darkness of a new Ideational epoch."[130]

Sorokin responded that Hart misinterpreted his prognostications. They were not scientific predictions but simply *guesses*.[131] As such Professor Hart was free to make his own guesses, and these were as justified as his own. Sorokin acknowledged that, like Hart, he preferred Idealistic culture, but his reading of the evidence suggested that it would not be the form of the future. Given, however, that he and Hart are guessing, then the future would tell.

As to their different interpretations of the data, Sorokin argued that Hart violated good statistical procedures in his reorganization. Hart's method of averaging, which is so vital to his criticisms, ignored the basic method used to derive the figures he was weighing. Therefore, the results were computational artifacts and not meaningful indicators of the phenomena being discussed. Because Hart's method was flawed, so were his conclusions. As a result, the criticisms, while "serious and well-intended," were not well grounded enough to threaten the integrity of *Dynamics*.[132] Sorokin's rebuttal of Hart's statistical criticisms are well founded. Hart's computations are too gross to support the reinterpretations he offered.[133]

Equally important as the sociological reviews were those by Harvard scholars—three in the *Harvard Guardian* and a fourth in the *Southern Review*. Abbot Payson Usher reviewed the volume on truth, ethics, and law for the *Guardian,* arguing that Sorokin's reliance on ideal types for his analysis was poorly conceived. The period covered was too long, and the number of cultures studied were too many for this method. The technique was most effective when used in brief, highly generalized essays. In longer studies such as this, there was an unfortunate tendency to treat the ideal types as "organic social entities." Unhappily, reifications permeated the work and seriously compromised its value. Usher was also suspicious of Sorokin's arbitrary and dogmatic interpretations of history, which colored his analysis and raised issues of credibility. On the whole this review was balanced, substantive, and neutral.[134]

D. W. Prall, however, found the volume on art disappointing. The tone of his review is derisive, and Prall castigates Sorokin for intellectual arrogance. He, further, charges that the volume was opinionated, logically flawed, and missed all that is important about art. Sorokin's writing was inexcusably prolix and his analysis too biased and naive to be taken seriously.[135]

William Yandell Elliott, the political theorist in the Department of Government, was much more balanced in his review of the volume on social relationships, revolutions, and war. While disapproving of Sorokin's methods of data collection and analysis, Elliott had deep questions about the specific details of much of the analysis. Also problematic were Sorokin's naive interpretations of Dilthey, Windelband, Rickert, and Weber. This, combined with a lumping together in footnotes of citations that did not necessarily belong together, and the failure to point out the differences, led Elliott to question whether Sorokin properly understood the authors he was citing. However, on the positive side, and anticipating criticisms like Prall's, Elliott observed:

The great feature of Professor Sorokin's work is that he seems to be bold enough to ask the right questions, and to try to do in the grand manner what sociologists are so afraid of attempting because of the scope of special disciplines relevant to their own conclusions. It is inevitable, and Professor Sorokin is modest enough to recognize it, that any such effort will have tremendous shortcomings, and will be pulled to pieces by the specialists in disciplines which he has attempted to bring into his schematic treatment. But, if one takes the works that have attempted such a grandiose plan beforehand, it seems to me that the first two hundred pages of Volume I contain far more significant analysis of social behavior and of the relation of ideas to culture than can be found in the whole range of Pareto.[136]

A fourth reviewer was Crane Brinton, whose acidic essay was tartly entitled "Socio-Astrology."[137] This was the domain of the social sciences and other forms of human speculation that attempt to nonscientifically predict the future. Sorokin's *Dynamics*, as "an attempt to plot the whole past, present and future of mankind," was in this genre. Sadly, the work was long on prose and short on originality. The Ideational and Sensate taxonomy was among the simplest theories of change used in philosophy of history studies, but it was, Brinton argued, the battering ram that Sorokin used to knock down the open doors of linear evolution, art, history, science, theology, and philosophy. Sorokin's naive understanding of these enterprises was combined with emotional bias and an intellectual arrogance that produced not a work of science but one of prophecy. Indeed, one so flawed that we can have no intellectual trust in it and no faith either. The fault was not only with Sorokin but with the social sciences and philosophies of history. None was capable of answering the questions they asked. Consequently, the socioastrologer has little or nothing to say that is useful or accurate. This was particularly true of *Dynamics*. Brinton's is a well written, hard-hitting review. No hurried job, it dissects *Dynamics* and Sorokin with a razorlike intellect and learning.

Sorokin, however, struck back in his own aptly titled essay "Histrionics." Classing Brinton's criticisms as three types—those irrelevant to the validity of his study; attacks against the reviewer's self-created straw men; and genuine criticisms of real issues—Sorokin addresses them in order. The first are a product of critical incompetence, compounded by unduly repetitious writing, emotionalism, and ineptness. The second are picayunish and have the critic destroying self-created bogeymen that have nothing to do with *Dynamics*. Brinton simply ascribes to the work "qualities and propositions not found in the volumes." Third, most of the genuine criticisms are minor, and Sorokin disposes of them in short order. On the two important ones Brinton is wrong, and Sorokin illustrates his errors of reasoning, scholarship, and interpretation. Finally, Brinton is dismissed as a careless scholar who has failed to understand the principal arguments of *Dynamics*.[138]

With this rebuttal Crane Brinton joined the long list of those who had confronted Sorokin over his magnum opus. While Sorokin often gave his critics as good as he got, there is little doubt that the reviews were damaging. They cost his stature among sociologists, Harvard scholars, and administrators. The reception of *Dynamics* may also have raised questions among graduate students about the general promise of Sorokin's sociology. These were indeed challenging times that dulled the edge of Sorokin's first decade as a Harvard scholar.

Prophetic Sociology

The years 1935 to 1940 were absolutely pivotal in Sorokin's career. By then the department was a fully established part of Harvard life. Though not without problems, the undergraduate program was in place and courses were well enrolled. The graduate program was the jewel in the crown. Promising students were attracted by the departmental faculty and by Harvard's prestige. Although he may not have been as popular with the graduate students as the younger Parsons, Sorokin established life-long relationships with many of them. Robert Merton, Wilbert Moore, Robert Bierstedt, and Jack and Matilda Riley would all remain loyal, although occasionally disobedient, friends. Equally long friendships and mentor relationships would continue with many others who became lesser leaders in American sociology. Sorokin was having his influence on the next generation of American sociologists.

Additionally, Harvard was at a point where it could become a vital, if not *the* vital, force in American sociology. Between the faculty, graduate students, and selected visiting members, a critical mass of talent existed that would come to shape many of the important contours of the discipline. However, Conant's appointment policy and the "up-or-out" directive dissipated this talented group to other institutions where they made their contributions. The result was that Harvard lost its best early opportunity to replace the University of Chicago as the center of power.

Sorokin also faced other internal problems. The difficulties with Parsons over his promotions in 1936 and 1939 greatly limited Sorokin's power in the department. It was clear by 1939 that Parsons and his loosely formed but influential association with the outside members of the department could exert substantial control over the direction and guiding philosophy of the program. Parsons's ties to L. J. Henderson, E. B. Wilson, Crane Brinton, O. H. Taylor, and Joseph Schumpeter gave him influence with Conant. This alliance occasionally proved more powerful than the intent of the sociologists. Now when it came to votes, Sorokin and the other sociologists were outnumbered in their own department. The implications of this situation would become clearer over the next five years.

There is little doubt that from 1935 to 1940 Talcott Parsons became the second most influential member of the department. This resulted not only from his influence at the university but from his rising significance in the discipline. Parsons's *Structure of Social Action* and Sorokin's *Social and Cultural Dynamics* were both published in the same year but with marked differences for their authors' careers. Sociologists were not accepting of a work they defined as either an attempt at prophecy or at best a philosophy of history; consequently, few gave the last volume of *Dynamics* the attention it required.

The response to *Dynamics* by significant sociologists and other social scientists signaled real trouble for Sorokin. As noted, most had serious difficulties with the work. There was widespread agreement among critics that Sorokin was biased in favor of Ideational and Idealistic cultures; unscientific, metaphysical, and often authoritarian in his analysis; guilty of reification; theoretically simplistic in the development of concepts and use of ideal types; statistically naive and empirically unsatisfying; historically inaccurate and frequently imprecise in representing the works of his forerunners; culpable of poor writing, the overuse of neologisms, and prolixity; and dominated by his values and scornful of science. Indeed, as Lawrence T. Nichols has noted, Sorokin was in stark violation of the norms of the scientific community that were widely accepted and respected by American sociologists.[139]

Furthermore, Sorokin's "deviance" was compounded by the fact that he "responded to peer critiques in an increasingly combative manner and explicitly rejected the collective characterization of his work as 'unscientific.' "[140] This had the dramatic effect of raising alarming questions about the quality and objectivity of his research and, as he became more recalcitrant, led to his marginalization and isolation within the discipline and Harvard. Sociology had clearly cast its lot with science, and Sorokin had risen in the discipline as a staunch supporter of scientific sociology. It was on this reputation that he had been called to Harvard. President Lowell and the Committee on Sociology and Social Ethics had recruited him to establish the discipline as a "severe" field of concentration and to replace a marginal field of study with a science of society. Sorokin's sudden turn toward social criticism and the philosophy of history violated the expectations of both communities. His increasing combativeness and stubbornness soon moved him to the boundaries of a scholar's most important reference groups: his discipline and institution.

The consequences of *Dynamics* would prove to be severe. However, to look at the work as a blunder is to miss its significance for Sorokin and the next twenty years of his life.[141] Following Robert W. Friedricks's analysis of sociological traditions, *Dynamics* signals a shift by Sorokin from the priestly to the prophetic mode.[142] Friedricks uses these terms to describe broad periods of disciplinary history. He argues that they underlie and order the interpretations of society offered by sociologists at different points in history. The priestly practitioner accepts the canons of the natural sciences as the best (if not the only) template for the development of the social disciplines. These sociologists cover themselves with the cloak of value neutrality, abandon subjective standards for objective perceptions, and are skeptical of all forms of knowledge except the empirical. They dedicate themselves to the study of order and the discovery of empirical uniformities that can be used to predict and hence control the future patterns of phenomena. These priestly sociologists use a special language (mathematics), serve a long novitiate in graduate schools mastering the liturgy and rituals of research, and form a community committed to empirical truth rather than the truths of a transempirical world.[143] This priestly community may even take on a mediator's role between layman and society:

> They assert that there is only one escape from the consequences of irrationality: that is by the application of the scientific method. And this method can be used effectively only by the expert few. . . . Instead of attempting to make people more rational, contemporary social scientists often content themselves with asking of them that they place their trust in the social sciences and accept its findings.[144]

Unlike priests, prophets are driven by other principles and goals. Drawing on their disciplinary origins, they are committed not to an understanding but to an image of the future. Their sociology goes beyond a science of behavior toward the improvement of society. They are value committed, not value neutral, and truth is taken to be multiformed, not only empirical. Prophets are critics, activists, and polemicists who view the real object of science and sociology as service to humankind. Friedricks observed that prophets have had a long and respected history among sociologists. The European origins of the discipline, as they are normally reckoned, derive from the works of Auguste Comte and the "Prophets of Paris." The tradition crossed the Atlantic and was an important element in early American sociology.[145] He further notes: "In the decades preceding the sixties the prophetic stance came to center around the persons and writings of Karl Mannheim, Pitirim Sorokin, Robert Lynd, Robert MacIver, and Louis Wirth."[146] Robert Lynd captured the disruptive ethos of prophetic sociologists when he wrote: "It is precisely the role of the social scientist to be troublesome, to disconcert the habitual arrangements by which we manage to live along, and to demonstrate the possibilities of change in more adequate directions. Their role, like that of the skilled surgeon, is to get us into immediate trouble in order to prevent our chronic present troubles from becoming even more dangerous."[147]

As a participant in this process Sorokin became isolated as a prophet. The uncomfortable consequences for such a change are delineated by Howard Becker:

The Church of Science, moreover, applies "pressures." If a scientist strays off the straight and narrow path by injecting other preferences and ultimate values into his supposedly scientific work, he will soon find that his books are no longer in the Holy Canon, his articles can be published only in journals which lack the Imprimatur and Nihil Obstat, and eventually he may discover that all his writings are in the Index Expurgatorious or even the Index Librorum Prohibitorum. Worse still, the institutions with which he is identified may suffer Interdict, and he himself may be visited with excommunication.[148]

Indeed, much of this was happening to Sorokin, and Harvard would soon be distancing itself from the prophet or heretic in its midst.

Dynamics, however, is the exemplar for the next two decades of Sorokin's work. To understand it one must recognize it not only as a work in prophetic sociology but as one cast in the mold of Sorokin's emerging epistemology. To appreciate its value we must grasp the various forms of truth that it contains. Like Plato, Sorokin reasoned that truth came in three forms: the truths of faith, reason, and the senses. Each system of knowing corresponded to a different dimension of awareness: the body, the mind, and the spirit. In the first three volumes of *Dynamics* Sorokin attempted to demonstrate that salience has been given to each of these forms of knowledge and dimensions of humaneness at different stages of Western history. While one form dominated a particular period, the others were also more or less active. The most fruitful blending of forms of knowing and being occurs in Idealistic periods. These periods are dominated by Integralism, that is, the integration of the three channels of cognition—senses, reason, and intuition—into a fuller and more valid knowledge. Unfortunately, Sorokin did not present the theory of Integralism until the fourth volume of *Dynamics*, published in 1941, although it is an important key for getting at what he was struggling with in the first three volumes. The earlier works analyzed each type of truth. Unhappily, they did so through a centerpiece that focused attention on the elaborate compilation of data, the creation of indices, graphs, and tables, that steered the reader toward an empirical understanding of the work. This, as Park indicated, may have been Sorokin's concession to the dominant empirical mentality of the times; sadly, it is also the weakest part of the book. *Dynamics* is a philosophy of history that becomes cast as a quantitative study of social change. In his analysis Sorokin presented Western culture as facing a time of increased conflicts, revolutions, and

wars. To survive required a major change in values and a move away from
the partial systems of truth that defined the past. The present required an
Integral system of knowing that brought together the truths of reason,
science, and faith, that is, an Integral epistemology. This, however, does
not become clear until the 1941 volume. However, because of the flawed
empiricism of the earlier volumes, the message of *Dynamics* as a philosophy of history and theory of humanity is lost. This does not mean that
what Sorokin wrote was untrue but that he attempted to demonstrate it
improperly. Many of his arguments on art, philosophy, and social unrest
show substantial insights into their nature and the processes of change.
However, the method by which he demonstrates this (e.g., the measurement of inches of skin and text) was poorly selected. Unhappily, the
benefits of his analysis are undermined by the techniques through which
he attempted to demonstrate them. Many of Sorokin's critics were
correct in noting that much of the data presented is tangential or inappropriate for the points being made. The more intemperate and superficial critics grabbed at these flaws to bury the work in ridicule and to
totally obscure its value. They were so successful that by the time volume
4 came out, few sociologists were interested in what Sorokin had to say.

Dynamics, however, is an important part of an unfolding analysis of
Western civilization. In the works that follow, Sorokin analyzes the crisis
of our age and advances a method of dealing with it. Sadly, the reception
of the first volumes of *Dynamics* moved Sorokin toward the periphery of
the discipline, and most sociologists overlook his later analysis of the
contemporary crisis. Almost all fail to see that what began as a twenty-
five-hundred-year study of social order and change became a theory for
social action and reform. The ideas developed in *Dynamics* culminate in a
sociology of altruistic action whose goal was the reconstruction of society.
However, the response by sociologists to *Dynamics* moved this emerging
strategy to the backwaters of the discipline and away from serious consideration by scholars at Harvard and elsewhere. Sorokin soon became a
prophet in a priestly land.

5

Crisis and Confrontation: A New Harvard Decade

Peer Review and the Politics of Publication

THE 1939–40 ACADEMIC YEAR and those that followed were trying, challenging times. While Sorokin's new direction was adumbrated in the first volumes of *Dynamics*, other works were also in progress. One of these was a volume coauthored with Clarence Q. Berger, *Time Budgets of Human Behavior*, a work that originated from the large-scale unemployment study directed by Carle Zimmerman. Though sponsored by the federal government, the study was also supported by the Harvard Committee for Research in the Social Sciences.

The foci of the book, which was based on Berger's dissertation, were on how people spent their time, their motives for doing so, and their self-prediction of future patterns of behavior. The data came from diaries kept over a five-month period by white-collar Works Progress Administration (WPA) workers. On the basis of these records, Sorokin and Berger classified life's activities into eight categories. Their data showed that people spent most of their time (eleven hours) sleeping, eating, grooming, and exercising. Work and related efforts took seven hours. Only one and a half hours were given to pleasurable acts such as hobbies and games. Just behind leisure was intellectual activity. A meager hour and twenty-five minutes were spent reading, at school, or listening to the radio. Many current researchers were mistakenly worried about how people would spend their leisurely hours. According to Sorokin and Berger, at an hour and a half or less a day, it was simply not a problem.

Time Budgets also showed that 81 minutes were spent in entertainment; artistic activities were given 25 minutes; love and courtship got 8.6 minutes; religion received 8.3 minutes; and political activity received a scant 6 seconds a day. The observed religious apathy supported Sorokin's contention that society was moving toward the Cynical Sensate stage described in *Dynamics*.

Sorokin and Berger next explored why people use time as they do and how this related to prevalent behaviorist explanations. Their data suggested that people were motivated more by custom and tradition, religious considerations, and circumstances than by the desire to seek pleasure and avoid pain. Psychologists simply overused these principles when analyzing motivations.

In the third section of the book Sorokin and Berger observed that people regularly erred in predicting their activities for the next day. While physiological and economic actions were accurately anticipated, other elements of daily life were not. Furthermore, the longer the time frame, the greater the error. Respondents simply did not plan, and this made it very difficult to predict future patterns. Hence, predictions by social forecasters were simply "guesswork" and unjustified.

Time Budgets was not widely reviewed or discussed. Most reviewers were critical of the design, sampling, analysis, or conclusions. Sociologists also paid little attention to the work, and Berger later noted that it "soon earned the distinction of losing more money for the Harvard University Press than any book previously published."[1] But its publication came only after a battle between Sorokin and the Harvard Committee for Research in the Social Sciences. The exchange would prove costly for Sorokin and again raised questions within the Harvard community about the quality and importance of his scholarship.

When the study began in 1937, John D. Black, Sorokin's Minnesota colleague and early Harvard sponsor, chaired the committee. Even with Black's predisposition toward Sorokin, *Time Budgets* was in for heavy sledding. The preliminary reviews were critical and raised important questions. Gordon Allport wrote Dr. Elizabeth Gilboy, the secretary of the committee, "This study as a whole disappointed me." He argued that the sample was too small, class-specific, and nonrepresentative. Furthermore, the manuscript was too rough. There were blatant errors in the tables and text; references and citations were carelessly done; and curious statements jumped out at the reader. For example, "The 'average time' for pleasure activities 'per participant daily' add up to 27 hours?" Allport was further disturbed by the "overbold" generalizations, the nonpsychological definitions given to psychological terms, and the general lack of conceptual precision. However, if the committee was to support publication, then the manuscript must be carefully rewritten with attention to grammar and idiom, should be shortened, and should be put in a paper binding so as "to emphasize the monographic character of the work."[2]

E. B. Wilson was similarly put off by the draft and wrote, "I wish Professor Black had not asked me to look at the Sorokin-Berger manuscript." He had opposed the project when the government proposed it and had discouraged Zimmerman from taking it on. Thus, he felt biased from the start. Wilson was also reluctant to referee the project based on "his previous contacts with Sorokin as a statistician and to the . . . obvious fact that the project had to be statistical."[3] On more substantive grounds, Wilson objected to sample size and representativeness, the weakness of self-reported data, the authors' indifference to reliability concerns, striking computational blunders, lack of regard for statistical conventions, and overgeneralizing. In support of his objections Wilson argued: "Studies on the self reporting of items have indicated that even such an item as hair color was reported very badly and that more subjective items are reported so badly as to be worth very little."[4] On computational blunders he wrote:

On page 87 there is an amusing instance of this. In the table it is stated the average time spent per participant per day on pleasurable activities is 27 hours, 50.3 minutes. Note the precision of the statement to tenths of minutes and the fact that no day contains over 24 hours. . . . at the beginning of Chapter IV . . . it is stated that sleep takes an average of 528.4 minutes per day. In the next paragraph it is stated that the women sleep on the average of 520.8 and the men 491.6. It is an arithmetic impossibility that the average for all persons should exceed the average both for the women and for the men. This kind of indifference to perfectly obvious arithmetic inconsistence is found occasionally in other places. . . . One wonders whether any credence is to be put on the statistical work or rather the imitation of statistical work and the numerical value given by persons who are so wholly insensitive to rather obvious arithmetical laws.[5]

Wilson also adds some general observations on sociologists:

As a literary effort the copy is not so bad. It isn't any worse than most sociology but as a scientific exhibit as to how sociology is going to get ahead as a science it is on the negative rather than on the positive side. Now despite these various criticism and we can make more of them—in fact, we can go on indefinitely along this same line—I am not reporting that the committee should not subvention or otherwise help this book to see the light of day. Sociologists write this way. The fact that they write this way is one reason sociology doesn't get ahead any faster but if a person of Sorokin's international distinction wishes to write this way there is much to be said in favor of supporting him in the conscientious results of his study while the technical details are not so good and whereas they might have been really worked up in such a way as to contribute a substantial desirable impetus to doing these things the right way, nevertheless, sociologists don't do them that way and it is quite possible that a mature sociologist should be allowed to function as his conferees do. The book indeed may interest many people . . . and thus perhaps rebound to the glory of the university.[6]

Wilson's condescending attitude angered Sorokin, who responded strongly to Black that the treatment of sociologists by the committee was frequently one-sided and unfair. It was standard practice to have books by economists, historians, and psychologists reviewed by their peers. This was not done for sociologists, and such was clearly the case with *Time Budgets*. The situation was further complicated by personal animus and reviewers' bias against his earlier works. Given these circumstances, he was ready to withdraw the manuscript. In the interest of fairness, however, the committee should pass peer review rules and in split decisions inform authors who voted for or against them.[7]

Black wrote that he agreed on peer review but had not sent the manuscript to Parsons because he thought "that various circumstances might make this inadvisable." However, he would hire an outside reviewer if Sorokin desired. Black reminded Sorokin that it was committee procedure to seek judgments from colleagues in related fields when reviewing a manuscript, so reviews by a psychologist and a statistician of a book like *Time Budgets* were standard practice. Sorokin was free to take the manuscript elsewhere, but the committee had not rejected it for publication.[8]

Sorokin and Berger stayed with the committee and Harvard University Press. They worked with Gilboy to satisfy the committee's objections and eliminate ambiguities. On grammar and style Sorokin was not so compliant. He wrote Black that rarely did people agree on style. Furthermore:

I think the English of the manuscript is quite correct: It is clear. That is all that can be required in a scientific work. As a curiosity, the English of my *Dynamics* by one critic, Professor Brinton—was found poor; by several other reviewers such as Professor A. Livingston, and others it was characterized as "beautiful," "readable," "elegant." So there you are.[9]

The required changes were completed and the manuscript issued in 1939. Black did compromise with Sorokin on language. He sent the manuscript to an editor at the Harvard University Press with directions to "make any corrections in grammar and punctuation which you think necessary, but as far as English style is concerned and even peculiar sentence structure, we prefer to let Professor Sorokin's method of expression stand."[10]

Department Stresses and Strains

The 1939–40 academic year witnessed a change of deans in the Faculty of Arts and Sciences as the mathematician George Birkhoff was replaced by the historian William S. Ferguson. The new dean was concerned about sociology's internal problems and wrote Sorokin asking about the department's history and current situation. Sorokin took this opportunity to educate Ferguson on the current faculty shortage and plead his case for additional senior members. He pointed out that the department's size had doubled since 1931 and now served over 670 registrants, 81 concentrators, and 20 graduate students. In quality, the undergraduates were average or better and the graduate students were superior. Sorokin quoted Robert Park's paean to the graduate program and informed the dean that Park was "one of the most distinguished sociologists of Chicago University, which up to the present time was the monopolistic center of sociology in the United States."[11] Sorokin wrote that the graduate students brought great energy to the department and were making their marks "as leaders of the younger generation of American sociologists . . . and all this had been accomplished in eight and a half years with a budget that . . . decreased by $725. . . . this means the department has been rapidly growing while its budget has been slightly decreasing."[12]

A similar unhappy trend existed among professorial staff. The department had started with two and a half full professors (Sorokin, Cabot, and Carver as half-time), two associate professors (Ford and Zimmerman), and two faculty instructors. At present it had but one full professor, three associates, and two faculty instructors. If the dean persisted in his planned cut of a faculty instructor and a lecturer, then Sorokin feared this "would be the equivalent of cutting from the department—not its fat but its vital parts." A further reduction in staff would hamper the department's pedagogical mission and compromise its rising position in the discipline. When the department originated, Harvard was not "on the sociological map." Now, in spite of its small size, the department was a force in American sociology. The proof could be found in the successful placement of graduates; the volume of faculty publications; the quality of the journals in which faculty's work appeared; the number of translations of their books and articles; and the frequency with which their works were cited and used in other research projects.[13]

These successes "testify convincingly that the department, in spite of financial and other disadvantages . . . has been doing important creative work and showing certain signs of healthy and creative growth." All this has occurred in spite of the "indifference" shown the department by the university. Further cuts would add to the perception of "administrative indifference" and deepen the faculty morale crisis. Clearly no new cuts should be considered by the administration.[14]

Ferguson would not give more senior slots and suggested that Sorokin compensate with annual instructors. Sorokin argued that the department could afford only two and a half annual instructors, too few to meet the tutorial demands of growing enrollments. The only practical solution was to hire more of the lower-paid teaching fellows. Experience showed that fellows were excellent tutors and, without a budget increase, the best department strategy. The loss of Timasheff, Hutchinson, and Wilbert Moore made the situation worse. Without new funding, the department would be seriously understaffed, particularly at the upper ranks.[15]

In addition to staffing problems, the relationship between Sorokin and Parsons, now an associate professor, remained strained. In letters to Robert Merton, Parsons noted that "the same tensions are present as always." He recounted a recent conflict over a graduate tutor who had taken a fellowship in the Business School. Both the student and Parsons felt it desirable to keep a foothold in sociology since the student had an offer of a House tutorship. The dean was willing to make an exception, but it failed in the department by one vote: Sorokin's. Parsons commented:

P.A. chose to regard the [student's] request to change [his appointment] as a breach of contract, which was evidence of his defective character, and got so excited about it that apparently enough of the outside members did not want to ram it down his throat, so we were beaten. I think you will have little difficulty in surmising some of the other sentiments that direct moral indignation involved. Indeed, I was told that when he talked to the dean about it he got so excited that he could be heard all over the section of offices, and that he made a very painful impression on Ferguson.[16]

As another example, Parsons wrote that he deliberately held back a strong endorsement of two students for fellowships because "my recent experience is that if I propose anything outside the realm of my own work as such, that he will turn against it almost invariably."[17] As a case in point, Parsons reported that when he suggested Everett Hughes as a possible candidate for a visiting lectureship "he got royally sat on" and was quite sure "that the mere fact that I proposed his name was almost enough to defeat him."[18]

Parsons concluded by relaying a story in which Sorokin was embarrassed by Dean Ferguson in front of a group of faculty. The tone of the letter reflects Parsons's enjoyment of Sorokin's embarrassment. Clearly, both parties contributed to these strains. Parsons summed up the problem:

There is no immediate promise of any improvement in the departmental situation, but considerable promise of developments which will be of sociological interest. The Social Science Area Plan is now before the new committee on Educational Policy, of which I am a member, and has, I think, every prospect of going back to the faculty with a strong positive recommendation. So I think it will almost certainly go into operation for next year. Then the committee of distribution is recommending four elementary area courses, one of which would be in the social sciences. I think it very probable that this recommendation will be approved in principle. The two together would go a long way toward opening up channels of undergraduate work free of the most serious difficulties of the departmental concentration. What the repercussions would be on the status of the department is your guess as well as mine.[19]

Some of the repercussions would be very indirect and take years to play themselves out. Significantly, though, the plan raised the idea of cross-disciplinary teaching. At the same time, it gave rise to a faculty committee representing all six social science departments under Parsons's chairmanship. Also serving on this committee were Hobart Mowrer, a psychologist then affiliated with the Graduate School of Education, and Clyde Kluckhohn, the only social anthropologist in the anthropology department. They and Parsons tutored in the interdisciplinary experimental program and had an opportunity to deal firsthand with the problems of cross-disciplinary cooperation. Unfortunately for Parsons, the program did not last long, but it opened new discussions between himself, Mowrer, and Kluckhohn.

Parsons and Kluckhohn were already aware of their common interest in Freud. They, along with Gordon Allport and the clinician Henry Murray, often discussed the value of Freudian principles for their scholarship. For Parsons the interest came from his participant observation study of the medical profession. As a result, he spent a good deal of time at Massachusetts General Hospital, where ideas about psychosomatic relations and psychoanalysis were taking root. Stanley Cobb, professor of psychiatry at the hospital, was also the principal founder of the Psychoanalytic Institute in Boston. However, the decisive event that led Parsons to Freud came from Elton Mayo. On learning of Parsons's limited knowledge of Freud, Mayo strongly advised him to "seriously and comprehensively" study the Vienna analyst. Parsons did so, and it "proved to be one of the few crucial intellectual experiences of [his] life."[20] He supplemented this work in 1946 with formal psychoanalytic training as a Class C candidate at the Boston Psychoanalytic Institute.[21] Interestingly, Clyde Kluckhohn had undergone analysis in Germany, and the experience proved valuable for his Navajo studies.[22]

Parsons, Murray, Kluckhohn, Allport, and later Hobart Mowrer came to know each other well. And as Parsons observed, "We had engaged to an unusual degree in many informal discussions of substantial scientific problems . . . in the course of which the closeness of our interests became ever more obvious, so much so that our membership in different departments seemed increasingly anomalous."[23]

While psychoanalysis fueled their discussions, they also shared marginal positions in their respective departments. Allport and Murray were in a minority position in psychology. The program established by William James in the 1870s had by the mid-1920s an established tradition of high-quality work in experimental psychology. In 1922, Edwin G. Boring took over the department and accomplished the separation of psychology from philosophy in 1934. By then his department was clearly split into the biotropes (Karl Lashley, Boring, and Beebe-Center) and the sociotropes (Murray, Robert White, and Allport), with power in the hands of the former.

The schism was a product of different orientations to the proper study of humanity. Biotropes preferred an experimentally based scientific psychology; sociotropes sought a humanistic, ameliorative psychology emphasizing the social and psychoanalytic traditions. Henry Murray, who represented the psychoanalytic wing, was director of the Psychological Clinic, a privately funded operation, and did not have a permanent appointment in the department. The department considered his program marginal, and many of his colleagues were hostile toward it. Gordon Allport suffered less because his earlier works in imagery and memory were experimentally based. In time, however, his interests moved toward a humanistic social psychology, and he came to consider himself a maverick within the department.[24]

The antipathy between these factions peaked in 1943 when a new permanent position was given to the department. The sociotropes promoted Murray's appointment; The biotropes were opposed and successfully filled the position with S. S. Stevens. This broke the tenuous peace in the department. Stevens, a man of strong will, opposed the psychology practiced by Allport and Murray. With his appointment Allport no longer believed that there was any room in the department "for his candle to burn."[25]

This split between Harvard psychologists was typical of the discipline at the national level. J. F. Brown observed in 1940, "It would be useless to deny that there is at present a schism between academic psychology and psychoanalysis." Psychoanalysis had fared poorly in the universities, and practitioners often developed their own training centers off campus. Consequently, a great opportunity for mutual enrichment was missed, and "the result is an academic psychology which is precise but sterile and a psychoanalysis which is badly in need of scientific criticism, but vital and fruitful." This separation also led to a curious stereotyping. Analysts saw biotropes as "curious fellows in no way concerned with real problems," and the scientists saw the analysts as "mystics or cultists." As a result, a mutually reinforcing "disdain and suspicion kept the groups apart."[26]

Clyde Kluckhohn faced a similar problem in the Department of Anthropology. Kluckhohn had replaced W. Lloyd Warner and was the only social anthropologist in the department. Since its inception in 1866, the department had become a center of excellence in archaeology and physical anthropology. Kluckhohn, a central figure in culture and personality studies[27] was not popular with his colleagues. They were suspicious of his application of psychoanalysis to his Navajo field studies and alarmed by the unscientific nature of the project. This cool reception by the department edged Kluckhohn toward other like-minded scholars on the outside.[28]

Personal and professional dissatisfactions with their departments contributed to the emerging solidarity between Parsons, Murray, Allport, and Kluckhohn. The conflict in sociology was mirrored, to a lesser degree, in psychology by the ill feelings between Lashley and Murray, and the antipathy between Boring and Allport. A similar situation prevailed in anthropology between Earnest A. Hooton and Kluckhohn.[29] Therefore, personal, professional, pedagogical, and intellectual considerations were among the factors that unified those who would soon establish an independent Department of Social Relations.

The institutional tie between these scholars was provided by the university's interdisciplinary initiative to develop an independent area of study in the social sciences. Progress was slowed because "the student body was virtually melting away into military service and it proved necessary to suspend the program in 1942."[30] However, these scholars were hopeful that further cooperation might be possible in the postwar university. Toward that end, they proposed a department that included social anthropology, sociology, personality psychology, and social psychology. Support for such interdisciplinary programs was certainly in the air at the time, and the Yale Institute of Human Relations was a good example of the idea in action. Mowrer, a product of the Yale enterprise, provided the group with a general model for its program. In 1942 the "conspirators" proposed a Department of Human Relations to President Conant, but their proposal was ignored.[31] He was simply too busy with his war work to give the idea serious attention. But its time would come in the not too distant future.

While Parsons and his group were moving on these and other issues, Sorokin was busy writing and meeting the demands placed on the department. The European situation was making itself felt at the university. Hitler's aggressive move through Denmark, Norway, Holland, and Belgium and then deep into France increasingly concerned Americans. Public support against German expansion was growing, as witnessed by the 1940 passage of the Burke-Wadsworth Bill, which launched America's first peacetime draft. By the summer of 1941, Harvard was facing income and enrollment shortfalls. Administrative planning for 1941–42 anticipated a three-hundred-thousand-dollar deficit, which had to be met through internal economies. Every department had to reduce operating costs by 10 percent, and Dean Ferguson announced to department chairmen:

The decisions made since January in Washington to let the main brunt of the draft fall on men between the ages of twenty-one and twenty-five . . . has increased materially the chances of a shrinkage in our enrollment. There are two hundred men in the present junior class . . . who will have reached their twenty first birthday by July 1941, and the major part of the total enrollment in the Graduate School is in the same category. This shows how vulnerable we are.[32]

The administration's cost-reduction program eliminated all unnecessary services and expenses, left unfilled permanent staff positions that resulted from deaths or resignations, reduced the number of teaching fellows, required the permanent department staff to assume larger teaching loads, and opened all "primarily for graduates" courses to qualified Radcliffe students.[33] Cutting teaching fellows hit the sociology department hard. Sorokin had advised the dean that his permanent staff already tutored 40 or 50 percent of the department's concentrators. The loss of Timasheff, Hutchinson, and Moore, combined with a reduction in teaching fellows, would increase their load to the breaking point. Furthermore, the opening of the "primarily for graduates" courses to Radcliffe students not only increased the workload but reduced professorial income. (Sociology was the second-largest field of concentration at Radcliffe. Harvard faculty traditionally received extra compensation for the courses they taught there. Now they would be doing more work for less money). But this was not Sorokin's main concern. As he had noted earlier, the department did not have the funds to meet its tutorial obligations with annual instructors and must depend on the less expensive teaching fellows. With his permanent staff at the maximum for tutorial work; the fact that Hartshorne and Ford would be in Washington for the year, and that

Zimmerman was subject to military recall exacerbated the already critical staffing situation. To cut teaching fellows made an already difficult job impossible.

With these reservations and worries in mind, Sorokin sent Ferguson his tutorial plan for the academic year. Charles Price Loomis was returning on a visiting appointment and could, if needed, do part of the tutorial work. Sorokin asked for eight teaching fellows: R. Freed Bales, Rollin Chambliss, Walter Firey Jr., Luke M. Smith, Richard E. DuWors, Herbert Bowman, John Landword, and Gilman McDonald. Rollin Chambliss was soon drafted and replaced by Reed Bradford.[34] Sorokin noted that he could provide tutorial assistance to fifty-seven concentrators at Harvard and thirty-six at Radcliffe. In reply, Ferguson agreed that they might be cutting it close. Regardless, Sorokin was to make no provisions for extra tutorial assistance.[35]

The financial shoe would bind more tightly the following year. The new dean of the Faculty of Arts and Sciences, Paul H. Buck, wrote to the chairmen that they must follow stricter guidelines in their 1942–43 budgets. There would be no salary increases for any annual appointments, associate professors, or professors. Teaching fellows must be used carefully and additions made only after review by the dean. Annual appointees must be reduced below the 1941–42 level. Buck echoed Ferguson's desire for senior faculty to assume more tutorial work. Projections indicated that student losses would be heaviest for upperclassmen and graduate students. Predictions suggested that almost two-thirds of arts and sciences students would be freshmen and sophomores. The diminished need for upper-division courses would free senior staff for lower-division instruction. The new dean expected cooperation.[36] In response, Sorokin reduced the number of teaching fellows and tutors to four. Those reappointed were R. Freed Bales, Herbert Bowman, Walter Firey Jr., and Luke M. Smith.

Professional Struggles and Marginalization

The problems of staffing, declining enrollments, the loss of graduate students, and dissension in the department consumed Sorokin's time. In what remained he wrote. His major efforts were the final volume of *Dynamics, The Crisis of Our Age,* and an evaluation of contemporary American sociology and social science. At this time he was also selected by A. Lawrence Lowell to give the prestigious Lowell Lectures for 1941. Interestingly, Lowell was in the habit of writing select faculty and administrators seeking recommendations for lecturers. Among L. J. Henderson's suggestions was Talcott Parsons, whom he considered "a gentleman and a scholar and a very thoughtful person among men who rarely have two of these three qualifications."[37] Lowell ignored the suggestion and invited Sorokin,[38] who called his lectures "The Twilight of Sensate Culture." Lowell's selection boosted Sorokin's beleaguered image at the university and was also an expression of loyalty; Lowell was standing by him at a difficult time. As Sorokin later observed, "The lectures were well received and along with materials from my *Dynamics* would later be published as *The Crisis of Our Age.*"[39]

While preparing the Lowell Lectures, Sorokin delivered a strong, confrontational paper at the December 1940 meeting of the American Sociological Society. The paper attacked his critics and blasted contemporary sociology and social science. In a prophetic, arrogant tone, reminiscent of Goldenweiser's review of *Dynamics*, Sorokin brings the social science to trial before "The Supreme Court of History." In what will later be published as the "Declaration of Independence of the Social Sciences,"[40] Sorokin affirms that the predicted crises have arrived and his critics were wrong. Therefore, as society moves through the transitional period there will be a reevaluation of its values, which will also involve a judgment by the "Supreme Court of History" of the adequacy and value of contemporary sociology and social science. Sorokin offered his audience three scenarios of how the court would decide the issue. The verdict on the quality of sociology and the social sciences would be a grade of D. We have neither been satisfactory, nor have we failed completely. Just like a student so graded, contemporary social science was on probation.

Sorokin next explained why history rendered this verdict. Here he strongly criticized the social disciplines and particularly sociology. These fields failed because they were obsessed with copying the natural sciences and had no body of principles and methods of their own. This had several negative results. First, the natural science method produced only meager advances. Second, sociologists misunderstood natural science and became obsessed with sense data and fact grubbing. This oversimplification of the scientific method led to the abandonment of intuition and logic as tools for gaining knowledge. Third, the overreliance on sense data produced a mass of facts that distorted reality, led to incorrect generalizations, and yielded a rediscovery of the known. No new increment of knowledge was produced by this imitative behavior, and much was lost through the misinterpretation of the scientific method:

Having banished logic and thought, the social sciences now found themselves in the dilemma of having no means by which to organize an intractable mass of incidental and diverse facts. Lacking principles to order it into a logical, consistent system, they had only the binding of the book as a bond between unrelated chapters, only the paper of the page to hold together the motley array of facts printed upon it.[41]

Sociologists came to find that "their creativeness progressively dried up. Their understanding of socio-cultural reality thinned out. They failed to make great discoveries; their generalizations became . . . a painful elaboration of the obvious."[42] In short, sociology and the other social sciences became sterile.

Once aware of the problem, these scientists responded poorly. They created a ministry of truth and a cult of method. Specifically, a hierarchy of rank emerged among them, beginning with well-funded "super-fellows and super-researchers" at the top and "ending with the lower ranks of the active, contributing and tolerated members."[43] A Supreme Council of Research was developed whose own truth was taken as infallible. Finally, it was declared that certain techniques of scientific research delivered the truth to anyone who used them.

For a while the sociologists and others believed this and worked busily "mastering, applying, and computing the results of these marvelous techniques. . . . Unfortunately in the course of time, scientists and mortals began to notice that many an infallible prediction derived by an infallible technique proved all too fallible."[44] Thus their theories did not hold, and they could make no contribution to solving social problems. As a result, the prestige of the social disciplines declined. Therefore, the court judged them as doing poorly and was forced to send them into oblivion unless they changed their ways.

Sorokin clearly had the solution in mind and talked about it as the "Declaration of Independence of the Social Sciences." The social disciplines must abandon the insane ambition to be a natural science and reclaim their heritage. That is, they must develop principles and methods better suited to the study of human behavior. This required a fundamental revision in their systems of truth and knowledge. Blind empiricism must yield to an "integral system of truth, consisting of the organic synthesis of the truth of senses, truth of reason, and truth of intuition each mutually checking and supplementing the other."[45] Sorokin reiterates the failure of the social sciences to grasp the true nature of science and its interrelationships with logic and intuition. Summarizing material from *Dynamics,* he demonstrates the roles that intuition and logic have played in some of the great discoveries of science and technology. "Furthermore, social scientists must realize that the great social thinkers . . . make their most important discoveries through logical, epistemological and mathematical analyses. There is need to open the gates of science to reason, in all its qualitative and quantitative forms."[46] Social scientists must avoid the empirical blunders of the past and utilize all three sources of human cognition.

Having changed their system of learning and truth, the social sciences must develop new methods of research and principles of analysis. These should be particularly attentive to the role of meaning in human action. When such changes are made, our knowledge of the social world will improve and we can make a contribution to social planning, societal reconstruction, and enrichment. Only through this declaration of independence can the social sciences be liberated from their serflike relationship to the natural sciences and fulfill their historical promise.

Given the temper of the times, most social scientists did not warm to the message. Many were put off by Sorokin's arrogance and the fact that the paper was a simple reiteration of past work. However, Read Bain, editor of the *American Sociological Review,* with Sorokin's approval, sent the paper out for review. Due to a mix-up, however, he did not notify Sorokin of the negative decision until 27 February 1941. His letter of 23 January had gotten buried at the journal's office, and he found it by chance over a month later. Unhappily, the negative decision combined with the lateness of the notification caused a breach in their friendship that would last over a decade.

In the letter that reached Sorokin in late February, Bain states that the editors found too little "news" in the piece to merit publication. They felt that most of the society's members were already familiar with the message, and Bain speculates that the paper may have gotten "under the skin of the boys and they can't take it." Also, the style was "more forceful than we were accustomed to see in scholarly publications."[47]

Sorokin was furious. He regarded it as "inexcusable" that more care had not been taken to inform him and demanded the return of his paper. To this he added, "I can say that I amount to something in sociology. In the majority of the cases the papers published in the *Review* amount literally to nothing, so the decision of your political faction not to publish my paper . . . appears to me little justified."[48] Sorokin closed with a threat to drop his membership in the society.

Bain was stunned but stuck up for his reviewers. He argued that the *Review* published quality articles, and he resented the charge that politics was more important than substance. On a personal note, he regarded himself as one of Sorokin's friends, had admired his work, and hoped that their personal relationship would remain unimpaired.[49] However, Sorokin would have no part of it, and a bitter exchange of letters took place. Sorokin accused Bain of political chicanery, publishing trashy articles, and contributing to the general decline of the discipline. Sorokin demanded the reviewers' names and their specific charges so he could add a footnote to his paper soon to be published by *Social Science*. Bain sent a summary of their comments but no names. If Sorokin wanted somebody to blame, then blame him. He was the editor and had made the decision; the responsibility was his, and he would stand behind it.[50] When the paper was published, there was no footnote, simply a comment by the editor stating that it had been presented at the society's meeting on 29 December 1940. However, the depth and intensity of the break in their friendship are evident in a Christmas Eve 1941 letter from Bain to Sorokin:

Dear Sorokin:

The godly and ungodly usually make each other uncomfortable. The difference between us is I admit you may be right and I wrong. You think anyone who questions your opinions must be a personal enemy. Watch your ego, sir! You have delusions of grandeur and persecution and are beginning to look ridiculous to many people who are not dogs—or stupid either. I'm sorry to see this because I still like and admire you in many respects—Though I realize you will not believe this statement.[51]

Bain and Sorokin remained at odds for a long time. Not only had Sorokin's temper cost him a friendship, but he lost a potentially powerful ally in mainstream sociology at a time when his work would be increasingly under attack.

Later in 1941, both *Crisis* and volume 4 of *Dynamics* were issued. *Crisis* is a transitional book in two ways. First, it is an in-depth analysis of the transitional phase of a declining sensate culture. Second, it marks a significant continuation in the shift by Sorokin toward a prophetic sociology. *Crisis* grew from the last volume of *Dynamics*. By way of putting it in context Sorokin notes:

The preceding volumes of *Social and Cultural Dynamics* give a vast mass of relevant facts concerning sociocultural change. On the basis of this material the groundwork of the theory of sociocultural change was done and part of its frame was erected. . . . However, the building was not finished in three volumes. . . . Nor were the main principles systematically unfolded. These tasks were left to this volume.[52]

Sorokin's main theoretical concern was how and why sociocultural systems change. The answer advanced the principles of Immanent

Determinism and Limits put forward earlier, and introduced his emerging Integral philosophy. Sorokin reasoned that social systems, like biological ones, change according to their inherent potentialities. Immanent Determinism asserts that the internal dynamic organization of a system establishes its capacity for change. Systems, however, have limits. For example, as they become more and more Sensate, moving toward the extreme Cynical Sensate, they reach their limits of expansion. In a dialectical fashion, Ideational countertrends are produced that grow stronger as the system polarizes. These countertrends start to move the culture toward an Idealistic form. The dissonant changes reverberate throughout the culture, and violence increases as the system takes on a new configuration. Thus, Sorokin concluded that we should study social change by focusing on the internal organization (Immanent Determinism) and the Principle of Limits

Sorokin next asked why these changes happened as they did. The answer advanced his Integral philosophy. The character of a cultural system is determined by the principle that underlies its means of identifying truth and reality. Historical analysis showed that Ideational systems rested on intuitive truth, Sensate systems on the authority of the senses, and Idealistic cultures on the truths of reason. None of these principles alone, however, gives absolute truth. If a system of truth and the culture it maintained were absolutely true, there would be no historical rhythms. Conversely, if a system were completely false, it would not have lasted. Therefore, for the observed superrhythms of culture to occur, each system of truth and culture must be only partially true and adequate for human needs. Each, however, contains necessary elements for the adaptation of humanity to the physical, social, and cosmic milieu. But these truth systems change because each type of knowledge is incomplete and has strengths and weaknesses. When one dominates, it forces out others and prohibits holistic understanding of the world. The longer a mentality dominates, the more anomalies accrue. That is, people become increasingly aware that their knowledge system is too narrow to explain important aspects of life, and the usefulness of their system is called more into question. Other means are now needed to address these anomalies of culture and cosmos. It is at this point that the Principle of Limits comes into play. For example, as a Sensate system moves toward the cynical extreme, the scientific method is used to explain more and more of life. Soon people realize its limitations for explaining the spiritual and intuitive aspects of existence, and Ideational countertrends are introduced. These move the culture toward an Idealistic form and as they grow in strength the system takes on a new configuration. But these transitional periods are times of great personal stress and social crisis. Unhappily, the superrhythms of Ideational, Idealistic, and Sensate mentalities could go on forever without humans realizing either ultimate truth or peace.

Sorokin's solution to this endless cycle was the pursuit of Integral truth. This form of knowing "is not identical with any of the three forms of truth, but embraces all of them."[53] It combines the empirical truths of the senses; the rational truths of reason; and the superrational truths of faith.[54] Integral truth gives us a more complete and valid grasp of reality. In Integral philosophy Sorokin brought together the religious, scientific, and rational aspects of culture. Cultures change out of a need for a more adequate knowledge to deal with life's major questions. Sensate knowledge gives us science, technology, and physical comfort but tells us little of the spirit. The truths of faith address those issues but leave us relatively helpless in the face of nature. As each type of culture tries to provide what is missing the culture changes. Integralism, however, binds the truth of science, reason, and intuition into a comprehensive whole. It also broadens our understanding and deepens our knowledge of the other forms of knowing. As an example, Sorokin argues:

For thousands of years many empirical uniformities of natural phenomena were lying under "the eyes and ears" of the organs of the senses; and yet they were unable to grasp them. When they were "discovered," they were discovered only through the cooperation of other sources of cognition: logic and intuition. When these elementary verities are understood, it becomes clear how limited, poor, incoherent and narrow would be our knowledge, if it were limited to only pure sensory cognition. . . . Likewise, mere dialectical speculation . . . or intuition . . . misleads us much more easily when it is isolated from, and unchecked by, the other sources and systems of truths than when it is united into one integral whole with the others. Hence the greater adequacy of the integral system of truth.[55]

It is our means of obtaining a satisfying framework to comprehend life, cosmos, and the role of humanity in each.[56] Once obtained, it is the ultimate foundation for the good society.

Sorokin felt that Integral philosophy, in a Sensate age, would be difficult for many to accept. People acknowledged mathematics and logic as fruits of reason, and natural science as the product of the senses. However, the truths of intuition, inspiration, and revelation were more questionable. Sorokin addressed this barrier by pointing to the role of intuition in other forms of knowledge. Drawing on histories of science, mathematics, technology, art, and religion, he documented intuition's role in the process of discovery. Citing accounts by mathematicians like Poincaré and Birkhoff; scientists such as Newton, Archimedes, and

Galileo; creative artists like Mozart and Beethoven; the philosophers Plato, Nietzsche, and Kant; and religious leaders such as the Buddha, Mohammed, Zoroaster, and Saint Paul, Sorokin demonstrated the role of intuition in their works. However, he held little hope that men of science could avail themselves to the "trinity of truth."

The skepticism that would lead to its rejection was the same that had greeted his predictions in the closing section of volume 3. But, "While the sweet theories of the critics are entirely washed out by the inexorable course of events, my diagnosis and the theory underlying it need no correction. History, so far, has been proceeding along the schedule of *Dynamics*. The great crisis of the Sensate culture is here in all its stark reality."[57]

In *The Crisis of Our Age* Sorokin examined this condition and asked what could be done. The remedy "demands a complete change of the contemporary mentality, a fundamental transformation of our system of values, and the profoundest modification of our conduct toward other men, cultural values and the world at large."[58] The new mentality must include an Integral synthesis that fuses the truths of reason, faith, and science. A new Integral values system that treats truth, goodness, and beauty as integrated absolutes is essential for the new age.[59] Sorokin elaborates:

Though each member of this supreme [value] Trinity has a distinct individuality, all three are inseparable from one another. . . . The genuine Truth is always good and beautiful. . . . Goodness is always true and beautiful; and the pure Beauty is invariably true and good. These greatest values are not only inseparable from one another, but they are transformable into one another, like one form of physical energy, say, heat, is transformable into other kinds of energy, electricity or light or mechanical motion.[60]

The Integral transformation of worldview and values would be insufficient, however, unless it became part of human relationships and social organization. Sorokin was unsure as to how this might happen. He simply suggested replacing "the present compulsory and contractual relationships with purer and more godly familistic relationships."[61] While *Crisis* lacked a programmatic solution to current problems, Integralism became more developed as a strategy, and Sorokin pointed the direction he felt Western culture should take. As Nicholas Timasheff observed in his review, Sorokin considers "the destiny of a declining sensate culture is to give way to a new ideational or—what is less probable—idealistic culture." The essence of this crisis for Sorokin "is spiritual: it is the crisis of a culture which has rejected God and religion and has tried to get along without them." Therefore, "A new religion or the regeneration of an older one is the solution to the problem of over-ripe sensateness." While Sorokin does not predict which will occur, "he hopes for a revival of Christian culture."[62]

While Timasheff stressed the proposed outcome of the crisis, Rubin Gotesky's essay focused more on the analysis of the crisis and saw a different outcome.[63] Gotesky combines the fourth volume of *Dynamics* and *Crisis* in his review. While he was aware of the bruising reviews of the earlier volumes of *Dynamics* by sociologists, Marxists, and cynics like Crane Brinton, he concludes that volume 4 "is a brilliant book and an important contribution to theoretical sociology."[64] He is impressed by Sorokin's use of "the Law of Immanent Change," and "the Law of Limits," and "the Law of Limited Possibilities of Change" to diagnose the advent of the current crises. It is to this theoretical assessment that he directs his praise of *Dynamics*. In turn, *Crisis* adequately renders the condition of modern civilization but errs in the prescribed solution. Here Sorokin confuses religion and socialism and improperly rejects the latter. Gotesky argues that a world in which private property, nation-states, and political compulsion cease to exist and humans become tied to each other as members of "a world family" is socialism's image of the world. Sorokin is guilty of misinterpreting the socialistic doctrine and minimizing its importance. But, other than this, the book is a fine contribution to understanding the current condition.[65]

Equally positive reviews were given by the sociologist Joseph S. Roucek and anthropologist M. F. Ashley Montagu. Roucek believed it hard to overpraise *Crisis* because of its deep and perceptive view of the forces that shaped modern society and its future direction.[66]

Other sociologists, however, were not as accepting of these works. In a piercing review of the last volume of *Dynamics*, Robert MacIver opens with a shot straight to the ego:

Happy Mr. Sorokin! He knows the secret of history (p. v.). . . . His supersystems of culture "seem to be, so far, the vastest supersystem among all the real systems of culture hitherto discovered." (p. 139) His propositions are free from all the shortcomings of current theory. (p. 577) He has discovered the true interrelations "of an enormous number of processes." (Ibid) He has answered all the important questions. (p. 773) Thrice happy Mr. Sorokin! . . . We admire his labors and we would not disturb his peace, even if that were possible. We are impressed with his vast Spenglerian antithesis, his more than Spenglerian erudition, and his utterly un-Spenglerian massing of statistics. We envy his short way with critics and his secure Athanasian stand. We genuinely applaud his vindication of the integrity of knowledge, his vehement polemic against positivists and pragmatists, neo-realists and mechanists. If we still cavil at the *Dynamics*, it may be only because the inner light that guides the author has not been vouchsafed to such critics as the present reviewer.[67]

Having wielded the sword, MacIver goes to work with the scalpel. "There are, it is true, minor blemishes, such as the curious looseness of language and a habit of using Latin words in a way that flouts the Latin grammar. We pass these by, we are concerned to look instead at the main theme of a work dedicated to the 'cardinal problem of sociocultural change.' "[68] Of the three main sections of the book, MacIver finds that only the first approaches adequacy. On the how and why of sociocultural change, Sorokin has little to offer. MacIver flatly rejects the Principle of Immanent Causation as simplistic, misdirected, and too heavily founded on an organismic analogy. In the second part, Sorokin discusses the rhythms of social change but introduces nothing new. Indeed, the focus here seems to be on poorly reasoned criticisms of dichotomous theorists of social change of which MacIver's is one. Sorokin's final discussion of the superrhythms, crisis, and advent of a new Ideational age leaves MacIver cold. There would be no joy in such a change, simply the return to the squalor and superstitions of a peasant society. MacIver reveals an important characteristic of the book when he comments: "It is in any event hard to convey a total picture of a work that voluminously combines pregnant observations and well-documented evidence with loose reasoning, dubious generalizations, prophetic utterances, and uncontrollable excursions to the Absolute."[69]

Wilbert Moore observed a similar quality in the fourth volume and commented, "Having freed himself of the constraints of conventional scholarship, Sorokin takes his reader on a free flight through the lands of speculation which is often entertaining, sometimes instructive, generally heavy going and always provocative. The latter quality should be underscored . . . [because] reviews will more often than not turn out to be polemics."[70]

The true polemical thrusts, however, were reserved for *Crisis*. Harry Elmer Barnes charged that the book was subjective, personally prejudiced, and loaded with value judgments. As such, it "affords the most elaborate vindication of Max Weber's contention that the interjection of value-judgements into sociology is fatal to scientific objectivity." Sorokin was next described as "the St. Augustine of contemporary sociology." Like Augustine he was the great prophet of an age of transition and "gathered together all the learning of his day to condemn the City of the Devil and to portray the glories of the coming City of God."[71] Additionally, neither of these harbingers of a new age was careful about their methods, nor fair to the legitimate points raised by their critics.

Read Bain, perhaps still stinging from his earlier exchange with Sorokin, condemned *Crisis*, finding that it contains nothing new; the style is poor and emotionally charged; it's opinionated and value laden; and it misinforms and misdirects its readers. Sorokin uses the term Sensate for everything he dislikes and Ideational for those traits he admires. No objective discussion of these cultural types is given. Instead, readers are told that the best solution to the crisis is a new Ideational culture. Sorokin's own account of history, according to Bain, identifies the last Ideational golden age as occurring between 500 and 1200. But Sorokin fails to tell his readers that this was a period of "filth, cruelty, ignorance, sensuality, disease, starvation, exploitation, persecution, revolution, war, bloody violence, and the denial of the dignity of men."[72]

Bain continues: "The way ahead is dark indeed but it is not so dark and dank as the medieval pit from which we have been digged. These dark days may be followed by a brighter dawn—or by oblivion. . . . We need prophets to lead us forward out of the Wilderness, not back into the Egyptian night."[73] Furthermore,

This volume then is neither science nor philosophy. It is infused with high purpose; it sounds like the anguished cry of a defeated idealist to whom the future looks very black and therefore lashes out against the world he does not like, and calls upon sinners to return to the comforting womb of the Absolute. Personally, I think this way is closed. . . . man must be master of his fate—if his fate can be mastered. We need more science, not less, and it must be natural science, not the pseudo-sciences of the ideational middle ages.[74]

A similar conclusion was reached by Sorokin's earlier critic Sidney Hook, who wrote: "Perhaps the strongest impression left with the reader is that this is a foolish book—not so much because of its utter lack of restraint and wisdom, but foolish in that it fails to recognize the alternatives that are still open and available to us in our existing culture."[75]

The publication of these books and sociology's "Declaration of Independence" kept Sorokin in conflict with important sociologists. Read Bain was the editor of the *American Sociological Review* from 1938 to 1942 and would become the society's vice president; MacIver was the society's president in 1940. People listened to these men and others like them. They had the respect of many of America's scholars, and their treatment of Sorokin's sociology moved him toward the backwaters of the discipline. It was getting to the point that sociologists were moving away from Sorokin, and many would soon ignore him completely.

The Decline of the Sociology Department and the Rise of Social Relations

While Sorokin was engaged in these activities, new social science programs were being discussed by Buck, Allport, and others.[76] Conant's war involvements had led him to ignore the group's earlier petitions, but Buck responded to Allport that he was "much interested in what you as a group would propose on the subject. . . . consequently I am appointing you as an informal committee to explore the problem and submit a report directly to me."[77] On 1 October 1943 the committee gave Buck its tentative plan for the "Reorganization of the Social Sciences at Harvard." In the cover letter Gordon Allport observed that the committee "feared that certain readers, without adequate preparation, might misinterpret our motives and our intentions." The committee realized that its report inadequately covered the Departments of Government, Economics, and History and encouraged the dean to explore the issue with members of those departments. However, the committee "was also apprehensive lest our colleagues in the Departments of Psychology, Sociology and Anthropology take offense at our negative recommendations regarding these departments.[78]

This sweeping document suggested creation of the following: a Division of History, combining the existing programs in history, archaeology, history of art, history of science, and history of religion; a Division of Biology, including human biology, botany, infrahuman zoology, and medical sciences; a Department of Basic Social Sciences, combining staffs of social anthropology, social and clinical psychology, sociology, and a "social biologist"; and a Graduate School of Human Relations staffed by the Department of Basic Social Sciences with representatives to be added later from the School of Education, the Littauer Center, the Department of Industrial Relations, the Department of Geography, and the Law School. To these recommendations were added the outline for an undergraduate and two graduate programs, guidelines for staffing, and a blueprint for cooperative arrangements with other departments and faculties.[79]

The guts of the document was the Department of Basic Social Sciences. The most profound changes discussed would be in the parenting departments and the careers of Joseph Ford and Pitirim Sorokin. The committee recommended that

the existent departments of anthropology, psychology, and sociology be dissolved. They represent compartmentalizations which are the result of the accidents of historical development rather than divisions of labor which correspond to coherent and well-delimited terrains of investigation. Indeed they promote intellectual confusion and personal friction by unrealistic juxtaposition of very divergent, though equally legitimate, interests which attract temperaments likely to be antagonistic.[80]

While no specific recommendations are found in this memo for the biotropes in psychology, the fates of Ford and Sorokin are explicit. "We recommend that Professor Sorokin and Professor Ford be given extra-departmental status: the former as professor of the philosophy of history, the latter as associate professor of social ethics."[81]

The conditions, however, were not right for implementing the report and moving toward what would become the Department of Social Relations. Shortly after Buck received the report, Mowrer moved away and Kluckhohn and Murray became involved with government war activities. However, Buck was impressed by the potential of interdisciplinary work for improving the quality of the social sciences and with how war projects demonstrated its problem-solving utility. Interdisciplinary social science

played a part in the selection of men and women for particular jobs, in the maintenance of morale both in the armed forces and at home, in the prevention and treatment of neuropsychiatric disorders, in propaganda analysis, in selling war bonds, in studies of the social and psychological make-up of the enemy, in training military government personnel for dealing with many kinds of people from Germany to the Pacific islands, and in numerous other operations.[82]

Interdisciplinary problem solving weakened disciplinary boundaries in a cooperative search for solutions. In the process, sociology and anthropology became more psychological and vice versa. Buck and the founders of social relations realized that what worked in the war might also be a potent model for academic reorganization and progress. Additionally, many of the founders had firsthand experience with interdisciplinary war research: Henry Murray and Gordon Allport with the Office of Strategic Services (OSS); Clyde Kluckhohn with the Foreign Morale Analysis Division (FMAD); Talcott Parsons with the School for Overseas Administration and as a consultant to the Energy Branch of the Foreign Economic Administration; and Samuel Stouffer as director of the Research Branch of the Education and Information Division of the War Department.

Though Buck saw the proposal's potential, immediate implementation was not advisable. But this changed in March 1944 when Northwestern University approached Parsons. It had recently received a great deal of new money and wanted, among other things, to expand its social science programs. Northwestern offered Parsons a well-paid full professorship, the chairmanship of the Department of Sociology, and a free hand in building the department. Given the current situation at Harvard, he was interested.

As fate would have it, Parsons made a trip to Chicago, and by accident he and Paul Buck were on the same train and even stayed at the same hotel. This gave them an opportunity to discuss in detail the situation in sociology, the reorganization plan, and the great promise of a new approach to the social sciences. When Parsons returned, Allport encouraged him to continue reorganization talks with the dean and to see if alternatives could be found to the Northwestern offer.[83]

Parsons put his proposal to Buck a few days later when he wrote:

That after our various conversations I think that it may be well to put my own position on paper so that misunderstanding of it on your part can be avoided so far as possible. I have greatly appreciated your willingness to talk to me frankly and somewhat as a personal friend as well as in your capacity as an administrative officer of the University. Hence I am taking the liberty of giving you my own point of view in a similar vein, speaking with complete frankness. Perhaps you will be willing to regard this more as a personal communication than as an official memo. I think that the essential thing from my point of view is that the offer from Northwestern has brought the whole complex situation here to a head in such a way as to force the crucial questions of the future role at Harvard, and particularly in the policy of its administration, of the kind of scientific work with which my own career has become identified. I want to use my own personal case as "pressure" only in the sense of helping to bring the administration to face issues of policy which I feel it will have to face sooner or later anyway. . . . The great advantage [of the Northwestern offer] to me would be a free hand, an opportunity to develop something much more in accord with my own ideas than anything which has heretofore existed at Harvard.[84]

Parsons then discussed various social science departments within the university and specified their strengths and weaknesses. For sociology, he made the following observation:

The sociology experiment was made and very badly bungled. Sorokin should never have been appointed to lead a great development in the first place. The administration should never have allowed him to secure a permanency for Zimmerman. But having made these mistakes the thing has been allowed to stew in its own juices, and continue as one of the sorest spots in the faculty. In the meantime a very big scientific development has been rapidly gathering force. . . . I will stake my whole professional reputation on the statement that it is one of the really great movements of modern scientific thought. . . . like all really big pioneer movements it is not understood by the majority of the established high priests of social science. Like all such movements it lacks an adequate institutional framework for developing its potentialities, and the development of such a framework is hindered by the vested interest of those already in the field. . . .

This general situation is particularly pronounced here at Harvard, as I have outlined above. The essential question to me is whether Harvard is going to seize the opportunity to be a great leader in this movement or is going to move only as it is forced to do so by the competition of other institutions. Which it is going to be seems to me will constitute a considerable factor in how far Harvard will, in the next generation, maintain a general position of leadership in the academic world or will depend for its position mainly on its wealth and past prestige.

Parsons further shared with Buck the content of previous discussions with President Conant about a "basic social science program" at the university and the situation in sociology. He reported that Conant favored the former, saying, "You don't need to try and convince me, I agree with you." On the unsatisfactory state of the sociology department, Conant commented, "It's pretty bad when three out of the four permanent members are the wrong people." (The third was James Ford). On the offer from Northwestern Parsons was clear:

To return to the immediate practical problem, I think I am clear in my own mind that merely a raise in salary, even a prospect of full professorship soon, without a change in the organizational situation, is not enough. I would rather go to Northwestern.

As I have repeatedly told you, I don't think that any substantial improvement in the Department situation is possible while Sorokin is Chairman. I greatly appreciate your assurances that his chairmanship will terminate soon. Frankly, however, two more years of it are not an attractive prospect to me. I should consider that justified only by the prospect that very substantial improvements would come immediately after that time. Also I frankly feel that your assurance that Zimmerman will not succeed him is an essential condition of a tolerable situation in the Department for me.

In closing, Parsons discussed several forms of organization for a new department and the alternatives for its chairman. The tone of the rest of the letter was such that a substantial reorganization was a precondition for his staying at Harvard.[85]

This letter was written in April 1944, but the administrative decision to support Parsons and the Social Relations alternative was a product of more than Parsons's pressure for change. There seemed to be dissatisfaction with Sorokin's leadership, and the department was somewhat of an embarrassment to the administration. Parsons's alternative remedied the situation without an extensive output of resources. Reorganization required only two new positions, and the new program would be accomplished largely through internal reorganization. Consequently, it was an attractive alternative for a variety of reasons.[86]

Buck had to move quickly and decisively if he was to keep Parsons. The dean went to Conant and with his consent offered Parsons an immediate full professorship and appointment as chairman of sociology beginning 1 July 1944. Parsons was also told to plan the merger of sociology, social and clinical psychology, and social anthropology. While the administration did not commit any new permanent appointments, it did offer support in getting the reorganization through faculty review.[87] The first step in this new direction was to replace Sorokin as chairman.

On 5 April 1944 Sorokin received a letter from Buck saying that his chairmanship had ended. The dean pointed out that in May 1940 the Faculty of Arts and Sciences had passed a bylaw that limited the maximum term of a chairman to five years. For a variety of reasons, the rule was implemented gradually and the time had come to apply the policy to sociology. Buck stated:

You have carried the burden of chairmanship since 1931 and deserve relief. I am, therefore, suggesting that your term as chairman come to an end at the conclusion of this current year, that is, on 30 June 1944, and a new chairman take office from that time. I shall appreciate your writing me your advice as to the member of your Department you feel best suited to assume the chairmanship.[88]

Within days Sorokin also received a request to give his opinion on the promotion of Parsons to full professor.[89]

To the resignation request Sorokin wrote: "I am very glad that finally after thirteen years and after my at least fourth request to free me from the duties of chairman, the administration found it possible to do so." However, when it came to a replacement he did not see any great differences between any of the permanent members. Given Parsons's ties with the School for Overseas Administration and his present interest in two or three other social science departments, he might not be a good choice. Of the two remaining, Zimmerman was his recommendation because he was an ex-serviceman, could get along with people, and was attractive to students.[90] In regards to Parsons's new rank Sorokin wrote that he could see no special reason for promoting Parsons without doing the same for Ford and Zimmerman. "If anything the total index of merit for Professor Zimmerman would probably be slightly higher than for Professor Parsons. Such is my honest opinion."[91]

Having made his recommendation, Sorokin awaited the outcomes. Buck wrote on 26 April that "President Conant . . . has decided to appoint Professor Parsons as your successor . . . and I trust that you will cooperate in the transition.[92] Sorokin did cooperate, but a small detail in this great transition proved troublesome and problematic for him–the fate of Marjorie Nobel, longtime personal and departmental secretary.

George Homans has observed that Mrs. Nobel, with Sorokin's acquiescence, had made life "an administrative Hell for Parsons."[93] Parsons could do little to get rid of Sorokin, but Mrs. Nobel was another matter. In May 1944 Parsons told her she would not be needed after he took the chair. Sorokin appealed the case to Dean Buck: "Though I possibly understand the reasons for such a decision of Professor Parsons, the decision does not appear to me just or best under the circumstances. . . . Mrs. Nobel has faithfully served the University for several years and in the most excellent manner. Dismissal of any member of any organization under such circumstances appears to me unjustifiable."[94] Sorokin questioned Parsons's decision on several grounds: it was university policy to change chairmen, not secretaries; with the new rotating chairmanships, the unexpected termination of secretaries at the end of their boss's tenure would make it hard to get and keep good people; it has been past practice to keep chairman's secretaries when a new man has come on, as Sorokin did when he replaced Cabot. However, if Buck chose to support Parsons's decision, then would they consider an alternative to dismissal–specifically, to keep Mrs. Nobel as a part-time secretary for the rest of the department and allow her to continue in charge of the department's library? This could be done at only a modest increase in cost.[95]

Sorokin's argument and alternatives were rejected, and on 12 May 1944 Parsons wrote Mrs. Nobel:

I understood you to say in our conversation Wednesday that you were planning to resign as Secretary to the Department as of June 30th. Hence, I shall take steps to find a new Secretary to start work when I assume office as Chairman July 1st. I realize that after having served the Department so long it must be difficult for you to leave. However, I appreciate greatly your generosity and tactfulness in preferring to do so. I share with the other members of the Department an appreciation of your efficient and faithful service to it, and hope you will succeed in finding a congenial and interesting new position.[96]

Mrs. Nobel's terse reply followed:

Thank you for your letter of May 12. Perhaps this note will make clear any misunderstanding of our conversation. I did not plan to resign as I had already told you I would accept your decision that my services as secretary to the Department "were not needed" when you assumed the chairmanship.[97]

And so Mrs. Nobel's term ended on 1 July 1944. Parsons wrote E. Y. Hartshorne, who was away on active duty, a few weeks later, giving him the following news of the department: "Since Harvard affairs are so remote from you, you probably have not heard about the revolution in the Department. The immediate visible sign is that I am now sitting in your old office with the sign 'Office of the Chairman' outside the door . . . [and] the department secretary you will be interested to hear is no longer Mrs. Nobel."[98] Along with this was the news of Joe Ford's death, Zimmerman's military discharge and return to active teaching, and Parsons's elevation to full professor. Hartshorne was further informed, "Back of this lie rather extensive plans for reorganization not only of the Department as such, but of those parts of social science outside History, Government and Economics. It seems a pretty strategic time to be working on such a plan so that we can be ready a year from now to start off on a new basis for the post-war periods."[99]

With Parsons's installation as chairman of the Department of Sociology, an important step toward reorganization was completed. Sorokin's power within the department and the Division of Arts and Sciences had been neutralized, and Parsons was in a position to move the department in a new direction. Furthermore, Ford's death created an open permanency in the department. After substantial discussion of the opportunities and alternatives offered by this vacancy,[100] Dean Buck converted it into two permanent associate professorships.[101]

The department voted in its 10 September 1945 meeting to appoint George C. Homans to one position and Robert K. Merton to the other. Homans accepted but Merton did not.[102] Merton's demur resulted in a position for an expert in methodology and research. Conant, Buck, and Parsons were becoming more convinced about the promise of interdisciplinary research and the increasing importance of organized research facilities to support and maintain it. In the spring of 1945, Buck asked Parsons to visit and report back on government and university programs that combined these elements. Parsons studied the programs at the Yale Institute of Human Relations, the Columbia Bureau of Applied Social Research, the North Carolina Institute of Social Research, the Research Branch in the Information and Education Division of the War Department, and various others.[103] From this followed the belief that an effective interdisciplinary program would require a department for the facilitation of research. Hence, before the end of 1945 it was decided to offer an appointment to Samuel A. Stouffer, professor of sociology at the University of Chicago and director of research in the Research Branch of the Education and Information Division of the War Department. Stouffer was an accomplished methodologist and expert on organizing and running a corporate research department.[104]

In light of the end of the war and the expected return of students to the university, Dean Buck called together members of the sociology, anthropology, and psychology departments to discuss reorganizations. A decision was made to organize a committee–made up of A. M. Tozzer and Donald Scott from anthropology, E. G. Boring and G. W. Allport from psychology, and Parsons and Zimmerman from sociology[105]–charged with drawing up a plan for the combination of the departments. "The committee was instructed first to report to each of the three Departments independently and if its report were ratified by them, to submit it to Faculty."[106] The plan was ratified by the other departments and debated in sociology on 8 December 1945. Only three members of the department were present. Zimmerman and Parsons voted to approve the recommendations. Sorokin abstained.[107]

At the beginning of 1946, the following plan was approved by faculty:

1. That there shall be established under the Faculty of Arts and Sciences a Department of Social Relations which shall exercise all the functions and assume all the responsibilities appropriate to a Department of this Faculty.
2. That the Department of Social Relations shall offer instruction beginning the Summer Term of 1946.
3. That the Department of Social Relations shall, in general, offer such instruction as at present lies within the Department of Sociology, and within the fields of social and clinical psychology as offered in the present Department of Psychology, and within the field of social anthropology as offered in the present Department of Anthropology.
4. That the Department of Sociology be dissolved since it will be incorporated in the Department of Social Relations.
5. That the Department of Social Relations be authorized to offer a field of Concentration in Social Relations to undergraduates and to recommend candidates for the bachelor's degree with or without honors.
6. That the present Concentration in the Area of Social Sciences be discontinued, and the Committee on Concentration in the area of Social Science be dissolved.
7. That the Department of Social Relations be authorized to offer instruction leading to the A.M. and Ph.D. degrees and to recommend

candidates for these degrees with the following subjects recognized for the Ph.D.: Sociology, Social Psychology, Clinical Psychology, and Social Anthropology.[108]

The new department was opened on 29 January 1946. The permanent members of its faculty were G. W. Allport, G. C. Homans, C. Kluckhohn, H. A. Murray Jr., T. Parsons, P. A. Sorokin, R. W. White, and C. C. Zimmerman.[109] A succinct statement describing the new department and the forces that gave it life is found in an article by G. W. Allport and E. C. Boring, who described the department as originating from:

1. The realization that the rigid lines of department organization at Harvard did not reflect the emerging synthesis of sociocultural sciences and psychology that has come about over the last decade.
2. The term Social Relations characterized this new synthesis. One which began over twenty years ago with the emergence of "culture and personality studies" and was intensified by the cross-fertilization of disciplines during the War.
3. This new fusion requires the continuous development of a common body of theory, and shared methods of research brought together through a common Laboratory of Social Relations.
4. The new Harvard program realigns its departmental structure "to encourage a genuine fusion of the three specialties hitherto kept separate by traditional departmental lines of demarcation."[110]

To these may be added the personal and professional dissatisfaction of important members of the faculty; their wartime experiences; and the forceful administrative vision of Paul Buck.

Institutional Conflict and the Rise of a Hegemonic Tradition

This was a very important period in Sorokin's career and in Harvard sociology. It also provides a rare insight into the dynamics of institutional life, scholarship, and discipline building. Sorokin's commitment to the humanistic tradition of prophetic sociology was crystallized in his works of 1940–45. In turn, Parsons's priestly adherence to the values of science and theoretical development adumbrated the struggle that emerged over the fate of the Department of Sociology. During its history the department provided extensive intellectual resources for either of these scholars to develop a major intellectual tradition. However, the Parsonsian group emerged as dominant, and Sorokin was driven to the boundaries of the discipline. To answer the question of why Parsons's star rose and Sorokin's waned, one must systematically examine not only the situation at Harvard but also the state of theoretical development in the discipline and the position of these scholars in the broader community of sociologists and other academics. Such an analysis not only systematizes our understanding of the period but gives insight into the rise and demise of theoretical traditions.[111]

A useful model for this analysis is found in Edward Tiryakian's concept of the theory school.[112] The Tiryakian variant of the school approach allows one to examine the development of idea systems within a discipline in terms of their substance, their significant theoretical figures, their social structure, and their relationship to the profession and to the larger scholarly community. It points to a satisfying sociological dimension in the study of theoretical development and diffusion. The school, in the Tiryakian sense, is a group of scholars integrated around an intellectually charismatic leader. The founder-leader's function is to develop the group's main frame of ideas or, as depicted by Imre Lakatos, its "Scientific Research Program" (SRP).[113] The SRP is a model of empirical reality used to guide investigation and specify hypotheses. Although the core formulations are those of the founder-leader and are usually expressed in that person's exemplar, the full-blown theory typically is a group effort.

The status-role structure that defines the organization of the school consists of the founder-leader and various types of colleagues and fellow intellectuals. Of central importance in the inner circle of the founder-leader is the role of the interpreter, a scholar who has a mastery of the SRP and insights into the founder-leader that allow him to explain and defend the program so outsiders can understand its significance.

The remainder of the initial inner circle is drawn from a group of "converts" who are contemporaries of the founder-leader. Being of the same generation, these scholars share similar historical backgrounds with the leader. Although they are often successful, recognized scholars in their own right, they find something in the work of the founder-leader that either reinforces and refines the direction of their own work or is a revelation for them. Thus, they actively contribute to developing, elaborating, and testing the group paradigm. Their established professional reputations give the emerging school visibility and often prestige.

Younger members of the school, usually students or new entrants to the lower academic ranks, are "lieutenants." They, too, are active in spreading the message. They participate in professional organizations, pursue grants, and publish from within the paradigm and often the social network of the school. When they are away from the center of activity, they send their students back to the founder-leader for further education and professional development.[114]

A successful school often receives support from the ancillary structures of academia. Foundation executives, publishers, and journal editors may frequently be proponents of a school's vision of the world. Additionally, the school may find a person who assists its activities financially and other supporters who advocate them politically and socially.

Tiryakian further develops the concept into that of a hegemonic school; a school exerts hegemony when the profession accepts its SRP as the way to perform "normal science." That is, the discipline finds that the general theoretical accounting and methodological guidelines for research provided by the school produce substantial new increments in knowledge. As a result, scholars spend their energy toiling in the vineyard of the master's SRP.[115]

If Sorokin would have formed a school in the Tiryakian sense, or more specifically a hegemonic school, he would have done so at Harvard between 1930 and 1944. The question of why Parsons succeeded in this milieu and Sorokin did not is an interesting one. The intellectual environment at Harvard was characterized by the continuous presence of talented and productive graduate students. Scholars such as Robert Merton, Kingsley Davis, John Riley, Logan Wilson, Robin Williams, and Wilbert Moore overlapped with or were followed by Bernard Barber, Marion Levy, Albert Cohen, and Francis X. Sutton. Some who arrived after the war were Harold Garfinkel, David Alberle (anthropology), and James Olds and Gardner Lindzey (psychology). Still later, in the 1940s, came Morris Zelditch and Neil Smelser. Clearly, a remarkable pool of talent was available to both Parsons and Sorokin. Indeed, both established many valuable working relationships with this cadre of sociological talent, but Parsons did so to a much greater degree and with substantially more success than Sorokin. It was in this network of relationships that the Parsonsian system was formulated and emerged to compete for hegemony within the discipline. To understand how Parsons did this requires examining a variety of additional factors.

To comprehend the dynamics of securing an institutional base at Harvard demands we consider a set of factors internal to the university and certain external conditions in the discipline of sociology. The internal factors include the character and level of development of Functionalism and Integralism in the works of Parsons and Sorokin; the perception among graduate students and faculty of the potential for success of each form of theorizing; the relationships between each scholar and his collaborators; Harvard's "Olympus Complex"; the intellectual style and charisma of the major figures; and their relationships with graduate students and other scholarly groups within the university. External considerations include the level of theoretical development in the discipline and opportunities for new approaches to emerge and take hold.

During the early years of the department, Parsons enjoyed a theoretical advantage over Sorokin. This had to do with the stage of development that characterized his theory. The Parsonsian system at that point was seminal, open, and showed a strong promise for success, making it particularly attractive to graduate students. By 1930 Parsons had published his translation of Weber's *Protestant Ethic and the Spirit of Capitalism*, and by 1936 he was doing the last preparations for *The Structure of Social Action*. He was at the very beginning of his theoretical development and actively incorporating others into his projects and concerns. Not only was he in continuous dialogues with Henderson, the Pareto Circle, and colleagues in other departments, but he was actively involved with graduate students through the Adams House group. Robert Merton, Kingsley Davis, Robin Williams, and Wilbert Moore, along with others, were regular participants in this informal but important theory group. It was at Adams House over beer and ideas that lifelong friendships and interests were formed around the seminal work of Parsons.[116]

The openness and promise of the Parsonsian system were reflected in students' comments. As John Heeren noted, "They had a strong sense of having a very powerful scientific kind of sociology."[117] This, combined with Parsons's willingness to enlist followers, allowed students to take an active part in the emerging tradition, make minor changes, and advance it.[118] There were many theoretical and empirical issues to be dealt with that required participation from competent researchers. Consequently, students saw an opportunity to advance their work and obtain a position in the discipline through their relationship with Parsons. They were also quite enthusiastic about the originality of his work and its potential for success.

In comparison, Sorokin's work can be viewed as mature, and with an intermediate and controversial position in the discipline. Sorokin's exemplar, *Dynamics*, was a joint venture but not a creatively cooperative one. The four volumes represented a completed system that appeared when Parsons's fecund early works were beginning to emerge and elicit interest from Harvard and the discipline. The cooperation with several Russian scholars on *Dynamics* was not the type that involved them with Sorokin or his ideas. Most of his collaborators were paid to do specific specialized projects. They followed a schedule developed by Sorokin and were in the dark as to the hypotheses and theoretical interest that informed the work. The group was also geographically dispersed throughout the United States and Europe. Thus, the relationships between Sorokin and his collaborators explicitly precluded the involvement and contributory partnerships typical of Parsons and his collaborators.[119] Additionally, Sorokin's books after *Dynamics* were independent ones, and those published after 1946 moved further away from science and value-free empiricism toward ideological justifications for an integrated moral society. Thus, while *Dynamics* offered some possibility of cooperative work, it did not produce the intellectual involvements necessary to form a school. In addition to Sorokin's work having an independent quality, its reception was too controversial and students were skeptical about its promise. Thus Sorokin's reception, his attitude, and his professional conflicts made his work appear less promising to graduate students and potential future collaborators.[120]

Alvin Gouldner provides good contextual insights into other factors that contributed to Parsons's ascent.[121] In *The Coming Crisis of Western Sociology*, he suggested that Parsonsian theory reflected a detachment from the emotions of the depression and World War II that was consistent with Harvard's institutional ethos. Both appeared aloof and clinical about the conditions of society and therefore able to be objective about the world around them. This institutional Olympus Complex gave the Harvard scholars support for a theoretical conceit that, in Gouldner's mind, was necessary to produce bold, detached, and innovative social theory.[122] Students in the department believed that the most important contribution they could make to resolving societal problems was to develop a scientific sociology that provided society the understanding needed to handle the current crises. Therefore, their private interests as scholars and academicians were consistent with the public interest of society. Through becoming good scientific sociologists, they could maximize their contributions to the country. Their orientation to society was removed and scientific. This attitude, like the Charles River, provided a buffer and a certain emotional distance from the mundane considerations of a world in pain. Indeed, the emphasis on objective, impersonal, detached scientific understanding made the values of the emerging sociology consistent with those of the institution. The character of Parsonsian theory fit the ethos and image of Harvard.

Although not explicitly noted by Gouldner, Harvard's ethnocentrism and nativism may have played a role in the Olympus Complex and had negative implications for Sorokin. The institution's history is wedded to Anglo-Saxon traditions, and, as a bastion of Brahminism, it may have had difficulty coping with Sorokin's style. There is ample historical evidence of antipathy in Boston toward the new immigrants. Indeed, Harvard's policy and the opinions of many of its notable figures were not immune to this general mood.[123] Additionally, the confrontational, challenging style of Russian intellectual exchange and pedagogy may have grated on the nerves and ears of Sorokin's students and colleagues. Add to this the flair, passion, and hyperbole characteristic of Russian expression and a style results that was at odds with the ethos and ambience that Gouldner calls the Olympus Complex.

Furthermore, Sorokin's work during most of this period was a product of both affect and intellect. He wrote with an involvement and passion foreign to the Parsonsian style. While his scope was broad and his erudition established, he was emotionally tied to his work. His writings thus have a flavor different from that of dispassionate science. The man who would describe himself as a "wild Jackass always kicking everything about"[124] may have fitted poorly into the society of Harvard University. Indeed, while the scope and flavor of Parsons's work fit well with the institutional ethos, one wonders if perhaps Sorokin's style, use of language, and passion were not an embarrassment to the department and to Harvard and, as such, tended to keep him from being taken more seriously by students and colleagues.

Tiryakian has further observed that founding a successful school depends, to a significant degree, on the charismatic qualities of the founder-leader's personality. Tiryakian uses charisma in this context to refer to the message of the leader. It is a revelation, a truth, an intellectually compelling body of work. The leader himself may have little or no personal charisma. Indeed, many students felt this was the case with Parsons; it was the work, not the fire of personality, that attracted their attention. This type of charisma requires that the personality be open, supportive, and sensitive to the ideas and contributions of others. Here again, there were substantial differences between Parsons and Sorokin. Sorokin conducted his classes as monologues. While students were impressed by the scope and power of his intellect and arguments, they also found him to be distant, demanding, and denigrating of their scholarly endeavors. Furthermore, because of his style and position as chairman, there were problems in communicating with Sorokin. Parsons, however, had different relationships with his students. There was a certain openness about him that implied that one's opinions counted for something. This was encouraging and attractive, and contributed to students' interest in him and his work.[125] Other factors that seem important in assessing the differences between these two theorists as teachers are their respective ages and the amount of informal contact they maintained with students. Parsons was fourteen years younger than Sorokin and thus closer in age to the first cohort of graduate students. This not only led to long-standing friendships with Merton, Davis, and others but also made him more approachable than was Sorokin, as elder statesman of the department. While Parsons most certainly was engaged actively with other members of the Harvard faculty, interests such as the Adams House discussion group gave him a special relationship with students, one that Sorokin did not have.[126]

From this discussion, it appears that Parsons was successful in obtaining a sound institutional footing not only in the Department of Sociology but also in the university. He had important and privileged ties with President Conant and Dean Buck. He maintained good relationships with L. J. Henderson, Crane Brinton, Joseph Schumpeter, and many members of the Society of Fellows, the Pareto Circle, and the Saturday Club. These brought him favorable attention from many Harvard notables.

During this and later periods, Parsons fulfilled other requisite conditions for founding a school. He was fortunate to have significant scholars like Edward Shils and Robert Merton work with him on developing major theoretical statements. The interpreter's role was approached, to a degree, by various scholars. Indeed, Kingsley Davis's *Human Society*, multiple editions of Robin Williams's *American Society*, and Marion Levy's *Structure of Society* shared fundamental insights into Parsonsian theory with a broader range of intellectuals, students, and social scientists. In this regard, Harry Johnson's excellent text is also noteworthy.[127]

Furthermore, Parsons won important positions in regional and national professional associations and had a particularly good relationship with Jeremiah Kaplan of the Free Press, who published a substantial portion of his works and those inspired by him. Thus, when the opportunity appeared for theoretical dominance within the profession—that is, the situation was ripe for a new perspective and sociology open for organizational change—Parsons was in a superb position to compete. The theoretical anomie that Tiryakian sees as a precondition for a new school to emerge was characteristic of sociology in the mid-1930s.

In 1935 the hostility toward Chicago's domination of the American Sociological Society and its official journal, the *American Journal of Soci-*

ology, was at its peak. Indeed, the result of the confrontation between the establishment and the rebels was to shift the control of the society away from Chicago and to replace the *American Journal of Sociology* with the *American Sociological Review* as the society's official journal.[128] Henrika Kuklick has argued that this rebellion reflected a broad pattern of theoretical reorientation in which hegemony shifted from Chicago toward the emerging structural functional perspective being developed at Harvard and Columbia.[129] Whether or not this thesis is correct, there was a theoretical and professional lacuna for Parsons to expand into. Thus, it appears that the state of sociology in the mid-1930s was structurally conducive to the emergence of a new theoretical direction.[130]

Given this opportunity, Parsons was able to put together Norbert Wiley's three-legged throne of ideas, theory groups, and control of the means of production and to enjoy this privileged perch for more than three decades.[131] Parsons's success in assuming the leadership of a department and later an emergent school resulted from significant differences in personality, style, and ideas between him and Sorokin. Parsons's presentation and manner were well suited to the institutional image of Harvard University. He understood the traditions, ethos, and character of the institution and therefore was able to interact with colleagues, administrators, and students in such a way as to preserve and extend the domain assumptions that structure the life world of Harvard. His ideas about education, social science, and sociological theory were innovative at a time when both Harvard and the discipline were looking for this particular type of innovation. These characteristics attracted a core of senior administrators and scholars, publishers, foundation officials, and promising graduate students. Combined with the fecundity and promise of his ideas, these features gave rise to an important intellectual tradition in sociology, a tradition that brought the man, his theory, and Harvard to a position of leadership at the cutting edge of sociology's development.

Sorokin's career went in another direction, and he established no school in the Tiryakian sense. This is attributable, at least in part, to what Don Martindale called the "primitive-warrior" element in Sorokin's character.[132] Indeed, Sorokin acknowledged this when he described himself as follows:

I seem to belong to the lone-wolf variety of scholars who, if need be, can do their work alone without a staff of research assistants or funds. On a small scale and with some reservation I can repeat what Albert Einstein said of himself: "I am a horse for a single harness, not cut out for tandem or teamwork; for well I know that in order to attain any definite goal, it is imperative that one person do the thinking and the commanding."[133]

6

Social Reconstruction

A New Direction

IT IS SAID THAT when God closes a door He often opens a window. This was the case for Sorokin after the fall of the Department of Sociology and the rise of the Department of Social Relations. The conduit was the Indianapolis philanthropist and entrepreneur Eli Lilly. Lilly, a man of broad interests, was deeply concerned about the tide of materialism engulfing society and retarding the development of character and spirituality. Indeed, he sensed that spiritual development lagged a century behind material progress and produced a crisis in which we lacked the character and values necessary to humanistically control our fate. In a 1936 conversation with his friend Glenn A. Black, Lilly mused about the caliber and spirituality of children. Was it possible to conduct experiments in character formation and develop a calculus for moral and spiritual development? What did we know about deepening moral values and preparing ourselves for the difficult future that awaited us? Lilly explored the problem and in the process discovered Sorokin.[1] Lilly wrote Pitirim in April 1942, saying:

Your book *Crisis of Our Age* has created a most favorable impression and influence among my friends and practically all are certain that your theories are correct. Our main interest now is what can we do about it. You say on page 320: "The best method for making the familistic relationship the foundation of future society is a purely technical matter not to be discussed here." Is there any place where the best methods . . . are set out? If you can answer the question it will be greatly appreciated.[2]

Sorokin replied that he had not written much in English about improving social relationships but more was forthcoming in *Man and Society in Calamity,* and "If my time and energy permit, I may soon write [even more] about it."[3] However, Sorokin's first major statement on human reconstruction would not come for some time. In addition to his departmental troubles, the next few years would witness his struggle with priestly and prophetic sociology. From 1942 to 1948 his efforts would be

166

split between the study of the modern crisis as evidenced in World War II and the extension of his system of sociological theory. But *Calamity* and his 1938 and 1944 works on war did set the stage for the emerging altruism studies.

In "A Neglected Factor of War"[4] Sorokin noted the astounding number of causes for war cited by investigators. These included sunspots, the alignment of the planets, instincts, overpopulation, the struggle for existence, economics, politics, Providence, and so on. The list was long, and many theories were loaded with inconsistencies, but the ultimate absurdity was the argument for multiple causation. Proponents argued that because no one factor caused war, it must result from several interrelated causes. Often these causes were such a hash that they defied unification and common measurement. Multiple causality became "a cloak that hides a profound ignorance . . . and prevents understanding the causes of war."[5] Theorists also failed to deal with the history and facts of peace and conflict. Sorokin suggested they start with the historical patterns of war and contributed his own data on 967 wars. His survey spanned eighteen hundred years and measured intensity by the number of casualties.[6] An adequate theory would account for these fluctuations in incidence and intensity. No existing theory did.

Sorokin next probed for the cause of war and peace. He observed that peace prevails when relationships between nations are based on stable, clearly understood, and shared values. Conversely, conflict ensues when relationships are based on a weak and unstable value consensus. Correspondingly, the more discongruent the values within a nation, the more likely internal conflicts. When these propositions were applied to the data, he found a provocative fit. The Middle Ages, a time of stable social relations, was relatively peaceful. But the thirteenth-century change from an agrarian to an industrial order was a time of upheaval and an escalating war curve that continued until the seventeenth century. A new order stabilized in the eighteenth and nineteenth centuries, and the curve declined. By the end of the nineteenth century that order was cracking. In the twentieth century the tempo of change became feverish, and "we entered the bloodiest century in the whole history of the Western World."[7] Sorokin encouraged acceptance of a shared body of values to stabilize and integrate the contemporary global system. They were humanity's best chance for a peaceful world.

The outline for a global consensus is found in "The Conditions and Prospects of a World Without War."[8] Peaceful consensus is based on acceptance of an Integral epistemology and reality in which science moves beyond empirical truth, toward new ethical norms shaped by the transcendent values of the great world religions. In such a world humans are again seen as incarnations of the divine rather than "mere biological organisms . . . or psychoanalytical libidos."[9] These values eliminate old institutions and change the foundation of social solidarity. The system of contractual relations crumbles and is replaced by one of familistic relationships. Economics and politics no longer exist for profit or power but to provide service to society. The differences between rich and poor, the rulers and the ruled are minimized, and society becomes a public trusteeship based on familial norms. If humankind does not move toward this, peace will evade us and we will face bigger, more terrible wars.

What are the chances for such a change? Isn't it unrealizable and utopian? Sorokin believed not, because these conditions were not new to human history: "In spite of the gravity of the great crises . . . human beings have always been able somehow to create new forms of culture and society that have eventually terminated the crisis. . . . there is no evidence whatsoever that a new sociocultural renaissance is impossible. . . . [Indeed] there is every reason to suppose that it can recur in the future."[10]

The catalyst for the renaissance is discussed in *Man and Society in Calamity*. There Sorokin explored how hunger, disease, and war affected mind and led to the deterioration of social behavior and organization. To restore a humane order we must move toward an Integral culture, which requires that Integral knowledge and values be transformed into personal and collective action. The trigger for transformation was altruism. All other solutions were inadequate:

None of the prevalent prescriptions against international and civil wars . . . can eliminate or notably decrease these conflicts. . . . Tomorrow the whole world could become democratic and yet wars and bloody strife would not be eliminated because democracies happen to be no less belligerent and strife-infected than autocracies. . . .

The same goes for education in its present form. . . . Since the tenth century . . . education has made enormous progress . . . and yet the international wars, the bloody revolutions . . . have not decreased. On the contrary, in the most scientific and most educated twentieth century they have reached an unrivaled height and made this century the bloodiest among all. . . .

The same goes for religious changes when these are not backed by increased altruization of persons and groups. Without a notable increase of unselfish, creative love (as ideally formulated in the *Sermon on the Mount*) in overt behavior . . . in social institutions and culture, there is no chance for a lasting peace.[11]

The solution to the crisis of modern civilization is an integral society, and the bridge to this new order is the altruization of humanity.

Sorokin's struggles with the roles of prophet and priest are captured by Read Bain in his review of *Calamity*. Bain praises *Calamity* as:

a return to the method and manner of *The Sociology of Revolution* and *Social Mobility* which, with *Contemporary Sociological Theories* are his best books to date. . . . it is a systematic and objective analysis of the impact of war, revolution, famine and pestilence upon social life. It fails to be convincing mainly when it is tied up to the trendless-flux, sensate-ideational dichotomy, and the clarion call to return to the Kingdom of God.[12]

The scholarly value of the work is its factually based, analytically driven disaster theory of social change. While not without problems,[13] Sorokin's use of data and his development of insightful propositions recall

the natural-science, preprophetic Sorokin we used to know. . . . however . . . when he tells us that the way out is a return to the Kingdom of God . . . he becomes a prophet of doom rather than deliverance. . . . A scientist should not prophesy, but if he must he should prophesy for the future not the prescientific past. . . . if these sensate-ideational, Kingdom of God ideas are overlooked, we could almost believe that Sorokin is returning to the earlier type of work for which he is justly famous.[14]

However, such ideas cannot be overlooked. J. L. Gillian's review cites Sorokin as using the tools of both an inductive scientist and a prophet. While agreeing with Sorokin's emphasis on the values of the Kingdom of God as the best way of preventing calamities, Gillian points out that this is a judgment of "faith, not a scientific deduction."[15] Others, like H. A. Reingold, Floyd N. House, and Orville Prescott, see the book as suggestive but also as "the obvious pompously proclaimed,"[16] "full of humorless truisms,"[17] and a reiteration of the obvious.[18] Thus, while it has some theoretical value, the evangelical insistence on the Kingdom of God as humankind's only hope for salvation limits its utility as a work of science. At best it is "a basis for further study."[19]

Sorokin's next book returned to theoretical issues. In the fourth volume of *Dynamics* he acknowledged that his theory of culture change was incomplete and promised a more comprehensive framework in *Sociocultural Causality, Space, Time*.[20] Sorokin believed new concepts were needed for theoretical growth and to liberate the social disciplines from imitation of the natural sciences. Causality, space, and time, he argued, are equally important in both, but for social analysis they must be different.

Sorokin's sociocultural system had three components: individuals, objects/artifacts, and the system of ideas that gave them unity and meaning. Sociocultural space was also distinguished by three planes: the planes of meaning, vehicles (objects), and agents (social actors). Social time reckons intervals by behavior or patterns of activity and not solar equivalents. Societies often keep their histories in terms of social beginnings, times of challenge, and golden periods of achievement. Years are reckoned as seasons or periods of planting, tending, and harvesting. Similarly, the days, weeks, and months are defined by personal and collective activities that establish a rhythm for life. Hence social time is different from the quantitative units used by the physicist or mathematician. To better understand social life requires explanations that integrate individuals, objects, and events into a comprehensible system of meaning. This Sorokin called meaningful-causal explanation.

The incorporation of these new concepts with the historical material in *Dynamics* significantly advanced Sorokin's Integral sociology. This new theoretical approach, while foreshadowed in *Dynamics,* was now more explicitly developed and grounded in Integralist epistemology and the trinity of truth. Here Sorokin again asserts that human beings are three-dimensional and that social life is a special reality not reducible to biological or psychological explanations. What makes humankind unique is that we are creatures of meaning, and to understand our world requires a special field of study. The meanings that direct social life are unlike the forces that direct the physical and biological worlds. Cultures are not hardwired and deterministic; instead, their changes exhibit a quality of choice derived from the collective decisions that members make when confronting specific situations. The qualities of these meaningfully constructed, willfully driven realities distinguish them from the organic and inorganic worlds. Hence, different concepts are needed to describe and analyze sociocultural systems.

Sorokin takes his next theoretical step in *Society, Culture, and Personality: Their Structure and Dynamics: A System of General Sociology.* Much of this volume integrates earlier works. The discussion of society and culture draws heavily on *Dynamics,* while the resulting generalizations point to problems described in *Crisis of Our Age.* The "news" is in the sections on personality, where Sorokin brings the systems together and focuses on social organization and the development of the self. For Sorokin personality is relentlessly molded by society and culture. Even before birth, culture shapes us biologically through norms of exogamy or endogamy, monogamy or polygamy. Culture may also limit conceptions within social groups or mandate infanticide for certain genders or social strata. At birth we inherit advantages or disadvantages in the forms of race, gender, religion, and social class. Culture also sets the parameters for a predictable life cycle through which members acquire certain skills, attributes, and characteristics. Culture, in this sense, is a playwright who assigns us specific positions and then writes our roles.

Beginning with the family, school, and adolescent peers, we are continuously socialized to meet expectations of specific and generalized others. To the degree that our reference groups are homogeneous, we develop a unified sense of self. Heterogeneity segments our personality and increases role ambiguity and conflict. This often results in poorly integrated personalities with a proclivity toward deviance. As we advance through the life cycle, each stage challenges us to make new decisions that form our identity and temperament.

At the microsociological level culture sets the routines of daily life. These time budgets determine the conscious or unconscious priorities that frame our identity. They result in weekly, monthly, and yearly rhythms that contextualize our lives and identities.

The tendency toward consistency and stability is shaken by rapid social changes that produce emotional and spiritual dislocations requiring a search for new normative structures to reestablish meaning. Personal adjustment is often accompanied by pain and loss as individuals attempt to adapt. People deal with these stresses and strains in various ways. Some refuse to take them seriously and instead cynically accommodate to structures that they find meaningless. Others become neurotic or melancholic, escaping through alcohol, hedonism, or suicide. Still others see change as an opportunity for enrichment and growth, and accommodate to it in ways consistent with their characters. When change produces a better life, personal pressures are reduced. When it is disruptive and overpowering, many lose their equilibrium and, like ships without rudders, become characterless, superficial, and uncertain.[21]

Because personality is externally determined, one wonders how to account for differences in individuals who are bound by the same social and cultural conditions. Furthermore, are there social configurations that maximize harmony and facilitate well-adjusted personalities? Sorokin's answer to the first is unsatisfying because he explains differences only as a product of the "creative x," then tells us little of its character. However, he is more explicit about the Integral social arrangements that sustain well-formed personalities. Such a culture and social structure emphasize cooperation over competition and collectivism over individualism; they have few distinctions in wealth and power. Force as an arbiter of human conduct is abolished, and behavior is directed by norms based on the Ten Commandments and the Sermon on the Mount. Social institutions are guided by familistic values, not contracts or coercion. With these changes and a new system of Integral truth, an age of certainty replaces one of uncertainty. Humans realize their potential and become less egoistic, violent, and antisocial. This new society gives rise to a new humanity and produces a world free of violence, war, and brutality.[22]

The integrative character of this work is clearly evident and was grasped by many reviewers. For most it was an asset because it pulled together a complex, historically grounded body of work into a sociological system that was systematic and provocative. Floyd N. House favored Sorokin's focus on meanings, values and norms, and the holistic approach to society, culture, and personality. The work made explicit many sociological principles conceived in previous efforts and synthesized them into a suggestive, challenging model. While the book was not without critics, House concluded that it merited "respectful consideration."[23]

Nicholas Timasheff praised it as a comprehensive supersystem that filled the gaps of previous works with new ideas. Among them were the studies of group formation and change, cooperation and conflict, and personality development. However, Sorokin's sociocultural universe, like his ideas on personality, was overly deterministic and obscured the voluntary and spontaneous elements of social action. Furthermore, Timasheff questioned Sorokin's focus on values as the glue of the sociocultural order. He found the approach Platonistic and favored one based on culture as a response to human needs:

Men, the real men forming social groups, interacting, creating, transmitting and modifying culture, do that to meet their needs. The contemplation of this aspect of sociocultural life gives rise to the functional approach centering around the problem: What social groups really do. The integration of the functions of the various social groups into the total social process is probably the very key to the understanding of the innumerable facts to be covered by general sociology.[24]

In spite of their important differences, Timasheff viewed the volume as an outstanding contribution to general sociology.

Sidney Hook blasted Sorokin for attempting to make "historical destiny" a scientific rather than a poetic or religious concept.[25] While reading the book is a grueling task because of its "barbarous terminology and underbrush of tables, graphs and footnotes" this difficulty pales when compared with the inadequacy of Sorokin's theory of social change. Hook's first volley is directed toward the principle of immanent causation, which he finds tautological. It is of no use to say that people die or societies change because it is their nature to do so; we want to know the nature of death and change, what drives them, what factors must be controlled to preserve life and alter social order. Furthermore, Sorokin never *proves* that his cultural types are based on distinctive concepts of reality. As is, they blur tremendous differences among contemporary cultures. Consequently, his explanations of order and change lack precision, are pompously and dogmatically stated, and provide little theoretical understanding of either.

These flaws are clearer when one concentrates on Sorokin's causes for wars, revolutions, and murder. Simply stated, they result from the incompatible value systems of the belligerents. Therefore, peace will prevail when the basic values of all humanity are shared and taken from the Sermon on the Mount and the Golden Rule. This assertion overlooks two historical facts: such values have never actually prevailed in any nation-state, and we have enjoyed long periods of peace. Sorokin is dissatisfied with anything less than a utopia. Indeed, his position is akin to one that maintains that "there is no point to curing a man's illness unless we can give him an assurance of immortality."[26] Furthermore, explaining war as a result of incompatible values is either "an empty tautology or an utter absurdity."[27] Germany and Turkey fought against England and Russia in World War I. Are the values of English and Russian culture any less compatible than those of English and German culture? Why nations war is much more complex than a difference in values, and value consensus will not in and of itself produce peace. What is needed is an accepted body of rules and procedures that allow us to negotiate our differences with a minimum of coercion.

Sociocultural Causality, Space, Time was also critically reviewed in the major sociological journals. Floyd N. House, in *Social Forces*, found the book suggestive, but Sorokin "does not convincingly show that sociocultural space and time must be used in the social sciences as *substitutes for* the highly generalized space and time of the physical sciences. . . . In some passages he seems to be arguing about the *words* to be used in the social sciences rather than the concepts to be designated by the words."[28] Kurt Wolff, in a thoughtful and careful review, observed that Sorokin's "systematic insistence on space and time as referential principles of sociology . . . seems more of an imitation of the natural sciences than 'a declaration of independence' from them."[29] An anonymous critic in the *American Sociological Review* caustically wrote the following:

Some more Sorokinese! Why Duke University Press found it advisable to publish a systematized collection of key paragraphs from *Social and Cultural Dynamics* passeth human understanding. Sorokin, of course, can be understood. . . . one may speculate as to why our eminent author has not yet been called into the State Department as a special adviser; surely his principles of integralist sociology would fit well with what seem to be our official tendencies toward clerical Fascism.[30]

Sorokin's struggles with sociologists over theoretical issues and the resentments they engender may result from the task he has set for himself: to develop a generalizing descriptive science of the social world. Is such a science possible? Rushton Coulborn argues, probably not. The order inherent in the physical world and the repetitions in events that it produces are not the same as those found in the psychological and sociological realms, where events resemble each other but their repetitions are far less exact.[31] Conformities emerge in the physical world from a tremendously large number of observations. Even so, the evidence from the hard sciences suggests a probabilistic, indeterminate universe. Patterns of repetition are strong there, but events are not identical and uncertainty is a characteristic of order. Indeterminacy increases in the superorganic world, and we do not have the data on which to establish universal laws of sociocultural order and change. Indeed, the study of large civilizations à la Toynbee, Spengler, and Sorokin go back no more than eight thousand years, a tiny cosmological moment that would contain only the merest hints of uniformities if we had the methods and database to detect them.[32]

Instead of pursuing a classificatory system for the social sciences, Sorokin should pursue his earlier and more productive focus on how societies evolve. Indeed, Coulborn argues that "the evolution of cultural 'supersystems' is his most important contribution to knowledge, however much it is marred by his peculiar methodology."[33] Lessons from the history of science, philosophy, and the philosophy of history suggest that "the historical evolutionary method, dealing with development, is the primary mode of knowledge, and that systematic, classificatory, purely descriptive method is secondary."[34] Clearly, Sorokin is on the right track, but his desire for classification and precision carry him far beyond the facts we can accurately observe. This quest for an unprovable certainty is the root from which many critics derive their objections. Sorokin's method simply will not sustain his arguments with the precision he desires. Instead, he should realize that what he has produced in *Dynamics* and the works that follow is a broad and valuable philosophy of history. It is a start, not a science, and at this time cannot become one.[35]

Prophetic Sociology and the Struggle for Identity

Sorokin became more resolute in his move toward prophetic sociology as he put the finishing touches on *Society, Culture and Personality*. Recalling this volume and *Causality* he observed:

I was glad to have these works published. Even while I was working on *Society, Culture and Personality* the relentless occurrence of calamities . . . persistently disturbed me and seriously interfered with the book's completion. The pressure of these crises grew so strong that it prompted me to decide . . . I would devote all my free time to the investigation of the means of preventing the imminent annihilation of the human race and ways out of the deadly crisis. . . . Motivated by it, I rushed the completion of my work and then began to orient myself in the little-explored field of these problems. . . . This . . . led me to the establishment of the Harvard Research Center in Creative Altruism and to the new phase of my studies.[36]

Shortly thereafter Sorokin wrote to Eli Lilly, saying:

In 1942 I had the privilege of receiving from you two letters that expressed your interest in the ideas expressed in my *Crisis of Our Age*. This . . . prompts me to take the liberty of writing to you about the following matter. If the matter appears to you unimportant, just disregard my letter. . . . As a result of a long study of human affairs and the present situation I have come to the conclusion that, unless human conduct and relationships become really more altruistic and nobler, nothing can save humanity from the third World War and apocalyptic destruction: neither UNO, nor World Government, nor armed power.

Meanwhile we know little how to make human beings good and especially how to make them to practice the noble ideas they preach. . . . Billions are spent for invention of devilish means of destruction and nothing . . . for how to make human beings more mutually loving, respecting, solidary. . . . Such a knowledge becomes now the most important thing, the question of life and death of humanity itself.

Motivated by these reasons I decided, from now on, to devote all my free time to the study of these problems. . . . A successful attack on these problems [requires] . . . at least as great a concentration of brains as [produced] the atomic bomb. . . . In other words, a special research Institute in which such brains are brought together. . . . For the Institute some funds are necessary. Hence my letter to you. Perhaps you may be interested in helping to organize such an Institute and becoming one of its initiators? . . . On my part . . . I offer my humble services, time, and energy, without any remuneration whatsoever. I have no strictly personal aims in this matter. The only reason of my initiative is the pending catastrophe of humanity, if human actions and relationships remain as they are.[37]

Lilly promptly responded, giving his endorsement of the idea and a pledge of financial support.

The letter which you wrote on April 11, is most inspiring and anyone that would argue with the points made would be foolish indeed. . . . It would or will indeed be a privilege to assist in such an effort, but unfortunately commitments have been made involving a high percentage of any funds available to me for such fine purposes for the next year or two. If, however, a sum of $10,000 or $20,000, together with contributions from others, would back you in getting the work started, I shall be very glad to give that sum as soon as you feel a practical plan has been made. Later I hope additional and more substantial sums could be forthcoming.[38]

Lilly's commitment allowed Sorokin to advance his plans for the Harvard Research Center in Creative Altruism. Sorokin's review of the literature showed that altruistic love had been largely ignored by the scientific community. Curiously, while many "modern sociologists and psychologists viewed the phenomena of hatred, crime, war and mental disorders as legitimate objects for scientific study, they quite illogically stigmatized as theological preaching or non scientific speculation any investigation of the phenomena of love, friendship, heroic deeds and genius."[39] However, the Center would view altruistic love as a power capable of stopping modern calamities. Sorokin was committed to discovering its nature and learning how to produce, accumulate, and use it to form better human beings and more altruistic social relationships.[40]

Writing to Lilly in May 1946, Sorokin reported that the financial and organizational plans for the Center were gaining ground. Two personal friends, Serge Koussevitzky and Igor I. Sikorsky, were deeply interested in the project and had pledged financial support. Combined with the Lilly grant, the Center now had a budget approaching fifty thousand dollars.[41] To minimize red tape Sorokin, on the advice of President Conant, had established a university account for the Center. This simplified tax concerns, made contributions easier, and still gave Sorokin control. Sorokin also suggested creating a board of trustees to advise on nonscholarly matters.[42]

The initial selection of scholars and projects began in the summer of 1946. Sorokin concentrated on physical anthropology, clinical psychology, and Hindu systems of mind development to map out six studies of altruism. He also wrote Lilly that the resulting publications would acknowledge his contributions and support.[43] Lilly responded that he preferred anonymity, but that Sorokin should do what was necessary for proper record keeping.[44] With these arrangements completed, Sorokin finished *Society, Culture and Personality* and turned full attention to the Center's exemplar: *The Reconstruction of Humanity*.

In *Reconstruction* Sorokin analyzed the shortcomings of the peace plans discussed in his 1944 "Prospects" article. He concluded that all such plans were flawed by their neglect of altruism. Whatever else peace required, it would not come without more sympathy and love. These are the foundations of the altruistic, familial relationships necessary for peace. He next asked what makes individuals and groups more altruistic.

Knowing these variables could promote the social and personal improvements necessary for a peaceful social order.[45]

Sorokin began *Reconstruction* by defining altruism and its forms. Altruism is action that produces and maintains the physical and/or psychological good of others. It is formed by love and empathy, and in its extreme form may require the free sacrifice of self for another.

Altruistic acts vary in type and intensity. Sorokin described these with an egoism-altruism continuum. Egoism, at one extreme, is the pursuit of one's own good even at the expense of others. Next is the nonaltruistic behavior typical of those who help others *only* because they are paid for the service. This is followed by the pseudoaltruism of love preached but not practiced; in its hypocritical form it sets standards for others that one does not follow. At the other extreme is genuine altruism, which is based on love and focused on the good of another. While personal pleasure may result from such acts, it is not the motivator. These kindnesses would be given even to the disadvantage or suffering of the doer.[46]

Altruism also varies in scope and intensity. Scope is the social reach of a person's altruism. One may be kind to family, friends, and coethnics while being nonaltruistic or egoistic toward all others. These are intragroup altruist and extragroup egoist behaviors. Intensity varies from small acts of kindness motivated by expectations of rewards to a boundless all-giving, all-forging love. At the top of the scale are those who love not only their intimates but their enemies; Jesus, Gandhi, Francis of Assisi, and the Buddha are examples.[47]

Because altruism is a social act, Sorokin asks if certain groups are more altruistic than others. The answer was yes, but this part of his analysis is also primitive. Primary groups (family and friends) are more altruistic than secondary groups (businesses, political parties, trade unions). Cooperative groups, bound by affective ties, are frequently altruistic, but as competition increases altruism declines. While many groups fall between these extremes, modern society is dominated by secondary groups.[48]

Sorokin tied human emancipation to progressive altruization. Specifically, change must happen at three interrelated levels: personal, cultural, and social. Individual changes precede social and cultural transformations. Sorokin argued that mindful people must learn to give their superconsciousness increasing control over their consciousness. He equates consciousness with intelligence but sees no close relationship between it and superconsciousness. Intellectual growth shows no measurable association with prosocial behavior. If we index intellectual development using educational attainment, literacy rates, university attendance, and the number of inventions and scientific discoveries, we would see great progress from the twelfth century to the present. However, no decrease in crime, wars, and violence has resulted. This led Sorokin to conclude: "Either the conscious intellect is impotent . . . or is not the factor positively connected with altruistic phenomena generally or their sublime form particularly."[49]

If intelligence is not the key, then what is? Sorokin's answer is an integral epistemology in which superrational intuitions guide our rational insights. Superrational intuition is a dimension of knowing inaccessible through cognition or sensory awareness. It is a form of insight that allows us to see the eternal in the ordinary and to feel things that transcend the ordinary with an unquestionable certainty. We learn it from great religious leaders and creative artists, among others. Acceptance and cultivation of this form of knowing are essential to an individual's altruistic progress.

When one accepts supernatural intuition as a form of knowledge, then awareness can grow by exercises that mobilize our higher powers. One may practice yoga, search for perfection through selfless good works, seek asceticism and solitude, or pursue enlightenment through creative work in art, religion, and philosophy.[50] In short, greater awareness must be transformed into action.

These actions should guide our performance of social roles. For example, as a parent, one takes care of family and children in ways that benefit their character and development. As an artist or politician, one stops producing vulgarized trash or unjust legislation. As a scientist or inventor, one discovers and invents constructively rather than becoming part of the arsenal of destructive minds that push us closer to nuclear madness. As a teacher, one develops in students a critical quality of mind that seeks truth and good rather than the creation of mindless entities whose expertise is found in the blind application of a paradigm to problems that may be destructive to humankind. As a businessman, a laborer, a mechanic, or a clerk, an individual performs his or her role informed by either altruism or egoism and consequently contributes to the prosocial or antisocial climate of society. For Sorokin culture is the product of millions of small individual acts and deeds. If each of us simply avoids the selfish abuse of our functions, then the world is improved. But if each, because of a deep sense of responsibility, attempts to altruize our actions, then the world is enriched.[51]

Sorokin devoted much of the remainder of *Reconstruction* to cultural and institutional criticism. Modern, materialistically dominated, sensate society must be moved toward Integralism. As in *Dynamics,* he demonstrates the problems faced by science, technology, the arts, religion, and philosophy, and the need for change if we are to advance.[52] He continues with an institution-by-institution description of modern society. The family has been the most effective agent of altruization. Unfortunately, it is now in decay. Divorce, adultery, materialism, self-gratification, and personal happiness have replaced love, duty, honesty, and responsibility as the basis of family life. Family has become trivialized and must be restored to a place of importance. To do this, family members must be less egoistic and more responsible for each other's good. Public opinion must renounce permissiveness and pressure people to return to traditional family values. Legislation must stabilize the family and reassert moral community.[53] Schools are the next influences on personality development and conduct. From kindergarten to the university the school is in partnership with the family to properly socialize new members of society. It is an agent for the development of sound values, controlled behavior, integrity, and character. It teaches not only a group's knowledge but how to think critically and responsibly, and to move beyond the known. The school can also be an important agent for inculcating altruism as a personal value and social condition of behavior.[54] Combined with their commitment to truth, learning, and critical thought, schools could make us more socially responsible. Sadly, modern schools fail in many of these responsibilities.[55]

On the other hand, Sorokin finds the world's major religions "supremely edifying." Like different languages that denote the same objects in their own ways, religions express distinct notions of God, humanity, and the paths to God. Religions abound with ethical imperatives to guide human actions. However, the vital sense of God in society has been lost. Modern religions are now challenged to recreate genuine religious experiences; to foster ethical behavior; to become "universal in the sense that everyone, regardless of his race, . . . creed, age, sex or status is regarded as a sacred end . . . ; to come into harmony with existing science and logic."[56]

This fusion of religion with the truths of the senses and rationality unites them as a "team dedicated to the discovery of the perennial values and to . . . shaping man's mind and conduct."[57] This is the trinity of integral truth that allows us to grasp ultimate reality. To reach it, religions must develop new and better techniques to spiritually and ethically transform humankind. It is to these techniques, among other things, that the Harvard Research Center in Creative Altruism would later be dedicated.

Sorokin ends his institutional critiques with observations on the state and economy. The state can provide altruistic social services for all or be the tool of a selfish minority. It has long been humanity's master but now must be reformed. States must first follow the same laws that bind citizens. If a citizen cannot kill, then neither can a state. A new world order must redefine sovereignty and particularly the rights to wage war and suppress, punish, and execute citizens. Correspondingly, research and social policy should develop new methods of conflict resolution and, along with universal laws and a global bill of rights, promote peace and cooperation. The political process must become focused on service, not power.[58] Such changes require new economic norms that redefine the distribution of wealth and the nature of wages, competition, and cooperation, and that promote equitable national and global economies.[59]

Sorokin's analysis ends with a map for social "reconstruction." Humankind must discover, develop, and use love to transform primary and secondary relationships. We must broaden and deepen the scope and intensity of our altruism. Sorokin argues that social perfectibility begins with individuals and spreads from their primary and secondary groups to concerted action at the institutional level. Coordinated institutional transformations result in systemwide sociocultural change. Social and cultural change is thus driven by the efforts of altruistic individuals acting in primary groups and formal organizations. It is part of their political function to teach altruism and convince ever-larger segments of society of the urgency and feasibility of their proposed reconstruction of humanity. Each organization focuses on specific challenges and coordinates its efforts to transform altruistic values into personal and social actions that progressively alter the character of nations and move them in the desired direction. Thus individual behavior, cultural values, and social institutions are modified in an orderly fashion, and eventually the entire sociocultural system becomes more peaceful and creative.[60] It was to this vision of society and character that Eli Lilly was most deeply drawn.

The Harvard Research Center in Creative Altruism

By the time that *Reconstruction* appeared, Lilly had incorporated several of Sorokin's ideas into his writings and speeches. Lilly was moved by Pitirim's insistence on the primacy of family, love, and religion. The harmony in their thoughts is captured in Lilly's essay "The Nemesis of Materialism."[61] Lilly writes:

Pitirim's younger brother, Prokopiy, holding his daughter. Velikiy Ustyug, 27 July 1929.

Sorokin on the Martha Washington, *1923. By permission of Sergei P. Sorokin.*

Pitirim the sociologist-in-exile, and Elena, as a graduate student at Charles University, Prague 1922. By permission of Sergei P. Sorokin.

Sorokin with colleagues and students from the University of Minnesota. Left to right: T. Lynn Smith, Carle C. Zimmerman, Pitirim, Gorrado Gini, Mr. and Mrs. Elio D. Monachesi, Sir Alexander M. Carr-Saunders, and Irene Barnes–Taueber.

In the Minnesotan cornfields, summer of 1926. Left to right: Yuri (George) Anderson, Elena Sorokin, and Pitirim. Elena had received her Ph.D. in botany from the University of Minnesota in 1925 and was then an active participant in studies on diseases of cereal crops. By permission of Sergei P. Sorokin.

Carle C. Zimmerman and Pitirim A. Sorokin in Minnesota, probably in 1929.
By permission of Sergei P. Sorokin.

Crimson *cartoon of Sorokin lecturing.*

The Sorokin's home in Winchester, Massachusetts, in May 1934. Elena is holding the newly arrived Sergei as a proud father takes the picture. By permission of Sergei P. Sorokin.

The boys grow up. Peter and Sergei in 1948. Peter had just entered Harvard, and Sergei was a junior at Winchester High School. By permission of Sergei P. Sorokin.

Sorokin and audience at the Harvard Faculty Club. By permission of Sergei P. Sorokin.

Pitirim and Elena at the Harvard tercentenary celebrations, Cambridge, Massachusetts, 1936. By permission of Sergei P. Sorokin.

Pitirim Sorokin as president of the International Institute of Sociology, Paris, late summer of 1937. By permission of Sergei P. Sorokin.

A characteristic picture of Sorokin working at home in Winchester, Massachusetts.

The mature Sorokin, 1954. By permission of Sergei P. Sorokin.

At the American Sociological Association, New York, late August 1960. Left to right: Georges Gurvitch (Sorbonne), Pitirim, Robert M. MacIver, and T. Lynn Smith. By permission of Sergei P. Sorokin.

Pitirim and Arnold Toynbee at the first Synopsiskongress *of the International Society for the Comparative Study of Civilizations (ISCSC), October 1961. By permission of Sergei P. Sorokin.*

Peter, Elena, and Pitirim at the Sorokin's summer cottage at Lake Memphremagog. There Pitirim, an avid fisherman, provided daily catches for the table and never read a serious book or wrote a line. The family vacationed at the cottage for two months each year. By permission of Sergei P. Sorokin.

At home reading the paper, sometime in the mid-1960s. By permission of Sergei P. Sorokin.

We must push back materialism into its real place. . . . We must know that truth, goodness and beauty are absolute values. The precepts of the Sermon on the Mount must be established in all human relationships. There must be a spiritualization of mentality and an ennoblement of conduct. Expedience, pleasure and utility must give way to duty. Licentious freedom must be given up for justice. Coercion and egotistic selfishness must be replaced by all forgiving love.[62]

Shortly after the appearance of *Reconstruction*, Lilly phoned Sorokin, saying he would be in Boston in April and would like to meet.[63] They agreed on lunch at the Parker House and there began a warm friendship. At lunch Sorokin reported spending only $248 from the original $20,000 to write *Reconstruction* and that the remaining money would support his work for some time. Lilly was surprised and asked if he could "put more steam into this business." Sorokin quickly affirmed that he could, but it might require millions of dollars. This was beyond Lilly's reach, but through the Lilly Endowment he offered $100,000 to be paid over a five-year period. Excitedly, Sorokin asked for time to discuss this with colleagues and to think about the opportunities it presented. Shortly afterward, he accepted the offer.

Leaving Boston, Lilly returned to Indianapolis and explained to his brother J. K. Lilly Jr. the substance of the meeting and his plans for the Lilly Endowment's support of the Harvard project. His brother was less enthusiastic but agreed that the proposition could go to the endowment board in January. Lilly then wrote Sorokin, asking for a budget and statement of objectives for that meeting.[64]

Sorokin outlined the goals, immediate tasks, staffing, and budget for the Center in a 14 December 1948 letter to Lilly. Deriving its direction from *Reconstruction*, the Center's objective was to discover and develop techniques that could increase altruistic actions at all levels of society. Staffing would be minimal so that more money could go to researchers. Sorokin sent a list of prominent scholars, their projects, and plans for two volumes reporting the results. The cost was $25,000. This would be met by the pledged $20,000 for the year and the carryover of $19,500 from Lilly's previous support.[65]

Lilly sent the proposal to board members and selected advisers. Few were prepared for Sorokin's extravagant, unidiomatic style, and some worried that it might be a cover for a lack of focus, substance, and direction. J. K. Lilly Jr. responded with a simple "Phew!!!" Another member queried, "Is there no one but the Lilly Endowment to help finance this?"[66] That there was some concern about the project and Lilly's commitment to it is captured in the philanthropist's reply to

Sorokin. Lilly wrote: "Thank you for your letters of December 14 and 21. We have a meeting of the Board of the Lilly Endowment on the 3rd of January, but I will give you some advance information that if for any reason they feel they cannot back the project to the tune of $20,000 a year for five years, I will do it myself, so you can pursue your plans."[67] Lilly, perhaps at the suggestion of the endowment staff, also wrote that the payments would be made in March of each year. He continued: "I think possibly there should be some proviso however, that if the $20,000 is not spent during the year, we will be called upon to subscribe only a sum equal to the amount spent because we would not want to see the funds piling up on you. Would you have any objection to such a provision?"[68] Sorokin's reply was one of appreciation, and he raised no objection. He promised his best efforts to produce useful results and suggested that they name the Center after Lilly.[69]

This exchange reveals much about the character of Eli Lilly and the nature of his philanthropy. James Madison, in his biography of the Hoosier millionaire, observed that

philanthropy at a distance did not much appeal to Eli Lilly. He told an interviewer in 1972 that in deciding about grants his selection [was] simply made on the basis of personal interest and often on the basis of friendship. . . . His largest contributions were made not because he was asked but because he actively initiated the gift. And that initiation came because he developed, often on his own, ideas and programs he believed worthy of support. . . . His interest in character education reflects this central feature of his philanthropy and reveals a major facet of his deepest and most enduring interest.[70]

Lilly was also attracted to Sorokin's focus on religion and family. Early on, Sorokin had attributed to the family important responsibilities for the development of altruistic people and social institutions. Sadly, the modern family was in crisis and its potential for good was being lost. Personally, Lilly's family was a source of both happiness and pain. His father and his second wife, Ruth, provided love and stability. On the darker side, he carried the failure of his first marriage and blamed himself for its telling effects on Evie, his daughter. Her life never developed a proper focus, and she endured two divorces and bouts of alcoholism. Lilly acutely felt his daughter's pain and lack of purpose. Looking back on his divorce and the granting of custody to Evie's mother, he blamed himself. These decisions, he wrote, "haunted me to this day as a betrayal of Evie to an affectionless mother, to be raised by nurses until 15 or 16 years old, in a group of youngsters down east of not too high a type. To this denial of love and security I attribute most of Evie's troubles. I pray for forgiveness for my part in this sad affair."[71] In many of Sorokin's works Lilly frequently underlined passages about families without love producing children without self-control and the qualities necessary to behave lovingly and responsibly toward others. Indeed, Lilly's nephew J. K. Lilly III believed there was "a close connection between his uncle's interest in character development and Evie."[72]

Regardless of their reservations, the endowment directors voted unanimously to support the Harvard project, but two qualifications were added to the previous proviso: if Sorokin's leadership ended before five years, then grants would continue only if the university and the endowment agreed that the funds would be wisely spent; and the Lilly name should be left out of any printed publicity. Paul Buck was similarly notified, and the Corporation approved the Center in February 1949.[73] The new research institute became the Harvard Research Center in Creative Altruism and was housed in Emerson Hall.[74] Now, with his new direction clearly established, Sorokin reduced his teaching to half-time and put "more steam" into this shared project.

Social Science and Social Action

In spring 1949 Sorokin began a sabbatical leave to work on three volumes: *Altruistic Love, Explorations in Altruistic Love and Behavior: A Symposium,* and *Social Philosophies in an Age of Crisis.* All were published in 1950. *Altruistic Love* is a curious juxtaposition of a study of 3,090 Christian saints with that of a sample of "good neighbors" drawn from Tom Breneman's radio show *Breakfast in Hollywood.* Breneman's audience sent the names of kind, helpful "good neighbors" from whom Sorokin took five hundred of the more altruistic for further study. All were queried on what it meant to be a good neighbor; to what personal and social forces they attributed their altruistic outlooks and actions; how they became open to people different from themselves; and their social and personal characteristics.

Most good neighbors were motivated by the Golden Rule and a love of humanity.[75] For them altruism came from religion, parents, and family. Most were from large families, female, married, over forty years old, middle-class, and from rural origins. There was no relationship between their altruism and education, but 90 percent regularly attended religious services and were classified by Sorokin as "religious altruist." Good neighbors were also regular participants in voluntary organizations, and 86 percent belonged to between one and five such groups.

The data showed two main altruistic routes. The first was that of "fortunate altruists" who were born into large, well-adjusted religious families committed to the welfare of others. From youth on, they lived in a climate of altruism. The second path was that of "catastrophic altruists." They discovered their humanity through an unexpected event, "a conversion experience," that changed them from egoists to altruists. Regardless of type, Sorokin observed that both types of altruists lived longer, happier, and more peaceful lives—not lives without trouble but ones in which adversity was not destructive. Tragedy was a vehicle for growth, and altruism enriched and stabilized their lives.

For comparative purposes, Sorokin studied biographies of 3,090 Catholic saints taken from H. S. J. Thurston's revision of Butler's *Lives of the Saints*.[76] He found that even with the increase of female saints beginning in the eighteenth century, men accounted for 82 percent of the canonized. The sample also reflected a class bias, with 78 percent coming from wealth, nobility, and royalty. Most (57.2 percent) were from religious orders, and about a third of these were high church officials.

As with good neighbors, Sorokin wanted to know how people became saints. Butler reported the road to sainthood for only 27 percent of the group, and these Sorokin also labeled as fortunate or catastrophic. Family influence was strong for 43 percent of saints. These "fortunates" were self-consecrated to God at an early age. Their souls "were born before the fall of Adam," and they always felt a strong tie to the Deity. Others found God through a life-altering event. For these the route to God was one of spiritual growth through prayer. Many were martyrs who had no outstanding altruistic activity before their sacrifice. This was a common route for many saints before the advent of the Holy Roman Empire in the fourth century. At that time a "new model" emerged that found perfection through prayer, solitude, and asceticism.[77]

On the future of saintliness Sorokin was not optimistic. Saints had declined in number since the seventeenth century, and only one was canonized between 1900 and 1926. The downturn was due in part to the rise of sensate cultures and the end of religious wars (the largest source of martyrs) in the seventeenth century. In today's world Sorokin saw little place for saints: "Unless a renaissance of ideational or idealistic culture recurs as the dominant supersystem, the stream of saints may actually dry up, and the Christian-Catholic saint may become extinct."[78] Actually, the number of saints has increased substantially. Kenneth Woodward's recent study of saints shows that there were eight canonizations between 1903 and 1922, seventy from 1922 to 1978, and twenty-three from 1978 to 1989. In the latter period Pope John Paul II has also beatified 123 more potential saints. Beatification is the penultimate step in the making of saints, and John Paul II has canonized more saints than any other pope.[79]

While genuinely concerned about the future of goodness in a sensate world, Sorokin drew three conclusions from his studies. One, the capacity to love others has tangible rewards for the altruist; they live longer, more vital lives, and enjoy a deep sense of peace and happiness. Two, the potential of love for improving human relationships is tremendous. Three, now is the time to intensely study the energy of love and how to incorporate its power into a broader range of social relationships. It is to this theme that Sorokin addressed his next work, *Explorations in Altruistic Love and Behavior.*

Sorokin began his *Explorations* by differentiating the forms of love into the religious, ethical, ontological, physical, biological, psychological, and social. The discussion shows love to be a universal binding force that ties humans to God and to each other. It unites matter and bonds our transcendental values into a unity of truth, beauty, and goodness. It is a glue to integrate our personalities and bind us socially. Sorokin focused, however, on the "psychosocial empirical aspects" of love.[80] As an empirical phenomenon love has five measurable dimensions: intensity, extensiveness, duration, purity, and adequacy. Clearly Sorokin is referring here to observable qualities rather than precisely measurable ones.[81] Hate is the zero point for love's intensity. Its maximum is freely giving what we value most to or for another. Extensiveness refers to the range of people we love. Egoism, love of self, is its lowest point, and extensiveness increases as we come to love family, friends, countrymen, and then all humanity. Duration is how long love lasts, and purity refers to the motivation for love. Do we love another out of love alone, or do we seek our own material, political, or sexual satisfactions? Adequacy refers to how well love benefits those to whom it is directed. For example, a mother may handicap her child through overprotection and overindulgence. Her love would be more adequate if it prepared the child to deal with the world directly and in a less dependent way.

After discussing the interrelationships between these dimensions, Sorokin asked if love could be produced, accumulated, and distributed. Observing that "solidarity and peaceful relationships . . . do not fall . . . from heaven, . . . they have to be produced"[82]; and that this is done through actual social processes, the issue of "production" then becomes more than a figure of speech. Sociologically we can state the following: Love is produced by certain interactions among human beings; the more intense these interactions, the greater the production of love. Love is more intense and pure in small, primary groups and lessens as group size and diversity increase. Interactions that produce love are spontaneous and not organized to increase production, although a few individuals (e.g., great religious leaders and teachers) have attempted to do so. Similarly, groups like the family, close friends, religions, and small voluntary organizations also increase the amount of love in a society.

Sorokin speculated that society would benefit if love was organized and embedded in the ongoing actions of human groups. This would require society to produce more "creative heroes of love": great religious leaders like Jesus and heroes of intellect and beauty such as Newton and Mozart. They are role models for love, beauty, and truth. Their impacts transcend death, and through history they have influenced increasingly larger numbers of people. While such examples exceed the reach of the average person, the rank and file can increase the amount of love in the world "if they would cut in half their daily actions of hate and double their daily good deeds."[83] This simple change would greatly increase humane behavior in society and is easily within the individual's reach. However, Sorokin warns that the greater the devotion to one's primary groups, the more hostility there is toward out-groups. We must learn to reach out to socially distant groups and humanize our heretofore impersonal relations. These changes will create new normative expectations for relationships among society's key institutions. The question is How does one do this?

An individual's love grows by habituation. When we habituate prosocial behaviors, our capacity to treat people dearly increases and becomes part of our character. Just as exercise strengthens the body, loving builds the capacity to care. The more you do it, the greater its strength. As norms become organized on the principles of love, society becomes more altruistic and responsive to human need. The more we institutionalize love, the greater its impact on individual and collective actions.

The other essays in *Explorations* explore several related issues raised by Sorokin. Biological factors in altruism and peace are discussed by Therese Brosse, M. F. Ashley Montagu, and Trigent Burrow. Gordon Allport, J. B. Rhine, and S. David Kahn each write on different psychological approaches to love, hate, and friendship. Other essays cluster around developing altruism, and the volume concludes with empirical studies of prosocial and antisocial behavior. The book is indeed an exploration into altruism.

The third book to appear in 1950 was *Social Philosophies of an Age of Crisis,* which describes and criticizes the theories of eight social philosophers: Nikolai Danilevsky, Oswald Spengler, Arnold Toynbee, Walter Schubart, Nikolai Berdyaev, F. S. C. Northrop, Alfred L. Kroeber, and Albert Schweitzer. Sorokin concludes with "Toward a Valid Social Philosophy," where he discusses the areas of agreement between these theorists and their relation to his works.

In the macrosociological-philosophical sections all thinkers agree that civilizations, though small in number, are identifiable and real historical entities. All but Spengler assert that they go through periods of growth, decay, and transition but do not die. Furthermore, all civilizations illustrate a meaningful-causal unity based on acceptance of an ultimate value that defines their character. For Sorokin it was the sensate, ideational, and idealistic. Toynbee wrote of a dominant potentiality of a civilization: aesthetics for the Hellenic, religion for the Hindu, and science for Western societies. Berdyaev refers to the barbaric, medieval, and humanist. All also view periods of transition as times of crisis.

Sorokin finds most in common with Alfred Kroeber. Each worked inductively from a broad base of data and was concerned about the dynamics of creativity in science, music, art, and other institutions. They agreed that not all cultures pass through the same stages; there is no master pattern for cultural development; there is no law that once a culture blossoms it must decline without a chance of revival; no culture has been uniformly excellent in all its institutions; and cultural transitions are times of crisis that lead to better-adapted cultures. Many of the other key theorists also agree on several of these points. Sorokin ends the book with a discussion of values and the importance of social philosophy in times of cultural crisis.

Along with *Reconstruction*, these volumes introduced sociologists and the intellectual public to the new Harvard Center. Social science reviewers were struck by Sorokin's continued shift from empirical sociology to the philosophy of history, and then mysticism. E. K. Francis comments that with *Reconstruction* "Sorokin frankly relinquishes the chair of the social scientists for the lectern of the utopian philosopher."[84] Harry Elmer Barnes pairs Sorokin with Toynbee and labels both as neo–medicine men coming into their own.[85] Robert Rockafellow, in the *Annals of the American Academy of Political and Social Science*, concludes his review with "it is fitting that the book [*Reconstruction*] is dedicated to Mohandas K. Gandhi."[86] Harry E. Moore speculates that:

Professor Sorokin poses an interesting problem. Here is a man who has produced works which have gained the admiration of his colleagues; notably his *Contemporary Sociological Theories* and the *Source Book* in rural and urban sociology of which he is senior author. How to account for the change in attitude and technique, to say nothing of faith, which is distressingly apparent when one compares these works with *Reconstruction of Humanity*, or the fourth volume of *Social and Cultural Dynamics*?

The present work might be dismissed as evidence of an unfortunate digression, or even as a tragic diversion of a line of development. But the vital question would not be answered. That question is: What has turned Sorokin into the mystic he now is?[87]

An answer for a reflective scholar is to see Sorokin's transition as grounded in his identity as a sociologist honestly challenging his discipline. William Kolb poses this approach when he confronts Sorokin and the discipline with his thoughtful review of *Social Philosophies of an Age of Crisis:*

Who reads Sorokin? Whatever the answer to that question, sociologists generally are not included in the attentive group. To be sure *Social Mobility* and *Contemporary Sociological Theories* are frequently cited by sociologists and are used by them in teaching and research. But the *Dynamics* and all its progeny, among which can be included the book under review, are lost in sociological limbo. They are no longer even criticized, simply ignored. The present work offers a ground on the basis of which we can get some idea of why Sorokin now finds himself at the far edge of the sociological endeavor. . . . The superficial reasons are easily discerned. Sorokin is now a philosopher of history.[88]

This new designation carries with it all the weaknesses associated with that field: vague concepts and categories, inability to prove hypotheses, argument by illustration, and evaluations of others based on their judgments of one's work. But is Sorokin "as guilty of these offenses against the scientific canon as he has been charged with being?"[89] Kolb observes that with the rise of contemporary functional theory Sorokin's discussion of a cultural system exhibiting a "causal-meaningful unity" is not as strange as it once was, and his notions of cultural integration and change are likely better than those of many of the philosophers of history reviewed in the volume. But even if the charges against Sorokin are valid, it is important that he not be ignored.

To ignore the contemporary philosophers of history is to risk the loss of our sociological souls, because, in the right or wrong fashion they are grappling with the essential problem of the moral and practical significance of social science in our contemporary society. . . . the picture of modern society which these men present has tremendous relevance. Atomization, fragmentation, alienation, bureaucratization, terror, the loss of human choice—all are the realities of our time. We need to know if these phenomena are the inevitable result of attempting to organize a society on a basis of individual freedom and dignity, or if there can be a viable social order in which arbitrary authority, coercion, and the violation of the human being are at a minimum. The predictions of the philosophers of history are conservative, whatever may be their own value preferences. We must accept these predictions or show that a sociology of possibility, unbound by the uniformities of the past although recognizing their significance, can find conditions in which freedom and order are not incompatible, and where stress on the person does not result in atomization and anomie.[90]

Considerations such as these show us why "Sorokin is ignored today." The questions he raises are of little concern to sociologists, they appear value driven rather than value neutral, and they cannot be approached using the accepted methodological canon. Sociologists' reluctance to raise similar questions and challenge the present social order closes "the door to a sociology of possibility." Indeed,

Contemporary social science is profoundly symptomatic of what the philosophers of history regard as the decline of our society. Its scientistic concentration on human manipulation represents an extreme form of the reduction of the human being to pure object. Sorokin is predicting our role in the future, and we do our best to make him right. But actually the choice is ours. There can be a sociology of possibility, although its findings *may* prove the human dream an illusion. To develop this science, though, we must return to a consideration of the basic problems, the whence and whither of man, society, and humanity: the conditions of various types of social organization; the status and function of reason and values in social life; the possibilities of human choice and human dignity. If we make such a return, Sorokin will again become a central figure, even though it be as the representative of an opposition hypothesis. Dare we ignore him now?[91]

Most sociologists will, and future works by Sorokin and others at the Center will have a wider audience among the lay intellectuals. The exception was *Fads and Foibles in Modern Sociology and Related Sciences*, published six years later.

Social Reconstruction and the Science of Amitology

The foundation for *Fads* originated from many of Sorokin's earlier works but was restated and given a sharp new edge in *S.O.S.: The Meaning of Our Crisis*. This work also builds on *Dynamics, Crisis of Our Age*, and *Reconstruction* for its analysis of history and restatement of the contemporary crisis. At the beginning of *S.O.S.* Sorokin asserts that the "Murderous Trends" of our times result from the greedy, brutal, and selfish acts of an elite pursuing its own interests. Using strong hyperbole and overstatement, he presents the crisis as a struggle between good and evil. Sorokin intentionally abandons the dry language of scientific description "in favor of a dramatic, impressionistic-expressionistic portraiture" in the traditions of Erasmus's *Praise of Folly*, Thomas Carlyle's *Sartor Resartus*, and Friedrich

Nietzsche's *Thus Sprach Zarathustra*.[92] In this impassioned plea the forces of the dark side, the "Great Destroyer," are incarnated in the social elite and their legal, propagandistic, and scientific epigones. In sixty-six biting pages of satire Sorokin expresses the powerlessness of the masses and ends with the humble prayer of "Supplications of Little Mortals to the Big Immortals."[93] However, the victims will soon see through their exploiters and, surprisingly, respond in a nonaggressive manner. Drawing on his *Sociology of Revolution*, Sorokin asserts that social emergencies are opportunities used by elites to expand their control. During these periods domination becomes more complete. Victims may respond with frustration, aggression, passivity, or submissiveness. However, they may also respond with an increase of altruism and creative spirituality. This is Sorokin's law of polarization, which asserts that the forces of the Great Destroyer will be dialectically checked by a movement for the "re-enthronement of the soul." Life will be recast along the lines of the Ten Commandments and the Sermon on the Mount. This spiritual response by dissidents will stimulate a reintegration of culture along Integralist lines. The methods of achieving such a transformation are discussed later in *Forms and Techniques of Altruistic and Spiritual Growth: A Symposium* and *The Ways and Power of Love: Factors and Techniques of Moral Transformation*.

In *S.O.S.* Sorokin also indicts social scientists for their role in maintaining the power of the Great Destroyer. The text is castigating and biting. Continuing with the satiric prayer he writes:

Proud Descendent of Prometheus! Learned Weaver of Words into Meaningless Carpets. Exactest Psychometricians, Sociometricians, and Econometricians precisely measuring the Immeasurables! And You, Manufacturers of Psychosocial Tests, Testing Nobody Knows What! . . . Your erudition and word polishing are wonderful. Your historical, philosophical, political, economic, sociological, and psychological researches are astounding. . . . Still more incomprehensible are the measurements of Your Metromaniacs, the objective tests of Your Testophreniacs, and the techniques of psychosocial research of Your Technomaniacs. . . . Only the Pythias of psychology, the Oracles of psychiatry, the Clairvoyants of socio-anthropology can unravel the mysteries of the mass-manufactured tests . . . and other basic problems of the social and humanistic sciences which they study with the marvelous techniques of anti-mathematical statistics, anti-logical semantics, anti-observational psychoanalysis, anti-rational operationalism, and the thoroughly nondirective interviewing of . . . clinical psychologists, sociologists, and anthropologists.[94]

Having reprimanded the practioners and ridiculing their sciences, Sorokin condemns them as weak sycophants and apologists for the Great Destroyer. "While the mighty and the exploiters directly suck the blood of the ruled and the exploited, you get your living as parasitic servants of the bloodsuckers. In this sense you are the vegetarian suckers of the carnivorous leeches of humanity."[95]

His acidic assessment sets the stage for *Fads* and is contextualized for Eli Lilly in a letter reporting future plans for the Center.

In addition to continuing the research of the Center a part of my time will be given to writing a new volume: *Fads and Delusions of Modern Sociology, Anthropology and Psychology* . . . and to a revision of my *Contemporary Sociological Theories* in order to warn the younger generation of social scientists against the sterile fads and unscientific delusions temporarily prevailing in American sociology and related sciences. This return to strict sociology and social science indirectly serves the purposes of spiritual and moral regeneration of scholars and scientists, and through them of the society at large. Wrong "scientific" theories may be as poisonous as any ignorant and perverted ideology. For this reason they have to be combatted, exposed, and discredited. This is the purpose of my two volumes in sociology mentioned.[96]

Having set the stage for a more comprehensive and condemning criticism of the social disciplines, Sorokin returned to the development of Amitology as a means of saving humankind from the Great Destroyer. Writing in 1951, he defined Amitology as the applied science or art of developing friendship, mutual aid, and love in individual and intergroup relations. Its goal was to stem the tide of Machiavellianism by providing a blueprint ("guidebook") for mutual service, cooperation, and amity. Amitology focused on determining the characteristics of the altruistic personality; the techniques for developing and using love as a force in social interactions; the influence of "significant others" on prosocial relationships; and the characteristics of an environment that promote altruistic actions. The Harvard Research Center in Creative Altruism was committed to discovering these traits, techniques, and conditions. Drawing on the earlier research of the Center, and particularly *Explorations*, Sorokin reported what had been learned thus far. Emphasizing the characteristics of good neighbors and saints, he asserted that more must be learned so this "lofty power" can be used to alleviate evil and build a nobler, happier, and wiser humanity.[97] In tandem with the Amitology article, Sorokin also attempted to broaden the awareness of the Center by circulating to social scientists, interested lay readers, and public organizations the brief brochure "Harvard Research Center in Creative Altruism." This piece provided a short history of the Center, statements of the problems being addressed and their sociohistorical context, an overview of past and planned publications, and a request for contributions. He reported that the Center wished to expand its small staff to include specialists from physics, biology, psychiatry, and other disciplines. This required an annual budget of \$120,000, and all who were interested in the Center's work were asked to help.[98] Similar requests were sent to major foundations, including one to Charles Dollard, then president of the Carnegie Foundation.[99] Dollard, a supporter of Parsons and several projects in the Department of Social Relations, replied with regrets.[100] Existing evidence shows that these solicitations did produce a number of small contributions but no significant awards from foundations. The Center's research continued primarily under the patronage of Eli Lilly.

The year 1954 witnessed the publication of two major works by Sorokin: *Forms and Techniques of Altruistic and Spiritual Growth: A Symposium* and *The Ways and Power of Love*. In *Forms* Sorokin grounds altruism and spirituality in religious traditions. Altruism is "conduct as close as possible to the Sermon on the Mount or similar norms."[101] Spirituality is finding one's true being through a personal identification with God. One's soul (supraconsciousness) is the fountainhead of life, and it guides the body and mind. To ignore it oversimplifies the triadic nature of the human being, a common fault of the psychosocial disciplines. *Forms* is a book about the development and care of the soul. Simply stated, the soul is our capacity to know God and establish a personal relationship with Him. We develop this capacity by practicing a set of precepts that foster spiritual growth. Directions and spiritual exercises are provided by the great religions and show us how to discipline the mind and body, behave cooperatively and lovingly toward others, and become more directed by the spiritual part of our character. Religious exercises develop the soul much as physical exercises change the body. However, technique and repetition are not enough. To grow spiritually and become one with God requires grace. Sorokin and his coauthors studied these processes in a variety of communities: Hindu, Buddhist, Islamic, Tibetan, Orthodox and Roman Catholic, Hutterite, and Mennonite. The care of the soul broadens to understanding spiritual community, factors that promote amity and cooperative-supportive relationships, and how to transform inimical relations into friendly ones. Through *Forms* and *Ways* Sorokin lays the foundations for the science of Amitology and thus provides a mechanism to check humankind's rush into a declining sensate epoch.

The first section of *Forms* introduces readers to a number of perspectives on the nature of reality and humanity's relationship to God. The book opens with a well-crafted ontological essay by Roger Godel that presents the divergent approaches of East and West, and how these are being distilled in the crucible provided by the experiences of modern quantum physics. To perceive genuine reality, Western philosophy became embedded in a dualism of subjectivity and objectivity, and turned outward to explore the external world. Eastern seekers explored ultimate reality by turning inward toward their own being and for twenty-six centuries sought their answers from the inside. These were separate paths until Western science began its exploration of the quantum world.[102] Each approach has its strengths. For the Hindu, finding reality is becoming perfectly integrated with nature. When this occurs, there is a fusion of subjectivity and objectivity. The techniques of yoga have freed seekers from the body and moved them beyond dualism to the point where they are absorbed into "a permanent substratum that cannot be fathomed."[103] Psychotechniques can go further, and the more subtle will lead thought to the frontier, where transcendent intuition receives and calls it. The psychotechniques go no further: "Arrived at this stopping place, no one gets beyond without being summoned. Here he has already discerned the peace of the confines where life and death indifferently exchange their masks."[104] Here one waits for the appearance of God.

Westerners have regularly asked how one reaches this form of knowing and unity. What are the methods and techniques? Godel is clear that attaining ultimate awareness and unity with God is not formula driven and that techniques go only so far. The liberative experience does not result from gymnastic exercises and training. While they expand our awareness and prepare us, the ultimate liberative experience is a gift, a flashing reality given to us by grace. So Easterners and Westerners must wait prepared, in perfect awareness and hope for the gift of unification.

Western religions have also developed techniques for control of the body and growth of the soul. Anthony Bloom, in his essay "Yoga and Christian Spiritual Techniques," describes three general forms of ascetic exercises. Mortification methods, or "Christian Yoga," yield different spiritual benefits. First are those that discipline the body directly, and the mind and soul indirectly. Fasting, vigils, hard labor, and chastity are examples. Meditation and certain forms of prayer put the mind and spirit to work and have bodily effects. Finally there are exercises that habituate the body to certain conditions, and have direct effects on the mind and indirect effects on the soul. These are the focus of Bloom's essay. Orthodox Christian monks, of which he is one, believe that every psychic activity has physical repercussions. Conversely, specific movements of the body can provoke special mental states. So the monks over the centuries developed exercises that sustained positive spiritual experiences. Several of these are described in the article.[105]

Bloom also provides insight into motivations for mortification and the triadic nature of human beings. Humans are sovereign beings whose relationship to God was redefined by the Fall from grace. At the moment of the Fall, God's spirit ceased to be the channel through which life poured into the human soul and vivified the body. Humans became mortal, physical, and could only die. Cut off from the eternal, we became part of the material world. No longer its master but an element in and of it. Humans became flesh.[106]

Flesh is the body without divine life. It exists only in the material order and belongs to the fallen world. The body is human material permeated by the spirit of God, restored to harmony, and liberated from its fallen nature. The struggle against flesh is for the revivification of the body. Mortifications are constructive exercises that fit us to receive the divine life of God.[107] Different forms of mortification yield specific benefits: fasting increases intellectual acuity and radiance, while thirst is necessary for progress in inner prayer. Yet all these techniques are not enough to bring us to God; they simply focus our attention and prepare us to pray and meditate. It is with this preparation for grace that technique ceases to be effective and the real spiritual work begins.[108]

More typical of the Christian experience than asceticism and mortification is prayer. Prayer is an exercise and a discipline that focuses attention on God and allows one to praise, petition, and perform acts of penance. Pierre Marinier asserts that prayer may be a cultural universal with specific psychological and physiological rewards.[109] While this essay devotes itself more to the somatic effects of praying, Marinier affirms that for most it is the road to moral recovery, comprehension and acceptance of the real, and the direction to God. It eases the body, helps us deal with difficulty, and directs the soul toward a unity with God. It is a transcendental universal in the pursuit of grace.

Most of the essays in this section deepen understanding of one or another path toward transcending ego, disciplining the flesh, and developing the supraconsciousness (soul). These may well be viewed as exercises that prepare one to move toward and hopefully beyond ego-centered altruism in the direction of exceptional altruism. Sorokin asserts that ego-centered altruism is based on a diadic conception of humanness that sees us primarily as bodies with minds. This form of altruism does not require transcendence of ego. Instead, ego is viewed as a positive element in moral development. A well-ordered ego allows us to accept and love others so that we will be loved: "To serve others in order to be served, respect others in order to be respected, be friendly to others in order that others be friendly to you. In such altruistic actions ego is trained to cooperate with others for mutual benefit, profit and pleasure."[110]

However, the techniques of the Buddhist, the Christians, the Hindu, and the Muslim allow us to go beyond ego and develop our souls. Such methods, on the one hand, facilitate inner growth, pure spirituality, and supraconsciousness. On the other, they increase the intensity, duration, purity, adequacy, and scope of our love and altruism. Such are the characteristics of the exceptional altruists. They reflect the triadic concept of humanity in which ego is left behind and the mind and body are given energy and life by a soul in harmony with the transcendent.

This section is followed by case studies of altruistic communities; an analysis of amity and enmity; and explorations of various methods for changing inimical relationships into friendly ones. In approaching altruistic communities, Sorokin's contributors study the Mennonite and Hutterite traditions. The Mennonite case explores the boundaries of altruism, and the Hutterites illuminate socialization practices that pass these traditions from generation to generation.

The Mennonite community scores high on all five of Sorokin's dimensions of love. Its altruism is broad in scope, extensive, and goes well beyond the community to the nation and the world. It is with intensity and purity that Mennonites help others for the glory of God, without expectations of personal rewards. These acts are institutionalized in their culture and inculcated by socialization into their personalities (duration). They help others in order to empower them to grow and become independent. Hence the acts are adequate in Sorokin's meaning of the term. Mennonites are, in Sorokin's mind, an exceptional altruistic community. So what can be learned from them and the Hutterites about communal altruism?

The Mennonite community is devoted to God, prayer, and good works as the essentials for salvation. These commitments bind them to and drive their altruism. Mennonites reach beyond the brethren to all who experience loss and suffering, and the community is remarkable for its organized programs. Typical of these are maintaining hospitals, orphanages, homes for the elderly, banks, cooperatives, credit unions, insurance companies, and burial societies that serve Mennonite and non-Mennonite alike.[111] Their worldwide relief efforts are also notable. These are staffed by volunteers who work only for maintenance and regularly involve their home congregations with their mission. Along with cash, these congregations frequently send food, clothing, tools, and medicines. There are regular children-to-children projects that tie young Mennonites to less fortunate youngsters. Such practices frequently result in feelings by the dispossessed that others truly care.[112]

What motivates people to do this, and how is their altruism institutionalized and passed to new generations? An answer, while partially given in the Mennonite article, is more developed by Eberhard Arnold in his essay on the Hutterites in Paraguay.[113] Both groups are direct descendants of the Swiss Anabaptists and share a core of conventional practices. Their altruism arises from the Bible, and these teachings prevail in home, church, and school. Lessons in neighborliness and charity are part of church teachings and regular themes in children's conversation and literature. The young learn early that as Christians they are stewards of their time and resources, both of which are to be used for the work of the Kingdom. These values carry over into behavior as individuals participate in special relief projects, provide neighborly assistance, and listen to missionaries relate their experiences. As Arnold reports for the Hutterites, however, adult role models are the key to how children learn to behave and live. They demonstrate egoless behavior, personal responsibility for one another, and Christian love. Adults give children freedom to make decisions at the same time that they provide a clear set of shalls and shall nots. Adult examples are carried by older children into peer society, where they take responsibility for younger, weaker members. They handle the antisocial behaviors of their charges by working them out among themselves. Peer groups are never exclusive, serve as normative points of reference, and sanction behavior, but leave open clear paths on which the unruly can return to full membership. The family is the most important vehicle for internalization of common values and the community's ethos. There children learn all the required skills for life in society. The examples of parents and others teach that marriage is a commitment to loyalty, love, responsibility, and mutual aid. It bonds mates into an insoluble spiritual and physical unity.

Having laid the groundwork, the Hutterites give children in late adolescence the opportunity to leave for education, job training, or other experiences to expand their personalities. From such experiences they can freely decide whether or not to live out their lives in the community. Most do, and thus assume their position as role models for the next generation.

These studies suggest several important things about altruism: ego can be transcended; religions provide powerful principles for moral development and social responsibility; humans are capable of individual and collective acts of helpfulness that can be institutionalized beyond the primary group for the greater good of socially and geographically distant fellow humans; and in a sensate age of individualism a collective spiritual and physical good is pursued by a large number of individuals, most of whom live in altruistic primary groups and communities.

Forms continues its exploration with studies demonstrating how to change inimical relationships into more amicable ones, and with an investigation of the prerequisites for an effective body of international law. Gordon Allport's essay explores techniques for reducing group prejudices.[114] The larger issue is that out-group altruism can potentially be increased at the macrosociological level to the degree that we can reduce antipathies based on race, culture, and national origin. Seven methods have been widely touted for the reduction of these antipathies: legislation, education, contact and acquaintance programs, group retraining, mass media, exhortation, and individual therapy. Allport assesses each but warns that the methods and data required for precise judgments are lacking. However, scores of evaluative studies do exist and, if taken with a grain of salt, suggest certain strengths and weaknesses for each strategy.[115]

Legislation is a favored method for reducing discrimination but rarely, if ever, has a direct impact on prejudice. For education the impact is more discernible but still not precisely attributable to specific techniques. Allport summarizes the evidence on six types of educational interventions by noting: "We are not yet able to say categorically which of these six approaches brings the greatest return. While it is fairly certain that desirable effects appear in approximately two-thirds of the experiments, and ill effects very rarely, we still do not know for sure what methods are most successful."[116]

Contact and acquaintance programs work only when they occur between equals working in pursuit of common objectives. The group dynamics approach does not directly attack prejudice but aims at more general attitude changes. It is most effective with those who want to change and are in a supportive social context.[117] The mass media, as currently used, have had no appreciable impact on prejudice but could if they systematically used the techniques developed in advertising and propaganda studies. To date, however, this has not been the case.

Exhortation and group therapy produce limited effects. The exhortations of clergy likely strengthen the good intentions of the converted, who without such reminders might not maintain their brotherly efforts. However, "for the character conditioned bigot, and for the conformist who finds his social environment too powerful, hortatory eloquence is likely to have small effect."[118] Because of its depth, the amount of time required, and the small number of people who pursue it, group therapy does not have a broad impact. Furthermore, the goal of therapy is rarely to change ethnic attitudes. Such change occurs only in the context of other shifts in perspective, and group therapy is poorly suited to changing the attitudes of a society. Clearly, other methods are better.

Allport concludes that while all these methods have limitations one should not overlook their known results and future promise. It would be   .

a grave error to assume that the plodding and serious investigations here reported have nothing to contribute to the improvement of human relationships. Education and religion, mass media and legislation, child training and psychotherapy—these and all other channels of human effort must be followed in order to produce a race of men who will seek their individual salvation not at the expense of their fellows but in concert with them.[119]

Similar problems of converting hostile relationships into friendly ones are pursued at the microsociological level by other contributors. J. Mark Thompson's study of a small group of inimical relationships showed that they become more amicable when a member of the dyad deliberately performed good deeds for the other person. While the rates of change varied, the trend was clear, and showed that changes in behavior produced changes in the feelings people held for each other. Thus, if you wish to like and be liked by one to whom you are not initially attracted, behaving with kindness and consideration is a good beginning.[120]

Inimical relationships between nurses and patients in a mental hospital were studied by Robert Hyde and Harriet Kandler. Their main concern was resolving the antipathies that arise between nurses and their charges in a complex setting that demands more than a clinical understanding of the patient's disorder. Relationships improved when nurses and patients established an empathetic relationship. That is, each attempted to imaginatively project him- or herself into the other to feel, see, and react as the other did. This allowed both to go beyond their respective roles and view one another as human beings. Typically there was a reduction of hostility on both sides, an increase in candor, and a corresponding improvement in the relationship. The longer the nurses and patients persisted, the better the relationship became and the more effective the nurses were in the care of their patients.[121]

The essays in *Forms* move discordantly up the levels of sociocultural integration. Altruization begins with the individual, expands to the primary group, then to secondary institutional relationship (e.g., school, economy, church), and on to the community, nation, and global order.[122] These are the building blocks of Sorokin's blueprint, drawn from prevailing practices and current research, which demonstrate that the altruization of humanity is possible and specify some of the techniques by which it is accomplished at various levels of social organization.

In his next book, *The Ways and Powers of Love,* Sorokin summarizes the Center's work of the previous six years and attempts a systemization of the techniques that can lead to humanity's improvement and reconstruction. His methods are founded on the belief that almost all of us will be ego-centered, not exceptional altruists. Ego-based altruism requires not control of mind and body by the soul but a simple harmony of our egos and basic drives with those of other people. Drawing on the influences of Pavlov and Bekhterev, Sorokin asserts that this can be accomplished by repetition, habituation, the development of conditioned reflexes to internalize cooperative behaviors, and reasonable coercion.

Sorokin's techniques begin with the body and cover a broad range of social behaviors. The individual must be in a biological state conducive to cooperation and friendly behavior. This requires that physical needs are met and under the control of the conscious will. Meditation and a healthy body predispose one toward cooperative behavior. Social sanctions can then be gently applied to effectively channel behavior away from selfishness and toward prosocial acts. These sanctions must be consistently and broadly reinforced by public opinion. Primary and secondary groups must learn and use established methods to reduce animosity and inimical conduct. Antisocial acts and emotions must be immediately addressed and resolved. Hostile individuals should be paired with good role models and put to work solving a common problem. Good moral examples must be widely reported and imitated. There must also be a clear understanding by group members of the norms and values that guide individual and collective life. The emotional identification and practice by group members of these norms and values is more important than simple intellectual acceptance. Empathy is enhanced when one directly experiences another's problem, so controlled deprivation (asceticism, mortification) can strengthen commitments to the welfare of others. The fine arts contribute to creative growth and should be part of group life. Creativity should be encouraged, particularly in cooperative groups facing a common problem. These groups may become therapeutic communities that encourage and support social development and the transcendence of ego. Individuals can build on progress made within the therapeutic community by intensifying their identification with unselfish love; by isolating themselves from groups that contradict or reject the values of their community; through personal and liturgical prayer; through self-examination and exploration for faults; through public and private confession accompanied by binding vows of charity, selflessness, and good works; and through commitment to meditation, prayer, and good deeds for growth of the soul and movement toward a less ego-centered, more exceptional altruism.

Ways introduces and organizes more of the elements in Sorokin's blueprint for societal reconstruction. While these focus on the individual and community, he returns to national and international levels in *Power and Morality: Who Shall Guard the Guardians?*[123] This work was coauthored by one of Sorokin's former students from Minnesota and Harvard, Walter A. Lunden. The first half of the book is a broad history of power and corruption stemming from Genghis Khan to New Jersey's Frank Hague. It encompasses not only monarchs, rulers, and political leaders of democracies and totalitarian states but covers corruption in city and state government, in industry and finance, and even that of Catholic popes when their authority extended over sovereign states. Clearly supported by these findings is not only Machiavelli's assertion that "a prince who wishes to maintain the state must often do evil" but Lord Acton's dictum, "Power tends to corrupt and absolute power corrupts absolutely."[124]

Today's rulers are not much different from those who preceded them, but nuclear power provides an unprecedented capacity to destroy the world:

For the past few years [nuclear and bacterial] weapons have been manufactured on a gigantic scale by the governments of the United States, Soviet Russia and Great Britain. At the present time, the number of stockpiled weapons . . . is sufficient to bring about the aforementioned calamity [extermination of the human race, and life itself]. The danger in this situation is intensified by the fact that this immense fund of deadly power is monopolistically controlled by a mere handful of governmental rulers, . . . leaders of science and technology and captains of industry and finance. . . . Thus the power which they hold is infinitely greater and more absolute than that of any of the monarchs, dictators, or military conquerors of the past.[125]

The overriding question is Who shall guard the guardians? To this age-old query Sorokin and Lunden suggest a government of scientists, sages, and saints that will move us from sensate government to Integral leadership. Surprisingly, they are optimistic about three current trends in the qualifications of new world leaders: a growing requirement for intelligence and wisdom; an increasing demand for moral integrity; and pressure to replace tribal (nationalistic) perspectives with more universal outlooks toward the good of humankind.[126]

Increasing intelligence is rightfully or wrongfully associated with the emergence of scientists and experts as administrators who plan and control important government programs. Sorokin and Lunden argue that politicians are increasingly becoming figureheads and implementers of policies developed by their more scientifically competent advisers and committees. As this trend accelerates, we will see the statesman-politician replaced by the scientist.[127] But will this mean better government or simply a replacement of one oligarchy by another? Indeed, the argument can be made that modern instruments of destruction and suppression have been developed largely by scientists. Furthermore, the knowledge of a scientific administrator is too specialized and narrow to provide the leadership currently required; it must be directed by the wisdom of the sage. That is, a pansophic intellectual capable of integrating scientific understanding into a broader blueprint for reconstruction and progress.[128] To be successful, the blueprint must contain a body of moral principles that serve a universal good. Therefore, pansophic leaders must also be ethical leaders capable of steering humankind through moral relativism to a set of universal norms similar to the Judeo-Christian Commandments that can be applied cross-culturally.[129]

Unhappily, there has been a lag in moral development. Scientific truths are universals, but moral standards remain circumscribed by the boundaries of the tribe. Humankind today is a unified, tangibly interdependent group in which all are dependent on the whole for survival. This universal interdependence suggests that parochial tribal morality and its nationalistic expression are obsolete and dysfunctional. Consequently, world leadership must focus on the development of a code of conduct capable of integrating all nations into a moral community. This imperative has gone beyond being a pious wish and has become an urgent necessity.[130]

Global morality requires that governments include people who can provide such leadership. Practically, this is not as difficult as it appears. Many of those scientists, scholars, and philosophers who are active in government are people of eminent moral integrity and leadership who have already contributed ethical guidance to public policy.[131] However, their effectiveness would be substantially increased if they participated in discovering new techniques for moral development and transformation such as those studied by Sorokin's Center.

Moral transformation also requires the active participation of religious leaders and the spiritual involvement of exceptional altruists and holy ones. These apostles would provide role models around which others could rally to promote change. These religious leaders must also promote more ecumenical moral education. Collectively, they have access to a substantial portion of the world's population. In the past, great religious leaders have decisively changed the course of history. The demands of a new international moral order now challenge current leaders to rise to past historical accomplishments.[132]

To be effective, moral change must be sustained at the grassroots level. The faithful, working in their neighborhoods and communities, are the foundations for ecumenical change, and must be supported by local and national leaders. The faithful are the key to moral transformation. They, along with guardians of the guardians, will move us toward a new global moral community directed by the Integral leadership of scientists, sages, and saints. The present government of politicians is a symptom of the decaying sensate order. It has ruled through two world wars and now governs human relations in a thermomodern age. By mobilizing its altruistic potential, humankind may prevent these leaders from plunging us into an apocalyptic war. If altruism can buy us a few decades of peace under the guidance of a unified creative force, then the most dangerous part of the declining sensate transition will pass and a solid foundation for the emerging Integral order will be built. This demands that a new benevolent elite of scientists, sages, and religious leaders assume increasing control now. With their Integral leadership a new Integral and emancipatory social order will emerge.[133]

The body of work between *Reconstruction* (1948) and *Morality* (1959) not only is a blueprint for social reconstruction but also contains the domain assumptions and operationalizations of a nascent discipline. *Power and Morality* completes the outline for the new applied science or art of Amitology, beginning with ego transcendence and culminating in a new moral community for the brotherhood of nations. The Harvard Research Center in Creative Altruism provided an answer to the questions of whether a moral society based on prosocial behaviors is possible, and if so, how it can be attained. The current issue was whether scientists, intellectuals, and citizens would rise to the challenge. That is, will they deepen their understanding of altruism, institutionalize the codes of values and norms necessary for social improvement, and move us toward an Integral social order?

From the scientific side there was little interest in Sorokin's last four works. The only sociological review of *S.O.S.* was done by Theodore Abel, and even popular reviewers found little of interest in the book. Luke Ebersole, writing in the *Crozier Quarterly*, observed that Sorokin's vivid imagery "and satire never quite come off. It does not hurt; it does not irritate; it does not tickle. . . . The effect is bitter rather than sharp." Hence, his text on the Great Destroyer and the prayer of supplication miss their mark. Indeed, even his scholarship is found wanting: "Whenever Professor Sorokin writes he reveals cogent insights, but neology and erudition will not be confused with profundity . . . and he has not yet separated himself from those who he calls the 'word weavers of scholarship' or the scholarly nonmystical mist makers."[134] A similar observation was made by Rudolf Allers for *Commonwealth*. "It is hardly possible to summarize the first part [of this book]. These pages are filled with bitterness and despair, with sharpest irony and moving appeal." However, instead of a "mist maker," Sorokin's work for Allers has a ring of truth: "The author is entitled to claim that the history of the last ten years has supported what he foresaw earlier. . . . This slender volume deserves to be read thoughtfully."[135]

Abel was similarly overwhelmed by the hyperbole in the first part of *S.O.S.*, referring to it as "the fanciest appellations to ever appear on the printed page."[136] Happily, this does not carry over, but the rest of the book is sociologically thin in terms of propositions and verifications. "The least that can be said by way of criticism of this book is that it shares the fundamental weakness of most other books that deal with the present crisis. It stresses what *should* be, but fails to indicate *how* this can be accomplished."[137] Abel's criticism was squarely faced in the next two volumes from the Center: *Forms and Techniques of Altruistic and Spiritual Growth* and *The Ways and Power of Love*.

Both *Ways* and *Forms*, however, met with a similar sociological silence. The latter attracted little attention, and perhaps its best review was a joint review of the two works by Richard L. Simpson. He treats *Forms* in a dry manner, briefly explicating the content with occasional mention of some of Sorokin's more esoteric examples. *Ways* is seen as the best reflection of Sorokin's current thinking because supraconsciousness, love, altruization techniques, and social change are intertwined. Simpson, however, has little faith in either a personality theory predicated on supraconsciousness or the techniques advocated in both volumes for developing it and prosocial behaviors. Sorokin's rejection of sensate personality theorists is too quick and emotional, and his own theory, while "firmly grounded in sociology and psychology, . . . leaves much of human behavior unaccounted for."[138] The value of both books in Simpson's mind is limited, and he cynically observes:

In both books much space is devoted to esoteric techniques like Yoga which . . . will never sell to the public at large . . . since practitioners must withdraw from society. About all the general public could hope to get from them is improved breathing and posture. Perhaps Sorokin will concentrate in the future on studying friendship and benevolence among ordinary folk and leave spiritual athletics to the few who can benefit from them.[139]

More confrontational is Arnold W. Green's review in the *American Journal of Sociology*. *Ways,* he writes, is blemished by Sorokin's sad abandonment of sociological theory and methods in his quest for social reconstruction. The resulting theory is based on "wish," not fact, and the evidence used is too superficial, historically selective, and one-sided. Consequently, the results are speculations and hopes, and as such carry little scholarly weight or conviction. Sorokin's unsatisfying argument is tied to a naive shortsightedness and absence of critical reasoning:

Sorokin does not recognize that love in a naughty world can be victimized, even crucified. . . . A complete acceptance of the Sermon on the Mount, at the present moment in world history, would lead to the involved paradox of surrendering to Communism. The lives of the saints support the stated probability that most of them would have surrendered. Few modern Americans would do so and nowhere does Sorokin indicate that a tragic ethical dilemma does in fact exist: Whether, at best by remaining silent, to promote the possibility of Armageddon or to embrace unqualified pacificism and accept the consequences of a foreign-dictated peace not only for ourselves as individuals but also for millions of others who do not want to pay that price for love or peace.[140]

The systematic quality of *Ways* was captured in Oliver R. Reiser's review, who grasped the logical progression of the chapters and saw the book as a program for moral transformation. Indeed, it is "an impressive work" but "one that lacks a proper place for fumbling, fallible, but self-corrective human intelligence." Regardless, it is "a masterpiece of systematic synthesis."[141]

The reception of *Ways,* and later *Morality,* was more positive in the popular press and religious publications. But by and large the research of the Center failed to start a significant mass movement or to institutionalize the study of altruism in the social sciences.

The Moral Reconstruction of Social Science

In between *Ways* and *Power and Morality* appeared *Fads and Foibles in Modern Sociology and Related Sciences*. Published in 1956, the volume was a "cleansing operation" intended to free social scholarship from "the half-truth, sham-truth, and plain error taken for the last word of science, 'operationally defined, empirically tested and precisely measured.' "[142] Sorokin points out that the operation will be painful and provoke anger but is necessary, and if well done will benefit all. Sorokin then acknowledges his guilt for many of these sins but cuts into the viscera of the social disciplines, attacking the pathological practices of scholarly amnesia by the New Columbuses' excessive jargon, pretentious scientific language, misguided operationalism and slavish imitation of natural science, excessive reliance on invalid tests and projective methods (testomania), misuse of experimental methods in the social disciplines, the poor quality of small group research, the excessive misuse of mathematics (quantophrenia), and the use of platitudes and predictive statements in place of a genuine theoretical understanding of social and cultural systems.

For each pathology he selects the works of specific scholars great and small as examples. Among the New Columbuses are Samuel Stauffer, Anatol Rapoport, Clyde Kluckhohn, Ralph Linton, Talcott Parsons, Edward Shils, Kingsley Davis, and Wilbert Moore. These scholars are guilty of two related offenses: a poor grasp of the history of their research fields (amnesia), and unmerited claims of priority and discovery (the discoverer's complex). Amnesia and rediscovery produce a thin and wasteful scholarship. Such scholarship, combined with the prominence given to methods and technique in graduate education, is creating a new generation of practioners with little understanding of the essence, meaning, and past accomplishments of their disciplines.

The defects of jargon and slang are manifested in several forms. The three most odious are blindly transferring natural science terms to the social sciences; disguising platitudes as profundity or original thought; and the use of neologisms. Among the guilty are the psychologists Raymond Cattel, Dorwin Cartwright, and Edward Tolman; and the sociologists George Lundberg, G. K. Zipf, Talcott Parsons, and Edward Shils. On neologisms Sorokin states, "The collection of examples of this sort of speech disorder can be increased by hundreds taken from the two volumes of Parsons and Shils."[143] Sorokin makes his point by quoting from Ellsworth Faris's satirical imitation of Parsons in his review of *The Social System*.

Knowing you to be an individual in whom the general value-orientation pattern of achievement-universalism, specificity, neutrality, and collective orientation is well established, I have long cathected you and still cathect. Let us look forward to an integration of ego (you) into a role complementary to that of alter (me) in such a way that the common values are internalized in ego's personality and/or alter's, and our respective behaviors come to constitute a complementary role-expectation-sanction system.[144]

Having pointed out these two minor pathologies, Sorokin turns to the more serious "internal cancers that are eating up the organism proper."

What follows is a familiar litany of "cancers" such as physicalism, quantophrenia, testomania, and technomania. At the core of all these mal-
adies lies the belief that the principles and methods used by physicists
and other exact scientists can be used in the social sciences, and will
produce comparable truth and predictability. Consequently, many social
scientists expend their energies developing tests, questionnaires, and
experiments that they mistakenly assume will isolate the essential qualities of social phenomena. These errors (of misplaced precision and
concreteness) are then compounded when the data are mathematized
and manipulated as if they satisfy the requirements of measurement
inherent in most physical phenomena and their indicators. These are the
main flaws of operationalism, testomania, and quantophrenia. Sorokin's
study of the latter tells the reader much about the others.

Mathematics has been correctly called the queen of sciences and has
earned its venerated position. However, it becomes less noble in the
hands of social scientists who try to quantify qualitative things. These
modern "numerologists" count the uncountable, then manipulate these
false units mathematically in the belief that their findings will tell them
something useful. The belief is so deep that mastery of numerology is the
gateway to the doctorate. Once the degree is earned, the practioner must
continue in the quantophrenic cult in order to publish, receive grants, and
rise in the profession. Sorokin's list of operationalists, quantophrenics,
testomaniacs, statistical cultists, and their faults laces the middle 250
pages of the book. Among them, mixed with no apparent regard for
merit, are some of the best and the poorest representatives of the social
disciplines. Then, having taken the reader through this long exercise,
Sorokin asserts not only that the methods are inappropriate but that
social imitators are practicing a dead form of science.

In chapter 12 of *Fads* Sorokin argues that *all* the previously discussed
faults derive from the use of an obsolete philosophy of science and a
mistaken theory of cognition. Social scientists are, in fact, trapped in a
philosophy of work that misses the recent lessons from quantum mechanics. Consequently, they misunderstand dualism and complementarity, as well as the true nature of prediction and the ideal limits of
knowledge. Clearly, Sorokin is referring to the scientific revolution that
developed from the clash between the Newtonian determinists led by
Einstein and the proponents of Niels Bohr's complementarity principle
at Copenhagen in 1927. However, he does not fully explicate the nature
of the controversy or its full significance for the social sciences to his
readers.[145] While the issue of debate was the essence of light, the underlying significance had to do with the nature of reality and its proper study.

Einstein was a Newtonian dualist who accepted, without question, the existence of an objective physical world that operated according to immutable laws that were independent of the observer.[146] Newton's laws gave an image of the universe (the great machine) that was both immutable and independent of human will. The machine operated with such precision that the position of heavenly bodies could be known one hundred years in the future or in the past. Many agonized over the role of the Deity in natural law. But scientists increasingly became observers of an objectified order over which the act of observation was willfully and epistemologically neutral. Subjectivity (how we think about things) led to distortion and was to be strictly controlled.

This seventeenth-century view of science dominated inquiry until unresolvable anomalies appeared, most significantly over the nature of light. Young's 1803 experiments had settled the issue of light's basic nature in favor of wave theory. Einstein, however, later described light as a particle, and specifically as a photon. Experimental evidence supported both the particle and wave theories; the anomaly lies in the fact that these characteristics are mutually exclusive features in scientific theories and assumptions about the physical world. The dilemma at Copenhagen was "How can the mutually exclusive wave-like and particle-like behaviors both be properties of one and the same light?"[147] Bohr resolved the problem with his famous complementarity principle: they are properties not of light but of the scientist's linguistic and experiential attempts to come to grips with the nature of light. Treat light like a wave and it behaves like a wave; treat it like a particle and it behaves like a particle. In quantum theory the real world is taken to mean not only that which exists for the senses but that which exists to the scientific intellect as well. In this orientation we have a different unit for the beginning of knowledge: the world is as it presents itself and the intellect's treatment of the world, once presented. In short, it is a position intermediate to strict objectivism and strict solipsism, and consistent with a phenomenological orientation, that takes reality as a consciously constituted object. The mathematician and philosopher Edmund Husserl had argued that the difficulty with empiricism was that we are asked to accept the principle of the uniformity of nature and its correlate of the past as a predictor of the future without access to the only connecting medium that allows them to make sound empirical sense a posteriori. That medium is the observer. If one wishes to avoid apriorism, one must provide the link between uniform events in nature, as well as between past and future. The link is the conscious knowable mind. The issue is not that the observer creates the uniformity in nature. Its existence is not the issue. But the investigator is the bridge between discrete occurrences, and the meaning of the uniformity is constituted in the consciousness of the observer.[148]

Max Born, however, described the generation of Einstein and himself as one that watched an objective, independent universe as an

audience watches a play in a theater. Einstein still believes that this should be the relation between the scientific observer and his subject. Quantum mechanics, however, interprets the experience gained in atomic physics in a different way. We may compare the observer of a physical phenomenon not with the audience of a theatrical performance, but with that of a football game where the act of watching accompanied by applauding and hissing, has a marked influence on the speed and concentration of the players, and thus on what is watched. In fact, a better simile is life itself, where audience and actors are the same persons. It is the action of the experimentalist who designs the apparatus which determines essential features of the observations. Hence there is no objectively existing situation, as we supposed to exist in classical physics.[149]

Thus, Sorokin's remarks not only criticize contemporary sociological methods but bring closer together heretofore diverging paths in Eastern and Western approaches to reality and how to best seek truth.

Another lesson from colleagues in atomic physics that had not been understood by social scientists had to do with the character of explanation and prediction in science. Again, the Copenhagen interpretation and the dialogue between Einstein and Bohr is illustrative. Einstein accepted the particle-wave duality, but the problem for him was that this evidence raised fundamental epistemological issues. He approached the world as a Newtonian determinist. Like Newton, he searched for unifying principles.[150] Newton's laws of gravitation had proven that the same force that pulls objects to earth also holds heavenly bodies in planetary orbits. With one stroke, he formulated the laws by which the universal great machine operated. Einstein believed this was the proper role of the scientist, and that we should develop theory that contains exhaustive explanations of objective reality. For every element of reality there is a corresponding element of theory. This is the ideal limit of knowledge.

The fact that the subatomic realm is not completely determined was difficult for Einstein to accept. Indeed, Heisenberg's Uncertainty Principle showed that it was impossible to obtain complete information about the position and momentum of a particle in the subatomic realm. The best that can be done is to know both approximately, but the more we know about one, the less we can know about the other. It is well known that Einstein did not like this interpretation because it introduced an element of chance and uncertainty in what he believed should be a completely knowable universe. For Einstein, the good Lord did not play dice with reality, and it was incumbent on physicists to find a unified field theory. It was toward this end that much of his later work was oriented.

It is important to note that what produces the "uncertainty" in the Heisenberg principle is not the consciousness of the observer but the way nature presents itself. Imagine that we want to know both the position and the momentum of an electron, and that we have a supermicroscope that allows us to locate one. This microscope cannot use conventional light waves since such wavelengths are too wide to detect the much narrower electron. Instead, gamma rays must be used, as explained by Gary Zukav:

If we hold a strand of hair between a bright light and the wall, the hair casts no distinct shadow. It is so thin compared to the wavelengths of the light that the light waves bend around it instead of being obstructed by it. To see something we have to obstruct the light waves we are looking with. In other words, to see something we have to illuminate it with wavelengths smaller than it is. For this reason Heisenberg substituted Gamma rays for visible light in his imaginary microscope.[151]

Gamma rays have shorter wavelengths and higher energy levels than visible light. Thus, when the gamma ray strikes the imaginary electron it will illuminate it and show its position. But it also will change the direction and momentum of the electron. Light that will not disturb the momentum of the particle, will, however, have a wavelength too great to show its position. Consequently, the more exactly we know the position of an electron, the less we know about its momentum.

Heisenberg's principle reveals that totalizing phenomena is sometimes impossible, and the best one can do is to state universal conditions as probabilities rather than as immutable laws of invariance.[152] Another lesson of quantum mechanics is that uncertainty is as much a part of the order of things as are the Newtonian natural laws. The uncertainty principle has two further implications for the theorist in the human disciplines: (1) some things in nature, because of nature, cannot be completely known and are not perfectly predictable; and (2) the act of observation alters that which is observed.

The impact of the Copenhagen interpretation, the Heisenberg principle, and the work that resulted from them has some specific implications for sociologists. Physicists in 1927 brought humans back into science. They were no longer the passive observers of the great machine, but instead, science and order are grounded in the structure of the scientific intellect. This tells us that good science need not and cannot be independent of the subjective processes of consciousness.

The Copenhagen interpretation also brought a new perspective to the issue of integration between macro- and microsociological spheres. Just as heavenly bodies follow one set of principles and subatomic particles another, the same may be the case for micro- and macrosociological relations among human beings. Different sets of principles may be necessary for understanding each. Consequently, good sociological theory need not be judged on either the ideal limits of knowledge or a unification of the individual, society, and history. Indeed, to paraphrase Merton, it may be premature to require this of a science that has not yet had its Newton, much less its Einstein or Bohr.[153] A fruitful path for methodological and theoretical development may be found along the lines suggested by the phenomenological sociologists, for it is they who deal best with a consciously constituted reality intermediate to solipsism and objectivism. This path seems consistent with the epistemology of the successful sciences and allows for pragmatic theoretical development to occur at both macro- and microsociological levels of discourse.

Having pointed to the foolishness of this obsolescent philosophy of science in the social disciplines, Sorokin finds in the new physics support for the "complementarity" for which he has long argued. Sensory perceptions are not the only channel of cognition. There is a role for intuition or supersensory perception in science, and these often provide the flashes of insight necessary for progress. Thus, a more adequate social science must be built on a theory of cognition that accepts, at least partially, "that it is possible for the knower and the known to merge into one unity; that some degree of merging is necessary for any approximately accurate cognition of an object; that a complete merging is the only way for the adequate cognition of the ultimate or true reality."[154]

Sorokin next argues that if we are to avoid the "blind alleys" of a mistaken empiricism there must be a basic reconstruction of sociology and psychology along integralist lines. This means using a three-dimensional conception of reality that combines the sensory, the rational, and the suprarational. Integral science requires the use of all these forms of knowing to grasp what is real. We use our senses to determine the physical characteristics of a phenomenon, our mind to grasp rational characteristics, and our intuition to comprehend superational elements. To grasp the total phenomenon requires the unified use of all three methods. This exhaustive examination "yields a fuller and more adequate understanding than any single method of cognition."[155]

Sorokin concludes:

The prevalent empirical psychosocial science has delivered, especially during the sixteenth, seventeenth, eighteenth, and nineteenth centuries, important knowledge of man and of his sociocultural universe. Helped in part by the logico-mathematical method, this empirical science has labored strenuously for several centuries. At the present time it is tired and has become somewhat neurotic and less creative. It urgently needs much greater help from the other two methods of cognition. This means there should be the closest cooperation and unification of all three methods into one integral conception of reality, an integral system of truth, and an integral method of cognition. Only such an integral way can lead today's psychosocial science out of the blind alley onto the royal road of a recreated sociology and psychology.[156]

Reviews of *Fads* were largely critical. Gresham Sykes however, in a nonconfrontational and balanced assessment, asserts that *Fads* should not be "dismissed as an intemperate, spiteful or irresponsible attack for at least two reasons. . . . many of the criticism are justified; and Professor Sorokin's many contributions to a science of society entitle him to a careful hearing."[157] Even so, most sociologists will not see the problems of the discipline as resulting from too strong a commitment to empirical research, nor will they adopt Sorokin's insistence on intuition as the path to genuine knowledge. Sociology as a young and vigorous discipline must be self-critical if it is to advance. Unhappily, Sorokin's critique is too opinionated, self-serving and depreciating of others to be of much constructive help.

On the other side of the Atlantic, Jean Floud reviewed *Fads* for the *British Journal of Educational Studies*. After heaving a sigh of relief that the attack is against American sociologists, Floud goes to what is considered the heart of Sorokin's criticisms,

the failure of social scientists to understand that which they are trying to imitate. Their efforts reveal a conception of principles and procedures in the natural sciences which is at best ill-informed and antiquated, and at worst downright false. If social scientists only knew how the notions of physical determinism and causality have been overtaken in the natural sciences by developments in quantum mechanics and atomic theory, they would be less anxious to flaunt their supposedly "scientifically objective" approach to the social reality in which they are, in fact, inextricably involved; and they would find release from the thraldom of fruitless analysis of meaningless "congeries of sociocultural facts" and from arid insistence on the importance of quantification and the achievement of results with predictive value.[158]

Having said this, Floud asserts that Sorokin fails to make a convincing case against the fads and foibles or for his alternatives. Instead, one gets a sputtering, eruptive polemic, with indignant and arrogant overtones.[159] Furthermore, many of Sorokin's key arguments are better made by other scholars (mostly British), and it's difficult to judge what contribution, if any, this volume makes to a better social science.

Sociologists also fell under scrutiny of the popular media when *Fads* was reviewed by the *New York Times* and in the *Times Literary Supplement*. The most biting review came from London in Richard McLaughlin's review in the *Literary Supplement*:

No one who has had occasion to examine selections of the current American outpouring of sociology can refrain from raising a cheer when he reads this catalogue of some of its main shortcomings and blemishes. Who has not been amazed at the evident ignorance many of these contributions exhibit about previous work in this field from Plato and Aristotle onwards? Who has not winced at the ponderous platitudes, the tautologies, the barbaric, incomprehensible style, the false air of precision sought through ill-defined or meaningless equations and pseudo-mathematical formulas, the question-begging use of scientific terms imperfectly understood and borrowed from a now outmoded and superseded physics, the importation of language from atomic theory or cybernetics, the reliance upon dubious psychological tests, the pathetically misplaced faith in psychoanalysis, the boastful claims to originality and the effort to gain credit for self or friends from pretended great discoveries which lead nowhere and are usually nothing but old views restated in new jargon? . . . Fads and foibles are terms too mild for many of the follies he exposes. The sword of justice and avengement which he wields ought to fall heavily upon perversions which have every promise of blighting the hopes, stunting the minds and misleading with false doctrine the ingenuous young, enrolled in their hundreds of thousands in the sociological faculties of scores of American universities. Exposed as they now are to masses of indigestible rubbish masquerading as the latest pronouncements of science, it would be serious indeed if they were to be allowed to accept it, to repeat it and in turn, maybe, to teach it; and shocking if they were forced to do all this as a price of success in their academic careers. For their sakes as well as for the advancement of learning Professor Sorokin has done well to publish his courageous and incisive manifesto. May it rally to his standard a goodly army of allies.[160]

Sociologists did not rally to the standard, and the mood of many was captured in a review by Donald Horton in the *American Journal of Sociology*:

Fads and Foibles is not an appeal to sociologists but an attack upon them. The derogations and ridicule in this book can be interpreted only as an appeal to third parties against sociology as a science and a profession. The distorted picture presented here of the problems, methods, and achievements of American sociology and the demagogic charge that its "negativistic theories" have "tangibly contributed to the present degradation of man" are a disservice to our discipline from which only the enemies of rational social inquiry can possibly benefit.[161]

Furthermore, Sorokin's motivations may not be only scholarly:

A number of passages indicate that Sorokin considers himself to have been treated shabbily by American sociologists—categorized as an "armchair theorizer," plagiarized by his immediate colleagues, disowned by his students, and disregarded as researcher, theoretician, and prophet. If Sorokin is no longer regarded as a creative power in sociology, it is because of the increasingly irrational and idiosyncratic character of his work, not because of any conspiracy against him. Professional isolation is the fate invited by any man who builds private systems of thought outside the collaborative development of the science to which he is nominally attached. If personal and professional difficulties have pushed Sorokin along this divergent route, this is to be regretted.[162]

Horton concludes his review with the claim that *Fads* is "a pitiable climax to a distinguished career."[163]

Sorokin replied intemperately in the next issue of the *American Journal of Sociology:*

To the Editor:

I heartily welcome Professor Donald Horton's review of my book *Fads and Foibles in Modern Sociology and Related Sciences, American Journal of Sociology,* LXII (1956), 338–339. The strongly disparaging character of the review is a good omen for the book because of a high correlation between the damning of my books by the reviewers of the *American Journal of Sociology* and their subsequent career. The more strongly they have been damned (and practically all my books were damned by your reviewers), the more significant and successful were my damned works, the more were they translated and the more voluminous the scientific literature in the form of substantial articles, Ph.D. theses, and books about them, the greater the space given them in various sociological and philosophical lexicons and encyclopedias, and the more substantial the chapters in texts and monographs on sociological, historico-philosophical, religious, ethical, political, and aesthetic theories devoted to my "emotional outbursts." Even more frequently my "yarns" have been appropriated by some of the damning reviewers a few years after publication of their reviews. So far, thirty-four translations of my volumes have been published, and several additional translations are under way. The total world literature about my "yarns" probably exceeds that about the works of any living sociologist highly praised by the reviewers of the *American Journal of Sociology.*

. . . In conclusion, I would like to know who or what authority entitled Professor Horton to speak on behalf and in the name of all American sociologists? So far as I know, no such authority empowered Horton to be an official or unofficial mouthpiece of American sociology. Neither can Horton claim such a right by the virtue of his great contributions to sociology, to my knowledge, his contributions have been very modest, if any at all. In brief, Professor Horton can speak only for Horton and for nobody else.

As to Horton's laments about the professional interests of sociologists being possibly hurt by my book, these laments are either insincere or naive. If by the "professional interests of sociologists" he means the pursuit of valid sociological knowledge, then no competent and sincere criticism of sociological theories can hurt such interests. If by "professional interests of sociologists" he means "the existential interests" of various "sociological" Tammany Halls and "Mutual Back-scratching Cliques," the less the number of such Tammany Halls and cliques in sociology, the better for the science of sociology.[164]

Pitirim A. Sorokin
Harvard University

With this letter the cult of silence more completely enveloped Sorokin and he was further removed from the serious consideration of practicing sociologists. Two years later, in 1959, he would retire from Harvard as a marginalized and caricatured figure, with little hope for return to the mainstream. His contributions would be ignored, and he would be remembered only for the imperfections of his personality.

Other Avenues: The Final Years of the Harvard Research Center in Creative Altruism

The signals from sociologists and other social scientists were clear by 1955: there was little interest in either social reconstruction or altruism. Cynicism and criticism were followed by an indifference that combined with hostility after the publication of *Fads*. Sorokin responded by attempting to organize and broaden the base of scholarly involvement for those already committed to his program. For several years he wrote Eli Lilly of the growing international awareness of the Harvard Research Center in Creative Altruism. As early as 1952 he reported increasing translations of the Center's publications and a growing demand by print and electronic media for more information. Sorokin responded with a number of popular pieces on the family, love, sexual behavior, and morality. He also gave interviews freely and spoke on a number of radio and television stations to broaden popular awareness of the Center's existence and research.

In 1955 he informally started to cultivate the involvement of like-minded scholars. Realizing the rather specific mission and limited resources of the Center, he proposed a new, more broadly based organization. Writing to Eli Lilly in September 1955, he observed that a growing number of scholars were interested in altruism and sought a forum to share ideas and develop the study of prosocial behavior. Seventy had responded to his proposal and were willing to be founding members. He envisioned a professional society with membership requirements, annual meetings, and a quarterly journal. Many encouraged Sorokin to lead the process, but he worried that this would drain energy from the Center's work. What did Lilly think?[165] The Hoosier entrepreneur was encouraging: "It seems that your proposed association for the application of creative altruism is a fine move. The broader that you can get the base of your interested people the more will be accomplished, I should think."[166] Lilly also sent Sorokin's proposal to the Lilly Endowment board.

The Lilly board adopted a conservative approach to the proposal and sought advice from Harvard's president Nathan M. Pusey. Endowment policies had changed in the late 1940s, when a generous gift from J. K. Lilly Sr. quadrupled its assets to thirty-nine million dollars. Correspondingly, annual grants reached two million dollars and required a more formalized and professional administration. This was done by Lilly's nephew J. K. Lilly III, who studied other foundations and incorporated some of their policies and procedures. J. K. Lilly III also hired G. Harold Duling as secretary of the endowment to oversee the routine operations. It was Duling who recommended consulting Pusey. Even with these changes, Eli Lilly remained a force within the organization. Though consultative, "he usually had his way, particularly in granting money, and was reluctant to adopt the more formal procedures of the Endowment."[167]

In regards to Sorokin, Lilly was steadfast in his commitment, though others did not share his appraisal. In February 1951 Duling sent Lilly a memo stating:

In the February 16, 1951 issues of *Counterattack*, Dr. Sorokin is listed as one of the sponsors of the banquet given in honor of Dr. W. E. Dubois, who, according to *Counterattack*, has a long record of pro-communist activity. The August 18, 1950 issue of *Counterattack* mentions Dr. Sorokin as having signed a "peace" petition which had been exposed as a communist device. In Mr. Robnett's paper issued by the Church League of America, we also noticed a reference that Dr. Sorokin was listed among others, in an article contained in the *Daily Worker* as a guest at a similar banquet on a previous occasion. The above references have caused some "lifting of the eyebrows" in this office and we have questioned what, if anything, we should do about it. As you know, Mr. J. K. Lilly, III recently spent two days with Dr. Sorokin and I am sure that he came away with confidence in the fine work Dr. Sorokin is performing. However, the repeated references to his questionable association have caused us some concern.[168]

J. K. Lilly Jr. followed up and asked Mr. E. Beck to "make some special inquiry into this Dr. Sorokin matter so that we may be guided in our Lilly

Endowment endeavors by your findings."[169] Beck responded two weeks later with a list of thirteen suspected communist organizations for which Sorokin either had been a sponsor of events or had signed statements or petitions. Beck concluded that "it seems this individual is associated with people who do not have very good records, and is sponsoring several activities that are very questionable."[170] J. K. Lilly Jr. passed Beck's report to his brother Eli, commenting, "My personal opinion is that this additional information adds something to the data previously supplied, and not of a favorable nature."[171] Eli Lilly discussed the report with his brother and set a meeting with Duling to talk over the Sorokin matter.[172] However, he was unconvinced and "refused to change his views about the Harvard professor."[173]

In 1956 Lilly Endowment staffers again raised questions about Sorokin. This time they wondered about his continuing ability to make a scholarly contribution. Manning M. Pattillo observed that, since 1955, Sorokin had lost touch with affairs at Harvard; though Sorokin was still active and writing a book, in Pattillo's "considered opinion further grants to support the research and writing of Dr. Sorokin would be imprudent. I do not believe that he is now in a position to make an important contribution to social thought."[174] Eli Lilly believed otherwise and continued to support Sorokin's writing and research.

These instances aside, Sorokin's newly proposed association posed administrative difficulties for the endowment. Duling's letter to Pusey in October 1955 reported Sorokin's desire to convene a small meeting of founding members to ascertain the depth of their commitment. If positive, Sorokin would begin incorporation and obtaining the association's tax-exempt status. Once established, Sorokin wanted Harvard to transfer the Center's funds to the new association. Was this possible?[175] On the advice of McGeorge Bundy, dean of Arts and Sciences, Pusey wrote to Duling that Harvard preferred to return the endowment's money but would continue to oversee the grant until the new association was established and then make the appropriate transfer.[176] But this was only part of the problem for endowment officials. Several worried about the quality of the association and whether Sorokin could continue his research while editing a quarterly journal and taking on a major administrative responsibility. There was also the question of whether the remaining two years of support for the Center (thirty thousand dollars) should be extended to the new organization. On these issues the endowment staff took a wait-and-see attitude. Sorokin was advised of these decisions by Duling on 1 November 1955.

On 29 October 1955, however, Sorokin had already brought together several interested scholars to discuss the feasibility of a new association.

Present at the convening meeting were Melvin Arnold of Harper and Brothers; E. Francis Bowditch, dean of men at MIT; Dean Walter H. Clark of the Hartford School of Religious Studies; the Reverend Duncan Howlett and Swami Akhilananda of Boston; Fritz Kontz of the Foundation for Integrated Education; U.S. Senator Ralph E. Flanders; Henry Margenau of Yale University; Chancellor Daniel March of Boston University; Abraham Maslow of Brandeis University; F. S. C. Northrop of Yale University; James Schrader and Robert Ulich of Harvard; and Igor I. Sikorsky, president of Sikorsky Aircraft. Together they decided, as charter members of the Research Society for Creative Altruism, to develop a constitution and incorporate the society in Massachusetts. Sorokin then wrote to Duling, thanking the endowment for the transfer of funds to the society, and announced a larger meeting of founding members in January or February 1956. The society would develop alongside the Center until December 1956, when, in collaboration with President Pusey, the continuation of the Center at Harvard would be decided. In the meantime, a constitution was being developed and a temporary executive board was conducting the legal and logistical affairs of the society. This board had I. I. Sikorsky as president, F. S. C. Northrop as vice president, Francis Bowditch as treasurer, and Sorokin as executive director and secretary.[177]

Nineteen fifty-six was a slow year for the society, but it did complete the Massachusetts incorporation process. Most of Sorokin's attention was directed toward preparing grant applications for the society, finishing his book *The American Sex Revolution*, published in January 1957, and putting the last touches on *Fads*, published in May 1956. Indeed, the publication and activities surrounding *The American Sex Revolution* and the society's first major conference were the key events for Sorokin in 1957.

Sex Revolution was the result of one of Sorokin's most popular articles. As he noted in the preface:

The appearance of this little book is due to a voluminous reaction of the readers to my article, "The Case Against Sex Freedom," published in *This Week* Magazine, January 3, 1954. The write-up was reprinted in several magazines [and] excerpts from it were reproduced in a number of other periodicals. The article was translated and published in several foreign countries. . . . Finally, a sizeable stream of letters . . . has come to the author. At least ninety per cent of these . . . have expressed the wish that the author publish a more developed version of the article [for] the intelligent lay-reader. This book is my answer to these suggestions.[178]

Intending it for a popular audience, Sorokin kept the format and language of the book nontechnical. He also believed that many readers would be displeased because his analysis was inimical to prevailing opinion. Thus the book might meet either an unfriendly or a "silent reception" from the partisans of sexual freedom.

He did receive a "silent reception" from social scientists. They completely ignored the volume for review. But the popular response was satisfying and lively. In *Sex Revolution* Sorokin argues that any significant change in the patterns of courtship; marriage; premarital, marital, and extramarital sexual relationships; and care of children would have significant consequences for society. Following J. D. Unwin's *Sex and Culture*, Sorokin asserts that societies tend to blossom, be creative, and grow when the sexual mores favor exclusivity, monogamy, fidelity, responsibility, and family stability. Conversely, when mores encourage permissiveness, sexual exploration, serial monogamy, easy divorce, and brief and changeable family relationships (particularly with children), then societies become unstable and alienating, and they decline. His thesis was that America was undergoing a sexual revolution that threatened the continued moral growth and vitality of our culture. As evidence he cites the increasing rates of divorce and desertion, the growth of single-parent households, a decline in fertility, poor adjustment to and rising unhappiness with marriage, less attention to children, more adultery and infidelity, increasing promiscuity and illegitimate births, exploding numbers of sex crimes, and a growing preoccupation with sex. These changes in primary relationships had been accompanied by a growing sexualization of American culture, media, art, literature, music, and political life.

Even science, and particularly the psychosocial sciences, had not been immune to the trend. Prominent among the guilty were Sigmund Freud and Alfred Kinsey:

The extraordinary popularity of Freudianism is a most convincing evidence of the sexualization of American psycho-social disciplines. One can hardly imagine a more degrading theory than the pan-sexual phantasmagories of Freud, which would hardly have had any serious chance among supposed scholars if today's psychology, psychiatry, sociology, education, and anthropology had not, in a sense, been infected by a growing sex obsession. In spite of the utterly unscientific nature of these [psychoanalytic] theories, and notwithstanding their extremely degrading effect; in spite of the fact that they drag into filthy sewers almost all the great values of humanity, beginning with love, marriage and parenthood . . . these theories continue to be accepted by many so-called scientists, and to win an ever-growing public. Their outstanding success is a tragic sign of sexual obsession.[179]

Equally harmful is Kinsey's theory. According to Sorokin, existing evidence shows that overindulgence in sex undermines physical and mental health, destroys morality, diminishes creativity, and increases guilt while undermining future prospects for happiness.[180] But if one believes the unscientific, poorly researched claims of Alfred Kinsey that indulgence shows no harmful effects upon health and vitality while restrictions of libido may cause serious illness, then we are again misled by a prominent and accepted dictum of psychosocial science. The truth is that existing "evidence points clearly to the fact that excessive sexual activity, particularly when it is illicit, has markedly deleterious effects."[181] Unhappily, a large number of gullible Americans overlook the truth and accept Kinsey because it provides a scientific justification for sexual excess and irresponsibility. In this way the psychosocial sciences contribute to a false awareness and feed the sexualization of society.

Newspapers throughout the country found *Sex Revolution* a good source for attention-getting articles. The news even reached the Hoosier state and the attention of some at the Lilly Endowment. While Sorokin was proud of the volume's popular appeal, he was more concerned about defining the research mission of the Research Society for Creative Altruism and with Francis Bowditch's obtaining the money to support that research agenda.

The agenda for the society was clarified in 1956, but securing funding proved more difficult. The research program had five elements and extended the Center's work and Sorokin's blueprint for reconstruction. Specifically, the research initiatives would broaden and deepen understanding of the following: the main forms of altruism and egoism; determination of the values most conducive to the maintenance of egoism and altruism at individual, institutional, and societal levels; which factors produce altruistic and egoistic personalities; the specific social institutions that maintain egoism and altruism; and the most effective techniques for the altruistic transformation of persons and groups. To these long-term projects was added a list of twenty-one more specific short-range initiatives.[182] To accomplish these goals, the society would create its own Research Institute of Moral Phenomena and Values, staffed by six eminent scholars with their assistants and associates. This group would grow to twenty as more funding became available. In January 1957 the executive board had identified two foundations to approach with requests for an annual operating budget of half a million dollars and a total fund of five to fifteen million dollars; one of these was the Lilly Endowment. The proposal was reviewed by the Lilly board at its February 1957 meeting and rejected.[183]

Duling and Pattillo were skeptical about both the research society and the Center, considering the grandiose plan put forward by the society "a pipedream." Now that a decision had been made, only Sorokin's request for the thirty-thousand-dollar extension of the Center's budget remained before the board. A review of the Center's account showed a balance large enough to support its work until 30 June 1957. Therefore, the board delayed a decision until later in the year. In November, under the gentle prodding of Eli Lilly, it approved a terminal grant of fifteen thousand dollars to complete the work of the Center.[184]

Much of the responsibility and work to develop the research society was shifted from Sorokin to Francis Bowditch during 1956–57. In early 1957 Bowditch became the administrative director of the society and began planning a major conference on "New Knowledge in Human Values" to be held on 4 and 5 October at MIT. The conference focused on the general question of whether a science of human values was possible and to what degree there was a convergence of conclusions on this issue by serious scholars. Participants, many of them nationally and internationally known scholars, came from a broad range of disciplines. They included Gordon Allport (psychology), Jacob Bronowski (mathematics and science), Ludwig von Bertalanffy (biology and systems theory), Theodosius Dobzhansky (genetics), Erich Fromm (psychology/psychoanalysis), Henry Margenau (physics), Abraham Maslow (psychology), Daisetz Suzuki (philosophy), and Paul Tillich (philosophy and theology). The conference attracted over a thousand participants, and a volume of the major addresses, edited by Maslow, was published in 1959.[185]

While the conference was successful, it unhappily signaled the demise of the research society. F. S. C. Northrop and several other charter members resigned during the planning stage. Others became less interested with the passage of time and failure to attract financial support. Equally discouraging was the inability to establish a base of membership to sustain the society intellectually. Altruism was not of sufficient interest to the community of scholars, and they were not attracted to the new ground that Sorokin was cultivating. The lay public had no interest in the progress of the society, and scholars were not attracted to the more popular works of Sorokin. Consequently, the society quietly ended in early 1958, and with it any hope that Sorokin carried for broadening the dialogue of social reconstruction and Amitology among scholars and lay audiences. The silence enveloped him, and in 1959 he retired from Harvard as a professor emeritus. With his full retirement came the termination (by policy of the Corporation) of the Harvard Research Center in Creative Altruism. However, he continued his writing and research in Winchester with the support of his friend Eli Lilly.

7

From Outcast to Elder Statesman

The Silence of Retirement

BY RETIRING IN STAGES, first from teaching and later as director of the Harvard Research Center in Creative Altruism, Sorokin increasingly gained control over his time and activities. Leaving teaching in 1955, he fully committed himself to writing and the work of the Center. Research was tempered by a series of lectures and seminars given during the summer of 1955 at the University of Oregon. As on earlier trips, Pitirim, Elena, and Sergei traveled by car across the United States to enjoy the marvelous scenery of the Northwest and parts of Canada. Time was spent camping and fishing, along with the good company of faculty from the university. The classes were stimulating and the change from the pressures of Cambridge welcomed.

Sorokin is clear in *Long Journey* that he retired from the Department of Social Relations in 1955 to be free from professional duties.[1] It is equally clear that he was not happy in that department, rarely attended its meetings, and nursed a residue of animus. Writing on the consequences of the transition from sociology to Social Relations, he observed:

I am not responsible for whatever has happened to the department . . . , either for its merging with abnormal and social psychology and cultural anthropology to form a "Department of Social Relations," or for the drowning of sociology in an eclectic mass of the odds and ends of these disciplines, or for any other change that has occurred in this department since 1942. The Department of Social Relations has certainly expanded in its staff, budget, research funds, and self-advertising. But it has hardly produced as many distinguished sociologists as the Department of Sociology did during the twelve [sic] years from 1931 to 1942 under my chairmanship. I give anyone complete liberty to dismiss these remarks as the biased grumblings of an old man. However, if such "interpreters" will check my grumbling observations they will probably find them fairly accurate.[2]

Sorokin's "grumblings" were more clearly expressed to the president of *Time* magazine, Roy E. Larsen, who chaired the 1954 Visiting Committee

221

to review Social Relations. Recalling a meeting of the department with the Visiting Committee, Sorokin wrote Larsen:

In a way, I am sorry that at the meeting of the Visiting Committee my criticism offered in all sincerity, and free of any desire to cast aspersions on any of the members of the department, was taken as a personal insult by some of the members. This reaction was particularly surprising to me, in view of the fact that the offended members of the department very often have criticized, not only the Harvard Research Center in Creative Altruism, but also my published works and even my own personality. Naturally, I would have preferred that such a clash would not have occurred, but, on the other hand, I do not offer any particular apology for my critical remarks, because sincere and frank criticism is one of the main duties of a scholar, even when it concerns his own department. Delivering them, after approximately eight years of observation, I was discharging only my duty of a scholar and of a member of this great University.[3]

Following this letter is Sorokin's appraisal of the department, in which he outlines several key criticisms. First and foremost was the department's failure to achieve a theoretical synthesis of sociology, social psychology, clinical psychology, and cultural anthropology into one scientific system. Sorokin asserts, "These four disciplines are as much apart under one roof of the Department of Social Relations as they were before their unification under this roof."[4] Secondly, undergraduate and graduate programs have failed to provide students with the skills and understanding necessary for developing an interdisciplinary perspective supported by sound interdisciplinary research. Sorokin notes that the undergraduate program required only one or two half courses intended to introduce students to the "vague field of social relations." Students are then required to select either sociology, social psychology, or cultural anthropology as a field of concentration. Obviously, the program does little to deliver the integrated social scientific understandings that were promised. The same is the case for the graduate program. Students concentrate and write their dissertations in one of the subfields; they undergo extensive "regimental training" in statistical methods of dubious value; and they receive almost no training in the content and methodologies of integrated social science. This unfortunate situation is compounded by the fact that training within the specialties is only "moderately satisfactory."

For these eight years I have been often unpleasantly surprised by the concentrators' ignorance of either history of the discipline of their concentration or of important currents, theories, methods, and techniques of such a discipline. I cannot help having the impression that graduate and undergraduate students have to waste a considerable part of their time and energy in studying various unimportant techniques or half-baked notions, instead of being trained in a solid and substantial knowledge of the discipline of their concentration. This situation is possibly responsible for the fact that several universities, and especially institutions which require competent sociologists, competent psychologists, and competent anthropologists have not always been anxious to employ graduates or Ph.D.s coming from this department, saying that they are neither specialists nor integrated scholars.[5]

Beyond doubt, these failures contributed to the reluctance of other prominent universities to adopt the social relations model of teaching and research.

Sorokin concluded by observing that almost all of the research by faculty and graduate students had been unpromising and methodologically misdirected. He suggested that only two constructive routes were open to the department: disband, as suggested by a survey of student opinion, or become truly interdisciplinary.[6]

One cannot but ask whether Sorokin's comments were solely the product of a seething anger and resentment or whether they had a foundation in fact. Existing evidence shows that the most systematic, impressive attempt at theoretical integration by the Department of Social Relations was *Toward a General Theory of Action*. This work was supported by a Carnegie Foundation grant and brought together Edward Shils, the erudite sociologist from the University of Chicago; Edward C. Tolman, the eminent psychologist from Berkeley; Richard C. Sheldon, Harvard social anthropologist and member of the Russian Research Center; and Talcott Parsons for concentrated work on theoretical issues. Their goal was to make a significant advance toward the theoretical unification of the social sciences. Committee meetings were held weekly from September 1949 to January 1950. The four principles met regularly with Allport, Kluckhohn, Murray, Sears, and Stouffer and occasionally circulated their work to other members of the department. Responses from both groups were used to revise, clarify, and extend the manuscript. The result of these deliberations was *Toward a General Theory of Action*, published in 1951. Parsons's feelings on the process and product are expressed in the preface:

This volume . . . is the product of nine individual social scientists, . . . four psychologists, three sociologists and two anthropologists. . . . The process has not been easy. Some of us have been closely associated over a considerable span of years. But when we tried to drive mutuality of understanding to deeper theoretical levels than was usual in our discourse, we frequently found unexpected and apparently serious differences. . . . However, with patience and perseverance, we have found it possible to make what, to us, is substantial progress toward agreement.

This fact . . . seems to us to bring out with peculiar vividness the fact that these many streams of thought are in the process of flowing together. We feel that the present effort belongs in the context of a major movement, whose significance to the future of social science far transcends the contributions of any one particular group. If we have helped to deepen the channel of the river and remove some obstacles to its flow, we are content.[7]

The belief that substantial agreement had been reached and progress made toward an integrated social theory was again demonstrated in the "General Statement" that introduces the volume. There Parsons states this treatise is

intended to contribute to the establishment of a general theory in the social sciences. . . . This statement does not purport to be the general theory. . . . it is rather a formulation of certain fundamental categories which will have to enter into the formulation of this general theory, which for many years has been developing through the convergence of anthropological studies of culture, the theory of learning, the psychoanalytic theory of personality, economic theory, and the study of modern social structure. . . . This present discussion will begin with an exposition of the fundamental concepts from which it is intended to develop a unified conceptual scheme for theory and research in the social sciences.[8]

This General Statement is signed by all nine of the participating social scientists.

Toward a General Theory of Action was widely read in- and outside of Harvard but did not have the desired groundbreaking impact. Cambridge scholars and others did not feel that a substantial synthesis, which could shape the future of the social sciences, had been achieved. While it was influential in the program, it never became departmental orthodoxy. As George Homans observed:

I too thought little of the "Yellow Book," because I was beginning to suspect that the authors' view of what constituted a theory was bound to lead their "approach" up a dead-end street: it would not even begin to move towards a theory of action. . . . Parsons himself laid the "Yellow Book" before a meeting of the whole department, including both tenured and nontenured members, urging us all to read it and implying, though without quite saying as much, that it ought to be adopted as the official doctrine of the department to guide future teaching and research. I was going to have none of that, if I could help it. Accordingly as soon as I was really satisfied that Parsons had finished, I spoke up and said in effect: "There must be no implication that this document is to be taken as representing the official doctrine of the department, and no member shall be put under any pressure to read it." Indeed there can be no official theoretical doctrines in science. A dreadful silence followed my attack, and I thought no one was going to support me. But finally Sam Stouffer, a tenured professor and a member of the senior committee, spoke up. He was always a fair-minded man—which did not mean he always agreed with me—and much to his honor but, I felt, somewhat reluctantly, he declared that the Yellow Book ought not be treated as departmental doctrine. There the matter dropped. Afterwards many of the junior members thanked me for what I had done. My seniors at last realized I was a bit of a rebel. No further official effort was made to integrate theory for the Department of Social Relations. Practically, for some years the structural-functionalism of Parsons was the dominant school of thought among our graduate students in sociology.[9]

The failure by senior scholars to provide an integrated foundation for social science was reflected in the character of work done by others in the department. While a good deal of varied research was conducted, very little of it was interdisciplinary, much less synthetic. An analysis of over five hundred research papers done by department members between 1946 and 1956 shows the following: over three hundred were single-authored works; the remaining two hundred were overwhelmingly co-authored by members of the same discipline. This crude index suggests that very little interdisciplinary research was taking place. While the Department of Social Relations was explicitly organized for interdisciplinary cooperation, it was not forthcoming. Members appeared to follow research and publication patterns typical of traditional departments. Instead of an interdisciplinary ethos unifying the department, they remained multidisciplinary.[10]

The failure of the department to achieve theoretical integration of disciplines was felt throughout the program. Sorokin is correct in stating that the graduate-level seminars did not show students how to achieve synthesis and integration in their work. The failure of formal instruction led to dependence on informal means, and emphasis turned to personal relationships between faculty and students. The dissertation research became the major mechanism for working at interdisciplinary synthesis. However, an examination of dissertations shows they were overwhelmingly confined to specific disciplinary interests rather than interdisciplinary topics. This multidisciplinary character of the program was reinforced by faculty appointments. New additions were made on the basis of disciplinary work and reputation rather than interdisciplinary interests and contributions.[11]

Similar problems were encountered by undergraduate concentrators. No one course gave an exposure to the full range of disciplinary interests, no courses demonstrated the goal of integrative social science, and no role models of integrative scholars were present on the faculty. The undergraduate program had also grown too quickly, and the quality of students had slipped. By the late 1940s social relations was the second-largest department in the college and had a reputation for giving easy courses. The program continued to attract a disproportionate number of students from the lower ranks. This created some unique problems but also made any meaningful integration of social science at the undergraduate level much more difficult.[12]

As to the overall quality of graduate students compared with those in the early sociology department, Sorokin was not equally accurate. Talcott Parsons refers to the first decade of the Department of Social Relations as "a true golden age" for graduate students. Among the promising scholars were Bernard Barber, Albert K. Cohen, James A. Davis, Harold Garfinkle, Joseph Kahl, Marion J. Levy Jr., Theodore Mills, Kasper Naegele, Thomas O'Dea, Fred L. Strodbeck, Francis X. Sutton, Edward A. Tiryakian, Jackson Toby, Morris Zelditch, Renee C. Fox, Robert N. Bellah, Neil J. Smelser, and Ezra Vogel. Clearly, this group was not without significance for sociology, and Sorokin's assessment should be taken with a grain of salt.

Sorokin's report to Larsen of the failure by Parsons and his collaborators to achieve an integrated theory may also reflect irritation over his own related works' being ignored by them and his personal exclusion from the process. After the publication of *The Social System* and *Toward a General Theory of Action* in 1951, Sorokin widely circulated two hundred copies of a mimeographed document entitled "Similarities and Dissimilarities Between Two Sociological Systems."[13] In this document he intimates that Parsons was guilty of either sloppy scholarship, amnesia, or at worst plagiarism. In the introduction to the document Sorokin writes:

Reading *Toward a General Theory of Action*, especially its most important part: "The General Theory of Action" representing the collective work of all the participants of the volume . . . then reading T. Parsons' *The Social System*, I was pleasantly surprised at finding the readings in some parts easy and feeling myself in these parts pasturing at very familiar grounds. The more I read these works, the more familiar I felt, at least, in their basic conceptual framework and in their main concepts. Soon I discovered the reason for this familiarity. It was a striking concordance between the basic conceptual scheme of the authors and my own conceptual framework. In a preliminary form my sociological framework was published first in my Russian two-volume *System of Sociology* (1921). In its fully developed form I have been hammering it in my courses at the Universities of Minnesota and Harvard since 1928; and since about the same time in several of my publications. Finally, it was published in its final form in the first three volumes of my *Social and Cultural Dynamics* (1937) and then in its fourth volume (1941). Then it was reiterated in an abbreviated form in my *Sociocultural Causality, Space, Time* (1943) and in my *Society, Culture, and Personality: Their Structure and Dynamics* (1947). While there is a multitude of dissimilarities between the two conceptual systems, there is hardly any doubt that the basic framework of the authors exhibits a notable resemblance to my framework. The subsequent points of similarity show this. Real similarity in these basic points goes, however, further than the given short quotations show: each of these basic concepts is fully developed in my works, is worked into the empirical phenomena, and is documented by a vast body of the logical and empirical evidence.

Now the points of similarity follow.[14]

Sorokin then lists nine areas of theoretical convergence or concordance: meaningful interaction as the basic process; subjects of interaction; trinity of personality, society, and culture; three forms of meaningful culture patterns; the concept of system; cultural system; social system and its properties; change of social systems; and personality system. He demonstrates each similarity by comparing quotes from his earlier volumes, *Society, Culture and Personality* and *Social and Cultural Dynamics*, with texts from the later Parsonsian works. Sorokin then observes:

The total body of these similarities is so evident that though my theories are neither mentioned nor referred to in both volumes, I contend that none of the numerous theories gratefully mentioned by the authors (M. Weber, V. Pareto, S. Freud, E. Durkheim, L. Henderson, and others) are so similar to the framework of the authors as the conceptual framework developed—logically and empirically—in my courses and publications. Even more, there is no sociological, anthropological, or psychological theory in the whole field of the psychosocial sciences as similar to the basic conceptual framework of two volumes discussed as my framework or, more exactly, my re-formulation, development, and test of the theories of many earlier eminent social thinkers. The basic framework of the new volumes is notably different even from that of T. Parsons' *Structure of Social Action.* His new framework shows a very tangible departure from the semi-nominalistic and singularistic standpoint of the *Structure of Social Action* with its main axis of the "means-end schema." Now this standpoint and schema are practically abandoned in favor of "a more generalized level" of analysis (S.S.,9) and the Weberian semi-nominalistic and singularistic framework of "actions," "actors and roles" is embraced by a more adequate "realistic standpoint" of "social system," "cultural system" and "personality system," or by the larger framework of *"the whole play"* in which "roles, actions, and actors" are but components. This shift explains why Parsons' present framework is more similar to my basic system than to that of his *Structure of Social Action.*[15]

Dissimilarities are many and originate from Parsons's inability to free himself from the theoretical orientation of the *Structure of Social Action.* Sorokin concludes:

Side by side with the basic similarities there is a multitude of dissimilarities between the two sociological theories compared. These dissimilarities concern important but mainly secondary points. Among many factors for these dissimilarities one is due to Parsons' uncompleted transition from his previous standpoint to the new one. For this reason "the sins" of the previous framework continue to visit upon, to crop up in, and to vitiate the new framework. Hence a peculiar eclecticism of his new stand-point. The incompatible elements of [the] two different frameworks, put together, [thus] clash and do not allow a consistent logical integration into one system. They fill the new basic framework with many "logico-meaningful congeries." It is earnestly hoped that the transition will eventually be completed and will lead to an elimination of these congeries.[16]

Sorokin may well have resented his work's being excluded not only from the theoretical tradition emerging at Harvard but from the lexicon of volumes that define American sociology from 1951 to the mid-1960s. This tradition of structural functional analysis would combine many of the elements common not only in the works of Parsons and Sorokin but in those of Robert Merton, Kingsley Davis, George Homans, Samuel Stouffer, Marion Levy, Edward Shils, R. Freed Bales, and Robin Williams. By asserting a claim for position in this legacy, Sorokin may have been doing more than warring with Parsons; he could have been struggling for a continued theoretical presence in the development of what Nicholas Mullins called "Standard American Sociology." But "Similarities" was considered by most as an attack on Parsons and a poorly reasoned claim for priority in developing concepts by then considered part of the public domain. Typical of this position is Robert E. L. Faris's account of Sorokin's attempt to publish "Similarities" in the *American Sociological Review*:

Even more absurd was a request from Pitirim A. Sorokin, who demanded that I publish a statement accusing Talcott Parsons of plagiarism from Sorokin's works. This was not the product of a reasonable mind; his principle argument was that Parsons had based a theory on the three elements of society, culture, and personality—an idea that was clearly in the public domain. On receiving a rejection, Sorokin responded with an angry letter, threatening to publish the statement elsewhere and to add that it had been refused by me, Editor of ASR. I terminated the correspondence by writing that if he did, he should add that the Editor had submitted the statement of every associate editor and that each one had recommended against printing it. I never learned if he attempted to publish it elsewhere.[17]

Sorokin would later publish portions of "Similarities" in *Fads* and almost the entire document in *Sociological Theories of Today*.[18]

Given the clashes over departmental affairs and their scholarly differences, it is likely that both Parsons and Sorokin expressed gentle sighs of relief when the latter's retirement from active teaching came in 1955.[19] Sorokin's transition to emeritus status in 1959, however, stimulated a more reflective response:

My reaction to this event was, on the whole, positive; nevertheless it did have some pensive notes. Retirement reminded me of the fact that the morning and the noon of my life were over and that it was now entering its late afternoon, to end eventually in the darkness of death. Since, however, after the death sentence passed upon me in 1918, the awareness of mortality had become habitual with me, this mood was neither depressive nor debilitating. Like elegiac music in some minor key, it was rather light, sweet, and consoling. After all, the thirty years of my association with the great university had been enjoyable and fruitful; during this period I had served the university and mankind as well as I could, and in turn they had effectively helped me to unfold my modest creativity. Of course, in these thirty years of my work for and in the university there had been painful and disheartening moments, but they were lost in the ocean of joyful experiences.[20]

Full retirement did not diminish Sorokin's activities or engagement with the profession. Along with writing and publication, he took a major role in the International Institute of Sociology meetings in Mexico and the American Sociological Association meetings in New York. Mexico was a wonderful experience. There Sorokin presented two papers: "A Quest for an Integral System of Sociology" and "Mutual Convergence of the United States and U.S.S.R. to the Mixed Sociocultural Type." Both addresses were published, and the latter was also translated into German by Adolph Grabowski and printed in the December 1960 number of the *Zeitschrift für Politik*. Combined with the hospitality of the Mexican scholars, receptions at several embassies, and the opportunity to visit local historical sites and the National University of Mexico, the congress proved to be a memorable event.

A similarly felicitous experience did not prevail at the ASA meetings in New York. Although Sorokin had withdrawn from the activities of the association for several years, he was strongly encouraged by Howard Becker, then president, and Rollin Chambliss, the chair of the theory section, to participate in a plenary session commemorating the centennial of Herbert Spencer. After substantial coaxing from Chambliss, he accepted and read his paper "Variations on the Spencerian Theme of Militant and Industrial Types of Society." The session was quite successful, and Chambliss wrote him that "the program drew the largest crowd I have ever seen at any meeting of the Association. . . . They came there,

I do believe, to hear *you*."[21] Based on the reception and solicited status of the paper Sorokin, submitted it to the *American Sociological Review*. It was rejected.

In a letter to Chambliss Sorokin wrote that he was neither surprised nor irritated by this and accepted the judgment humorously.[22] There was little humor, however, in his reply to Harry Alpert, then editor of the *American Sociological Review*, or in his account of the event in *Long Journey*. He ends his letter to Alpert ominously: "Without any difficulty, I can publish it in a number of scientific journals. For the present and future generations of sociologists, I will mark this incident in my Autobiography and possibly in other publications of mine. Like most of my books the Autobiography probably will be translated into several languages and in this way this remarkable incident will be known to the sociologists of many countries."[23] His mocking account of the incident appears in *Long Journey:*

When I humorously mentioned this fact to some of my scholar friends, they asked me Who is this Alpert?

"As an office administrator he has been doing well. Now he is a dean of the graduate school of Oregon University. As a scholar he is just a third-class sociologist, who, so far as I know, wrote only one poor book about Durkheim."

"Then how did he dare reject your paper?"

"For the same reason for which the papers of incomparably greater scholars than I happen to be rejected by midgety editors. Don't you know, I added facetiously, 'that Leibnitz's nurse and servant never understood why so many important people, even royalty, paid such great respect to their seemingly plain master?' Don't you know also that the ways of clerical administrators are inscrutable?"

Of course, my paper was not particularly important, but certainly it was at least as good as the rank and file of papers published in the *Review*. Since several American and foreign journals had already offered to publish the paper before, I sent it to *Social Science* where it was published in the next issue; since then it has been republished in translations in European, Latin-American and Asian scientific journals. So much for this humorous incident.[24]

Harry Alpert was not a third-class sociologist, nor was his book on Durkheim a poor one. Charles Page, in his autobiographical *Fifty Years in the Sociological Enterprise: A Lucky Journey*, writes: "Harry Alpert's *Emile Durkheim and His Sociology* (1939) . . . is a study in biography and the history of sociological theory which for decades, I believe, was the outstanding work on the great French scholar. The appraisal holds notwithstanding Talcott Parsons's detailed treatment of Durkheim in *The Structure of Social Action*."[25] As to Alpert's career Page states, "Alpert's later feats as splendid scholar-teacher and as a distinguished administrator in the National Science Foundation, UNESCO, and in the academy comprised a record rivaled by the careers of very few of his contemporaries."[26] An index of his stature among colleagues can be gleaned from the positions to which they elected him, including presidencies of the American Association for Public Opinion Research, the Pacific Sociological Association, and the Sociological Research Association. He was also vice president of the American Sociological Association and from 1960 to 1962 served in the appointed position of editor for the *American Sociological Review*. Alpert also made a substantial contribution to the social sciences during his five-year stint at the National Science Foundation, where in the face of great difficulty and resistance he established a separate Program for Social Science Research and served as its first director.[27]

Most of Sorokin's other involvements with professional organizations were less contentious. In 1961 he was elected the first president of the International Society for the Comparative Study of Civilization and attended its meeting in Salzburg, Austria. It was again a memorable event at which he was regally treated. Attending the meeting were Arnold Toynbee and his wife, who were housed in the same hotel as Sorokin and had long conversations over meals and drinks. While his duties as president were light, he did take responsibility for funding publication of the conference *Proceedings*. He obtained this support from Eli Lilly, who responded to his request with a personal check for five thousand dollars.[28]

Nineteen sixty-two was the capstone year for conference activities. The Sorokins attended three meetings in Washington, D.C., between 30 August and 5 September, and Pitirim spoke in key sessions at each. His presentations covered a wide range of topics. At the Fifth World Congress of Sociology he spoke on the uses of the historical method in the social sciences. For the Catholic Sociological Society he analyzed Teilhard de Chardin's *Phenomena of Man*. Most significant was his return to the American Sociological Association to present "The Practical Influences of Impractical Generalizing Sociological Theories." The session, chaired by Robert K. Merton, marked a key event in their relationship, as Merton recalls:

In a profound way, your paper in this session will round out a circle for me. I believe it was about 25 years ago—about 1928 or 1929, that the Sociological Society met in Washington. As a sophomore or junior in college, I attended that convention: my first such experience. It was then that I heard you give your paper on Hornell Hart's current ideas. As a result, I definitely decided upon two matters: first, that I would devote myself to sociology and second, that I would do all I could to begin my graduate studies under you.[29]

Sorokin was no doubt pleased by Merton's recollection, and these meetings ended on a happy note.

The Silence Is Broken

As Sorokin settled into the life of an emeritus, three processes were unfolding that would transform his relationship with professional sociologists. The first was initiated by his visit to Mary Washington College of the University of Virginia for a lecture in November 1958. The second came with a seventieth-birthday greeting from Ed Tiryakian in January 1959. The third resulted from a conversation over a brown-bag lunch among O. D. Duncan, his wife, Beverly, and Albert J. Reiss in early January 1963.

Sorokin met Philip J. Allen at a dinner at Mary Washington College in Fredericksburg, Virginia, after he had addressed the college's students and faculty. There Allen spoke of his idea for a series on "outstanding contemporary sociologists" that he wished to inaugurate with a volume on Sorokin. The anticipated series, "The American Sociological Forum," would follow a format developed by the philosopher Paul Arthur Schilpp for his "Library of Living Philosophers" volumes. Specifically, there would be an intellectual autobiography, followed by critical articles from leading experts in the field, the reply of the scholar to critics, and a complete bibliography of the subject's work. Sorokin expressed interest, and Allen soon sent him a preliminary outline for the volume.

The outline suggested topics and critics. Allen pointed out that he had included many nonsociologists in hopes of stimulating a cross-disciplinary dialogue, and had also excluded critics he felt could not, at this point, be objective and dispassionate (excluding here Talcott Parsons and Read Bain). But

to select only your friends might subvert the intent and purpose underlying the series, in general, and this volume in particular. MacIver and Lundberg . . . may be expected to give you the ungloved treatment, as also may one or two others. But if I estimate your character correctly, you will heartily welcome these as a challenge and an opportunity to clarify some of your misrepresented views. Anyway, you will have the last word in your Reply.[30]

Allen also noted that he had sent a prospectus for the volume to the editor of Oxford University Press and would notify Sorokin when he received a reply.

The answer from Oxford was encouraging but noncommittal. The press was interested, but the market would be narrow, and they would make no commitment without the completed manuscript. From April to December 1959 Allen tried to find other publishers and failed. He thus wrote Sorokin shortly before Christmas 1959 that he had cast "all caution aside and decided to go ahead with the volume, despite the reluctance of publishers to make a formal commitment."[31] Allen's faith was justified, but it was over two years before Duke University Press agreed to publish the volume with the assistance of a Ford Foundation grant. The results of his efforts, *Pitirim A. Sorokin in Review,* came out in January 1963, shortly before Sorokin's seventy-fourth birthday.

The contents of the volume changed greatly over the four years. Of the original contributors, only Arnold Toynbee and T. Lynn Smith delivered their solicited essays. To their works were added essays by Robert Merton and Bernard Barber on the sociology of science, Joseph Ford on integralism, Matilda White Riley and Mary E. Moore on methodology, Gosta Carlsson on social mobility, David Mace on sex and society, Othmar Anderle on culture, Alexandre Vexliard on psychological theories, Alex Inkeles on Soviet-U.S. relations, and Nicholas Timasheff on law, revolution, social calamities, and war. To these essays were added personal assessments of Sorokin's contributions by F. R. Cowell (England), K. M. Munshi (India), Gorrado Gini (Italy), and Lucio Mendietta y Nunez (Mexico). The work is valuable, and in one volume summarizes Sorokin's contributions, fairly criticizes them, and provides readers with a well-qualified defense. The essays by Ford, Toynbee, Timasheff, Anderle, and Vexliard introduce Sorokin as a philosopher and theoretician. His views on science and methodology are put forth in the essay by Merton and Barber and that by Riley and Moore. Specific studies are analyzed by Smith, Carlsson, Inkeles, and Mace.

The reader begins the venture into Sorokin through an autobiographical essay tracing the development of his mental life. He captures his audience with the candid disclosure that "in the late afternoon of my life . . . I have a personal interest in understanding the reasons and factors that determined the course of my mental life and, especially, the character of my sociological theories and other 'mental productions.' "[32] His inquiry is directed by the sociology of knowledge, and he centers his analysis on changes in the cultural mentalities that he experienced. Thus the assessment of his mental life at the microsociological level parallels his theoretical considerations of social change at the macrosociological level in *Dynamics*. In the closing section of his essay, Sorokin delineates a series of very specific relationships between events in his life and his scholarship. Among them are his peasant origins and studies of rural sociology; his six imprisonments and the volume *Crime and Punishment, Service and Reward;* his wayfaring and wildly changing life as the foundation for his study of social change in books like *Dynamics, Social Mobility, The Sociology of Revolution, Man and Society in Calamity,* and *Reconstruction of Humanity;* living through two world wars and two revolutions as the source of his abhorrence of violence and his firm commitment to sympathy, mutual aid, and love as the preferred mechanisms for social change. This, of course, led to the Harvard Research Center in Creative Altruism and the volumes on the development and power of altruistic love and its uses in social reconstruction.[33]

Sorokin ends his account with a discussion of the character of his theories and his commitment to them. He declares that these theories are more adequate and true than all other competing theories.[34] He asserts this not from arrogance but out of commitment to the scholar's responsibility "to find and tell the truth" regardless of any consequences. This commitment has driven him, and he has pursued it to the limits of his energy and ability. It is now for the reader to assess how well he has done. This essay provides not only an articulate exposition of the changes in Sorokin's thinking but a compelling introduction to the man and his work.

An anonymous reviewer for Duke University Press grasped the power of Sorokin's essay:

The autobiographical sketch by Sorokin himself makes fascinating and informative reading. The frank revelation of the impoverished background of his youth, his self-support after the age of ten, his self-education until 14, his three imprisonments under the Czars and three more under the Communists, his sentence to death by the Communists and his grant of amnesty by Lenin, and his final banishment from the Soviet Union, throw a flood of light on his personality, character, and achievements, his willingness to tackle almost superhuman tasks in the way of research and scholarship, his persistence against obstacles and discouragements which few have equaled and almost none have surpassed, his firmness in support of his theories which have sometimes at first met with skepticism and occasionally with downright hostility (which Sorokin himself acknowledges as "bull-headedness")–all this reminds one of Toynbee's challenge-response theory of the development of civilizations applied to the individual.[35]

Sorokin's lucid style and scholarship are also shown to advantage when he faces his critics. Between the autobiography and Sorokin's "Replies," however, is a coherent collection of essays that introduce apprentice and journeyman sociologists to the complexities and range of his sociology.

Sorokin the theoretician and philosopher is revealed in the essays of Toynbee, Timasheff, Anderle, Vexliard, and Ford. Readers will benefit by studying Toynbee first to get the historical boundaries and analytical concepts from which Sorokin forms his theory of social change. The essay on social structure by Anderle is a disappointment, but one can gather Sorokin's concepts of social organization from his reply to the Austrian. Timasheff explores disasters (wars, revolutions, calamities) as forms of social transformation that broaden Sorokin's use of Immanent Determinism. Alexandre Vexliard's well-crafted essay on personality develops Sorokin's notions on culture and personality as well as delineating his contributions to psychology and personality theory. Ford's essay on Integralism can then be read as an umbrella piece that puts these contributions under one philosophical and theoretical system. The beginning student would benefit by first studying Sorokin's brief overview of Integralism that introduces his reply to critics.

Toynbee explicates the philosophy of history that serves as the basis of Sorokin's mature works and Integralism. The historian begins with the insightful claim that Sorokin's efforts must be taken as a whole and correctly launches his analysis of the oeuvre with a masterful exegesis of the four volumes of *Dynamics*. He quickly addresses a key objection by Sorokin's earlier critics to the use of statistics in the study of social change. This is not a blunder but a pioneering approach to historical method and the statistician's craft. Sorokin has moved both out of the safety zone and into a wilderness full of risk and promise. The more timid settlers of the historical and statistical landscape will rise in alarm as the pioneer quantitatively explores and reports his finding on changes in art, ethics, values, and cultural subsystems. *Dynamics* is a big target, and the critics will come after him. What they do not realize is that Sorokin has seized the initiative and they are

pounding after him into fields that they would perhaps never have trodden except in hot pursuit of a heretic. Laboriously, they will pick perhaps as much as 90 per cent of Sorokin's findings to pieces. But Sorokin will come out strategically victorious from any number of tactical defeats. It will have been he, not his pursuers, to whom the credit will have been due for this involuntary but nonetheless fruitful broadening of the conventional statisticians' horizon; and the result will have been a solid gain for one of mankind's common causes: the drive to increase human knowledge and understanding.[36]

Sorokin also blazes new trails for the historian when defending his quantitative approach to their vocation.

There is scarcely any historical work . . . where, explicitly or implicitly, quantitative judgments are not given in verbal form. What historians of ideas, human thought, science, religion, art styles, political systems, or economic processes do not use quantitative expressions like the following: "the period was marked by an increase of riots, revolts, and disorders," "the period was marked by a decline of idealism and religion," "Kant was one of the greatest philosophers," "It was an epoch of the rise and triumph of materialism, nominalism, the Gothic style, or socialistic doctrine," and so on? . . .

The above quotations and thousands of other statements of historians and social scientists are quantitative and also verbal quantitative. The procedure used here [in Sorokin's own work] is numerical quantitative. The first makes quantitative statements but in an indefinite verbal form without the use of figures or numerical indicators. The second describes the quantitative change with the help of figures. Which method is preferable?[37]

Toynbee's contextualization of Sorokin's methodology is followed by a succinct delineation of his key concepts and propositions. Sorokin's focus on societies in motion reflects the keen insight that change is the essence of sociocultural phenomena. *Dynamics* is well named, and the concept of immanently driven superrhythms is well reasoned in that it does not pretend to be all-inclusive. Sorokin scrutinizes patterns of change in five major cultural systems and their derivatives but makes no claim that the observed changes affect the entire culture or typify its entire history. The observed changes are the consequences of actions within the total culture (immanent causation), specific to it, and not generalizable to other similar cultures. Sorokin fails to give due weight to external factors as motors of change, according to Toynbee. However, his principles of immanent causation and alternation of recurrent states (the patterns of the superrhythms) show a strong independent concordance with theories of Empedocles, Ibn-Khaldūn, and Chinese scholars of the yin and yang. Sorokin's rediscovery of the principle in the previously unstudied laboratory of Greco-Roman culture and its derivative Western culture provides convergent validation. This convergence between minds working in markedly different time periods and cultures "is surely most impressive." Toynbee is not implying that Sorokin was unaware of his predecessors, for he clearly deals with them (among others) in chapter 13 of the fourth volume of *Dynamics*. "But his knowledge of them is not incompatible with his having made the same discovery independently; and if Sorokin did arrive at the idea independently, its discovery at least four times over suggests that there is likely to be something in it."[38]

While Sorokin's theory of change and its empirical testing in Western culture is clearly a contribution, it is not without flaws. Among the more prominent are Sorokin's attribution to culture the dominant power in the shaping of personality. This leads to a one-sided, overly determined concept of humanity and fails to grasp the dynamic interplay between personality and culture. Toynbee also argues that there are places in *Dynamics* where poor operationalization of ideas led to inappropriate measurement. This is particularly true for the sections that attempt to assess progress in the arts and sciences. Sorokin also does not give due weight to external factors as change agents, nor does he reconcile his implicit belief that all cultural systems generate the forces of their own replacement with his assertion that sociocultural systems have the power to be at least partially self-determined. If the last is true, then why is each system bound to fail in time? Putting these small criticisms aside (and both scholars do), there is great agreement in their works:

But it is, of course, as an intellectual pioneer that Sorokin has made his mark on the history of thought about human affairs. A pioneer condemns himself to be corrected and surpassed. This fate is on the pioneer's own head, because in the intellectual field, at any rate, one need not be a pioneer unless one chooses. At least, one need not report one's findings and thereby draw fire (and Sorokin has, fortunately, reported his findings circumstantially). A pioneer's sketch map will be corrected by his less enterprising successors, the surveyors; his trail will be progressively straightened out, underpinned, surfaced, and double-tracked; his axe's blaze marks on tree trunks will be replaced by neon signs. All these improvements will overtake his pathfinding work; and, the quicker they do, the more eloquent will be their testimony to his achievement. Later generations do not spend time and energy on improving pioneer trails that lead nowhere. The trail on which they work is always one that has proved its value; and, in all their subsequent improvements on it, there is one thing that they cannot do to its discoverer. They cannot supersede him. Even when his work has been completely overlaid, it will still remain invisibly on the map. Daniel Boone's trail, for instance, still lives today in the radar beam that a pilot gratefully follows in navigating his plane from Washington D.C. to St. Louis.[39]

Further exploration of Sorokin's ideas on social structure and change is found in the essays by Anderle and Timasheff. Anderle regrettably attempts to make Sorokin a cultural morphologist. Rather than extending Sorokin's ideas on social structure and organization, he attempts to win support for the morphologists. His argument would influence only the uninitiated. Even a novice in the study of social change would quickly realize the deep conflicts between the two approaches and recognize that Anderle's essay is no more than proselytizing. Sorokin firmly distinguishes his position in the "Reply" and elaborates on his taxonomy of groups and social organization.[40] His response is uncharacteristically restrained. This may result from his previous association with Anderle, who was Secretary General of the International Society for the Comparative Study of Civilization during Sorokin's presidency.

Timasheff's essay begins with a look at the role of law in Sorokin's theory of order and change. Correctly identifying their mutual debt to Petrazhitsky, Timasheff observes that Sorokin is one of the few sociologists to use law as a key concept in his studies of statics and dynamics. Legal norms differ from other moral rules in that they are imperative, attributive, and enforceable. Laws ascribe rights to one party and duties to another. Other norms are only imperative; they specify what one should do but do not give the others a right to demand such an action. Thus they are not enforceable. Legal norms organize interaction, guide the personality system, and are a major mechanism for orderly social change.

Revolutions and wars are mechanisms of disorderly change. Timasheff traces Sorokin's thoughts on these forms of hostility from the *Sociology of Revolution* to *Social and Cultural Dynamics, Man and Society in Calamity,* and *Society, Culture and Personality.* In the later works Sorokin abandons behaviorism and develops a more sociological approach to these processes. A revolution is a comparatively rapid, extensive, and violent change of a society's laws and the values they represent; it is a forceful change involving a significant proportion of the native population.[41] Sorokin analyzed and reanalyzed the data from *Dynamics.* In his first nonbehavioristic interpretation he asserts that revolutions are a part of the life process of society; that is, they appear regularly in the history of a nation. This finding is refined in *Society, Culture and Personality.* The observed pattern in *Dynamics* is a consequence of fluctuations in value integration. The more integrated, compatible, and stable the system of values among citizens, the greater the chance of peace. When integration declines, particularly if the decline is sharp and sudden, the greater the chances of civil war. Thus Sorokin's explanations for revolutions evolve from a stimulus-response model, to a determination of their historical occurrences and correlates, and end with a model based on changing patterns of social solidarity.

For wars Timasheff reports a similar process. Wars are an external, violent intergroup disturbance between or among nations. To analyze their frequency and traits, Sorokin and his assistants developed a data set of 967 wars. These conflicts were organized by country and reported for intervals of twenty-five and one hundred years, from as early as 901 to 1925. The aggregated data reflected no strong pattern of increase or decrease, but wars were more frequent during periods of political and territorial expansion. They also increased during times of national decline and decay. These periods corresponded with major transitions between cultural epochs. Sorokin interpreted these fluctuations using the same patterns of social solidarity that he observed for revolutions. So the common denominators for changes in frequency of internal and external social conflict are stability and change in the integration of values.

From these forms of hostility Sorokin moves to a more generalized study of large-scale tragedies in *Man and Society in Calamity*. The disasters of famine, disease, floods, and earthquakes are also analyzed as stimulants of social change. He studies their impact first on individual behavior and then on social institutions and organization. The results are similar to the processes of disintegration produced by war and revolution, and are explained with similar theoretical tools, for example, the law of polarization. However, the analysis of all these forms of calamity and disaster does broaden and augment Sorokin's grasp and understanding of change. His model covers in a general way orderly processes of transformation in society, disorderly processes (war and revolution), and transformations as a result of natural and social disasters. He has a scope rarely matched by other theorists of social change.

Alexandre Vexliard's essay[42] is an excellent overview of Sorokin's contributions to general psychology and personality theory. Vexliard emphasizes the latter and shows how Sorokin develops a theory of basic personality and relates its form and content to his theories of cultural mentalities and supersystems. His grounding of personality in culture and history does not, in Vexliard's mind, lead to the overdeterminism suggested by Toynbee. Instead, it is based on Sorokin's antiformalism. That is, social reality intertwines with personality in such a way as to have existence only in discernible mental processes and social behavior. Vexliard demonstrates this weaving of personality, cultural mentality, and supersystems in his discussion of the sensate, ideational, and idealistic cultural types and their derivatives.[43]

The vital part of this essay arises from Vexliard's acknowledgment that Sorokin's most important contributions to psychology are in his techniques for transforming the personality. Sorokin's ideas, while directed toward increasing a person's altruistic development and actions, apply to the majority of important psychological and moral characteristics. Hence, knowing how to change and develop character contributes substantially to the development of other methods of individual and collective therapy aimed at personality problems and the formation of a desirable nature.[44]

Furthermore, to grow and improve, one must go beyond the bio-conscious and socioconscious level of personality and develop the supra-consciousness, that is, the spirit or soul. To do this requires focusing on spiritual development in our lives and reorganizing our egos and group affiliations for a closer identification with the supraconsciousness. Humans have developed several unified systems to promote this type of growth, most of which incorporate in one way or another the twenty-six techniques discussed by Sorokin in *The Ways and Power of Love*. Thus Vexliard sees in Sorokin's psychological theories a method for the development of the total personality; a good model for examining the complex micro- and macrosociological interactions between the individual and the group; and a methodological and substantive critique of Freud and modern psychology that deserves careful attention.

Sorokin's philosophy of history, his theories of social order, personality, and social change, and his ontology and epistemology coalesce in his Integralism. Joseph Ford's scrutiny gives the reader a broad assessment of Sorokin as philosopher.[45] However, Sorokin takes the opportunity of "replying to his critics" to lay out for new readers a concise outline of Integralism as a philosophy, system of cognition and truth, and theory of humanity and culture. As a philosophy, Integralism expands materialistic and idealistic philosophies by adding to the world of matter and mind a third element of spirit. Sorokin's ontology takes the ultimate reality of the world as a creative, changing synthesis of these elements. Correspondingly, cognition and truth are three-dimensional. We know matter through our senses, we derive rational aspects of truth through reason and mind, and we grasp the suprarational through intuition and spirit. Each is a powerful form of knowing; when combined, these elements yield a more potent and exhaustive comprehension of the world. For Sorokin humans are integral creatures consisting of body, mind, and soul. The sociocultural realities that they create and inherit result from their nature and are best understood when all aspects of their existence are examined and analyzed. Hence Integralism is an ontological, epistemological, and sociological doctrine for understanding the dynamics of our existence.[46]

Ford demonstrates how Sorokin marries sociological discourse to broader concerns in philosophy and at the same time is condemned by sociologists and largely ignored by philosophers. Ford's exposition clearly shows the historical and philosophical common ground that is the basis of Sorokin's Integralism and theory of change. But what has this done to Sorokin? While it has marginalized him in both disciplines, it crystallized his identity as a pioneer, allowing him to freely explore the mountains and boundaries of both disciplines, searching for and charting the pass that united them. This he did with substantial significance for both. Ford observes:

More than any contemporary social scientist, and probably as much as any contemporary philosopher, Sorokin affirms the crucial role of the major philosophic premises of a culture in the total articulation and, indeed, in the very quality of continued existence of the society and the culture. Not only does the main philosophic premise "define the situation"; it defines the future, the very potentiality of survival. In the current sociocultural crisis, he sees the only hope in a new integralist philosophy which can and must become the basis for a new integralist culture.[47]

In short, philosophy and culture coalesce in humanity's struggle for survival. What we know, how we know it, and how we use it combine to produce the ideas and their sociological expressions that will advance us as a species.

"But how shall we evaluate Sorokin's integralism as a philosophy?"[48] Ford puts the ball in play by raising several questions about the strains and contradictions in the Sorokinian system. Are philosophically reconcilable opposites reconcilable in social systems, as Sorokin asserts? Can the validity of Integralism as a system be demonstrated rationally or empirically? If neither, is it then a matter of faith? If so, where does this leave us? What about values and moral philosophy? Has Sorokin made a distinctive contribution, and if so, what is it? Additionally, Integral truth is most closely associated with the Idealistic system. This is the least stable and shortest-lived of all the systems. What does this suggest about the viability of an Integral social order? Ford raises many more questions about Integralism's philosophical and sociological nature. Some he answers, and others are left to Sorokin for his "Reply." In combination, the article and its rejoinder provide the careful reader with a deeper understanding of Integralism and its limitations. Combined with the other essays in this section, it also provides a provocative introduction to Sorokin as philosopher, sociologist, and historian. The remaining essays challenge and assess his contributions to the sociological enterprise.

Central to this reappraisal are the piece by Merton and Barber and that by Riley and Moore. Merton and Barber[49] use the sociology of science as a springboard to criticize Sorokin's idealistic philosophy of history. They find that focusing on the three supersystems and their corresponding mentalities restricts the analysis of ideas to what is consistent with the dominant mentality and eliminates important differences occurring in the same period. By reducing the flow of ideas to

this single source, a sociology of science results that has several significant weaknesses. It is overly deterministic; it does not account for the
effects of the social structure of the scientific community on the development of knowledge; and it leaves unspecified the mechanisms (and
contents) of selective accumulation of knowledge from one scientific
period to another.

In addition to their macro- and microsociological concerns, Merton
and Barber raise pointed methodological questions about the study of
science in *Dynamics* and the critique of statistics in *Fads*. Sorokin relies
heavily on quantitative data to demonstrate superrhythms. Statistics are
not, as Robert Park asserted in his review of *Dynamics*, a concession to the
current sensate mentality.[50] Quantitative information is essential to Sorokin's argument and is used as a vehicle for confirming his theory.

However, Sorokin's use of such data in *Dynamics* poses key theoretical
and methodological problems for Merton and Barber. On the theoretical
level:

Sorokin describes empiricism as "the typically sensate system of truth." The last five
centuries, and more particularly the last century, represent "sensate culture par
excellence!" Yet even in this flood tide of sensate culture, Sorokin's statistical indices
show only some 53 per cent of influential writings to be characterized by "empiricism." Furthermore, in the earlier centuries of this sensate culture, from the late
sixteenth to the mid-eighteenth, the indices of empiricism are consistently lower
than the indices for rationalism (which, in the theory, is associated with an idealistic
rather than a sensate culture). The statistical indicators, then, show that the notion of
a "prevailing" system of truth needs to be greatly qualified, if it is to cover both the
situations in which it represents a bare statistical "majority" and even a statistically
indicated minority in the writings of a period.[51]

The authors are not concerned with the gap between theory and data nor
what is suggested about sixteenth- to eighteenth-century science, but
rather wish

to suggest that, even on Sorokin's own premises, the general characterizations of
historical cultures as sensate, idealistic, or ideational constitute only a first step in the
analysis, a step which must be followed by further detailed analyses of deviations
from the central tendencies of the culture. Once Sorokin has properly introduced the
notion of the extent to which historical cultures are in fact integrated, he cannot, in all
theoretical conscience, treat the existence of types of knowledge which differ from
the dominant tendencies as evidence of a mere "congeries" or as a merely accidental
fact. It is as much a problem of the sociology of science to account for these
substantial "deviations" from the central tendency as to account for these tendencies
themselves. And for this . . . it is necessary to develop a theory of the socio-

structural bases of thought in a fashion that a cultural-emanationist theory does not permit.[52]

Methodologically, a comparison of *Dynamics* and *Fads* reveals Sorokin's deep ambivalence toward statistics. In *Dynamics* Sorokin employed independent experts to gather specific data. They were blind to the purpose and hypotheses of their work. These assistants were experts in the field but, given the time frame and range of the data they gathered, were not intimately familiar with the events or phenomena. However, in *Fads* Sorokin asserts:

Only through direct empathy, coliving and intuition of the psychosocial states can one grasp the essential nature and differences . . . of religious, scientific, aesthetic, ethical, legal, economic, technological, and other cultural value-systems and their subsystems. Without the direct living experience of these cultural values, they will remain terra incognita for our outside observer and statistical analyst. . . . These methods are useless in understanding the nature and difference between, say, Plato's and Kant's systems of philosophy, between the ethics of the Sermon on the Mount and the ethics of hate. . . . Only after successfully accomplishing the mysterious inner act of "understanding" each system of ideas or values, can one classify them into adequate classes, putting into one class all the identical ideas, and putting into different classes different ideas or values. Only after that, can one count then, if they are countable, and perform other operations of a mathematical or statistical nature, if they are possible. Otherwise, all observations and statistical operations are doomed to be meaningless, fruitless, and fallacious simulacra of real knowledge.[53]

Sorokin must deal with the discrepancy between "his actual practices" and "the far more demanding criteria for such quantification proposed in the *Fads*."[54] But Merton and Barber suspect that "what Sorokin actually does in the one case seems to us more compelling than what he says in the other."[55] It would also be a major contribution if Sorokin, in his reply, explicitly set out the criteria for the appropriate collection and use of social and cultural statistics. This would be methodologically helpful and a direct contribution to the process by which theory is validated in social science.

Merton and Barber conclude with several other challenges for their former teacher.[56] However, Matilda White Riley and Mary E. Moore narrow and soften the focus of Merton and Barber in their examination of Sorokin as a quantitative investigator of complex sociohistorical structures and processes. They are quick to acknowledge the tremendous imbalance between the then available methods and the goals of Sorokin's research. As a result, much of what he did was pioneering.[57] His commitment to an empirically informed macrosociological study of social processes and institutions began with *Social Mobility* and *Principles of Rural-Urban Sociology,* and reached its apex with *Social and Cultural Dynamics.* In each of these works Sorokin wrestled with fundamental and ardous methodological problems. In each he struggled to develop multidimensional definitions that captured the key elements of the object of study in such a way as to empirically document changes from one form to another. To analyze patterns of change he struggled with the gains and losses that result from aggregating and disaggregating data. All of his empirical studies reflected his awareness and frustration over the inherent dissonance between a concept and its indicator. Luckily, he did not give in to raw empiricism and reify data in order to proceed with analysis. Sorokin clearly understood that lack of fit between concept and indicator ended in a loss of precision that was amplified by statistical manipulation, and that with each operation the relationship between data and reality weakened. Yet he continued in the task of crafting an empirical macrosociology. Why?

Sorokin was more concerned about enriching our knowledge of the "what, how and why of human life" than with the techniques of research; techniques were "a mere means not the end of creative work." Sorokin cut through the Gordian knot of quantitative methodology by keeping his techniques simple and direct. The simpler the method, the fewer the arbitrary assumptions it contained and the more reliable the results. Secondly, the difficulty in precisely defining the multidimensional phenomena that he studied made superfluous and misleading any attempt at precision. Thus Sorokin asserted, "In this type of research, my efforts at measurement and my cognitive ambitions have seldom aimed at results that were more than only *roughly valid.*"[58]

Riley and Moore further observe he avoided modern methods in *Dynamics* because they were based on sampling and he was using total enumerations; several seemed to rest on weak theoretical bases; they did not apply to what he was studying; and he was not convinced that the methods would deliver the promised goods. Consequently, he chose to work with direct enumerations and basic imputations. He also provided his readers with the raw data necessary to check his results or do their own analysis. Therefore, they conclude that his work should be judged not by technical shortcomings but on how adequately it grasps the fundamental realities of the human universe.

The quality of his data, statistical analysis, and the theoretical web that gave them coherence is open to further scrutiny in the essays that follow Riley and Moore's. T. Lynn Smith provides a first-rate history and appraisal of Sorokin's rural-urban sociology. Gosta Carlsson broadens the dialogue with his analysis of *Social Mobility*. These two essays, along with Sorokin's candid and focused replies,[59] give new and old readers a revitalized introduction to the power and scope of his science. The book, to this point, invites a reengagement with the man and his ideas.

Lamentably, the remaining essays contribute unevenly to the core discussed previously. The pieces by Alex Inkeles and David Mace criticize Sorokin's works on Russia and the United States, and *The American Sex Revolution*, respectively. These works were written primarily for lay audiences. Consequently, sociologists will get little that is helpful for understanding Sorokin's general theory, even though Inkeles's article is a good orienting statement to U.S.-Soviet relations.

Of the four assessment essays by Italian, English, Latin American, and Indian scholars, Gorrado Gini's is arguably the most provocative and informative. F. R. Cowell's piece covers worn ground, and those of Lucio Mendieta y Nunez and K. M. Munski are more personal comments and paeans than assessments. In combination with the other essays, however, they reflect a coherent body of work capable of beginning a reappraisal by the sociological community of one of its pioneering members.

This exploration of Sorokin and his significance for sociology continues in Edward A. Tiryakian's *Sociological Theory, Values, and Sociocultural Change: Essays in Honor of Pitirim A. Sorokin*.[60] Unlike Allen's volume, this is not a penetrating look into the complexities and contributions of Sorokin. Instead, it explores topics that were important in Sorokin's work and remain significant in the contemporary sociological enterprise. By and large the essays reflect the interests of the authors as they relate to the central themes of theory, values, and change. Talcott Parsons, Florence Kluckhohn, Thomas F. O'Dea, and Walter Firey are concerned with values. Parsons and O'Dea focus on religion, and Parsons's essay challenges Sorokin's notion of the current era as one of a declining Christian influence. Instead, Parsons argues that Christian values have become differentiated and institutionalized throughout the structure of secular society. They are not only shared with the varied Protestant denominations but extend to three other important groups: Catholics, Jews, and those who claim no formal denominational affiliation.[61] In other essays Charles Loomis summarizes his theory of social change; Carle Zimmerman argues for the convergence of four family systems into a common type; Wilbert Moore and Georges Gurvitch explore different qualities of time; Marion J. Levy opens the issue of necessary conditions for a theory of human nature; Robert Merton and Elinor Barbar investigate the concept of sociological ambivalence; Bernard Barber and Logan Wilson examine the dynamics of the business and academic communities, respectively; Nicholas Timasheff reintroduces the sociology of Don Luigi Sturzo; and only Arthur K. Davis directly reports on poorly learned "Lessons from Sorokin." While these essays are only tangentially related to Sorokin, the fact that so many first-rate sociologists came together to honor him could not escape the notice of the sociological community. Indeed, attention to both volumes was expanded by the reviews of prominent sociologists in the major sociological journals. For example, Charles Tilly reviewed the Allen volume in the *American Sociological Review*, Otis Dudley Duncan reviewed both works for the *American Journal of Sociology*, and Robin Williams reviewed Tiryakian's book in the *American Sociological Review*. Hence, by 1963 Sorokin was again in the mainstream of the sociological community.

These currents of interest deepened when later in the same year his autobiography, *A Long Journey*, made its debut and was also widely reviewed. This work broadens the glimpse of personal history he gave in *Leaves from a Russian Diary*. It is neither a revolutionary's history, an intellectual account, a hermeneutical guide, nor a personal document, yet it contains elements of all these. We get no systematic exegesis of his work and ideas, no agenda for interpretation, and no intimate insights into family, friends, or passions. There are snippets here and there: the softly stated joy at the births of his sons; his love for the outdoors, flowers, and music; the satisfactions and pride he derived from family life and good friends. But these figures and events stay largely in the background and are undeveloped. What we do have is a Sorokin without sharpness and acrimony. He gives the reader an accurate yet detached sense of himself as a man. While there are a few jabs at editors, journals, critics, and professional societies, this is largely a book without bitterness. As Wilbert Moore writes in his review, "He has mellowed . . . and he has kept his weapons of scholarly harassment concealed."[62] Thus there is no invitation to controversy, just a subtle, softly formed summons to move beyond the caricature.[63]

With the autobiography the aura of suspicion, animus, and indifference began to lift. As Tiryakian writes, Sorokin's "old admirers, critics and skeptics will all read this autobiography with interest. But it also deserves to be read by younger members of the profession who would like to get acquainted with Sorokin the man."[64] This widespread attention to Sorokin and his work received another synergistic boost in 1963 with the launching of a grassroots, write-in campaign to place him on the ballot for the presidency of the American Sociological Association. The catalyst for this event was O. D. (Otis Dudley) Duncan, the son of Sorokin's old friend and protégé Otis Durant Duncan.

Restoration: The Campaign

The idea originated from a luncheon conversation that O. D. Duncan and Beverly Duncan had with Albert J. Reiss Jr. They recalled that Sorokin, after losing in 1952 to Florian Znaniecki, had never received the customary renomination for the ASA presidency.[65] On 21 January 1963 O. D. Duncan wrote to some friends who might be sympathetic to correcting this oversight: C. Arnold Anderson, Walter Firey, Charles P. Loomis, Robert K. Merton, William H. Sewell, and T. Lynn Smith. The response and enthusiasm for redressing this omission were so unequivocally positive that a nascent movement for Sorokin's nomination emerged.[66] Duncan and the others agreed that they would start contacting ASA members before the official candidates were announced by the nominating committee. This would make it clear that the movement intended to honor Sorokin and not to repudiate any particular candidate. The campaigners decided to follow a three-step approach. First they implemented Robert Merton's suggestion for a "committee of correspondence." That is, "each of a relatively small group of us . . . say twenty or so . . . write to twenty-five or so members of the Association putting forward the case for Sorokin."[67] This, of course, required a central coordinator to oversee the project and avoid duplications. O. D. Duncan volunteered and with the help of Beverly Duncan became the campaign coordinator. They received substantial assistance from Charles P. Loomis, and the three of them carried the major portion of the committee's workload.

The second step was a mass mailing of postcards explaining the campaign and asking for support. The committee mailed the cards early in order to reach ASA members before the official association ballots arrived. The card read as follows:

Dear Fellow Members of the American Sociological Association:

Although the Nominating Committee has not yet announced its selections for President-Elect, the pattern in recent years has been to overlook one of our most distinguished members, P. A. Sorokin. We hope that it is not too late to remedy this oversight, without prejudice to the worthy nominees the committee may choose. According to our constitution, a write-in of a given candidate's name by 10% of the members voting will require a new election, including him as candidate (Feb. '63 ASR, p. 137). We urge that you consider the desirability of this course of action.

C. Arnold Anderson	Dudley Duncan	Walter Firey
Chas. P. Loomis	Robert K. Merton	Wm. H. Sewell
T. Lynn Smith	Herbert Blumer	

In order to broaden its geographical coverage the committee wanted a sponsor from the West Coast. At Loomis's suggestion, Duncan wrote Herbert Blumer of the University of California at Berkeley.[68] Blumer accepted their invitation,[69] and the foregoing "Committee of Eight" was complete. The third step required no formal action. Each member would simply contact as many colleagues as possible, put the issue before them, and solicit support.[70]

The Committee of Eight began the process with each member writing a minimum of twenty-five colleagues. They enclosed a memorandum that explained their objectives, described their position in regard to the official (and at this point yet unnamed) candidates, underlined their intention only to honor Sorokin, and described the procedures they would follow. Each recipient was then asked to contact twenty more colleagues who would be potentially sympathetic to the cause. Recipients were asked to move promptly in order to create a chain-letter effect and to make clear that the group's only intention was to advance Sorokin's candidacy. The Committee of Eight reached 677 correspondents with its initiating letters.[71]

The letters had their intended effects and stimulated a much broader network of correspondence and interest. Among the more active participants were Arthur K. Davis, Otis Durant Duncan, Joseph Ford, Harry Johnson, William Kornhouser, Edgar Schuler, Nicholas Timasheff, Edward Tiryakian, Robin Williams, Kurt Wolff, Milton Yinger, and Carle Zimmerman. The combined mailings of these and other sociologists reached an additional 1,026 voting members of the ASA.[72] These efforts also stimulated a third wave of contacts. It is estimated that at least 3,000 members were contacted through the postcard mailing and a minimum of 1,700 personally informed of the movement to nominate Sorokin.[73]

The official process of candidate selection was in the hands of the ASA Committee on Nominations and Elections, chaired that year by Professor Harold L. Wilensky of the University of Michigan.[74] The official procedures required that they take three ballots for the office of president-elect. On the first ballot each member nominated four candidates. On the second ballot each voted preferentially for two persons (first-choice votes getting two points, second-choice votes, one). The same procedure was followed on the third ballot. The two nominees receiving the most points became candidates for office.

The nominating procedures also advised committee members of the 10 percent write-in provision: "In the event that a person's name is written in for a particular office by at least one-tenth of those returning ballots, in no case less than 25 persons, he is considered nominated for office" (Article II, Section 3). In these cases a second presidential ballot must be prepared and mailed to the membership. The ballot was to be returned to the chairman of the committee within thirty days.

The designated procedure for balloting and mailing to members required that the Committee on Nominations and Elections have its slate to the ASA executive office no later than 1 March. Ballots were to be mailed to members by 20 March, and voting would close on 30 April. If a second ballot were required, it would go to members by 14 May. Voting would then close on 15 June.[75]

On the first nominating ballot Wilbert Moore had a clear lead, and with the returns from the second ballot, Wilensky declared him a candidate. The runoff voting for Moore's competitor was close, but Arnold M. Rose won. The procedure was acceptable to all members, but Roy G. Francis expressed the following thoughts with his return of the third ballot:

I really think that we have achieved sufficient consensus already. Further balloting only seems to me to be a device to secure someone other than Sorokin on the ballot.

I may be acting only out of sentiment; but, if so, here I would defend sentimentality. As an honorific post, the presidency "belongs" to a man like Sorokin. Surely, of the names still on the list, none has made the contribution he has.

The president of the ASA is not a major executive officer. Sorokin can ably handle whatever administrative chores remain: no office held for only one year can involve too much detail. Moore, Rose, Sewell, Bendix—and thousands of others—have many years left to secure the highest honor we as a group can bestow. Must we wait until Sorokin dies to begin to wonder how it was that a man of his stature never obtained the presidency? Or do we wish to continue a quasi-statistical mish-mash to make it certain that he never will be given such an honor?[76]

On 2 January 1963 Professor Wilensky reported the results of the balloting to the Committee on Nominations and Elections. He informed them that candidates Rose and Moore had already notified Secretary Talcott Parsons[77] of their decision to run.

The write-in campaign created a personal difficulty for Wilbert Moore. Sorokin had been a Harvard mentor, and a lasting friendship had developed between them. The concern of the Committee of Eight that their efforts be understood only as seeking an honor for Sorokin and not as a movement against the official nominees led O. D. Duncan to contact Moore on 28 January (only a week after the first mailing to those who would make up the Committee of Eight). Duncan sent Moore a copy of the original memorandum describing the intentions and procedures of the campaign and further noted: "As of this time there is no decision that a group of us will actually proceed on the plan I suggested. If so, every effort will be made to make it clear that our interest is in conferring due honor upon Sorokin, not in foreclosing the opportunity of any worthy nominee."[78]

Moore's reply made it clear that he found himself in an awkward situation. He had earlier told the Committee of Nominations and Elections he would have to refuse their call if it meant running opposite Sorokin:

Not only am I a former student but also I have stayed "closer" to him than have many others. (For example, I am dedicating my little "social change" book to Sorokin.) Put another way I not only never "broke with" Sorokin but I regard the Sorokins as close personal friends. Normally that would make no difference in professional matters. But I too have a measure of prideful ambition, and if I run for the presidency I should expect to vote for myself and I should hope to win. But if Sorokin is the opponent I could only support his candidacy.[79]

Moore goes on to ask if it would be best for him to withdraw. He also suggests that both official candidates could remove themselves.

Duncan wrote Arnold M. Rose, sending him a copy of the initial memorandum describing the purpose of the group.[80] Rose's response shows him sensitive to the committee's purpose but resolute in remaining a candidate:

My first reaction to your letter—and accompanying memo to the six outstanding sociologists supporting the effort to elect Sorokin president of ASA—was to respond that I would cooperate with you. I completely agree with several of your premises: (1) P. A. Sorokin is one of the greatest living sociologists. (2) He has been unfairly neglected (or rejected, I don't know which) by nominating committees of ASA for at least 25 years. (3) Wilbert Moore and I—as the officially nominated candidates for the presidency-elect of ASA—are young enough to have our candidacy postponed for a year in favor of the older man whose reputation is world wide. On the basis of these of your premises, I almost wrote you that I would withdraw from candidacy and support Sorokin.[81]

Rose goes on to say he has had second thoughts. Among them were that his withdrawal could be an injustice to Moore—a combination of his supporters together with Sorokin's might assure Sorokin's victory; he had made a commitment to run; the ballots were prepared; and to pull out now would throw a wrench into the operation. Furthermore, the nominating process needed structural changes. Although the committee might be successful in its advocacy of Sorokin, it would not remedy the problems inherent in the present system. In light of these considerations, Rose chose to remain a candidate.[82]

Duncan's reply confirms Rose's assessment, but a bit of unintended irony can be found in the letter:

Thank you very much for taking the trouble to set down your reaction to the move to nominate Sorokin. I fully agree that there would be nothing to be gained by your seeking to withdraw from the nomination at this point. For one thing, quite apart from any other consideration, the nominating committee has a constitutional duty to put up two candidates. Since Sorokin is not an official candidate and will not be unless he gets 10 per cent of the votes on a write in, withdrawal of one from the committee's slate would merely force them to choose a replacement. *Except in the improbable event that they selected Sorokin* [emphasis added], we would be back where we are now, and I think the feelings of those of us who are pushing the Sorokin nomination would be quite unchanged.[83]

Had Rose withdrawn, the nomination would have gone to either Reinhard Bendix or Sorokin, who had tied on the third ballot. Established practice for the Committee of Nominations and Elections required that the tie be broken by "an arbitrary device."

Had Moore followed his original inclination to withdraw, then Sorokin or Bendix would have run against Rose. However, in early April, Moore wrote to Harold Wilensky, saying, "I agreed to run for the presidency and I am running. . . . How in the hell did I get into this mess?"[84] Given Moore's genuine regard for Sorokin, there can be no doubt that this decision came from deep and difficult soul-searching in which no happy middle ground could be found.

By the end of February 1963, most voting members of the ASA were aware of the campaign for Sorokin. However, not all responses to the Committee of Correspondence were positive. A small group of sociologists clearly opposed Sorokin's candidacy. Some argued that this was a bad time for a purely honorific president. The president-elect and a new executive officer would take office at the same time. This could create organizational difficulties, particularly if the president were too old or too uninterested in ASA affairs to be an effective leader. Furthermore, as the ASA offices were being relocated to Washington, D.C., this would be a year of disorganization and logistical troubles. Both situations required that a competent administrator be chief officer.

Some members pointed out that Sorokin had not concerned himself with the ASA for a good number of years. Indeed, he had often been critical of the group and spoke disparagingly of its members. Others simply took the opportunity to label Sorokin as unfit for any office.

Sorokin was also opposed because of his sociology. Respondents argued that religion permeated his recent works and that electing him president would endorse a value-laden sociology. This would compromise the scientific standing of the discipline among the social sciences.

By 3 April 1963 the die was cast and the membership had spoken. Janice Hooper wrote to Sorokin, congratulating him on his nomination for the office of president-elect.[85] Following the established procedures, the second ballot was mailed on 16 April 1963. It is important to note that by then the committee supporting Sorokin had suspended its activities. As Duncan pointed out to Timasheff:

Now, I would like to respond to your query about the second election. It seems to me that once the nomination is achieved any effort on Sorokin's behalf must be purely personal and not on any organized basis. There are two good reasons for this. First, the very fact of having a second election will be so unusual, and the news of how the nomination was accomplished will be so widespread that hardly anyone will need to be reminded that he has an opportunity to vote for Sorokin. . . .

The second, and more important reason is this. . . . I think that any organized politicking about the election as such would be beyond the conventions now considered proper. . . .

. . . I intend to be involved in no organized effort on Sorokin's behalf once the nomination is made, and I think that others of the initial group of correspondents have the same intention. While we will argue for Sorokin's election with our friends, we will take the public point of view that the electorate must exercise its own judgment ultimately.[86]

Duncan's comments to Timasheff again demonstrate the desire of the Committee of Correspondence to avoid "politicking." It makes clear that the goal was to give Sorokin the traditional second chance. The committee was not concerned with opposing the official candidates or with securing the election for Sorokin. Such an honor was meaningful only if it represented a broad consensus among sociologists.

The ASA executive office expected a return on the second ballot of 1,600 to 1,700 votes. Instead it received 2,073, a return of 71.3 percent of the 2,906 ballots mailed. This seems high, particularly for a second ballot. A breakdown of the returns is found in the following table.[87]

It is clear that the ASA membership chose unequivocally to honor a senior scholar who had made a substantial contribution to the discipline. His election brought Sorokin out from the backwaters of silence and neglect that had enveloped him. Along with the recent volumes about the man and his work, it would allow a new generation of sociologists to see a legendary figure in action.

Election Returns: Second Ballot

Computer Decks	Moore	Rose	Sorokin	Total
Orange deck*	114	130	451	695
Yellow deck	130	109	456	695
Blue deck	112	134	437	683
Totals	365	373	1,344	2,073

Source: Records of the American Sociological Association, Box labeled "1960–63," Folder: "1963 Nominations and Election: IBM Results," American Sociological Association Collection, Library of Congress, Washington, D.C.

*The color of the deck indicates the sequence in which candidates were listed: orange = Rose, Sorokin, Moore; blue = Sorokin, Moore, Rose; yellow = Moore, Rose, Sorokin.

The Presidency and Theoretical Reengagement

Sorokin's reentry into the ASA was not without bumps and challenges for both. As president-elect, Sorokin and his vice president–elect, Robert Bierstedt, would serve on the executive committee under the leadership of George Homans. Homans wrote Sorokin shortly after the election to congratulate him, observing that the honor was long overdue and "it is preposterous, in every sense of the word, that you should be succeeding me in this office."[88] Sorokin responded with appreciation and a request for guidance in policy and procedures: "Since I know very little about the duties of president of ASA, I hope that you will help me in proper discharge of these duties. Though I expect that most of the functions of this office will be discharged by the vice president and the council, nevertheless a few of these functions I probably have to exercise myself."[89]

Homans correctly anticipated differences in administrative style between his former colleague and the association's staff. As he recalls in his autobiography:

One clause of its constitution required the president to "consult" with the chairmen of "sections" within the organization and come to an agreement with them about a particular issue. Sorokin asked me: "Does this mean that, when I'm president I can't just tell them what to do?" I said the clause meant exactly that. "But what if we don't reach agreement, can't I decide?" I said that no, he might not, but that men of good will ought to be able to reach a compromise acceptable to all. Sorokin simply could not understand: if one was head of an organization, one had full power over it. I doubt if he ever understood the nature of democratic institutions in the way one does who has been born to them.[90]

Sorokin's clashes with ASA staff, however, were relatively minor because he decided early on to be a "titular president" and was prohibited by health problems from becoming fully engaged with the politics of the association. Among the issues that concerned him most were the pronounced change of the ASA from a scholarly society to a professional organization (or, as he preferred to call it, a trade union); the tendency to limit appointments on important committees to a small circle of members; and the overbureaucratization of what should be an academically oriented scholarly group. Sorokin had actually drafted a memorandum of concerns, which he planned to take before the executive committee and the association's first full-time executive officer, Gresham Sykes, in early 1965. But, as he notes in a letter to O. D. Duncan, the memo "will not be presented . . . because I suddenly became ill and could not attend the meeting of . . . the Executive Committee. I . . . asked Bierstedt to preside over the meetings. Meanwhile I received a very apologetic letter from Dr. Sykes. Anyhow, for the present, any head-on collision is postponed. If it would be unnecessary in the future so much the better."[91]

Existing records suggest that head-on collisions were avoided and Sorokin gave his attention to planning the program for the 1965 meetings in Chicago. The program theme, "The Problems of Civilizations and Their Changes," not only was central to Sorokin's past works but blended with a reawakening of professional interest in macrosociological concerns and heralded a major theme in his concluding chronicle of developments in sociological theory. A focus on social change and theoretical development would be highlighted in the presidential address and developed in two major plenaries. There would be seventy-two sessions organized under eight sections. The meetings also celebrated the sixtieth anniversary of the association and the first ever to be presided over by a president elected under the provision for write-in candidates.[92] From 29 August to 2 September Sorokin had the scholarly attention of the American sociological community. He used that "bully pulpit" to stir interests in the revitalization of grand theory and a quest for a new theoretical synthesis.

Sorokin's presidential address, "Sociology of Yesterday, Today and Tomorrow," suggested several themes that would be developed in his coming volume, *Sociological Theories of Today*. In his speech the theoretical development of sociology was characterized by alternating periods of fact-finding and synthesis.[93] Yesterday's sociology was a grand sociology concerned with discovering broad cross-cultural and universal trends in group dynamics and sociohistorical reality. Today's sociology has moved away from the study of civilizations, global societies, and the social systems of history to focus more on methods, analytical fact-finding, and microsociological issues. The range of vision has narrowed to the study of small groups, specific forms of action (e.g., voting, union activities, courtship, and mate selection), and a growing concern with negative (crime, alcoholism, family violence) rather than constructive social phenomena. Sociologists are increasingly becoming technicians committed to improving measurement and gathering large amounts of data on increasingly smaller facets of the sociocultural world. Such research is now a collective enterprise in which "the steam shovels of numerous investigating crews have dug up an enormous mass of facts."[94] Lamentably, there is little cognitive gold to be found in this mountain of excavated data. Clearly, such gold as is found improves our understanding of detail but leaves uncovered the broad trends of discovery typical of earlier theories. Sadly, there are no new giants—"no new Platos, Aristotles, Newtons or Galileos of sociology . . . nor even leaders of the caliber of . . . Durkheim, Weber, Pareto, Scheler, Spengler, Ward, Sumner, W. I. Thomas or the like."[95] Instead, what we have is an increasingly specialized sociology that enriches our understanding of aspects of social reality but fails to integrate these "specks" of knowledge into a coherent body of understandings.

Clearly, this trend is reaching its apogee, and it is time for a return to broader patterns of theoretical synthesis. If we continue on the old path, we will learn more about less and the field will become stagnant and sterile.[96] But what are our chances of making such a return? Are there any signs that we are doing so? And what form will the sociology of tomorrow take?

The evidence from the history of science, in Sorokin's mind, confirms the inevitability of a new period of synthesis. Empirically, he also observed a growing concordance of findings among analytical researchers that reflected a common set of principles that would serve as the core for the new synthesis. This confluence of research findings takes social life to be superorganic and multidimensional. As a system of human action, its basic elements are interacting individuals, with collective systems of meaning, living in a world of shared material objects. More abstractly, social life is a constellation formed by the interplay of social systems and congeries, with cultural systems and congeries, and the personality systems. Theoretically, sociologists have been developing and refining taxonomies to conceptualize the elements of these three systems and sequence them from the simplest units to the most complex structures. Such classifications set the stage for powerful theoretical models that nomothetically integrate the systems internally and with each other. To Sorokin these developments signal and give shape to a new period of theoretical integration. Without doubt it will be a period of Integral sociology. But the grand synthesis does not come all at once. Instead, the future holds new cycles of analysis and unification. Each, however, brings us closer to the integral goal of an all-inclusive social theory. Such is the direction of tomorrow's sociology.

The bridge between the sociology of yesterday and that of tomorrow is constructed in the middle fifteen chapters of *Sociological Theories of Today,* a volume in which Sorokin examines the main currents of general sociological theory from 1925 to 1965. This book is a companion to *Contemporary Sociological Theories,* and its objectives are "essentially similar to those outlined in the earlier work."[97] While few readers likely referred to the 1928 objectives, one is significant for the current study. Sorokin points to this when he writes:

Sociology has not suffered during the period mentioned from a lack of theories. They have been . . . appearing like mushrooms after rain. . . . The field of sociology is overcrowded by a multitude of various and contradictory systems. . . . Therefore, one of the most urgent tasks of the contemporary sociologist is to separate what is really valid from that which is false or unproved. . . . Providing that it is done carefully, a critical analysis of the contemporary sociological theories may be of a real service to the science of sociology. This task is attempted in the book and is its primary purpose.[98]

This critical work assesses the major contributions by American and European writers to current thinking in general sociological theory.

Unlike the school approach used in 1928, Sorokin's new typology identifies three established theoretical streams: singularistic-atomistic theories, to which he devotes two chapters; theories of cultural systems, treated in seven chapters; and theories of social systems, analyzed in six chapters. These currents of thought are each divided into several sub-classes. What passes Sorokin's litmus test for veracity accumulates as elements for the construction of a fourth type of theory: the Integral system of structural and dynamic sociology.

Singularistic-atomistic theories are perhaps the least satisfying of today's theoretical developments. They are marked by

their preferential treatment of microsociological, concrete, sensorially perceptible phenomena; their imitation of the methods and terminology of poorly understood physical sciences; their concentration on the quantitative aspects of the sociocultural phenomena studied; and, finally, their negative attitude toward "philosophizing," "speculative theorizing," and "grand systems of sociology."[99]

The specific types of theorists included under this generic heading are physicists who want to be sociologists, sociologists who want to theorize like physicists, mathematical imitators and shorthand sociologists, sham operationalists and experimenters, mathematical modelers and statisticians, small-group theorists and cybernetic fisherman, and those committed to tests and scales for capturing meaningful personal and social characteristics. All of these were previously discussed in *Fads* as quantophreniacs, testomaniacs, cultists, social atomists, numerologists, metrophreniacs, and New Columbuses.[100]

Does this direction signal "real progress by sociology from the 'speculative and philosophical' to the 'scientific' stage?"[101] Sorokin sets three criteria on which to judge their progress. First, do these theorists depend upon the grand systems of sociology to explain, corroborate, and generalize the results of their own research? Yes, this is plainly the case, and frequently such studies are "mere illustrations of or variations on the themes of the grand system makers."[102] Second, do singularistic-atomistic sociologies produce rich universal or middle-range (à la Merton) insights into humanity, social behavior, and sociocultural processes? For Sorokin the answer is no: "The net result of their massive research is modest and has given us hardly any universal or middle range understandings of . . . social and cultural life."[103] Third, do these theories provide a new and better foundation on which to build a future sociology? Clearly not. Something has been achieved but is not enough to make the grand systems obsolete or to establish their own brand of sociology as "impeccably scientific." Sociology's gain from these efforts has been "only a few grains of real cognitive gold in the enormous amount of excavated pseudophysical, pseudo-mathematical, and pseudoexperimental stuff."[104] Therefore, they make no substantial contribution to the sociology of tomorrow.

Sorokin next asks what the disciple has gained from the recently developed systematic studies of social systems. In the six chapters addressed to this issue Sorokin examines the social action theories of Znaniecki and Parsons; the analytical theory of Marion J. Levy; the functional theory of Robert K. Merton; the psychological "nomenclature" theory of Charles P. Loomis; the dialectical theories of Georges Gurvitch, Jean-Paul Sartre, and Otto Kuhne; the pseudobehavioristic theory of George C. Homans; the taxonomical attempts of Robert Bierstedt and Lucio Mendieta y Nunez; and the studies of social change by a variety of theorists, including Talcott Parsons, Robert Bellah, Wilbert Moore, and Don Martindale.

After all of this, he finds little outside of his own contribution that has substantially advanced our knowledge of social systems. The social action models put forth by Znaniecki and Parsons are flawed:

In . . . Znaniecki one finds no systematic theory of sociocultural structure and types of personality, nor any classification of these types in their relationships with the social groups and cultural systems among which they live and interact. . . . So, we are left with social actions and relations void of all cultural meanings-values-norms and separated even from the individuals who perform them. This separation turns these actions-relations into formless, foggy ghosts floating somewhere in a mysterious universe and existing mysteriously by themselves without any human individuals to perform them.[105]

Parsons is more completely castigated. Sorokin briefly outlines Parsonsian action theory as it was developed in *The Structure of Social Action, The Social System*, and *Toward a General Theory of Action* and finds that it "has all the defects of Znaniecki's theory and several additional ones."[106] As revealed in *The Structure of Social Action*,

Parsons' own theory of action systems (or, rather, action congeries) contributes little to the extant knowledge of meaningful human actions. . . . Its limited heuristic value is still further decreased by the "analytical abstractions" in which Parsons presents his ideas. Parsons' intelligible abstract propositions rarely touch the prosaic empirical realities of human actions. As a result, his monograph hardly enriches our knowledge of empirical human actions generally and voluntaristic actions particularly. . . . We still have to wait for an adequate generalized theory of social action. . . . Parsons' valiant effort does not fill this bill.[107]

Sorokin next observes that while Parsons's action theory is very similar to Znaniecki's, "his theory of social cultural and personality systems turned out to be particularly reminiscent of the theories of earlier social thinkers as reformulated and developed in my works."[108] Sorokin then introduces the text of "Similarities and Dissimilarities Between Two Sociological Systems," the memo previously circulated in 1951.[109] While more space is given to dissimilarities than before, it is painfully obvious that Sorokin finds nothing original in Parsons's efforts. Furthermore, they contribute very little to our understanding of the structure and dynamics of social systems. Consequently, action theories show little promise of substantially increasing sociological understandings of social systems.

Similar fates are pronounced on the functional, behavioral, and taxonomic efforts to broaden sociological understandings of social systems. Functional contributions to our knowledge of social systems are modest because they simply put old wine in new bottles. As a theory, functionalism has no special method or body of ideas that distinguishes it from the general methods and ideas widely used in sociology and social anthropology. But, given that sociologists, at this point, refuse to abandon it, he takes Robert Merton's works on the basic problems of functional analysis and reference groups as the best examples of such thought on social systems. But Merton's efforts can be no better than his tools, and he fails to produce a comprehensive theory of social systems or substantial insight into their structure and properties.[110] As Sorokin further reflects:

> The main contributions of Merton to sociology consist not so much in his theory of functionalism and of reference groups as in his thoughtful studies in the sociology of knowledge and science, psycho-social anomie, bureaucracy, radio and film propaganda, manifest and latent functions, and other empirical investigations with specific social theories involved. Most of these studies represent Merton's variations on the themes of earlier masters. . . .
>
> Nevertheless, like Beethoven's variation on Mozartian themes or Brahms' variation on the themes of Paganini, Merton's variations are admirable. . . . He has also contributed significantly by his thoughtful criticism of the theories of other sociologists, including my own "yarns."[111]

It is evident that Sorokin sees much more of value in Merton than in most of the scholars he has reviewed to this point.

A similarly happy evaluation is not in store for another Harvard associate, George Caspar Homans. The strict behavioristic approach taken by Homans is found lacking because it tells us little about the complex operations of human groups. This is due to two faulty yet basic assumptions of behaviorism. First, all human behavior is *not* shaped by rewards and punishments. Second, human behavior is much more complicated than the animal behavior on which behaviorism is founded.

> Despite their behavioristic contentions, all these theories largely deal with such nonbehavioristic phenomena and terms as consciousness, mind, ideas, sentiments, feelings, emotions, wills, duty, rights, memory, inventions, values, symbols, and other inner experiences of human beings, not to mention such phenomena as science, religion, ideology, law, ethics, authority, esteem, and so on—phenomena hardly found in the animal kingdom.[112]

These mistaken assumptions taint the findings of Homans's books *The Human Group* and *Social Behavior: Its Elementary Forms*. Furthermore, by arguing that his generalizations applied to all relationships and groups instead of limiting them to exchange relationships, Homans pushed his findings too far and in the process undermined their validity. Behaviorism is decidedly not the route for developing a general theory of group dynamics.

The taxonomical efforts by Lucio Mendieta y Nunez and Robert Bierstedt are also unproductive attempts at specifying the structure of basic social systems. While Sorokin has a slight preference for Mendieta's work, neither he nor Bierstedt move beyond the classificatory scheme put forth earlier by Sorokin in *Society, Culture, and Personality*.[113] Sorokin concludes that his "survey of recent taxonomic theories indicates that this division of general sociology has been largely neglected. . . . To develop a truly scientific taxonomy remains the task for future sociologists."[114]

The dialectical theories of social systems advanced by Georges Gurvitch, Jean-Paul Sartre, and Otto Kuhne receive substantial attention from Sorokin. Gurvitch's work is extensively presented, and he is given more space than any other theorist in the volume.[115] This may be due to the similarities between his and Sorokin's theories[116] or to Sorokin's strong sense that there is something unique and powerful in the work of his former countryman. Sorokin believes Gurvitch's "methodological, philosophical, and sociological contributions remain among the most significant of our time. Each of his main works notably increases our knowledge of social realities, opens new dimensions of the multidimensional sociocultural universe, and teaches us not only by its scientific verities, but also by its errors."[117] Similar but not so elaborate praise is given to Sartre, whose philosophy of history Sorokin considers "a valuable contribution to the psychosocial sciences."[118] Even Otto Kuhne's theories, which suffer from vagueness and some logical inadequacies, are more adequate from a logical viewpoint than those of the structural functionalists. Indeed, Sorokin judges the dialectical theorists as having "contributed to our knowledge of and orientation in the multidimensional, bewildering human universe about as much as have most of the empirical, analytic, functional-structural and historic-philosophical currents of contemporary sociological thought."[119]

Sorokin is even less satisfied with most modern attempts to understand social change. Recent studies are particularly disappointing because they fail to produce a "physiology of social systems" and tell us nothing of the patterned processes that characterize their life histories. Instead, they focus on poorly conceived structural-functional theories. Such efforts have been of four types: those that develop basic social change concepts; abstract analytical and functional speculations on social change (e.g., Parsons and Robert Bellah); surveys of central problems in the study of change (Wilbert E. Moore); and monographic studies of change (Don Martindale). The only "bright spot" has been in basic conceptual studies. Significant advances have appeared in the study of sociocultural space, time, and causality; the pace and rhythms of change; and categories of cognition that underlie processes of transformations.

Theories developed in these areas "largely redeem the noted inadequacies and shortcomings of the bulk of the recent theories of social change."[120] Many of these theoretical results are "unique" and "truly revolutionary." Sorokin made major contributions to several of these topics, as did Gurvitch, Merton, Moore, MacIver, Barber, and others.[121]

Unfortunately, progress in the field has been uneven, and analytical functional efforts, when carefully examined, turned out to be "either platitudes dressed up in ponderous pseudoscientific verbiage or a series of empirically inadequate . . . propositions contributing little if anything to our understanding of empirical social change."[122] Wilbert Moore's study *Social Change* and Karl Popper's *Poverty of Historicism* fare better, in Sorokin's estimation, because they clarify problem areas in the study of change. Popper's observations on predictability and theoretical history are valuable, and Moore's criticisms of change theories are lucid, skillful, and helpful. However, the works are more concerned with what not to do than with providing direction and content for the development of theory. Don Martindale's study *Social Life and Cultural Change* invites Sorokin into a polemic, and much of this section is a clarification of his own work relative to Martindale's. To Sorokin, Martindale's historical study of social structure and creativity is one of the best of its kind but still inadequate and defective. Martindale's theory of the dynamics of creativity is simplistic; he omits intuition as an intellectual and creative force; his historical analysis of creativity is inaccurate; and his model is overly behavioristic.[123] The study would be greatly improved if Martindale incorporated Sorokin's concepts of creativity, particularly those dealing with the centrality of intuition.

Sorokin's final assessment of change theories is quite similar to his judgment of social systems theory. Both need a lot of work. True progress in understanding the structure and dynamics of change is yet to come.

The systematic study of culture completes the triad of current developments in sociological theory. In this section Sorokin moves away from the scornful judgments given singularistic and social systemic theories, and asserts that theories of the great civilizations (totalitarian and nontotalitarian macrosociologies of culture, in his terminology) are "despite their shortcomings perhaps the greatest achievements of recent sociologies and related sciences."[124] The premier theorists of this tradition are, however, primarily philosophers, historians, and anthropologists. The only sociologists included are Florian Znaniecki, Howard Becker, and, of course, Sorokin.

Among the most significant civilizational theorists are the eight key figures from *Social Philosophies of an Age of Crisis:* Nikolai Danielevsky,

Oswald Spengler, and Arnold Toynbee are joined in the all-inclusive totalitarian category by the Polish historian Feliks Koneczny. The cultural typologists and more specific theorists (nontotalitarians) from *Philosophies* (F. S. C. Northrop, Alfred Kroeber, Walter Schubart, Nikolai Berdyaev, and Albert Schweitzer) expand to include Florian Znaniecki, Howard Becker, Jose Ortega y Gasset, and F. R. Cowell.[125]

In his opening arguments (chapters 5 through 8) Sorokin critiques the systemic macrosociologies of the totalitarians. His analysis centers on Danielevsky's *Russia and Europe,* Spengler's *Decline of the West,* Toynbee's *Study of History,* and Koneczny's *On the Plurality of Civilizations.* To their works he adds a section on cultural morphology and Anderle's theories. In addition to agreeing that civilizations exist sui generis, have unique and clearly discernible characters, and are to be studied holistically, these theorists focus on the macrocultural, use both quantitative and qualitative methods, and favor the philosophy of history approach to that of scientific analysis.

Sorokin next analyzes the nontotalitarian approach. These theorists reject the notion of civilizations as totally unified causal systems. Such misperceived coherence results from reliance on vague theoretical concepts that imply but lack the precision and rigor to demonstrate unity. When more exacting criteria are applied, one clearly sees that civilizations are only partially unified entities. To study this orientation Sorokin reviews F. S. C. Northrop's *Meeting of East and West,* Alfred Kroeber's *Configurations of Culture,* Florian Znaniecki's *Cultural Sciences: Their Origin and Development,* and the dichotomous theories of cultural systems developed by Alfred Weber, Robert MacIver, William Ogburn, F. Stuart Chapin, and Thorstein Veblen. Additional topological theories worthy of attention are those of Walter Schubart, in *Europa und die Seele des Ostens;* Howard Becker's sacred-secular theories; Nikolai Berdyaev's *Meaning of History;* Jose Ortega y Gasset's *Man and Crisis* and *Revolt of the Masses;* Albert Schweitzer's *Philosophy of Civilizations;* and F. R. Cowell's *Culture in Private and Public Life.* Sorokin concludes his exploration with an analysis of studies of art taken from the aesthetic works of Sir Flinders Petrie, Paul Liget, Waldemar Deonna, and Frank Chambers.[126]

From this far-flung survey Sorokin forms his conclusions. Despite the differences in these studies, there are significant points of agreement. Importantly, there were and are past civilizations that functioned as real unities but were not totally integrated. They were few in number and coexisted with several cultural systems that had not reached their level of integration. The cultural supersystems (civilizations) exerted a considerable influence over the less integrated and smaller sociocultural systems, and a knowledge of the structure of supersystems was essential for comprehending the operations of the smaller units. The theorists agreed that these civilizations were integrated by a variety of mechanisms (e.g., prime symbols, cultural mentalities, or ultimate values), and key institutions exhibited a self-directing (immanent) process of change that was accelerated or slowed by external factors. Linear conceptions of historical processes were rejected in favor of cyclical and rhythmical conceptions, but much effort was given to discovering dynamic uniformities. However, civilizations had thus far exhibited more originality than repetitiveness. The reviewed theorists unanimously agreed that our time was one of great crisis from which, most believed, would come a period of "reunification of the supreme values of Truth, Beauty and Goodness."[127]

Sorokin took this concordance of results among distinguished theorists from a number of disciplines, using different methods and materials to suggest a powerful validity for their conclusions. This strong convergence yielded a body of understandings much more compelling and authoritative than those given by social system and singularistic-atomistic theorists. Thus,

Despite the shortcomings of these theories, each of them brings into the open one or more important aspects of cultural realities; each of them enriches our understanding of the structure and nature, . . . of macrocultural unities and, consequently, of the whole cultural universe, including our own personality and behavior. . . . For these reasons the examined theories represent possibly the most significant cognitive achievement among all the recent theories of general sociology.[128]

As such, these theories provide the best available material from which to configure the synthesis of a sociology of tomorrow.

This convergence among cultural macrosociologies is further enriched by the agreements among most sociologists on the basic axioms of their enterprise. Granted, the works discussed in *Today* show considerable differences within and between the theoretical and methodological views and practices of sociologists. However, this is largely due to the character of the taxonomy, which requires an emphasis on distinctions. But if we were to examine these works again and use the axioms of Integral sociology as benchmarks, we would more clearly see the similarities. Using this approach, we find an emerging consensus on the following Integral points: Social phenomena are superorganic and exist sui generis. Sociological phenomena consist of three components (actors, meanings, and materials), and as such there are three levels for analysis (ideological, behavioral, and material). The same three dimensions suggest that sociocultural phenomena have three interdependent aspects—social, cultural, and personal—and researchers must study them as a system. Each social element exhibits different degrees of integration (going from congeries to systems), and each requires special methods of study. Thus there exist social systems and congeries, cultural systems and congeries, and personality systems and disintegrated personalities. There is now an increasing drive to bring these systems together into an integrated theory. In the process, scholars are developing taxonomies to classify the basic elements of culture and society. These taxonomies begin with the simplest units and move to the most complex. New and powerful models are being developed to study systems and congeries: unique congeries are studied ideographically, and the theory is descriptive; patterns of congeries are studied statistically; systems are studied nomothetically. These developments move us toward a body of theory capable of integrating the great superorganic systems.

Accompanying the above trends is an increasing scholarly dissatisfaction with the type of work described as abstracted empiricism (facts without explanatory principles) and grand theories (principles without facts). The inadequacies of both are well known, and all sociologists seek to avoid them. In their place is a trend toward convergence between the forms of sociological theory discussed here and the findings of the period. The strands of truth from each form of theory can now be incorporated into a more multidimensional, unified, and adequate Integral theory. Sorokin cites his own Integralism as an imperfect attempt at such a synthesis.[129] But Sorokin is also optimistic:

In some divisions of sociology, the existing, partially true theories are already sufficiently numerous and correct as to permit their tentative synthesis into a multidimensional integral theory. In other divisions of sociology, particularly in its taxonomy of social and cultural systems, . . . the existing, partially true theories are still too few and too uncertain for such an integral synthesis at the present time. A great deal of research in these fields has to be done before such a synthesis becomes possible. The preceding survey shows that even in these less-developed fields of sociology an intensified study of basic problems is proceeding crescendo and that several significant theories with their relevant empirical evidence have already been formulated. Several others are in a statu nascendi.[130]

The fruit of this process will be a more inclusive social theory and a significant advance toward a grand synthesis.

Sorokin has now come full circle in both his last theoretical work and his presidential address. Sociology is at a crossroads: one road leads it to the new peak of great syntheses and more adequate systems of sociology;

the other leads it to a hackneyed, rubber-stamped, greatly mechanized set of dogmas devoid of creative élan and cognitive growth.[131] Which will we travel? For Sorokin the choice is clear and his faith in and hope for the profession certain:

My guess is that, of the two roads, sociology will choose the road of creative growth and will eventually enter a new period of great syntheses. I hope that this prognosis may be as lucky as my previous prognostications of the changes in the sociocultural life of mankind that I made at the end of the 1920s. With this hope, I say finis to this critical examination of the main currents of recent sociological thought.[132]

With a very similar statement, he made his exit from the presidency and said his farewell to the profession as a community.[133]

What did this book and the presidency of the American Sociological Association mean for Sorokin? Both signal his reengagement and acceptance as a respected elder statesman in the sociological community. The address and its publication in the *American Sociological Review* set the stage for a dialogue with a new cohort of sociologists. The speech, given in Chicago during September 1965, was followed by *Today* in 1966. The book is vintage Sorokin. In it many aspects of his career, style, and scholarship come together for the scrutiny of the sociologists of the 1960s. His panoramic scope and erudition again have an audience, and he honestly challenges them to a duel of minds.

The uninitiated reader will be struck by the range of ideas covered by Sorokin and will be challenged to independently assess the quality of his criticism. Do Znaniecki, Gurvitch, and many of the macrosociologists of culture deserve a praise that sometimes borders on panegyric? Are the style and substance with which Sorokin castigates and condemns the singularistic-atomistic sociologists, their progeny, and the social action, functional, and taxonomic theorists of social systems deserved? Martindale comments on the flavor of Sorokin's reprimands in his review of *Today*:

As always, Sorokin is most fascinating when moving against an opponent with a berserker's battle ecstasy. At such times there is a Rabelaisian superabundance in his performance as if no aspect of his opponent must escape destruction. Hence, as it were, he will pluck out his beard hair by hair, tear out his eyes, dismember his limbs joint by joint, saw his carcass into cord wood, split his long bones with an axe, shatter his vertebra with a hammer, run him through the meat grinder, flush him down the garbage disposal, and clean the equipment with a disinfectant. Sorokin may well find any single opponent to be operating with undefined terms, resting his argument on false suppositions, lacking familiarity with the literature, using illogical and nonempirical methods, failing to discover the major issues, dealing with trivialities, mixing up those he deals with, and contributing to the field primarily as a horrible example of what not to do. Particularly notable examples of such energetic acts of annihilation are Sorokin's reviews of the theories of his former Harvard associates, Talcott Parsons and George Caspar Homans.[134]

Along with Parsons and Homans, many other important sociologists are severely excoriated. The Chicago School is largely ignored, and significant minds such as Robert Merton, Robert Bierstedt, and Marion Levy abrasively treated (although Sorokin concludes with kind words for his former students). To what degree are these observations accurate? Is Sorokin delivering on his promise to discriminate between what is valid or false in these theories? Or is he simply determining their power and worth by their degree of similarity and agreement with his own work?[135] If this is the case, is it not "entirely legitimate on the part of an outstanding scholar like Sorokin to use his own convictions as the touch-stone with which to judge the contributions of others . . . ?"[136] Werner Stark thinks so but is troubled by a concern for how fairly Sorokin has represented the positions of his opponents. He feels that the treatment is often too brief, that it overlooks the fine points and subtleties, and that criticisms are frequently directed toward trivial concerns, mere peccadillos, while overlooking the true sins of the ideas under scrutiny.[137] Stark's essay ends with this assertion:

Contemporary sociology needs Sorokin. It needs his profound learning, so sharply contrasting with the narrowness of many sociologists; it needs his zest, so sharply contrasting with the coldness of the approach of many others; it needs his commitment to humanitarianism without which a science of society is but half of what it ought to be. But it also has a great demand to make on him: namely that he should enter deeply into the ideas of his peers and truly wrestle with them—not only repel them after the briefest of contacts. The present volume contains more of the case against the accused than the case for the defense, and for this reason it is not an entirely fair judgment of "sociological theories of today."[138]

Roscoe Hinkle appraises the book from a sociology of sociology perspective in the following assertion:

This volume is uncompromisingly and irrepressibly a testimony to Sorokin's intellectual and personal qualities in his relation with American sociology. *Sociological Theories of Today* is uncomfortably blunt, contentious in spirit, exasperatingly confident in tone, disturbingly erudite (though relieved by traces of haste), contemptuous of pretense, intolerant of ponderous neologisms and verbalisms, and iconclastic of the American sociological establishment. Certainly, American sociology is incalculably indebted to Sorokin for his part in revitalizing interest in general sociological theory during his more than forty years in this country. Yet, symptoms of mutual distrust, estrangement, and rejection have frequently characterized the encounters between American sociology and Sorokin, and these features are again apparent in his latest work. *Sociological Theories of Today* affords an indispensable perspective on the enigmatic relationship between its author and the discipline in America.[139]

Are Stark and Hinkle correct that *Today* is more a personally driven ad hominem attack on old enemies than a conscientious assessment of contemporary theory from the perspective of a philosopher of history? Clearly, the volume builds on Sorokin's earlier works, particularly *Fads* and *Philosophies,* and he casts his criticism under the theoretical umbrella developed in *Dynamics* and *Society, Culture, and Personality.* Missing from his criticisms of the singularistic-atomistic theorists, however, is much of the vitriol and mockery to be founded in *Fads.* His criticisms of social action and functional theories of social systems raise many genuine but perhaps overstated concerns about these enterprises, and his inclusion of the "Similarities" memo may have been intemperate, but was it unjustified? Is it the case that Sorokin is suggesting his own formulations as exemplars for the development of an integrated theory of sociocultural phenomena, or are there other theories better suited than Integralism to serve this function?

Sociological Theories of Today is a text in general sociological theory. As written, it invites journeyman and apprentice to critically assess not only the classified theories, and those of Sorokin, but their own personal theoretical and methodological commitments. Are Sorokin's formulations that good and those of the others so bad? If not, then why not? The book forces one unwittingly into confronting his or her own sense of what is true and right in sociology and to decide in what direction personal efforts and energy would be most productive. It engages the reader in an intimate and exhaustive exploration of sociology and social science. Here Sorokin is not only the pioneer and pariah but the catalyst to deep and independent scholarship. He is among the last of his kind, and he forcefully asserts his perspective and position. Based on the nature and quality of the reader's response in particular and that of the sociological community in general, a sociology of tomorrow is formed. Which direction it will take is both a personal and a collective decision. *Today* leaves the challenge clearly in the practioner's court.

It is fitting that Sorokin's last book reflects the range of his style and scholarship. The theoretical continuum from *Contemporary Sociological Theories* to *Sociological Theories of Today* shows him continually at the frontiers of the discipline. He had now been professionally honored and

recognized for his achievements, and when he died in 1968 it was with
the dignity of an accomplished scholar. But there would be other professional recognitions before and after his death. Among them were the
Sorokin Award and the spontaneous session held by student dissidents at
the 1969 ASA meeting devoted to "Sorokin Lives!" The difference in
these events reflects Sorokin's lifelong relationship to the discipline.

The Sorokin Award and Lectureship originated during Charles
Loomis's ASA presidency and was funded by a ten-thousand-dollar
donation from Ruth and Eli Lilly. The first recipients were Peter Blau,
Otis Dudley Duncan, and Andrea Tyree for their book *The American
Occupational Structure*.[140] The 1969 meetings brought recognition of
a different type. There, wearing the button "Sorokin Lives!" radical
students rebelled against a corrupt power structure, the Vietnam War,
and a servile, impotent sociology. During a long, unsanctioned session
in San Francisco, they confronted the issues faced for decades by
a kindred spirit who had stood up against war, irresponsible power,
and the hollowness of scientific sociology. They wanted life and scholarship to have substantive meaning, and saw their sociology and praxis as
deeply intertwined. In Sorokin they glimpsed a sociologist who understood and fought against human suffering. His was a strong, angry voice,
opposed to the brutalities of the modern age and committed to a science
of reconstruction. In his scholarship and social criticism they found much
that had value for the sociology of tomorrow. Sorokin was not only
relevant, he was essential, and on that day they celebrated the sociology
of the pariah.[141]

The Journey Ends

Sorokin's life ended with much more than the attention of his colleagues;
he had the love of a strong family and the respect and affection of good
friends. In an anonymous note found in the early Lilly records the writer
observes: "One of the constantly interesting things about Sorokin is that
he is an intellectual genius, who has arrived at truth about love and
altruism via this route and has wound up his life a bitter old man with no
young disciples. His interpreters are all old men, and as he once told me,
'Sorokin will be rediscovered a 100 years hence—'."[142] Clearly, Sorokin
had few young disciples or interpreters. The web of silence that had
enveloped his work for more than a decade removed him from the
attention of a generation of graduate students, and his style of teaching
and scholarship did not inspire or accept filial piety. He did, however, win

attention with good, well-argued ideas, and stimulated students who wanted to think for themselves. Happily, his rediscovery took less than one hundred years. His thirty-five books, over four hundred articles and almost sixty translations were opened to a wider audience in the early and middle 1960s.[143] Furthermore, when word of his illness spread in early 1967, sociologists and others of wide fame and reputation acknowledged their debts and appreciation to Sorokin. Some did so in print, others in private correspondence. The letters of appreciation go back to relationships formed in the mid-1920s and extend beyond the Harvard years.

Death made its presence known during a routine physical examination in late 1966 that revealed, along with several persistent infirmities of old age, a spot on Sorokin's lung. Later tests led to a diagnosis of cancer, and one physician tentatively gave him a year or so to live. Seven months later, however, there was no appreciable spread of the disease, and predictions for its course became more uncertain.

As Sorokin prepared for the inevitable, he also wrote good-byes to his friends. Among those he notified were Mr. and Mrs. Eli Lilly. Along with the description of his condition, he reported a depression that was just lifting. He planned to keep himself busy and was considering a new work to occupy his attention and help him combat the cheerless brooding and anxiety that accompanied the diagnosis. For now, though, he had made his peace and put the fate of "Brother-body" in the hands of Providence.[144] Ruth and Eli Lilly were dazed by the news and wrote Sorokin an encouraging, thoughtful, and tender reply; they continued regular correspondence up until Pitirim's last days. In December 1967 Sorokin wrote that he was cutting back on work because the disease was slowly progressing:

I hope to be alive at my 79th anniversary. . . . But I am not sure I would be alive to meet my 80th anniversary. The bugs of lung cancer and emphysema in one year turned me from a still fairly normal and vigorous man into a "skeleton" and weak, easily winded and tired shadow of myself. I leave the decision to the Good Providence, being resigned to "exit" from life at any time it finds advisable.[145]

The Lillys responded to Sorokin's Christmas letter with a letter and later a birthday poem to which Pitirim cheerfully and thankfully replied on 2 February 1968. His illness was growing worse, and he was still at home being cared for by Lena, "but my days are numbered and it would be for me and my family the purest and heavenly joy to meet again, as you have said quoting Stonewall Jackson 'after we cross over the river and rest in the shade of the trees.' . . . Forever yours, Pitirim."[146] Sorokin moved to the shade of those trees eight days later.

Before 10 February 1968 Sorokin had received letters from many of his students and colleagues, and others would write touching, powerful pieces to his family and for his obituaries. In these missives Sorokin's character as a teacher, critic, and friend was clarified. Robert F. Bales wrote of Sorokin, the scholar-teacher, now being rediscovered by a new generation of students and sociologists:

Although he was a severe critic, and loved criticism, even of himself, Sorokin's students also learned, in time, that he was a tender man. Tears were sometimes seen in his eyes. He loved beauty as he loved excellence, and he spent much effort in the nurture of both. . . . It was impossible, I should think, for a student to enter one of Sorokin's courses and not emerge stunned from the first few weeks of lectures. Sorokin was immensely involved in all he did and said. His lectures invariably started with an air of excitement that built up in the course of the hour to an electrifying pitch, if not a storm. But the real cause of the stunning impact was the breadth of his knowledge and the way in which he brought it to bear. He lived and thought in the knowledge of the full sweep of history, and the whole world of cultures. I remember sometimes feeling in his lectures as if I were suddenly lifted up, off the ground and to a point of great height, where ages and cultures could all be seen as if at one point in time. It was this tremendous comparative perspective that gave the power to his criticism. . . . His students were either inspired or terrified by the height—most often some of both, I think.

None of Sorokin's students is more than remotely like him—for those who knew him the impossibility of this is self-evident. But I think it is equally evident that many of them have been inspired by the qualities of his character and by the ideals of scholarship and humanism which he represented. It is consoling to know that the inspiration of Sorokin's life and work is very much alive today, and that it is being passed on to another generation of students and sociologists.[147]

Personal letters to Sorokin's family would come from Robert Merton, Robert Bierstedt, Charles Loomis, Edward Tiryakian, Robin Williams, Walter Firey, Joseph Ford, Edgar Schuler, C. Arnold Anderson, and dozens of others, testifying to Sorokin's influence as a teacher and the contributions he made to their development as scholars. Each wrote of debts earlier incurred and not yet discharged. While for each, and in different ways, he had been a life-altering influence, they were not disciples. Sorokin had stimulated and challenged them to be creative and independent scholars, not imitators, and therein was his gift.[148]

Sorokin's disputes and the tone of his critical exchanges were often taken as a sign of bitterness and anger rather than responsible acts of a scholar and teacher. He gives his own views on these in an exchange of letters with Otis Dudley Duncan in early 1960. Duncan had written him, asking that if taking the role of the severe critic was compatible with altruistic love. Sorokin replied:

My usual forward to my lectures on Altruistic Love is as follows:
"My lecturing on Altruism does not mean that I am one of the eminent altruists. Just as a lecturer on Criminology needs not be an eminent criminal or a biologist, studying fish, needs not be himself a fish, for the same reason one can study altruism without being an eminent altruist. In this respect I am probably fairly near to the rank and file of the population."

This forwarding entitles me in my scientific works to follow the usual critical procedures of scholars, including sarcastic and ironic criticisms.

. . . Unselfish love does not require an abstention from exposing a pseudo-truth as error, regardless as to whether such a criticism is pleasant or not to the authors of such an error. Love rather demands such a criticism, and such an exposure is an act of love rather than its opposite. Jesus does not hesitate to castigate in the strongest terms the falsifiers of truth (scribes and Pharisees) as "hypocrites," as "blind guides," as "fools," as "whited sepulchers, which indeed appear beautiful outward, but are within full of dead men's bones, and of all uncleanness" and "iniquity."

Similarly, practically all the eminent altruists: Buddha, St. Francis, up to M. Gandhi, castigated the mental and moral errors of their own and of others in strong words, including sarcasm, irony, etc. (So also does a loving mother in regard to the errors of her children).

In the "five-dimensional universe of love," the dimension of love's "adequacy" requires rather than prohibits such a criticism. In brief, the highest forms of love are not just a "sweet, apple sauce." They go hand in hand with the search for the purest forms of truth, and both have an element of asceticism and loving sternness. The old motto: *Amico Plato sed veritas amicissima* expresses well an additional "justification" of my criticism. Yes, any serious criticism of errors "cultivates" creative power of any real creator or scholar. It is only "the thin-skinned" little scholars who take it as a personal insult.

PS. As my personal habit, when I see the papers, books, praising uncritically my published "yarns," I hardly ever read such papers and books from the beginning to the end. But when I read the criticism of my "yarns" I read and often re-read them most carefully. If the criticism is stupid, I am reinforced in the validity of my "yarns"; if it exposes my errors I doubly profit from it by being shown my errors and by being given a chance and stimulus to replace the errors by something more true or valid.[149]

In a similar vein, after presenting a long list of distinguished students and associates, Sorokin wrote in *Long Journey:*

If I did not contribute much to their growth except perhaps by furnishing a few seminal ideas, at least I did not hinder the development of their creative potentials. As founder and chairman of the departments of sociology at the universities of Leningrad and Harvard, I never pressed students to accept my personal theories uncritically but rather, repeatedly advised them to follow the path of independent investigation and formulation of their own views regardless of their agreement or disagreement with my or any other conceptual schemes, methods, and conclusions. This attitude and policy have been fully justified by the subsequent development of these students, research-associates, and instructors into notable leaders of today's American sociology, psychosocial sciences, education, and other cultural activities.[150]

Sorokin was proud of his students, and at least part of that pride came from the independence and quality of their achievements. When he criticized them, as of course he did, it showed their acceptance as equals and pride in their accomplishments. As one student from the Minnesota years recalled: "Pitirim Sorokin was a stimulating teacher for undergraduate and graduate students. . . . He created and sustained intellectual excitement. . . . He often said that he didn't bother to criticize a theory or a man unless the work contained real substance. His critical review was a mark of esteem."[151]

Sorokin accepted and gave criticisms as a part of his scholarly role and did not seek intellectual fealty from peers or students. A more complete grasp of his character is expressed in a letter written by Otis Durant Duncan, a friend of forty-two years, to Elena Sorokin and her sons:

You do not need me, nor anyone else, to tell you of what Sorokin's greatness consisted. His mind was incomparably brilliant, his energy without bounds, his intellectual honesty absolute, and his personal integrity was flawless. Yet, to me, there was another element of his greatness which stood even above these, and that was the flame of human kindness that lay underneath his exterior. Despite his own attainments, he never forgot the young and struggling student whose wits were no match at all for his own.

The general agreement around the University of Minnesota . . . during 1926–28, was that I was . . . simply a country boob who did not know but one thing, that I was very badly in need of being taught. . . . Sorokin was one of the very few professors who seemed to believe that . . . a professor's obligation was to teach such a poor fellow, at least as far as he was able to go. In all the forty-two years of our friendship he never lost that attitude. . . . In my opinion, this is one of the most outstanding marks of a man of superiority.

In a personal way, we had a lot of fun together. We played handball, and goaded each other with incisive remarks. We often chatted at the meetings and exchanged repartee on many subjects. Whatever our discussions were about, I came out . . . having gained a new idea which proved helpful. I remembered that in Philadelphia I had breakfast with him, once. We were soon in the midst of a verbal slug fest, each giving the other all he had. Neither of us convinced the other of anything, but we got attention. It was a rough and tumble bout. When it was all over, a number of young fellows who had encircled us followed me. One of them asked, "How can you wade into Sorokin just as if you were as big as he is?" My reply was, "Because he likes it." He did enjoy having anyone stand on his own two feet and spar with him. He was a true champion in that respect.

As I wrote him last fall, I am proud that it was my son who was responsible, directly and ordinarily for the move to make Sorokin President of the American Sociological Association. That was an honor long past due him. . . .

Regretfully, human life is so short that I shall not live to see the world's appraisal of Sorokin as a thinker and scholar, after his writing has stood the tests of time. . . . He was one of those who belong not to an era, and not to a particular country, but to the ages and to mankind.[152]

Sorokin was a complicated, passionate man, and will remain among the most controversial and colorful of sociologists. At different times in his career he was a pioneer, priest, prophet, and pariah. While all such figures are to a degree outcasts, they are also necessary. Those who follow the beaten path at best contribute only incrementally to their societies or crafts. The brilliant, who are occasionally intemperate, challenging, and difficult, stimulate a reexamination of the accepted and promote growth and new discoveries. Sorokin was of this type. The elder Duncan was correct: Sorokin belongs to history.

Notes

1. Pitirim A. Sorokin, *A Long Journey: The Autobiography of Pitirim A. Sorokin* (New Haven, Conn.: College and University Press, 1963), 114.

2. Ibid., 117.

3. Russia used the Julian calendar until February 1918. The difference between it and the Western Gregorian calendar is thirteen days. By our reckoning the revolution occurred on 7 November 1917. However, the dates used in this section follow the Russian practice. Walter Kirchner, *A History of Russia*, 6th ed. (New York: Barnes and Noble, 1976), 241. For contrasting views on the Russian Revolution see Pitirim A. Sorokin, *Leaves from a Russian Diary and Thirty Years After*, enlarged edition (Boston: Beacon Press, 1950); Bertram D. Wolfe, *Three Who Made a Revolution* (New York: Dell, 1964); Alexander Kerensky, *Russia and History's Turning Point* (New York: Duell, Sloan and Pierce, 1965); and Robert K. Massie, *Nicholas and Alexandra* (New York: Atheneum, 1967).

4. Sorokin, *Long Journey*, 138.

5. This body was charged with implementing a democratic system in Russia. Elections were held in November 1917, and district representatives were elected by secret ballot. Of the 707 elected deputies, only 175 were Bolsheviks. The Bolsheviks argued that the slates of candidates had been selected prior to the October Revolution and represented the old regime. Thus the Constituent Assembly was nothing more than a screen for the counterrevolution, and the Bolsheviks dissolved it on 19 January 1918. For a description of the Bolshevik agenda and the Decree of Dissolution see William Henry Chamberlin, *The Russian Revolution* (New York: Universal Library, 1965), 1:491–495.

6. The Komi homelands border Finland. The Komi, as they are designated today, historically consisted of two groups: the Komi-Zyrans and the Komi-Pernyaks. The Zyrans are the largest of the two and speak Zyrian, Komi, Russian, Finnish, and several dialects. Most Komi are at least bilingual. The region is rich in coal, oil, and timber. The Komi are peasants living in small villages and towns and earning their living as farmers, livestock breeders, hunters, and fishermen. They are the third most literate group in Russia (the first two being the Russian Germans and Jews). The Komi are well known among the intelligentsia and have an impressive record of contributions to the arts, sciences, and humanities.

7. Sorokin, *Long Journey*, 23.

8. Ibid.

9. Sorokin would always be a religious man. The religious climate of his youth shaped his early beliefs, moral standards, and values. He was so deeply taken with his

faith that on several occasions he retreated to the forest for long periods of fasting and prayer, living the life of an early Christian ascetic. Komi music and art also influenced his aesthetic development and formed his standards for beauty. For a discussion of these influences see Pitirim A. Sorokin, "Sociology of My Mental Life," in *Pitirim A. Sorokin in Review*, ed. Philip J. Allen (Durham, N.C.: Duke University Press, 1963), 11–18.

10. The Sermon on the Mount and the Beatitudes are found in Matt. 5:1–7:29 and another version in the Gospel of Luke. The Beatitudes forecast religious happiness for those who are largely without wealth or position on earth: "Blessed are the poor, the sorrowful, the meek, the hungry, the merciful, the faithful, the peacemaker and the pure of heart for they all shall be comforted and rewarded." The Beatitudes specify characteristics of the social and spiritual world that, when possessed, yield religious rewards. The remainder of the sermon points to prescriptions and proscriptions for living a good spiritual and social life: overcome anger, conquer lust, love your enemies, be pure of intention, do not lie, fast to be purified, seek true riches, do not judge others, pray, and follow the Golden Rule. It was also in this sermon that Jesus gave his followers the Lord's Prayer.

Pitirim saw more than biblical injunctions in these passages. He saw prescriptions for a good life and a good society. If one wanted to eliminate social problems and evil, then fashion better people. The Sermon on the Mount told all how to do this. It and other sacred works would later inform the program of the Harvard Research Center in Creative Altruism.

11. The Russo-Japanese War (1904–5) was an attempt by Nicholas II to unify the Russian people and maintain the nation's position in Manchuria and Korea. It had disastrous effects: the Russian fleet was nearly destroyed at Tsushima; the czar had to settle for a negotiated peace and lost all holdings in the areas of contention; scarce resources were drained by the war, which had little support at home; and it was a major defeat at a time when the czar desperately needed a victory.

The revolution of 1905 began with Bloody Sunday, when czarist troops fired on demonstrating workers in St. Petersburg. The act shook the nation because it was believed that the czar had sanctioned the shooting. Disturbances spread throughout the land: strikes, protest, mutinies (e.g., *The Potemkin*), and armed peasant uprisings were common. The czar first met force with force but eventually made concessions. A Duma was convened, political parties and labor unions were legalized, and land reforms were introduced. The protests and challenges to the monarchy continued until the middle of 1907.

These two events seriously undermined the regime. The intelligentsia and masses became increasingly aware of the government's weaknesses and the ineptitudes of leadership. Failure in war and domestic unrest led many to confront the monarchy and look to revolution as the way of restoring order and progress. These changes shook Pitirim's political beliefs, and he sought ways of comprehending the regime's failure.

12. Pitirim joined the Social Revolutionary Party rather than the Social Democrats because of the former's wide base and views on history and social change. The Social Revolutionaries represented all laboring classes, and as a peasant and intellec-

tual Sorokin found this appealing. Also, the Marxist economic model of social change seemed too simplistic. The more open Social Revolutionary model, which emphasized ideas, voluntary action, and individualism, seemed a more adequate and satisfying philosophy of history. Sorokin, *Long Journey*, 44.

13. Ibid., 48–55.

14. Ibid., 58.

15. Ibid., 68.

16. The period of service for a draftee at this time was six years. University graduates were excused from most of their service but could still be required to serve six months. The Bolsheviks did away with the draft in January 1918 but later reinstituted it. Earlier draftees had served for periods of sixteen to twenty-five years. S. V. Utechin, *A Concise Encyclopedia of Russia* (New York: Dutton, 1964), 351–352.

17. These works were "A Historical-Statistical Sketch of the Zyryans," *Works of the Expedition to Investigate the Pechorian Lands* (St. Petersburg, 1910), with K. Jakov; "On the Problem of Evolution and Progress," *Herald of Psychology, Criminal Anthropology and Hypnotism* 3 (1911): 67–95; "The Main Theories of Progress in Contemporary Sociology," *Herald of Knowledge* 9 (1911): 777–791; "Remnants of Animism Among the Zyrians," *Proceedings of the Archangelsk Society for the Study of the Russian North* 20 (1910): 49–62; 22 (1910): 39–47; "On the Question of the Evolution of Family and Marriage Among the Zyryans," *Proceedings of the Archangelsk Society for the Study of the Russian North* 1 (1911): 34–41; 5 (1911): 356–361; "The Contemporary Zyryans," *Proceedings of the Archangelsk Society for the Study of the Russian North* 18 (1911): 525–536; 22 (1911): 811–820; 23 (1911): 876–885; 24 (1911): 941–949; "The Limits and Object of Sociology," *New Ideas in Sociology*, no. 1 (St. Petersburg: Education Press, 1913); "A Survey of the Theories and Fundamental Problems of Progress," *New Ideas in Sociology*, no. 3 (St. Petersburg: Education Press, 1914), 116–155; *Crime and Punishment, Service and Reward: A Sociological Essay on the Main Forms of Social Behavior and Morality* (St. Petersburg: Dolbyshev Press, 1913); "E. Durkheim on Religion," *New Ideas in Sociology*, no. 4 (St. Petersburg: Education Press, 1914), 58–83; and "The Laws of Development of Punishment, from the Point of View of L. I. Petrazhitsky's Psychological Theory of Law," *New Ideas in the Science of Law*, no. 3 (St. Petersburg: Education Press, 1914), 113–151. A more complete listing with annotations of Sorokin's work from 1910 to 1924 is now available. See Barry V. Johnston, Natalia Y. Mandelbaum, and Nikita E. Pokrovsky, "Commentary on Some of the Russian Writings of Pitirim A. Sorokin," *Journal of the History of the Behavioral Sciences* 30 (January 1994) 28–42.

18. Pitirim A. Sorokin, *Contemporary Sociological Theories: Through the First Quarter of the Twentieth Century* (New York: Harper and Row, 1928), 438. Sorokin errs in observing that de Roberty's ideas predated those of Durkheim. De Roberty published *A New Program of Sociology* in Paris during 1904 and *Sociology of Action* in the same city in 1908. Durkheim's *De la division du travail social: Etude sur l'organisation des societies superieures* was first published in Paris by Felix Alcan in 1893. The second edition, with the preface on occupational groups, came out in 1902. *Les Regles de la methode sociologique* was done in 1895 and *Le Suicide: Etude de sociologie* in 1897. De

Roberty spent several years teaching and working outside of Russia. If he knew Durkheim in Paris, it is not known to this author.

19. Sorokin, *Contemporary Sociological Theories*, 448–452. The names of the scholars discussed here are subject to a variety of spellings, for example, de Roberty, De Roberty, Petrajitzsky, Petrajitky, Petrajzychi, Petrazhitsky, V. W. Bekhtereff, V. Bekhterev, W. Bechterew, W. Bechtereff, and so forth. The spelling used in this text is as follows: (1) the spelling found in the *Encyclopedia of the Social Sciences* or a translated book; (2) if neither is available, the most consistent spelling to be found among sources; or (3) Sorokin's spellings in *Contemporary Sociological Theories*.

20. Ibid., 700–703.

21. Ibid., 703–704, and Lewis A. Coser, *Masters of Sociological Thought: Ideas in Historical and Social Context*, 2d ed. (New York: Harcourt Brace Jovanovich, 1977), 500–501. Coser points out that Petrazhitsky influenced two other Russian sociologists who would have lifelong relationships with Sorokin: Georges Gurvitch and Nicholas Timasheff. For more information on Petrazhitsky's work see Pitirim A. Sorokin, "Russian Sociology in the Twentieth Century," *Publication of the American Sociological Society* 31 (1927): 57–69, and his review/essay of Hugh W. Babb's partial translation of Petrazhitsky's *Introduction to the Study of Law and Morality*, in the *Harvard Law Review* 69 (1956): 1150–1157. Also P. A. Sorokin, *Society, Culture, and Personality: Their Structure and Dynamics* (New York: Harper and Brothers, 1947), 70–82. See also Leon Petrazhitsky, *Law and Morality*, trans. Hugh W. Babb (Cambridge, Mass.: Harvard University Press, 1955); Nicholas S. Timasheff, *An Introduction to the Sociology of Law* (Westport, Conn.: Greenwood Press, 1974); Georges Gurvitch, "Petrazhitsky, Lev Iosifovich," in *The Encyclopedia of the Social Sciences*, ed. E. R. A. Seligman and A. Johnson (New York: Macmillan, 1932) 12:103–104. Gurvitch notes that Petrazhitsky was absorbed in the relationship between justice and charity. This led him, through his "politics of law," to seek ways for reconciling law with the ideal of love. Sorokin's interests in altruism and social improvement were similar.

22. Kovalevsky was interested in the dynamics of village life and studied it in England, France, and Caucasia. He made three trips into the Caucasus Mountains, the range that divided the Soviet Union into its Asian and European components. His studies resulted in several books and monographs. He also wrote in-depth studies of England at the end of the Middle Ages and of prerevolutionary peasant problems in France. Other works that reflect his broad interests are *Modern Customs and Ancient Laws of Russia* (London, 1891); *Origin of Modern Democracy*, 4 vols. (Moscow, 1895–97), *Russian Political Institutions* (Chicago, 1902); *Economic Growth in Europe Up to the Rise of Capitalism*, 3 vols. (Moscow, 1898–1900).

23. Quoted in Julius F. Hecker, *Russian Sociology: A Contribution to the History of Sociological Thought and Theory* (London: Chapman and Hall, 1934), 202.

24. See Coser, *Masters*, 492–502; Hecker, *Russian Sociology*, 200–205; Sorokin, *Contemporary Sociological Theories*, 388–399; E. Spektorski, "Maksim Maksimovich Kovalevsky," in *The Encyclopedia of the Social Sciences*, ed. E. R. A. Seligman and A. Johnson (New York: Macmillan, 1932), 8:595–596; B. G. Veber, "Kovalevsky,

Maksim Maksinovich," *The Great Soviet Encyclopedia*, ed. A. M. Prokhorov (New York: Macmillan, 1974), 12:620–621.

25. P. A. Sorokin, *Hunger as a Factor in Human Affairs* (Gainesville: University of Florida Press, 1975).

26. Sorokin, *Contemporary Sociological Theories*, 35. Bekhterev was the founder of the institute and a significant force in Russian social science. His main work was on the associative reflex and the relationship between the nervous system and personality development in normal and pathological subjects. He applied many of his theories to criminology, child development, mental hygiene, suicide, and crime. He was a strict objectivist and laboratory scientist who had studied under Charcot and Wundt. J. R. Kantor, "Bekhterev, Vladimir," in *The Encyclopedia of the Social Sciences*, ed. E. R. A. Seligman and A. Johnson (New York: Macmillan, 1932), 2:498–499.

27. Sorokin, *Contemporary Sociological Theories*, 635. At this time Sorokin felt that attempting to deal with value judgments and ideas like Thomas's four wishes just muddied the waters. Careful laboratory studies were the way to proceed.

28. Sorokin, *Long Journey*, 92.

29. Sorokin bases his account on an editorial published in the *Ekonomist*, nos. 3–5 (1922). In quoting the article he states: "In view of the abolition of the advanced scientific degrees at the present time, the dispute was closed by the official announcement by presiding professor Grevs that the faculty vote unanimously approved the *System of Sociology* as fully meeting the requirements for which it was submitted, and that Professor Sorokin's defense of his dissertation was unanimously voted quite satisfactory." Sorokin, *Long Journey*, 95–96. This statement is, of course, in conflict with Sorokin's own on the restoration of advanced degrees. It is also interesting to note that I. I. Lapshin was one of his "official opponents." This great philosopher would later be a consultant/contributor to *Social and Cultural Dynamics*.

30. This region had been assigned to Pitirim because he knew it well. As a student preparing for the maturity exams, he had spent several months there with his Uncle Mikhail and Aunt Anna. There were also regular summer visits to their farm, and he had spent some time in the area as a revolutionary organizer. When he was elected to the Constituent Assembly, he had received the overwhelming support of the people from the province.

31. Sorokin, *Long Journey*, 163.

32. Whether or not his visitor was the commissar of justice or of public instruction is unclear. Sorokin states the former in *Long Journey*, 167, and the latter in *Leaves from a Russian Diary and Thirty Years After*, enl. ed. (New York: Beacon Press, 1950), 193.

33. Interestingly, there is no mention of this letter in *Long Journey* or *Leaves*. See V. I. Lenin, "Speech at a Rally in Lenin's Honor, November 20, 1918," in *Collected Works of V. I. Lenin*, ed. Jim Riordin (Moscow: Progress Publishers, 1965), 183.

34. Vladimir I. Lenin. "The Valuable Admissions of Pitirim Sorokin," in *Collected Works*, 28:185–194. Lenin's letter was published in *Pravda* on 21 November 1918.

35. Sorokin, *Long Journey*, 189.

36. Pitirim had known Masaryk as a scholar. They had become friendly when the Czechoslovakian leader was an émigré in Petrograd. Indeed, Masaryk was one of the

reasons that the Sorokins' wedding celebration had been cut so short; he and Pitirim met on that day to discuss Czechoslovakian independence. As editor of the *Will of the People,* Pitirim supported Masaryk and wrote about his problems in the newspaper. While Masaryk is most widely known as a philosopher, he was also an active sociologist. See Ferdinand Kolegar, "T. G. Masaryk's Contributions to Sociology," *Journal of the History of the Behavioral Sciences* 3 (January 1967): 27–37; Joseph S. Roucek, "Masaryk as Sociologist," *Sociology and Social Research* 22 (1938): 412–420; Thomas G. Masaryk, *Thomas G. Masaryk: Suicide and the Meaning of Civilization,* trans. William B. Weist and Robert G. Batson (Chicago: University of Chicago Press, 1970).

37. Among others, Pitirim was reunited with P. Struve, N. Lassky, and I. Lapshin.

EMIGRÉ SCHOLAR

1. Michael Novak, *The Rise of the Unmeltable Ethnics* (New York: Macmillan, 1973), xxxiii–xxxiv, 63. Novak attributes the acronym to Monsignor Geno Baroni.

2. U.S. Department of Commerce/Bureau of the Census, *Historical Statistics of the United States: From Colonial Times to 1957* (Washington, D.C.: U.S. Government Printing Office, 1960), 56–57.

3. Barry V. Johnston, *Russian American Social Mobility: An Analysis of the Achievement Syndrome* (Saratoga, Calif.: Century Twenty One Publishing, 1981), 1–16. For additional discussion of Russian immigrants and their social mobility see Jerome K. Davis, *The Russian Immigrant* (New York: Macmillan, 1922); L. J. Levinger, *A History of Jews in the United States* (Cincinnati: Union of American Hebrew Congregations, 1949); Moses Rischin, *The Promised City* (Cambridge, Mass.: Harvard University Press, 1967); E. P. Hutchinson, *Immigrants and Their Children 1850–1950* (New York: Russell and Russell, 1976); Vladimir Wertsman, *The Russians in America: A Chronology and Factbook* (New York: Oceania Publications, 1977); and Nancy Eubank, *The Russians in America* (Minneapolis, Minn.: Lerner, 1976).

4. Laura Fermi, *Illustrious Immigrants* (Chicago: University of Chicago Press, 1968), 139–172. While Fermi concentrates on intellectuals, scientists, artists, and other professions, the general achievements of all Russian Americans should not be overlooked. As Duncan and Duncan observed in their conclusions of a nationwide study of the effects of natural origins on achievement: "The survey results reveal fairly substantial differences among national-origin groups with respect to educational and occupational achievement. Especially distinguished by high achievement are the Russian-Americans, who outrank not only other minorities, but also the native-of-native majority." Beverly Duncan and Otis Dudley Duncan, "Minorities and the Process of Stratification," *American Sociological Review* 33 (1968): 360.

5. Sorokin clearly states in *Long Journey,* 209, that he arrived in New York City in October 1923. Indeed, many others writing about him cite that date as marking his arrival in the United States. For example, Coser, *Masters,* 487; Robert Bierstedt, *American Sociological Theory: A Critical History* (New York: Academic Press, 1981), 303. George A. Theodorson errs when he states that Sorokin "came to the United

States in 1924"; see Theodorson's preparation of a fourth edition of Nicholas S. Timasheff's *Sociological Theory: Its Nature and Growth* (New York: Random House, 1955), 325. The mistake is not in the third edition of 1967. Barry V. Johnston, "Pitirim Sorokin and the American Sociological Association: The Politics of a Professional Society," *Journal of the History of the Behavioral Sciences* 22 (April 1987): 104. There is some uncertainty, however, about the precision of Sorokin's recollection. In an 8 November 1923 letter to Sorokin from Henry Noble MacCracken, the Vassar president observes: "It is very surprising, and also very pleasant to learn of your arrival in the country. I was much interested in your coming, and naturally I desire to have you give at least one lecture at the college. Your letter is dated October 5th, and the letter has not been in the mail for a month" Henry Noble MacCracken to P. A. Sorokin, 8 November 1923, Vassar College Archives (hereafter referred to as VCA), MacCracken Papers. Sorokin replies, "I sincerely thank you for your kind letter. Of course, the date of my letter is my mistake. I arrived in this country on 3 of November" Sorokin to MacCracken, 9 November 1923, VCA.

6. "Russian Speaker Will Be Vassar's Guest Six Weeks," *Poughkeepsie Evening Star,* 12 November 1923, VCA. The book that MacCracken had reviewed was later expanded and published in English as *The Sociology of Revolution;* see Joseph Ford, "Life and Works of Pitirim Alexandrovich Sorokin (1889–1968)," *International Review of Sociology* 7 (1971): 827.

7. "Guest," *Evening Star,* 12 November 1923; "Russian Professor Is Guest at Vassar," *Poughkeepsie Evening Star,* 28 November 1923; "Russian Revolutionist Now Is Guest at Vassar College," *Poughkeepsie Evening Star,* 15 December 1923, VCA.

8. The material for this account is found in "Dr. Sorokine Talks to Vassar Students; Discusses Revolutions," and "Soviet Russia Will Continue Under Present Rulers, Belief of Professor Sorokin: Life of Government, However, Will End Within Three Years, Noted Sociologist Says; Addresses Rotary Club," from the *Poughkeepsie Eagle News,* 9 January and 24 January 1924, respectively; "Sorokin's Views of Russia's Fate," *Poughkeepsie Courier,* 28 December 1923; "Dr. Sorokine of Russia Gives Talk to Vassar Girls," "Dr. Sorokine Gives Lectures," and "Russia's Famous Cultural and Political Leader to Remain in Poughkeepsie–Watchful Waiting," all in the *Poughkeepsie Evening Star,* 12 January 1924, 15 January 1924, and 18 January 1924, VCA, respectively. It is interesting to note that at this time Sorokin was spelled Sorokine. This spelling occurs in several newspaper accounts, but, more interestingly, is also the spelling Pitirim used on his personal stationery.

9. The correspondence between Sorokin and MacCracken comes from two sources: the MacCracken Papers at the Vassar Library noted previously and the Pitirim A. Sorokin Collection, in Special Collections at the University of Saskatchewan, Saskatoon, Canada (hereafter referred to as USSA). Letters from 5 November 1923 (the one misdated 5 October) to 5 December 1925 can be found in the Vassar collection. Letters from 28 October 1924 to 15 April 1964 are found in the Saskatchewan collection. Thus there is a paper trail extending over forty years. The correspondence shows a warm, joking relationship between them. They often jested about getting fatter and older, the irony of certain experiences, and so forth. The two

men also recollect their experiences at Yelping Hill with affection. This was an intellectual retreat in Cornwall, Connecticut, where people went to rejuvenate themselves during the summer and other vacation periods. It had been established by faculty from Yale, and the MacCrackens owned a house there. MacCracken had been at Yale before going to Vassar.

10. Sorokin mistakenly states in *Long Journey*, 213, that Hayes passed away prior to his arrival to give the lectures. Hayes may have been away from the university for a variety of reasons, but he did not die until 1928.

11. Sorokin, *Long Journey*, 204–205.

12. Herman Ausubel, *Historians and Their Craft: A Study of the Presidential Addresses of the American Historical Association, 1884–1945* (New York: Russell and Russell, 1965), 95–97, 356; G. P. Gouch, *History and Historians in the Nineteenth Century* (Boston: Beacon Press, 1959), xxx–xxxi; Sorokin, *Long Journey*, 214, 252–253; *National Cyclopedia of American Biography*, (Clifton, N.J.: James T. White, 1954), 39:558–559.

13. Because of Ross's nativism, it's a bit surprising that he supported Sorokin. For a discussion of Ross's politics see Bierstedt, *American Sociological Theory*, 135–138; Ross's autobiography, *Seventy Years of It* (New York: Appleton-Century, 1936); and Julius Wineberg, *Edward Alsworth Ross* (Madison: State Historical Society of Wisconsin, 1972), 149–176.

14. Letter from Henry Noble MacCracken to Sorokin, 2 August 1924, VCA.

15. Most of this discussion of Minnesota sociology is based on Don Martindale's *Romance of a Profession: A Case History in the Sociology of Sociology* (St. Paul, Minn.: Wildflower Publishing, 1976), 37–62; Gary Alan Fine and Janet S. Severance, "Great Men and Hard Times: Sociology at the University of Minnesota," *Sociological Quarterly* 26 (spring 1985): 117–134; and Sorokin, *Long Journey*, 217–240. For a detailed discussion of the revolt against Chicago's domination of the American Sociological Society see Patricia Madoo Lengerman, "The Founding of the *American Sociological Review:* The Anatomy of a Rebellion," *American Sociological Review* 44 (1979): 185–198.

16. These articles were "The New Soviet Codes and Soviet Justice," *Michigan Law Review* 29 (November 1924): 38–52; "American Millionaires and Multimillionaires," *Social Forces* 4 (May 1925): 627–640; and "Monarchs and Rulers: A Comparative Historical Study," *Social Forces* 4 (September 1925): 22–35.

17. Sorokin, *Long Journey*, 217–218.

18. Letter from Sorokin to Henry Noble MacCracken, 17 August 1924, VCA.

19. Sorokin, *Long Journey*, 218.

20. Letter from Sorokin to Henry Noble MacCracken, 28 November 1924, VCA.

21. Sorokin, *Long Journey*, 233. Most American economists did not become aware of Kondratieff's contributions until 1939, when Joseph A. Schumpeter published his *Business Cycles: A Theoretical, Historical and Statistical Analysis of the Capitalistic Process*, 2 vols. (New York: McGraw-Hill, 1939). Indeed, the association of long cycles with Kondratieff became a case of eponymy as economists often refer to

the "Kondratieff cycle" or "Kondratieff waves." George Garvey, "Kondratieff, N.D.," in *The International Encyclopedia of the Social Sciences*, ed. David L. Sills (New York: Macmillan, 1968), 8:443–444.

22. The revolution cost Pitirim both of his brothers. Vassiliy also died at the hands of the Communists.

23. A. N. Nikolaieff, "Russia from Within," *New York Evening Post*, 3 January 1925.

24. Louis H. Wetmore, "Review of *Leaves from a Russian Diary*," *Commonwealth*, 4 March 1925, 469–470.

25. Johan J. Smertenko, "Review of *Leaves from a Russian Diary*," *New York Herald Tribune*, 14 March 1925.

26. Interview with C. Arnold Anderson, 14 June 1985. Professor Anderson was a student of Sorokin's at the University of Minnesota. He also followed Sorokin to Harvard during the first few years of his tenure as chairman. Professor Anderson retired as a professor emeritus at the University of Chicago.

27. *Leaves* came out again in 1950, published by the Beacon Press and carrying an expanded subtitle: *Leaves from a Russian Diary and Thirty Years After*. In the new chapter Sorokin wrote of the revolution as both a gigantic success and a colossal failure. The successes were far-reaching. First was its survival in the face of internal and external enemies. It quelled internal dissent, survived the Anglo-American-French invasion of 1918, and withstood all the forces of Hitler and the Second World War. Second, it completely transformed all the institutions of Russian society; it was a total revolution. Third was its unprecedented diffusion to other parts of the world. Finally, it undermined the sensate order of czarist Russia and cleared the ground for a new idealistic or Integral order. In the process, the revolution changed even its most stubborn enemies.

On the negative side, it stifled creativity in the sciences, humanities, and arts. The new intellectual leaders glowed with dimmer lights than those of the old order who had educated them. Through murder, imprisonment, and banishment, the intellectual capital of Russia was depleted. What replaced the past were "the works on Lenin, Bukharin, Deborin, Stalin and the petty prophets of Communism" (321–322). These were only pale, simplified, and vulgarized formulations of the deeper and more profound thinkers of Russia's past. Furthermore, the revolution has promised:

> a new communist or socialist form of society incomparably better than the capitalist or any other form of social organization known to history. Economically, politically, socially, mentally, morally, and even biologically this communist or socialist society of the Revolution was to be a sort of paradise on earth. Everyone would serve according to his capacity and would receive according to his needs. Poverty, inequality, exploitation, and injustice would be abolished. (328–329)

However, instead of a higher standard of living, the quality of life remained below the prerevolutionary level. Rather than more freedoms there were fewer. Instead of a government elected to serve the people, elections were meaningless and people existed to serve the government. Revolutions come into being to improve the lives of despairing and oppressed peoples. This is their justification for existence. In this purpose the Russian revolution had truly failed.

This later analysis showed little change from the prognosis Sorokin had delivered earlier on the campuses and to the service clubs in the East and Midwest. The last thirty years demonstrated the truth of his earlier observations. However, the failure of the revolution was not due to the Communists alone: "The Revolution is one of the main manifestations of the death of the sensate order, such agony, by its very nature, cannot be creative" (342). Revolutions are "most effective in destruction and entirely unfit for creative construction" (344). Because they are built on divisiveness and grow through terror, torture, murder, and hate, they are incapable of producing a new order based on kindness, justice, equality, respect, and love. While revolutions are "often conceived by idealists they all are carried on by murderers and profited from mainly by scoundrels" (345). Sorokin concludes that revolutions are not the way to produce a new and better order. The only hope for the reconstruction of man and society is in the prosocial emotions of kindness, love, and the unselfish help of others. These are the true values to be followed by social movements that aim to reconstruct humanity.

28. Interview with Edgar Schuler by Barry V. Johnston, 3 July 1985.

29. Martindale, *Romance of a Profession*, 61.

30. Ibid. "From the beginning, Sorokin was an intense competitor."

31. Fine and Severance, "Great Men," 119.

32. Martindale, *Romance of a Profession*, 62.

33. Letter from Lowry Nelson to Don Martindale, 28 April 1975. Quoted in Martindale, *Romance of a Profession*, 219.

34. Letter from Sorokin to Henry Noble MacCracken, 20 October 1924, VCA; Sorokin, *Long Journey*, 221.

35. Pitirim A. Sorokin, *The Sociology of Revolution* (Philadelphia: Lippincott 1925), 21.

36. Sorokin, *Leaves*, 3.

37. Harry Elmer Barnes, "Review of *The Sociology of Revolution*," *The Nation*, 10 June 1925, 669.

38. Wilbur C. Abbott, "The Working of Revolution," *Saturday Review of Literature*, 11 April 1925, 664.

39. J. Grierson, "Review of *The Sociology of Revolution*," *American Journal of Sociology* 7 (1926): 399. This review was important because the *American Journal of Sociology* was then the official journal of the American Sociological Society.

40. Robert E. Park, "Review of *The Sociology of Revolution*," *Annals of the American Academy of Arts and Sciences* 123 (1926): 231. Quoted in Lawrence T. Nichols, "Sorokin and the American Sociological Profession: The Dynamic Assessment of a Moral Career," unpublished paper, 1987.

41. I. M. Rubinow, "Are Revolutions Worthwhile?" *New Leader* 6 (June 1925): 4. The second contribution of the work is for the activist rather than the scientist:

If the professional propagandist and the agitator can force himself to read a book such as this calmly, he cannot help being impressed with the cost of any revolution. Nor can he help unless he intentionally wears blinders, being convinced that revolution as such is an event, a transitory process, at most a means to an end. To the judicious mind, therefore, the book will furnish evidence of the historic absurdity of the formula "revolutions en permanency." (4)

Rubinow also makes some observations on the quality of the translation Hayes had commissioned:

Professor Sorokin writes in a, to him, foreign language which he probably learned comparatively late in his life. Considering the circumstances, he does it extremely well, but the fact is quite obvious to the reader. As the book has been issued as one of a series (Lippincott Sociological Series) under the editorship of a professor of sociology of an American university, the latter must be held responsible for failure to give the book the necessary degree of editorial supervision and proof reading. The book abounds in un-English phrases and even faulty syntax, which would undoubtedly have called for the use of the red pencil had they occurred in a sophomore's essay. The lack of care which permitted such errors is, of course, an act of unfairness to the thoughtful author. (4)

The quality of the translation may have negatively influenced some reviewers, who could have taken the poor English as an indication of generally poor scholarship. Rubinow is correct in observing that Sorokin did "extremely well" with English, given the amount of time available and the circumstances under which he learned it. Many émigré scholars never developed a comparable facility with English.

42. In regards to theory, Sorokin states that he "stressed the behavioristic and biopsychological too much and [did] not sufficiently take into account the sociological." Pitirim A. Sorokin, "Foreword to the 1967 Edition," *The Sociology of Revolution* (New York: Howard Fertig, 1967). For a more complete discussion of the manifold characteristic of revolutions see *Social and Cultural Dynamics* (New York: American Book Co., 1937), vol. 3, chaps. 12–14; *Society, Culture and Personality: Their Structure and Dynamics* (New York: Harper and Brothers, 1947), chaps. 31–35; and *Man and Society in Calamity* (New York: Dutton, 1942), chaps. 9–12.

43. Ellsworth Huntington, "The Social Pyramid," *Saturday Review of Literature*, 3 December 1927, 370.

44. Gosta Carlsson, "Sorokin's Theory of Social Mobility," in *Pitirim A. Sorokin in Review*, ed. Philip J. Allen (Durham, N.C.: Duke University Press, 1963), 128–129.

45. Kingsley Davis and Wilbert E. Moore, "Some Principles of Stratification," *American Sociological Review* 10 (1945): 242–249. This piece is important because it has been extensively anthologized and sparked a major controversy between functionalists and conflict theorists of stratification. See, for example, Melvin Tumin, "Some Principles of Stratification: A Critical Analysis," *American Sociological Review* 18 (August 1953): 387–394; Kingsley Davis, "Reply," ibid., 394–397; Wilbert Moore "Comment," ibid., 397; Melvin Tumin, "Reply to Kingsley Davis," *American*

Sociological Review 18 (December 1953): 672–673; Melvin Tumin, "Rewards and Task Orientations," *American Sociological Review* 20 (August 1955): 419–423; Richard D. Schwartz, "Functional Alternatives to Inequality," ibid., 424–430; Richard L. Simpson, "A Modification of the Functional Theory of Social Stratification," *Social Forces* 35 (December 1956): 132–137; Walter Buckley, "Social Stratification and the Functional Theory of Social Differentiation," *American Sociological Review* 23 (August 1958): 369–375; Kingsley Davis, "The Abominable Heresy: A Reply to Dr. Buckley," *American Sociological Review* 24 (February 1959): 82–83; Marion Levy, "Functionalism: A Reply to Dr. Buckley," ibid., 83–84; and Walter Buckley, "A Rejoinder to Functionalist Dr. Davis and Dr. Levy," ibid., 84–86.

Besides exchanges in the journals, the debate became a part of most introductory textbooks in sociology and specialized texts in social stratification. This still remains the case. Of course, Moore and Davis were Harvard students during Sorokin's chairmanship. Carlsson observed that their paper contained few footnotes and that there was no reference to *Social Mobility*. He is not implying anything out of order, and his observation is true. However, Davis and Moore note in the first two sentences of their article that the paper builds on an earlier work by Davis ("A Conceptual Analysis of Stratification," *American Sociological Review* 7 [June 1942]: 309–321). Davis states in a note at the beginning of the article, "No claim is made that all concepts here utilized are original. Indeed, complete originality in a paper of this sort would probably be worthless. The aim, rather, is a slightly new synthesis of concepts already extant in the sociological literature" (309). Davis does develop ideas similar to those found in *Social Mobility* but through a quite different line of reasoning. He also attributes many of the ideas to informal discussions in the "Parsons Sociological Group" (319). This, of course, takes nothing away from Sorokin because, as Robert Merton has observed, good ideas are usually the product of multiple independent discovery. Sorokin is clearly in the lineage of these thoughts.

46. Pitirim Sorokin, *Social Mobility* (New York: Harper and Brothers, 1927), ix–xi. Sorokin's shift to a quantitative approach would be appropriate at Minnesota. The department's position in the discipline was partly a product of its leadership in the emergence of a "scientific sociology."

47. As one would expect, sociology has made substantial gains in the quality of cross-national research since the 1920s, although some of the earlier problems still persist. For an excellent account of more recent developments and problems see Melvin L. Kohn, "Cross-National Research as an Analytic Strategy," *American Sociological Review* 52 (February 1988): 713–732.

48. Franklin Giddings, "Sociology à la Carte," *Saturday Review of Literature*, 6 August 1927, 21.

49. Letter from E. A. Ross to Sorokin, 16 May 1927, USSA, Mrs. E. A. Ross file.

50. The field would not be explored for some time to come. Not only were there obstacles in terms of data, but the direction of class research was to take another tack. Milton Gordon renders the following judgment on *Social Mobility* in his superb book *Social Class in American Sociology* (New York: McGraw-Hill, 1963), 62:

Social Mobility must be considered a major addition to the class literature of American sociology of the twenties, attempting as it did the crystallization of the fields of social stratification and social mobility. Its most valuable contribution, to this writer's mind, is analytical. . . . Its failure to lead directly to a series of investigations based on Sorokin's conceptual scheme was due to other forces at work which were beginning to inspire an approach to the study of class phenomena through a fuller-bodied technique which Sorokin did not seem to envisage—the field studies of separate communities.

Here, of course, Gordon is referring to studies such as the Lynd's Middletown volumes, Warner's Yankee City series, and other studies by Dollard, Powdermaker, Blumenthal, and so on (see pp. 63–165).

51. Sorokin, *Contemporary Sociological Theories*, xiv–xvii.

52. Comment by Harry Elmer Barnes on *Contemporary Sociological Theories*, USSA, folder on *Contemporary Sociological Theories*. No date.

53. Comment by E. A. Ross on *Contemporary Sociological Theories*, USSA, folder on *Contemporary Sociological Theories*. No date.

54. Comment by Floyd N. House on *Contemporary Sociological Theories*, USSA, folder on *Contemporary Sociological Theories*. No date.

55. Robert M. MacIver, "Review of *Contemporary Sociological Theories*," *Annals of the American Academy of Arts and Sciences* 139 (1929): 216.

56. Edward B. Reuter, "Review of *Contemporary Sociological Theories*," *American Journal of Sociology* 34 (1929): 382. Reuter was American Sociological Society president in 1933 and MacIver in 1940.

57. A. B. Wolfe, "Review of *Contemporary Sociological Theories*," *American Economic Review* 15 (1929): 715.

58. Sorokin, *Contemporary Sociological Theories*, 758–759.

59. Ibid., 760.

60. Ibid., 759.

61. Carle C. Zimmerman, "My Sociological Career," *Revue internationale de sociologie* 9 (April–August 1973): 106–107.

62. Pitirim A. Sorokin and Carle C. Zimmerman, *Principles of Rural-Urban Sociology* (New York: Henry Holt, 1929), 5.

63. R. D. McKenzie, "Review of *Principles of Rural-Urban Sociology*," *American Journal of Sociology* 36 (July 1930): 135–137. Many of McKenzie's criticisms are debatable (definitions, analysis, etc.), and he completely disregards the intent of the book as a basic text.

64. Floyd N. House, "Review of *Principles of Rural-Urban Sociology*," USSA, folder on reviews of Sorokin's books.

65. Nels Anderson, "Review of *Principles of Rural-Urban Sociology*," *New Republic* 60 (1929): 328. He also wrote Sorokin privately, that "It is the most convincing work in the way of a text that I have read for some time." Letter to Pitirim A. Sorokin, 23 August 1929, USSA, "A" general file.

66. "Review of *Principles of Rural-Urban Sociology*," *Information Service* 9 (4 January 1930): 1–2. Published by the Federal Council of Churches of Christ in America

with the disclaimer that articles are not to be construed as declarations of official attitudes and policies of the council.

67. Anonymous, "Review of *Principles of Rural-Urban Sociology*," *Commonweal*, 7 May 1930, 17–18.

68. Zimmerman, "My Sociological Career," 103–105.

69. Ibid., 104.

70. T. Lynn Smith, "Sorokin's Rural-Urban Principles," in *Pitirim A. Sorokin in Review*, ed. Philip J. Allen (Durham, N.C.: Duke University Press, 1963), 198.

71. Ibid., 204–205.

72. Lowry Nelson, *Rural Sociology: Its Origins and Growth in the United States* (Minneapolis: University of Minnesota Press, 1969), 33–44. For a more detailed discussion of Galpin's life and career see his autobiography: *My Drift into Rural Sociology* (Baton Rouge: Louisiana State University Press, 1938).

73. Charles J. Galpin, "The Story of My Drift into Rural Sociology," *Rural Sociology* 2 (December 1937): 416–428.

74. Pitirim A. Sorokin, Carle C. Zimmerman, and Charles J. Galpin, *A Systematic Source Book in Rural Sociology* (Minneapolis: University of Minnesota Press, 1930), x.

75. Letter from Carle C. Zimmerman to Charles J. Galpin, 3 January 1938, USSA. This letter was never sent, although one similar to it was. Galpin refers to such a letter dated 17 January 1938 in his reply to Zimmerman, USSA, Sorokin Collection. Some additional details related to this letter are found in Zimmerman's "Memoir" as part of the final chapter in Nelson's *Rural Sociology*, 179–182, with particular attention to 181–182. Zimmerman notes that it was Galpin's idea to drop him from the *Source Book*. He further states, "It hit me like a bolt of lightning. However . . . Dean Walter C. Coffey simply said 'No books without Zimmerman.' So after a sleepless night I found my way back into the *Source Book*. And when it was published, since the work was all done by Sorokin and myself, I became the second author" (182).

76. Letter from Charles J. Galpin to Carle C. Zimmerman, 19 January 1938, USSA.

77. Letter from Carle C. Zimmerman to Charles J. Galpin, 28 January 1938, USSA.

78. Carl C. Taylor, "Review of *A Systematic Source Book in Rural Sociology*," *American Journal of Sociology* 37 (January 1932): 657–660. This review covers the first two volumes.

79. Carl M. Rosenquist, "Review of *A Systematic Source Book in Rural Sociology*," *American Economic Review* 22 (March 1932): 175–176.

80. Dwight Sanderson, "Review of *A Systematic Source Book in Rural Sociology*, Volume I," *Annals of the American Academy of Political and Social Sciences* 155 (May 1931): 245.

81. Eitaro Suzuki, "Review of *A Systematic Source Book in Rural Sociology*," *Proceedings of the Japanese Sociological Society* (November 1931): 124–129.

82. Sorokin, *Long Journey*, 235–236.

83. Roscoe C. Hinkle and Gisela J. Hinkle, *The Development of Modern Sociology* (New York: Random House, 1954), 3.

84. See Anthony Oberschall, "The Institutionalization of American Sociology," in *The Establishment of Empirical Sociology*, ed. Anthony Oberschall (New York: Harper and Row, 1972), 198.

85. Most of the community studies that contributed to Chicago's fame had not yet been done. Only Nels Anderson's study *The Hobo* (Chicago: University of Chicago Press, 1923) and R. D. McKenzie's book *The Neighborhood: A Study of Local Life in the City of Columbus, Ohio* (Chicago: University of Chicago Press, 1923) were published. Chicago's most explicit attempts to study the characteristics of class life in the city, Louis Wirth's book *The Ghetto* (Chicago: University of Chicago Press, 1928) and Harvey W. Zorbaugh's work *The Gold Coast and the Slum* (Chicago: University of Chicago Press, 1929), did not appear until after *Mobility*.

86. Sorokin, *Contemporary Sociological Theories* 502.

87. Ibid., 760.

88. Ibid., 520.

89. Ibid., 543.

90. Ibid., 745.

91. Anderson, "Review of *Principles*," 328.

92. A newspaper report observed that Sorokin's book *Contemporary Sociological Theories* "demolished most of the late conclusions of sociologists." If by this is meant the Chicago scholars, then the following limerick is quite telling.

> There once was a prof named Sorokin−
> Who kept on a-knockin' and pokin'
> At the isms and fads,
> Of the socio-dads,
> And now we know they were jokin'.

H. Sheperd, "Fads for the Dads," *The Hour Glass*, 3 May 1929, 2.

93. Andrew W. Lind, "Review of *Social Mobility*," *American Journal of Sociology* 33 (March 1928): 847.

94. Quoted in Sorokin, *Long Journey*, 227.

95. Rudolf Heberle, "Review of *Social Mobility*," *American Journal of Sociology* 34 (July 1928): 219–225. This was a solid review and pointed out many of the strengths and problems of the book.

96. Hinkle and Hinkle, *Development of Modern Sociology*, 25. This discussion draws heavily on chapter 2 of their book and on Oberschall's *Establishment of Empirical Sociology*.

97. Hinkle and Hinkle, *Development of Modern Sociology*, 18–22.

GOLDEN OPPORTUNITIES

1. Sorokin, *Long Journey*, 236. Three complimentary letters have been found in the USSA, Sorokin Collection. Two are from Frank W. Taussig and one from Carl S. Joslyn. In a 4 February 1928 letter Taussig wrote Sorokin, praising the "verve and acumen" of *Contemporary Sociological Theories*. Later, on 12 July 1929, Taussig wrote in praise of *Principles of Rural-Urban Sociology*, noting that the book showed "brains as

well as information," which was more than he could say about "many of the current American books on sociological subjects." Both letters from Taussig are found in the "Ta–Th" general file. It is also noteworthy that Sorokin had written positively about Taussig in *Contemporary Sociological Theories* and *Social Mobility*.

Carl S. Joslyn had reviewed *Social Mobility* in the *Quarterly Journal of Economics* 42 (1927–28): 130–139. The review was balanced and perceptive, and concluded that *Social Mobility* was "a pioneer work . . . [which] will undoubtedly occupy a permanent and important place in the literature of the subject" (139). However, Joslyn was concerned that Sorokin would take his other comments too negatively. He wrote:

> I had many things in mind of a favorable nature which I should have liked to have included in the review–but space forbade! As it is customary to say all the horrible things we can think of about a book on the occasion of its review–thus showing how superior we are to the author!–I adopted this practice, and failed, thru lack of space, to say all the favorable things that might have been said about it. So far as my opinion of your "Social Mobility" is concerned, you may be interested to learn that Professor Carver and I are using it in the course in Sociology in this Department.

Letter from Carl S. Joslyn to Pitirim A. Sorokin, 11 May 1928, p. 1, USSA, "J" general file. Joslyn also asked for advice on his dissertation and the American Business Leaders project that he and Taussig were working on.

Sorokin was mistaken in identifying the *Quarterly Journal of Economics* as the *Harvard Quarterly Journal of Economics*. Joslyn's is the only review prior to Sorokin's trip to Harvard. It is likely that his other works were acknowledged favorably in articles and research notes. Although no documents were found from Thomas N. Carver or John D. Black dated prior to Sorokin's visit, there is evidence that they too thought highly of him.

2. Sorokin, *Long Journey*, 223.

3. Letter from A. Lawrence Lowell to Pitirim Sorokin, 25 September 1929, Harvard University Archives, Pusey Library (hereafter referred to as HUA), Lowell Papers. In *Long Journey*, 237, Sorokin mistakenly recalled that this letter specified him as a unanimous choice and detailed the financial arrangements and other conditions of the offer.

4. Sorokin, *Long Journey*, 238.

5. James Ford, "Social Ethics 1905–1929," in *The Development of Harvard University Since the Inauguration of President Eliot 1869–1929*, ed. Samuel Eliot Morison (Cambridge, Mass.: Harvard University Press, 1930), 187–201.

6. Arthur K. Vidich and Stanford M. Lyman, *American Sociology: Worldly Rejections of Religion and Their Directions* (New Haven, Conn.: Yale University Press, 1985), 59–66.

7. Ford, "Ethics," 224–225.

8. Ibid., 226–228.

9. Edward Cummings's appointment is of interest because it shows an earlier formal recognition of the discipline at Harvard than is usually reported. Albion Small

is typically credited with the first chair in American sociology; he was appointed at the University of Chicago in 1892. Frank Hankins argues (*International Encyclopedia of Social Sciences*, 1968, 6:175) that this priority belongs to Franklin Giddins, who was a lecturer in sociology at Bryn Mawr in 1888 and the "the first full-time professor of sociology in the United States." Following Robert L. Church's, "Economists Study Society: Sociology at Harvard 1891–1902" in *Social Sciences at Harvard 1860–1920: From Inculcation to the Open Mind*, ed. Paul Buck (Cambridge, Mass.: Harvard University Press, 1965), 18–90, and Vidich and Lyman's, *American Sociology*, 70, it is clear that Cummings first taught a course in sociology at Harvard in 1891. He was responsible for Economics 3, "The Principles of Sociology–Development of the Modern State, and of Its Social Functions." Church, "Economists", 19. It is also clear from these sources that his appointment was in the Department of Economics.

However, Frank W. Taussig, in his essay "Economics at Harvard 1871–1929," in Morison, *Harvard*, 187–201, states: "Edward Cummings (A.B. 1883), whose appointment as Assistant Professor of Sociology in 1893 had marked another enlargement of the scope of Economics" (p. 191), and later, "It is true that Cummings was appointed Assistant Professor of Sociology in 1893" (p. 193). This opened a fascinating question: What was Edward Cummings's title in 1891? *The Historical Register of Harvard University 1636–1936* (Cambridge, Mass.: Harvard University Press, 1937), 171, shows that Edward Cummings was appointed as instructor in political economy in 1891. However, he was appointed as instructor in *sociology* in 1892–93. In 1893 he became assistant professor of sociology and held that rank and title until he left Harvard in 1900. Thus, Cummings has the unique priority of being Harvard's first sociologist and gives the university an earlier presence in the history of American sociology than previously believed.

10. On leaving Harvard, Cummings "was ordained minister of the South Congregational Society, Unitarian, of Boston and became the colleague of Reverend Edward Everett Hale, a distinguished clergyman and author of the nineteenth-century classic *The Man Without A Country*. Cummings became pastor in 1901. Charles Norman, *E. E. Cummings: The Magic Maker* (New York: Bobbs-Merrill, 1972), 15.

Edward Cummings was the father of e. e. cummings, and one gets a real sense of the man when his son describes him in the first of his Harvard Nonlectures:

> I wot not how to answer your query about my father. He was a New Hampshire man, 6 foot 2, a crack shot & a famous fly-fisherman & a firstrate sailor (his sloop was named The Actress) & a woodsman who could find his way through forests primeval without a compass & a canoeist who'd still paddle you up to a deer without ruffling the surface of a pond & an ornithologist & taxidermist & (when he gave up hunting) an expert photographer (the best I've ever seen) & an actor who portrayed Julius Caesar in Sanders Theatre & a painter (both in oils & watercolours) & a better carpenter than any professional & an architect who designed his own houses before building them & (when he liked) a plumber who just for the fun of it installed all his own waterworks & (while at Harvard) a teacher with small use for professors–by whom (Royce, Lanman, Taussig, etc.) we were literally surrounded (but not defeated)–& later (at Doctor Hale's

socalled South Congregational really Unitarian church) a preacher who announced, during the last war, that the Gott Mit Uns boys were in error since the only thing which mattered was for man to be on God's side (& one beautiful Sunday in Spring remarked from the pulpit that he couldn't understand why anyone had come to hear him on such a day) & horribly shocked his pewholders by crying "the Kingdom of Heaven is no spiritual roofgarden: it's inside you" & my father had the first telephone in Cambridge & (long before any Model T Ford) he piloted an Orient Buckboard with Friction Drive produced by the Waltham watch company & my father sent me to a certain public school because its principal was a gentle immense coalblack negress & when he became a diplomat (for World Peace) he gave me & my friends a tremendous party up in a tree at Sceaux Robinson & my father was a servant of the people who fought Boston's biggest & crookedest politician fiercely all day & a few evenings later sat down with him cheerfully at the Rotary Club & my father's voice was so magnificent that he was called on to impersonate God speaking from Beacon Hill (he was heard all over the common) & my father gave me Plato's metaphor of the cave with my mother's milk.

11. Vidich and Lyman, *American Sociology*, 70.

12. Ibid., 77.

13. Ibid., 79–85.

14. Letter from George W. Cram, secretary for the Faculty of Arts and Sciences, to Ralph Barton Perry, 5 October 1927, Records of the Committee on Concentration in Sociology and Social Ethics, HUA.

15. Ralph Barton Perry, "Sociology and Social Ethics," n.d., p. 3. Records of the Committee on Sociology and Social Ethics, HUA.

16. Letter from President A. Lawrence Lowell to Professor Richard C. Cabot, 9 February 1926, Records of the Committee on Sociology and Social Ethics, HUA.

17. Ibid.

18. Thomas N. Carver, *Recollections of an Unplanned Life* (Los Angeles: Ward Ritchie Press, 1949), 211. Carver was most impressed by the theoretical arguments put forward in the first three chapters, specifically, Black's analyses of the law of variable proportions, which Carver had earlier shown to be an extension of the law of diminishing returns. Black had elaborated on Carver's argument and introduced a number of new examples to illustrate its accuracy.

19. Ibid.

20. Ibid., 212.

21. Black contributed to Sorokin's hiring. He observed in a 23 October 1929 letter to Sorokin that the best strategy here is not to push a case yourself but have someone else do it. "I believe that I could have spoiled the chances of your favorable consideration here if I had urged you strongly in the economics faculty." USSA, "B" general file.

22. In this letter he also told President Lowell that his present salary was $6,900. The university paid $4,500 and the U.S. Department of Agriculture the other

$2,400. The contribution of the Agriculture Department would end in August 1930 when the manuscript for the last two volumes of the *Source Book* would be ready for printing. Letter from Pitirim A. Sorokin to A. Lawrence Lowell, 28 September 1929, HUA, Lowell Papers. Lowell responded that the university would offer him $7,000 a year should he take the position. Letter from A. Lawrence Lowell to Pitirim A. Sorokin, 2 October 1929, HUA, Lowell Papers.

23. Letter from Henry Noble MacCracken to Pitirim A. Sorokin, n.d., USSA, Henry Noble MacCracken file.

24. Letter from Pitirim A. Sorokin to A. Lawrence Lowell, 7 October 1929, HUA, Lowell Papers.

25. Letter from A. Lawrence Lowell to Pitirim A. Sorokin, 11 October 1929, HUA, Lowell Papers.

26. Letter from Pitirim A. Sorokin to A. Lawrence Lowell, 16 October 1929, HUA, Lowell Papers.

27. Letter from Howard W. Odum to Pitirim A. Sorokin, 5 October 1929, USSA, Howard W. Odum file.

28. Letter from Edward A. Ross to Pitirim A. Sorokin, 21 October 1929, USSA, Mrs. E. A. Ross file.

29. Sutherland also cautioned him that he might find himself caught between social ethics and classical economics and regret his decision. Letter from E. H. Sutherland to Pitirim A. Sorokin, 26 October 1929, USSA, "Su–Sz" general file.

30. Letter from Henry Noble MacCracken to Pitirim A. Sorokin, 22 October 1929, USSA, Henry Noble MacCracken file.

31. Letter from Joseph Lee to the Harvard Corporation, 29 November 1929, HUA, Lowell Papers.

32. Sorokin, *Sociology of Revolution,* 367.

33. Letter from Joseph Lee to the Harvard Corporation, 9 January 1930, HUA, Lowell Papers.

34. Robert K. Merton, "Remembering the Young Talcott Parsons," *American Sociologist* 15 (1980): 69. While social ethics had a distinguished past, it is also clear that Lowell saw the department as fraught with problems and was looking for an opportunity to change it.

35. The jingle was recounted by Merton when interviewed by Anna Di Lellio, "Le aspettative sociali di durata: Intervista a Robert K. Merton," *Rassegna Italiana di sociologia* 26 (1985): 16.

36. John D. Black wrote Sorokin: "You will be interested to know that Lowell devoted his summer's reading to works in sociology, and read your *Social Mobility* and *Contemporary Sociological Theory* [*sic*]. When he wants *you,* he *knows why* he wants you. You will start on a splendid basis, with his understanding and belief in you and your points of view." Black is, of course, referring to *Contemporary Sociological Theories.* Letter from John D. Black to Pitirim A. Sorokin, n.d., USSA, "B" general file. This letter, which is very long, was most likely written between 28 September 1929 and 16 October 1929.

37. The chairman of the board of tutors, Karl Bigelow, had been keeping Sorokin abreast of the committee's work since 23 October 1929. After learning of Sorokin's acceptance of the chair, he wrote him of changes in the program and the addition of new staff to the committee, specifically, Talcott Parsons and W. Lloyd Warner. Letter from Karl Bigelow to Pitirim A. Sorokin, 23 October 1929, USSA, "B" general file.

38. Lawrence T. Nichols, "The Establishment of Sociology at Harvard: A Case of Organizational Ambivalence and Scientific Vulnerability," in *Science at Harvard University: Historical Perspectives,* ed. Clark A. Elliott and Margaret W. Rossiter (Bethlehem, Pa.: Lehigh University Press, 1992), 207–209.

39. Letter from Karl Bigelow to Pitirim A. Sorokin, 28 April 1930, HUA, Records of the Committee on Sociology and Social Ethics.

40. Letter from Pitirim A. Sorokin to Karl Bigelow, 13 May 1930, HUA, Records of the Committee on Sociology and Social Ethics.

41. Karl Bigelow had accepted a teaching position in Buffalo and left Cambridge in the summer of 1930. When he resigned as chairman of the Board of Tutors, his duties were divided between Parsons and Joslyn. Parsons became secretary of the committee and Joslyn secretary of the board of tutors. Letter from Karl Bigelow to R. B. Perry, 4 June 1930, HUA, Records of the Committee on Sociology and Social Ethics.

42. Nichols, "The Establishment," 208.

43. "Report of the Committee on Sociology and Social Ethics on the Organization of a Division and Department of Sociology at Harvard University," 10 February 1931, p. 1, HUA, Records of the Committee on Sociology and Social Ethics.

44. Sorokin, of course, had the support of most of the major participants in the decision. C. J. Bullock, E. F. Gay, F. W. Taussig, T. N. Carver, W. T. Ham, and A. A. Young were senior economists favoring the move. Of lesser importance but not without influence were the workhorses of the committee, Joslyn and Parsons. John D. Black had observed in an earlier letter to Sorokin that "Harvard means to make itself *strong* in *sociology.* The economics group believe that a separate department is desirable." Letter from John D. Black to Pitirim A. Sorokin, undated (but likely written between 28 September and 16 October 1929), USSA, "B" general file.

45. Allen S. Debus, ed., *World Who's Who in Science from Antiquity to the Present* (Chicago: Marquis Publishing, 1968), 287; Albert N. Marquis, ed., *Who's Who in America 1938–1939* (Chicago: Marquis Publishing, 1939), 20:478. Ford, "Ethics," 226–228. Cabot's involvement with social work and social improvements lasted even after his retirement from Harvard. In 1935 he began a social experiment, the Cambridge-Somerville Study, to determine the impact of a delinquency prevention program on rates of juvenile crime. The field portion of this study of 650 boys began in 1939 and concluded in 1945. Sadly, Cabot died of a heart attack in 1939 and was unable to direct this unique and pioneering experiment. However, "The Cambridge-Somerville project . . . stands as a unique event in the battle against delinquency." William McCord and Joan McCord, *Origins of Crime: A New Evaluation of the*

Cambridge-Somerville Study (New York: Columbia University Press, 1959), quoted in Rodney Stark, *Social Problems* (New York: Random House, 1975), 68. For a complete report on the project see Edwin Powers and Helen Witmer, *An Experiment in the Prevention of Delinquency: The Cambridge-Somerville Youth Study* (New York: Columbia University Press, 1951).

46. Nichols, "The Establishment," 207.

47. "Report of the Committee," 1.

48. Sorokin, *Long Journey,* 242.

49. A complete biography of Henderson is yet to appear. However, overviews of his life and work in the social sciences are found in George C. Homans, "Lawrence J. Henderson," *International Encyclopedia of the Social Sciences,* ed. David L. Sills (New York: Free Press 1968), 6:350–351; Bernard Barber, *L. J. Henderson on the Social System* (Chicago: University of Chicago Press, 1970); and Cynthia E. Russett, *The Concept of Equilibrium in American Social Thought* (New Haven: Yale University Press, 1966). The Pareto Circle refers to an informal discussion group of faculty and students that grew up around Henderson after he began to offer his seminar on Pareto in 1932–33. For a discussion of this group see Barbara Heyl, "The Harvard Pareto Circle," *Journal of the History of the Behavioral Sciences* 4 (1968): 316–334.

50. Richard Norton Smith, *The Harvard Century: The Making of a University to a Nation* (New York: Simon and Schuster, 1986), 97–98.

51. Barber, *Henderson,* 7. There are some slight differences between sources on the role of different founders in the genesis of the society. These are usually minor differences. The most thorough account is that of Crane Brinton, *The Society of Fellows* (Cambridge, Mass.: Harvard University Press, 1959).

52. Morison, *Harvard,* 21. Dorothy Emmet, "Alfred North Whitehead," *International Encyclopedia of the Social Sciences,* ed. David L. Sills (New York: Free Press, 1968), 533.

53. Barber, *Henderson,* 5. For a fine biography of Wheeler see Mary Alice Evans and Howard Ensign Evans, *William Morton Wheeler, Biologist* (Cambridge, Mass.: Harvard University Press, 1970).

54. Dwight W. Hoover, "Schlesinger," in *McGraw-Hill Encyclopedia of World Biography,* ed. David I. Eggenberger (New York: McGraw-Hill, 1973), 9:447.

55. Letter from John D. Black to Pitirim A. Sorokin, 23 October 1929, USSA, "B" general file.

56. All of these negotiations were taking place while Zimmerman was doing field research in Siam (Thailand).

57. Letter from Pitirim A. Sorokin to Carle C. Zimmerman, 8 December 1930, HUA, Records of the Committee on Sociology and Social Ethics.

58. Letter from Pitirim A. Sorokin to Carle C. Zimmerman, 19 February 1931, HUA, Records of the Committee on Sociology and Social Ethics.

59. Minnesota was unhappy with his resignation. Zimmerman was a valued faculty member, the highest paid for his age, and well supported with research funds. The Minnesota deans, Coffey and Johnston, resisted his leaving because the

university would lose the benefits of his recent foreign experience and future promise. They also had made arrangements to match the Harvard offer with a combination of salary and other benefits (letter from Dean W. C. Coffey to Carle C. Zimmerman, 26 June 1931, USSA, Zimmerman file), but their offer had come after "the horse was out of the barn."

60. Merton recalls that, according to E. B. Wilson, John D. Black and E. F. Gay were pivotal in Parsons's appointment. They knew he was unlikely to receive a continuing appointment in economics and, knowing of his deep interest in sociology, supported his change of departments. Barry V. Johnston, "Sorokin and Parsons at Harvard: Institutional Conflict and the Origin of a Hegemonic Tradition," *Journal of the History of the Behavioral Sciences* 22 (April 1986): 111.

61. Sorokin, *Long Journey*, 244.

62. Letter from Clifford Moore to A. Lawrence Lowell, 29 May 1931, HUA, Records of the Sociology Department 1930–44. Moore is likely referring to Parsons's article "Wants and Activities in Marshall," *Quarterly Journal of Economics* 46 (1931): 101–140. Later in the same year, Moore's replacement as dean of Arts and Sciences would voice strong reservations about both Parsons and Joslyn.

> I am considerably disturbed by the situation of the two younger instructors in the Department, who, as I understand it, have not proved themselves fit for permanent position, and who, according to your statement, cannot relieve you as they should from some of the burden of course instruction. Don't you think it would be well to consider, at least, the possibility of replacing one of them this year by a new instructor who could share the work of teaching courses and thereby relieve the older men of some of the burden? Of course, I realize it may be difficult to find a man, but I think it is important, wherever possible, to replace relatively inefficient members of our staff by more efficient ones as promptly as possible.

Letter from Kenneth B. Murdock to Pitirim A. Sorokin, 16 December 1931, HUA, Records of the Sociology Department 1930–44.

Sorokin, in turn, wrote Murdock defending his younger colleagues:

> I want to add that if Dr. Parsons and Dr. Joslyn have not been quite successful in the most fundamental course to which they were assigned as lecturers, I should not like you to conclude from this fact that these men are either incompetent or below the standard of most of the instructors in other departments. The dryness of their lectures is the principal criticism to be made, and this is due not to intellectual, but to temperamental factors. In general, their work has been entirely satisfactory; and both men are good tutors, though scarcely of the highest caliber. Dr. Joslyn, especially, has shown himself to be an unusually competent tutor. These remarks are necessary in order that we may not do these instructors an injustice by causing you to undervalue them.

Letter from Pitirim A. Sorokin to Kenneth B. Murdock, 17 December 1931, HUA, Records of the Sociology Department 1930–44.

63. A full course lasted two semesters. Students could complete this requirement by taking five courses that lasted a year each or by mixing full and half courses.

64. *Bulletin of Harvard College, 1930–1931*, 340–341.

65. Letter from Pitirim A. Sorokin to Carle C. Zimmerman, 8 December 1930, HUA, Records of the Committee on Sociology and Social Ethics.

66. "Report of the Committee on Sociology and Social Ethics," 10 February 1931, 7.

67. Pitirim A. Sorokin, Mamie Tanquist, Mildred Parten, and Mrs. C. C. Zimmerman, "An Experimental Study of the Efficiency of Work in Various Specified Conditions," *American Journal of Sociology* 35 (March 1930): 765–782. Sorokin also reports the effect of social distance on altruism. He found that regardless of the seriousness of another's need (e.g., starvation as opposed to the passing of an exam), as social distance increased altruistic responses diminished. For details see pp. 771–774 and Pitirim A. Sorokin, "Experimente zur Soziologie," *Zeitschrift für Volkerpsychologie und Soziologie* (March 1928): 1–10.

68. Pitirim A. Sorokin, "Sociology as a Science," *Social Forces* 10 (October 1931): 20–27.

69. Pitirim A. Sorokin, "An Experimental Study of the Influence of Suggestion on the Discrimination and Valuation of People," *American Journal of Sociology* 37 (March 1932): 720–737.

These were not the only pieces to come out about this time. Sorokin also published "Metabolism of the Different Strata of Social Institutions and Institutional Continuity," *Metron,* nos. 1 and 2 (1932): 319–347; "Soziale Bewehungsvorgange," *Kolner Vierteljahrshefte F. Soziologie,* Jahrgang VII, Heft 2, n.d.; "Life-Span, Age-Composition, and Mortality of Social Organizations," *Mensch en Maatschappij,* 9e, Jaargagn, Nos. 1 and 2, n.d.; "Studien zur Soziologie der Kunst," *Sociologus* (March 1933); Allen, *Sorokin,* 503.

70. Sorokin, *Long Journey,* 245. The committee consisted of full professors from the Departments of Government, Economics, History, and Sociology. Sorokin was a member and Charles J. Bullock its first chairman. Sorokin received almost nineteen thousand dollars from the committee over its ten-year life. Records of the Committee for Research in the Social Sciences, HUA.

71. Sorokin, *Long Journey,* 245.

72. These assignments were compiled from Sorokin's acknowledgments at the beginning of various chapters in *Dynamics.* The designation "White Russian WPA" was given to the department by the Harvard *Crimson.* Robin Williams recalls that the term was initially coined by Porter Sargent. Interview of Robin Williams Jr. by Barry V. Johnston, summer 1985.

73. Letter from Pitirim A. Sorokin to James B. Conant, 20 March 1934, HUA, Records of the Sociology Department 1930–44. Sorokin was reporting to Conant on the department's progress since its beginnings in 1931.

74. It is quite difficult to compile an exhaustive list of the graduate students who studied in the department. This selective list is taken from the department budget

files from 1931 to 1934 and from the correspondence files between the department and the dean of arts and sciences office in the General Papers of the Sociology Department, HUA. Another source was an unpublished list generated by Lawrence T. Nichols dated 17 August 1981. This list contains the names of 172 graduate students from 1931 to 1945.

75. Letter from Robert Park to Pitirim A. Sorokin, 14 October 1936, HUA, Records of the Sociology Department 1930–44, "P" general file. This letter was often quoted by Sorokin to members of the administration as evidence of the department's quality.

76. Many of these students would have been seen by Park. Letter from Dean Kenneth B. Murdock to Pitirim A. Sorokin, 17 May 1933, HUA, Records of the Sociology Department 1930–44.

77. Letter from Pitirim A. Sorokin to Dean Kenneth B. Murdock, 22 May 1933, HUA, Records of the Sociology Department 1930–44.

78. Ibid. Letter from Pitirim A. Sorokin to A. Lawrence Lowell, 18 June 1932, HUA, Records of the Sociology Department 1930–44.

79. Letter from Sorokin to Dean Kenneth B. Murdock, 22 May 1933. HUA, Records of the Sociology Department 1930–44.

80. Letter from Dean Kenneth B. Murdock to Pitirim A. Sorokin, 23 May 1933, HUA, Records of the Sociology Department 1930–44. Lowell also suggested that the grading in the beginning sociology course be made "as severe as possible" so all weak students would be discouraged from pursuing the major.

81. Letters from Pitirim A. Sorokin to President A. Lawrence Lowell and Dean Kenneth B. Murdock, 14 December 1931, HUA, Records of the Sociology Department 1930–44. It was at this time that Murdock complained about Parsons and Joslyn; see note 62.

82. "At the time the division was organized, it was promised that two or three professorial members would be added during the next two or three years; but during the three years of the existence of the division not only has no professor been added but the department has lost two professorial members, T. N. Carver . . . and R. C. Cabot." Letter from Pitirim A. Sorokin to James B. Conant, 10 October 1934, HUA, Records of the Sociology Department 1930–44.

83. "Report of the Sociology Department," November 1932, HUA, Records of the Sociology Department 1930–44.

84. Letter from Pitirim A. Sorokin to Dean Kenneth B. Murdock, 30 January 1934, HUA, Records of the Sociology Department 1930–44.

85. MacIver had been broadly educated in the classics, government, and economics at Edinburgh and Oxford. He left Europe for Canada, where he spent twelve years at the University of Toronto. He came to the United States in 1927 as chairman of economics and sociology at Barnard College, Columbia University. Among his notable works at that time were *Community* (London: Macmillan, 1920); *Labor in a Changing World* (New York: Dutton, 1919); *The Elements of a Social Science* (London: Methuen, 1949) it originally appeared in 1921; and *Society: Its Structure and Change*

(New York: Ray Long and Richard Smith, 1932). For a discussion of MacIver's work see Bierstedt, *American Sociological Theory*, 243–297. Also see MacIver's autobiography *As a Tale That Is Told: The Autobiography of R. M. MacIver* (Chicago: University of Chicago Press, 1968).

86. Letter from Pitirim A. Sorokin to James B. Conant, 10 October 1934, HUA, Records of the Sociology Department 1930–44.

87. Letter from James B. Conant to Pitirim A. Sorokin 20 December 1934, HUA, Records of the Sociology Department 1930–44. Conant felt it would be in the department's best interest to seek a younger man.

88. Pitirim A. Sorokin, "Sociology Department 1931–1936," a report sent to President James B. Conant, 30 March 1936, HUA, Records of the Sociology Department 1930–44.

89. Ibid.

90. The President's Research Committee on Recent Social Trends, *Recent Social Trends in the United States* (New York: McGraw-Hill, 1933).

91. Herbert Hoover, "Forward by the President of the United States," *Recent Social Trends in the United States* (New York: McGraw-Hill, 1933), 1:v.

92. Robert C. Bannister, *Sociology and Scientism: The American Quest for Objectivity, 1880–1940* (Chapel Hill: University of North Carolina Press, 1987), 182. For a good discussion of disciplinary politics in sociology and the theoretical cleavages surrounding *Trends* see pp. 173–187.

93. For an example see Herbert Blumer, "Science Without Concepts," *American Journal of Sociology* 36 (1931): 515–533.

94. Pitirim A. Sorokin, "*Recent Social Trends:* A Criticism," *Journal of Political Economy* 41 (April 1933): 194–210.

95. Ibid., 198.

96. Ibid., 207–209.

97. Wesley C. Mitchell, "A Review of the Findings by the President's Committee on Social Trends," in *Recent Social Trends in the United States* (New York: McGraw-Hill, 1933), 1:xii–xiii.

98. Sorokin, "*Trends*," 203.

99. Ibid., 204.

100. Ibid., 210.

101. William F. Ogburn, "A Reply," *Journal of Political Economy* 41 (April 1933): 211.

102. Ibid.

103. Ibid., 218.

104. Ibid., 220–221.

105. Pitirim A. Sorokin, "Rejoinder to Professor Ogburn's Reply," *Journal of Political Economy* 41 (June 1933): 400–404.

106. Ibid., 401.

107. Ibid., 402.

108. Ibid., 403. The quote comes from Ogburn's "Reply," 215.

109. Ibid., 404.

PROFESSIONAL POLITICS AND PROPHETIC SOCIOLOGY

1. Sorokin, *Long Journey,* 259.

2. "The Course of Arabian Intellectual Development 700–1300 A.D.: A Study in Method," *ISIS,* February 1935, 516–524; "The Fluctuations of Idealism and Materialism, from 600 B.C. to 1920 A.D.," in *Reine und Angewandte Soziologie,* Eine Festgabe F. Toennies (Leipzig: H. Buske-Verlage, 1936); and "Form and Problems of Culture Integration and Methods of Their Study," *Rural Sociology* (September 1936): 121–141. All of these articles were based either directly on *Dynamics* or on materials gathered for it.

3. Pitirim A. Sorokin, "Le Concept d'equilibre est-il necessaire aux sciences sociales?" *Revue international de sociologie* 44 (1937). Pitirim A. Sorokin and Robert K. Merton, "Social Time: Methodological and Functional Analysis," *American Journal of Sociology* 42 (March 1937): 615–629.

4. Pitirim A. Sorokin, *Social and Cultural Dynamics,* 3 vols. (New York: American Book Co., 1937), esp. 2:125–132.

5. Morton Hunt, "How Does It Come to Be So?" *New Yorker,* 25 January 1964, 54–55.

6. Ibid., 55.

7. Letter from Robert K. Merton to Barry V. Johnston, 13 February 1987.

8. Ibid. Merton has also observed that graduate students came to the department for one or both of two reasons: to study with Sorokin or to be at Harvard. He "went there solely for the first reason." See Di Lellio, "Le aspettative sociali di durata," 15. This is also confirmed by a letter from Merton to Sorokin in which Merton discusses a paper that Sorokin is to present in a session at which Merton will preside:

> In a profound way, your paper in this session will round out a circle for me. I believe it was about 25 years ago–about 1928 or 1929–that the Sociological Society met in Washington. As a sophomore or junior in college, I attended that convention: my first such experience. It was then that I heard you give your paper on Hornell Hart's current ideas. As a result, I definitely decided upon two matters: first, that I would devote myself to sociology and second, that I would do all I could to begin my graduate studies under you.

Letter from Robert K. Merton to Pitirim A. Sorokin, 11 January 1962, USSA, Robert K. Merton file.

9. Robert K. Merton, "George Sarton: Episodic Recollections of an Unruly Apprentice," *ISIS* 76 (December 1985): 470. Sarton, the son of an engineer, was born in Ghent, Belgium, in 1884. As an undergraduate he studied the natural sciences, chemistry, and mathematics. Sarton graduated with highest distinction in chemistry in 1908 and completed the doctor of science degree in mathematics in 1911. He then started to fulfill his vision for a unified history of science. The first step was establishing *ISIS,* a publication Sarton envisioned to be "at once the philosophical journal of the scientists and the scientific journal of the philosophers, the historical journal of the scientists and the scientific journal of the historians, the sociological journal of the scientists and the scientific journal of the sociologists."

Quoted in Merton, "Unruly Apprentice," 473. *ISIS* would also serve "as the future focus of a new intellectual movement that would bring scientific studies and humanities together and help them become one single and coherent system of knowledge . . . what he later called the doctrine of the New Humanism." See Hosam Elkhadem, "George Sarton's Correspondence: Sarton and Irenee van der Ghinst," *ISIS* 75 (1975): 36.

10. Sarton's early career at Harvard was difficult and uncertain. The Carnegie support was vital to his remaining there after his two-year appointment. He kept his Widnener Library office by giving a yearly free course in the history of science. For details and insights into this great scholar see May Sarton, *I Knew a Phoenix: Sketches for an Autobiography* (New York: Norton, 1954); May Sarton, "An Informal Portrait of George Sarton," *Texas Quarterly* 16 (Autumn 1962): 101–112; I. Bernard Cohen, "George Sarton," *ISIS* 48, no. 3 (1957): 286–299; Arnold Thackray and Robert K. Merton, "On Discipline Building: The Paradoxes of George Sarton," *ISIS* 63 (1972): 473–495.

11. Sorokin, *Long Journey*, 257.

12. For Merton's contribution to *Dynamics* see vol. 2, pp. 125–180, 437–476. As a methodological innovation Sorokin and Merton's work may have paved part of the way for the development of prosopography: "The study of the common background characteristics of a group of actors in history by means of a collective study of their lives." Norman W. Storer, "Introduction," in *Robert K. Merton: The Sociology of Science: Theoretical and Empirical Investigations*, ed. Norman W. Storer (Chicago: University of Chicago Press, 1973), xiv. Merton and Sarton were deeply interested in the problem, and Sarton's use of biographical statistics pioneered the development of the technique. Thackray and Merton, "Discipline," 492. For more information see Lawrence Stone, "Prosopography," *Daedalus* 100 (1971): 46–79.

13. Sorokin and Merton, "Social Time."

14. Ibid., 629.

15. George Devereux, "Letter to the Editor," *American Journal of Sociology* 43 (May 1938): 967–969.

16. Ibid., 968.

17. Pitirim A. Sorokin, "Rejoinder to Devereux," *American Journal of Sociology* 43 (May 1938): 969–970.

18. A similar conclusion was reached by M. F. Ashley-Montague in his "Letter to the Editor," *American Journal of Sociology* 44 (September 1938): 282–284. He believed it was essential for social scientists to realize the lack of congruence between different time systems and work on its significance in the human sciences. Sorokin and Merton had performed a valuable service in that regard.

19. Robert K. Merton, *Social Theory and Social Structure*, enl. ed. (New York: Free Press, 1968), xiii–xiv. The relationship between Merton and Sorokin was lifelong and occasionally marked by disagreements. However, each valued the other, as is clear from the correspondence between them from 1946 to 1967. Merton further notes the differences in his relationships with Sarton and Sorokin when he recalls:

George Sarton was poles apart from another Harvard mentor, the sociologist Pitirim Sorokin. The contrast was palpable. An official sponsor of my dissertation, Sorokin took it as something of a cognitive rejection–even a betrayal–of his developing doctrine of historical cycles of ideational, idealistic, and sensate cultures that, in 1937, would animate the four volumes of his *Social and Cultural Dynamics.* Indeed, in the strongest possible language, he paid me the supreme compliment of concluding that I was clearly as mistaken as Ernst Troeltsch and Max Weber had been before me. That sense of my having badly let him down persisted, if one may judge from his ambivalent inscription in the one-volume edition of the *Dynamics* published twenty years later. Couched in amiable hyperbole, it reads: "To my darned enemy and dearest friend, Robert–from Pitirim." Sarton could no more have taken my divergence from his ideas and style of thought as betrayal than he could have engaged in the other extravagance of "dearest friend." In the tranquility of retrospect, however, I must conclude that it took no great effort to steer through the dangerous waters between the Scylla of Sorokin's passionate cyclicalism and the Charybdis of Sarton's Comtean progressivism. One need not agree fully with either of them to learn–quite different things–from both of them. (Merton, "Unruly Apprentice," 484–485)

Unhappily, Merton is yet to write an autobiography. This would no doubt be an important statement for a great many who toil in the academic enterprise. Interested readers may get other glimpses of Merton from Charles Crothers, *Robert K. Merton* (New York: Tavistock, 1987); Piotr Sztompka, *Robert K. Merton: An Intellectual Profile* (New York: St. Martin's Press, 1986); Caroline Hodges Persell, "An Interview with Robert K. Merton," *Teaching Sociology* 4 (1984): 470–486; David Caplovitz, "Robert K. Merton as Editor: Review Essay," *Contemporary Sociology* 6 (1977): 142–150; Lewis Coser, ed., *The Idea of Social Structure: Papers in Honor of Robert K. Merton* (New York: Harcourt Brace Jovanovich, 1975); and Thomas F. Gieryn, ed., *Science and Social Structure: A Festschift for Robert K. Merton* (New York: New York Academy of Sciences, 1980).

20. Letter from Pitirim A. Sorokin to Dean George D. Birkhoff, 24 January 1936, HUA, Records of the Sociology Department 1930–44.

21. Pitirim A. Sorokin, "Annual Report on the Condition and Activities of the Department of Sociology of Harvard University, 1934–1935," and letter from Pitirim A. Sorokin to Dean Kenneth B. Murdock, 11 January 1935, HUA, Records of the Sociology Department 1930–44.

22. Pitirim A. Sorokin, Sheldon S. Glueck, and Gordon W. Allport, "James Ford," *Harvard University Gazette* 40 (30 December 1944): 95–96. Sheldon Glueck had been a part-time member in Social Ethics and became one of the interdepartmental professors in sociology. He was a professor of criminology in the Harvard Law School. Wilbert E. Moore recalled James Ford as a very quiet and gentle man who gave graduate students their language exams in French. Interview with Wilbert E. Moore by Barry V. Johnston, 15 November 1985.

23. Letter from Pitirim A. Sorokin to Dean George D. Birkhoff, 17 April 1936, HUA, Records of the Sociology Department 1930–44. Sorokin was able to offer

Becker a competitive salary but not rank and tenure. Becker was a senior scholar ready for a full professorship. A position at the assistant level, without permanency, even at Harvard, was not attractive to him.

24. Pitirim A. Sorokin, "Department of Sociology: Brief Commentaries on Recommendations for 1936–1937," 3 December 1935, HUA, Records of the Sociology Department 1930–44.

25. Ibid. Timasheff had earned a magister of law degree (1914) and a doctor of laws degree (1916) at the University of St. Petersburg.

26. Letter from Pitirim A. Sorokin to Nicholas S. Timasheff, 17 January 1936, HUA, Records of the Sociology Department 1930–44. On the matter of language Wilbert Moore observed that Timasheff's English was better than Sorokin's. He speculated that Sorokin retained his thick Russian accent for the purposes of undergraduate teaching: "It let him get away with some of the corniest damn jokes because they sounded fine when they came out with that accent of his." Interview with Wilbert E. Moore by Barry V. Johnston, 15 November 1985.

27. Letter from Pitirim A. Sorokin to Nicholas S. Timasheff, 17 January 1936, HUA, Records of the Sociology Department 1930–44.

28. Letters from Pitirim A. Sorokin to Nicholas S. Timasheff, 20 July 1936 and 10 August 1936, HUA, Records of the Sociology Department 1930–44.

29. Letter from Nicholas S. Timasheff to Carle C. Zimmerman, 4 March 1936, and letter from Nicholas S. Timasheff to Pitirim A. Sorokin, 31 July 1936, HUA, Records of the Sociology Department 1930–44.

30. Letter from Pitirim A. Sorokin to Dean Kenneth B. Murdock, 26 October 1937, HUA, Records of the Sociology Department 1930–44.

31. After Harvard, Timasheff went to the Fordham University Graduate School as an assistant professor. He was promoted to associate in 1945 and professor in 1949 and contributed several substantial works to the discipline, including *Sociological Theory: Its Nature and Growth* (1955) and later editions in 1959 and 1967 (there was also a posthumous edition brought out in 1976 by George A. Theodorson; each was used by several cohorts of sociology students as part of their basic introduction to theory); *Three Worlds* (1946); *General Sociology* (1959); *The Sociology of Luigi Sturzo* (1962); and *War and Revolution* (1967). He also wrote over two hundred professional articles. Timasheff retired from Fordham in 1958 and spent the last part of his working life as coeditor of *Novyi Zhurmal* (New Review) a Russian literary magazine. So the invitation from Sorokin was a life-altering event, providing opportunities that not only improved his life but enriched American sociology.

This discussion of Timasheff is based on "N. S. Timasheff," *National Cyclopedia of American Biography* (Clifton, N.J.: James T. White, 1973), 54:592–593; Roman Goul, "N. S. Timasheff (1886–1970)," *Russian Review* 29 (July 1970): 363–365; Robert Bierstedt, "Nicholas S. Timasheff (1886–1970)," *American Sociologist* 5 (August 1970): 290–291; and Alex Simirenko, "Social Origin, Revolution and Sociology: The Work of Timasheff, Sorokin and Gurvitch," *British Journal of Sociology* 24 (March 1973): 84–92. Simirenko errs when he states, "As it happened all three scholars found themselves in the West, with Czechoslovakia providing their first refuge" (87). Timasheff lived in Germany before going to Prague.

32. Bierstedt, "Timasheff," 290.

33. Letter from Pitirim A. Sorokin to Kenneth B. Murdock, 8 November 1933, HUA, Records of the Sociology Department 1930–44.

34. In March 1937 the up-or-out policy was applied to the Department of Economics, with the result that Raymond Walsh and Alan R. Sweezy were given two-year appointments and would not be considered for promotion. Because Walsh and Sweezy were leaders of the Cambridge Teachers' Union, word spread that they were being discharged for political reasons. This case led to the creation of a faculty body known as the "Committee of Eight," a group charged with looking into the Walsh-Sweezy affair *and matters related to criteria and methods of promotion.* Conant and the Harvard Corporation found no merit in the committee's recommendations on Walsh and Sweezy, but on matters of rank and promotion the committee's suggestion were largely followed. It recommended that new faculty be appointed for five years without possibility of reappointment. The rank of assistant professor would be abolished, and the associate professor would be the first permanent rank. The committee thus accepted the principal of up or out. Instructors not promoted were out. For Conant's account of this policy and a review of Walsh-Sweezy see James B. Conant, *My Several Lives: Memoirs of a Social Inventor* (New York: Harper and Row, 1970), 157–179.

35. For discussions of Parsons's career and development see Talcott Parsons, "On Building Social Systems Theory: A Personal History," *Daedalus* 99 (1970): 826–881; Talcott Parsons, "A Short Account of My Intellectual Development," *Alpha Kappa Deltan* 29 (winter 1959): 3–12; Martin V. Martel, "Talcott Parsons," *International Encyclopedia of the Social Sciences,* ed. David Sills (New York: Free Press, 1979), 609–630. Interestingly, Laski had been in the history department at Harvard from 1916 to 1920. While there he was an outspoken advocate of the Boston police strike of 1919. This so outraged several members of the board of overseers that it appeared they might call for his dismissal. As a poignant example of Lowell's commitment to the free expression of opinion, Smith reports in *The Harvard Century,* 83, that while Lowell opposed the walkout and had no fondness for Laski, "when demands circulated for Laski's head he was immovable. 'If the Overseers ask for Laski's resignation,' he remarked to a friend while crossing the Yard, 'they will get mine.' "

36. Martel, "Parsons," 611.

37. Parsons, "A Short Account," 6.

38. Talcott Parsons, "Wants and Activities in Marshall," *Quarterly Journal of Economics* 46 (1931): 101–140; Talcott Parsons, "Economics and Sociology: Marshall in Relation to the Thought of His Time," *Quarterly Journal of Economics* 46 (1932): 316–347.

39. Talcott Parsons, "Sociological Elements in Economic Thought, I," *Quarterly Journal of Economics* 49 (1935): 414–453; Talcott Parsons, "Sociological Elements in Economic Thought, II," *Quarterly Journal of Economics* 49 (1935): 645–667.

40. Martel, "Parsons," 611.

41. Ibid.

42. Parsons, "A Short Account," 8.

43. Parsons, "On Building," 832.

44. Talcott Parsons, "The Place of Ultimate Values in Sociological Theory," *International Journal of Ethics* 45 (1935): 282–316.

45. In addition to the previously cited articles, Parsons had also published the following: his translation of Max Weber, *The Protestant Ethic and the Spirit of Capitalism* (New York: Scribner, 1930); "Malthus," in *The Encyclopedia of the Social Sciences,* ed. E. R. A. Seligman and A. Johnson (New York: Macmillan, 1933), 10:68–69; "Pareto," in *The Encyclopedia of the Social Sciences,* ed. E. R. A. Seligman and A. Johnson (New York: Macmillan, 1933), 11:576–578, and several other pieces in *The Encyclopedia of the Social Sciences,* ed. E. R. A. Seligman and A. Johnson (New York: Macmillan, 1933), on Jean Calvin 3:151–153; Samuel Smiles 14:111–112; Service 13:672–674; Society 14:225–232, and Thrift 14:623–626; "Some Reflections on the Nature and Significance of Economics," *Quarterly Journal of Economics* 48 (1934): 225–231; "H. M. Robertson on Max Weber and His School," *Journal of Political Economy* 43 (1935): 688–696.

46. Letter from Talcott Parsons to Pitirim A. Sorokin, 4 October 1935, HUA, Parsons Papers.

47. John Heeren, "Functional and Critical Sociology: A Study of Two Groups of Contemporary Sociologists" (Ph.D. diss., Duke University, 1975), 163. This stimulating and insightful study provides a substantial amount of information on Harvard and Columbia. The fact that Heeren leaves his quotations unattributed (perhaps to guarantee confidentiality) means we cannot assess the position of respondents in the discipline or their relationship to either Sorokin or Parsons.

48. Ibid., 176. By circumstance the author of this statement read a paper of mine in which this quote was used. He wrote that "starting in 1945 he [Parsons] did like disciples and from about that time on demanded more and more of them and especially more and more obeisances."

49. Ibid., 163.

50. Ibid., 176.

51. Ibid., 175–176.

52. Hereen dates the Adams House group from "about 1934 and continuing until the end of the decade" (173). Parsons, in his 1935 letter to Sorokin, definitely states "that the group has lasted for three years." Letter from Talcott Parsons to Pitirim A. Sorokin, 4 October 1935, HUA, Parsons Papers.

53. Merton, "Remembering," 70.

54. Robert Merton in an interview with Anna Di Lellio, "Le aspettative sociali di durata," 15.

55. Merton, "Remembering," 70.

56. Letter from Talcott Parsons to Pitirim A. Sorokin, 4 October 1935, HUA, Parsons Papers.

57. Letter from Pitirim A. Sorokin to Talcott Parsons, 21 November 1935, HUA, Parsons Papers.

58. Ibid.

59. Letter from Pitirim A. Sorokin to James B. Conant, 17 November 1936, HUA, Records of the Sociology Department 1930–44.

60. Letter from Joseph A. Schumpeter to the Harvard Committee for Research in the Social Sciences, 23 December 1936, HUA, Records of the Committee.

61. Letter from Lawrence J. Henderson to John D. Black, 4 January 1937, HUA, Records of the Harvard Committee for Research in the Social Sciences.

62. Letter from J. D. Black to L. J. Henderson, 9 February 1937, HUA, Records of the Harvard Committee for Research in the Social Sciences. In an undated letter, O. H. Taylor wrote Black that he had submitted his criticism directly to Parsons. Taylor states that even though "many things in it are open to much criticism and improvement, its general excellence seems to me beyond doubt." Letter from O. H. Taylor to John D. Black, n.d., HUA, Records of the Harvard Committee for Research in the Social Sciences.

63. Parsons, "On Building," 877.

64. Talcott Parsons, *The Structure of Social Action* (New York: Free Press, 1949). The original preface to the 1937 volume is included in this edition. See pages vii and viii.

65. Heeren, *Functional and Critical Sociology,* 171, 176. One student reports that a fight actually erupted during his oral examination (171).

66. The bad feeling between Parsons and Sorokin is known to many sociologists, and several of those I interviewed (e.g., George Homans, Edgar Schuler, Robin Williams, C. Arnold Anderson, Wilbert Moore, and Robert Bierstedt) acknowledged a firsthand awareness of the difficulty. Interestingly, none knew how it arose. Some state that Sorokin was jealous of Parsons's relationships with students, others believe that they were incompatible personalities, or that they simply had no respect for each other's scholarly work. Homans gives some support to the first of these when he writes:

> Sorokin's authoritarian tendencies may have been exacerbated by jealousy. For a small and young department, sociology by the 1930s had attracted an unusually large number of able graduate students, persons who were later to become distinguished in the profession. There were, to name only a few, Robert K. Merton, Robin Williams, Kingsley Davis, Wilbert Moore, Florence Kluckhohn, and the Rileys, Jack and Matilda. Many of these students wanted to study with Talcott Parsons, who had come to Harvard as an instructor, fresh from Heidelberg and enthusiastic for the work of Max Weber. He did more than anyone else to introduce Weber to American scholars. I have a slight suspicion that Sorokin may have been jealous of Talcott's popularity with the students. At any rate, he was said to have made life administratively unbearable for Talcott. (George Homans, *Coming to My Senses: The Autobiography of a Sociologist* [New Brunswick, N.J.: Transaction Books, 1985], 131)

67. Parsons, "On Building," 832.

68. Conant, *Lives,* 87.

69. Interview with Wilbert E. Moore, 15 November 1985, Denver, Colorado.

70. Conant, *Lives*, 87–90.

71. Parsons, "On Building," 832.

72. Letter from Pitirim A. Sorokin to James B. Conant, 25 May 1937, HUA, Records of the Sociology Department 1930–44. The others were Black, Ford, Tozzer, Wilson, Timasheff, Zimmerman, Hutchinson, and Merton.

73. "The Department also voted unanimously to recommend Assistant Professor Talcott Parsons for Associate Professorship beginning with the next academic year." Letter from Pitirim A. Sorokin to Dean George D. Birkhoff, 15 May 1939, HUA, Records of the Sociology Department 1930–44.

74. While speculating on how he came to be selected as Merton's replacement, Homans observed that he called on Sorokin from time to time when he was a junior fellow because he "had pretensions to becoming a sociologist." He further believed that he was selected because he was not a member of Parsons's circle and had the support of many of the "outside professors" of the department (particularly L. J. Henderson, E. B. Wilson, and E. F. Gay). See Homans, *Coming to My Senses*, 131–132, for the account.

75. Moore recalls that he was offered an instructorship at Harvard before leaving to join Davis at Penn State. He turned it down because he would not have been able to give his own courses. Instead, he would serve as someone's assistant. Interview with Wilbert E. Moore, 15 November 1985, Denver, Colorado.

76. Parsons, "A Short Account," 7.

77. William Buxton, *Talcott Parsons and the Capitalist Nation-State* (Toronto: University of Toronto Press, 1985), 285.

78. Ibid., 284.

79. Letter from E. B. Wilson to James B. Conant, 8 December 1934, HUA, President Conant's Papers.

80. Letter from Anonymous to James B. Conant, 6 April 1935, HUA, President Conant's Papers.

81. Letter from James B. Conant to Anonymous, 12 April 1935, HUA, President Conant's Papers.

82. Letter from Anonymous to James B. Conant, 23 July 1935, HUA, President Conant's Papers.

83. Letter from Talcott Parsons to James B. Conant, 28 September 1939, HUA, Parsons Papers. On 2 October 1939 Dorothy Bonn (Conant's secretary) wrote Parsons that she would be calling to arrange the meeting within two weeks. Letter from Dorothy Bonn to Talcott Parsons, 2 October 1939, HUA, Parsons Papers 1930–59.

84. Letter from Edward Y. Hartshorne to Talcott Parsons, 30 April (n.y.), HUA, Parsons Papers 1930–59, E. Y. Hartshorne file. The absence of a year poses a difficulty: When did Hartshorne draft it and the attached report? He notes in the report that it was written after three years as an assistant in Sociology A. Hartshorne came on board in the 1936–37 academic year, so the letter was likely written during the spring of 1939.

85. Edward Y. Hartshorne, "Report on Sociology A," HUA, Parsons Papers 1930–59, E. Y. Hartshorne file. Here Hartshorne is recalling a comment made by Sorokin at a faculty meeting.

86. Ibid.

87. Ibid. It's not clear whether this document or its substance was brought to Conant's attention by either Parsons or Hartshorne. Nevertheless, the memo expresses serious problems. Regardless of whether or not they were true, they could have gotten to Conant through any of the outside members of the department. Sorokin often noted that there were "many windows into the sociology department."

88. This coherence, though called logico-meaningful, may not actually be "logical unities in the formal sense of the word logic." Sorokin, *Dynamics*, 1:21.

89. Here Sorokin is using causal functional integration as a synonym for concomitant variation. Clearly, things may co-vary and not be causally associated. However, when co-variation is supported by knowledge of temporal sequence (the independent variable precedes the dependent variable in time), evidence that the hypothesized relationship is nonspurious, and provides us with a superior explanation of the phenomenon, then we can have some confidence of a causal association between events.

90. Sorokin, *Dynamics*, 1:32.

91. Ibid., 37.

92. Ibid., 51.

93. Ibid., 67.

94. Sorokin, *Dynamics*, 3:532–534.

95. Ibid., 535.

96. Ibid., 537–538.

97. Ibid., 539.

98. A. E. Tibbs, "Book Reviews of *Social and Cultural Dynamics:* A Study in Wissenssoziologie," *Social Forces* 21 (May 1943): 474.

99. Arthur Livingston, "Toward Another Civilization. Sorokin Predicts the Replacement of Ours by a Better Order," *New York Times Book Review*, 20 June 1937.

100. Ernest Sutherland Bates, "Charting the Coming New Age of Faith—An Erudite Russian Scholar Views the Past History of Mankind and Predicts the Future," *New York Herald Tribune*, Book Review Section, 30 May 1937.

101. Sidney Hook, "History in Swing Rhythm," *The Nation* 145 (July 1937): 48–49.

102. Alexander Goldenweiser, "Sociologus: A Platonic Dialogue," *Journal of Social Philosophy* 3 (winter 1938): 350–358.

103. Ibid., 354.

104. Ibid., 355.

105. Ibid., 358.

106. Ibid.

107. Letter from Pitirim A. Sorokin to Moses J. Aronson, 20 May 1938, USSA, Moses J. Aronson file. In an earlier letter Aronson informed Sorokin that Goldenweiser was commissioned to do the review "upon his own urgent request." Letter

from Moses J. Aronson to Pitirim A. Sorokin, 10 May 1938, USSA, Moses J. Aronson file.

108. Pitirim A. Sorokin, "Pseudo-Sociologus: A Reply to Professor Golden-weiser," *Journal of Social Philosophy* 3 (winter 1938): 359.

109. Ibid., 364.

110. Lewis Mumford, "Insensate Idealogue," *New Republic* 41 (14 July 1937): 283.

111. Sorokin replied to Mumford's theoretical criticisms in *Dynamics*, 4:732–733. He states that Mumford misunderstood his theory of change and should have been more careful in his reading. This comment comes after a lengthy discussion of linear and cyclical processes of social change.

112. Frank H. Knight, "Interpreting History," *Saturday Review*, 29 May 1937, 5–6.

113. Letter from Frank H. Knight to Pitirim A. Sorokin, 25 May 1937, USSA, *Social and Cultural Dynamics* file.

114. Sorokin must have found nothing serious in the review because Knight is not mentioned in the 1941 volume.

115. Robert E. Park, "Review of *Social and Cultural Dynamics*," *American Journal of Sociology* 43 (March 1938): 832.

116. Ibid., 831.

117. Ibid., 827.

118. Ibid.

119. Sorokin, *Dynamics*, 2:116. See also Sorokin, "*Recent Social Trends:* A Criticism," *Journal of Political Economy* 41 (April 1933): 196–202.

120. M. R. Rogers, "Fluctuations of Forms of Art," *American Sociological Review* 2 (December 1937): 920.

121. Ibid., 921.

122. John H. Randall Jr., "Fluctuations of the Systems of Truth, Ethics and Law," *American Sociological Review* 2 (December 1937): 922.

123. Ibid., 923.

124. Hans Speier, "Fluctuations of Social Relationships, War and Revolutions," *American Sociological Review* 2 (December 1937): 925.

125. Robert Bierstedt, *Power and Progress: Essays on Sociological Theory* (New York: McGraw-Hill, 1974), 2–3. The discussion of Bierstedt's essay that follows is based upon the reprinted version appearing in this volume, pp. 12–27. The original was printed in the *American Sociological Review* 2 (December 1937): 813–823.

126. Ibid., 17.

127. Ibid., 27.

128. Pitirim A. Sorokin "Rejoinder" in Bierstedt's *Power*, 27–30. The original was in the *American Sociological Review* 2 (December 1937): 823–825. As Bierstedt notes in *Power*, "I still enjoy the merry quip and the end where, in a footnote, he put me in my place" (3). The footnote reads: "In the fourth volume of my *Dynamics* I expect to answer all important and mature criticisms of my work." Sorokin, however, must have considered Bierstedt's criticisms important and mature because he did address them in volume 4.

129. Livingston, "Civilization," 1.

130. Hornell Hart, "Sorokin's Data Versus His Conclusions," *American Sociological Review* 4 (October 1939): 646.

131. Sorokin does state in *Dynamics* that his predictions about changes in art, literature, and epistemological foundations are guesses; see 1:504, 608, and 2:117 as examples.

132. Pitirim A. Sorokin, "Comments on Professor Hart's Paper," *American Sociological Review* 4 (October 1939): 646–651.

133. Ibid., 648–651.

134. Abbot Payson Usher, "Review of *Fluctuations of Systems of Truths, Ethics and Law*," *Harvard Guardian* 2 (November 1937): 5–8.

135. D. W. Prall, "Review of Fluctuations of Forms of Art," *Harvard Guardian* 2 (November 1937): 8–13.

136. William Yandell Elliott, "Review of Fluctuations of Social Relationships, War and Revolutions," *Harvard Guardian* 2 (November 1937): 13.

137. Crane Brinton, "Socio-Astrology," *Southern Review* 3 (autumn 1937): 243–266.

138. Pitirim A. Sorokin, "Histrionics," *Southern Review* 4 (winter 1938): 555–564.

139. Lawrence T. Nichols, "Deviance and Social Science: The Instructive Historical Case of Pitirim Sorokin," *Journal of the History of the Behavioral Sciences* 25 (October 1989): 338–339. The author is referring to the norms described by Robert K. Merton in Storer, *Robert K. Merton: The Sociology of Science*, 268–278. These norms are universalism, which requires that assertions be tested by accepted and impersonal standards, and therefore be capable of replication; communalism, which requires shared ownership of discoveries and ideas; disinterestedness, which demands that the scientist be committed to truth rather than favoring a self-serving goal; and organized skepticism, which charges the scientist to question results particularly when they are those that favor his theory or project.

140. Ibid., 351.

141. Lawrence Nichols misses this important characteristic of *Dynamics* in his article "Deviance and Social Science." Consequently, the role of this book in Sorokin's later works is obscured, and readers may remember *Dynamics* only for its part in shaping a "spoiled identity." Sorokin accepted the identity, but *Dynamics* was the bridge to the next phase in the development of his sociology.

142. Robert W. Friedricks, *A Sociology of Sociology* (New York: Free Press, 1970), 57–110.

143. Robert E. Fitch, "The Scientist as Priest and Savior," *Christian Century* 75 (26 March 1958): 368–370.

144. Reinhard Bendix, "The Images of Man in the Social Sciences: The Basic Assumptions of Present Day Research," *Commentary* 11 (1951): 190; quoted in Friedricks, *Sociology,* 109. The priest of science would now have an audience that must accept their truths on "faith."

145. Friedricks, *Sociology,* 69–75.

146. Ibid., 74.

147. Robert Lynd, *Knowledge for What?* (Princeton, N.J.: Princeton University Press, 1939), 125–126.

148. Howard Becker, *Through Values to Social Interpretation* (Durham, N.C.: Duke University Press, 1950), 196–198; quoted in Friedricks, *Sociology*, 74.

CRISIS AND CONFRONTATION

1. Clarence Q. Berger, *Fiftieth Anniversary Report* (Cambridge, Mass.: Crimson Printing, 1983), 42.

2. Letter from Gordon W. Allport to Elizabeth Gilboy, 31 March 1938, HUA, Records of the Harvard Committee for Research in the Social Sciences.

3. Letter from E. B. Wilson to Elizabeth Gilboy, 31 March 1938, HUA, Records of the Harvard Committee for Research in the Social Sciences.

4. Ibid.

5. Ibid.

6. Ibid.

7. Letter from Pitirim A. Sorokin to John D. Black, 8 May 1938, HUA, Records of the Harvard Committee for Research in the Social Sciences.

8. Letter from John D. Black to Pitirim A. Sorokin, 9 May 1938, HUA, Records of the Harvard Committee for Research in the Social Sciences.

9. Letter from Pitirim A. Sorokin to John D. Black, 11 May 1938, HUA, Records of the Harvard Committee for Research in the Social Sciences.

10. Letter from John D. Black to Dumas Malone, 21 July 1938, HUA, Records of the Harvard Committee for Research in the Social Sciences.

11. Letter from Pitirim A. Sorokin to Dean of Arts and Sciences, 14 February 1940, HUA, Sociology Department Annual Reports file.

12. Ibid.

13. Ibid., 2.

14. Ibid., 3.

15. Letter from Pitirim A. Sorokin to W. S. Ferguson, 28 February 1940, HUA, Sociology Department Annual Reports file.

16. Letter from Talcott Parsons to Robert K. Merton, 23 October 1940, HUA, Parsons Papers 1923–40.

17. Letter from Talcott Parsons to Robert K. Merton, 20 December 1940, HUA, Parsons Papers 1923–40.

18. Ibid., 2.

19. Letter from Talcott Parsons to Robert K. Merton, 23 October 1940, HUA, Parsons Papers 1923–40.

20. Parsons, "On Building," 835.

21. Ibid., 840.

22. Interview with George W. Goethals by Barry V. Johnston, 11 April 1990.

23. Talcott Parsons, *The Department of Social Relations at Harvard: Report of the Chairman on the First Decade: 1946–1956* (Cambridge, Mass.: Harvard University Press, 1956), 11–12.

24. Henry Murray had a broad, varied background. A man of wealth, he was prepared at Groton School and graduated from Harvard College in 1916. He then pursued a medical degree at Columbia and followed it with a two-year surgical internship. His medical studies were broadened by two more years of work in embryology and additional study in Cambridge, England, for a doctorate in bio-chemistry. Murray was deeply interested in the complex interactions between the physical, biological, and psychological aspects of life. Before leaving Europe, he "visited Zurich for what turned out to be a fateful encounter with Jung—this was the turning point in Murray's transition from biomedicine to the behavioral sciences. He returned to the United States committed to psychology." Gardner Lindzey, "Henry A. Murray," in *The International Encyclopedia of the Social Sciences: Biographical Supplement*, ed. David L. Sills (New York: Free Press, 1979), 566. Murray was a charter member of the Boston Psychoanalytic Society, had completed his training as an analyst in 1935, and had been director of the Harvard Psychological Clinic since 1928.

Gordon Allport was another lifelong participant in the Cantabrigian experience, receiving his bachelor of arts degree in 1919, his master of arts degree in 1921, and the doctorate in 1922. He was a man of broad psychological interests whose best-known contributions were in personality theory, attitudes, and the study of prejudice. Allport was committed to improving the human condition, believed in the unique-ness of the individual, and was critical of a psychology based solely on experimenta-tion. His first teaching position at Harvard was not in psychology but in social ethics under Richard Clarke Cabot, whose "influence on Allport's life and career was at least as important as that of any of Allport's teachers." Arthur Jenness, "Gordon W. Allport," in *The International Encyclopedia of the Social Sciences: Biographical Supple-ment*, ed. David L. Sills (New York: Free Press, 1979), 13.

Interestingly, Gordon Allport's career spans much of the history of sociology at Harvard. He began in Social Ethics, and was an interdepartmental member of the sociology faculty and a founding figure in the Department of Social Relations. Coincidentally, he ended his Harvard career as the first Richard Clarke Cabot Professor of Social Ethics, an appointment made in the Department of Social Relations at his retirement in 1966.

Allport's humanistic concerns made him a marginal figure in the psychology department and were compounded by his deep intellectual and personal interest in religion. Indeed, he played an important part in religion's becoming a legitimate topic of psychological study and was a founding member of the Society for the Scientific Study of Religion. Allport received many of the traditional symbols of success in psychology: he was American Psychological Association president in 1939, was the Eastern Psychological Association president in 1942, was a founder and 1943 president of the Society for the Psychological Study of Social Issues, and received the highest award of the American Psychological Foundation, its Gold Medal, in 1963. However, the most meaningful distinction may have come from his colleagues in clinical and abnormal psychology when, in 1951, he was named as the second most influential force in personality theory. The first was Sigmund Freud.

Over the years and in spite of their differences, a warm relationship was maintained between Sorokin and Allport. George W. Goethals suggested in an 11 April 1990 interview that this was because both "were deeply religious men." Insight into this aspect of Allport's life is found not only in his work but in his posthumously published *Waiting for the Lord: 33 Meditations on God and Man* (New York: Macmillan, 1978).

25. Patrick L. Schmidt, "Towards a History of the Department of Social Relations: Harvard University, 1946–1972," honors thesis, Harvard College, 1978, 26.

26. J. F. Brown, "The Position of Psychoanalysis in the Science of Psychology," *Journal of Abnormal and Social Psychology* 35 (1940): 30–43.

27. Marvin Harris, *The Rise of Anthropological Theory* (New York: Thomas Cardwell, 1968), 394, 597.

28. Clyde Kluckhohn was also broadly educated and made substantial contributions to anthropology. His initial training was in the classics, and he had a gift for languages. He was a Rhodes scholar at Oxford and there completed his classical education. On leaving England he spent a year in Germany, and while there underwent analysis. However, he contracted tuberculosis and on return to the United States went to the Southwest for health reasons. There he became fascinated with the Navajo, learned their language, and began his second career as an anthropologist. Kluckhohn was considered brilliant by many of his peers and had no interest in "stones and bones" anthropology.

29. George Homans, in a 20 October 1977 interview with Patrick Schmidt, observed that "Social Relations was a department built on personality conflicts—hate!" It was Homans's belief that these conflicts were an important factor in the emergence of the department. Professor Homans expressed the same opinion in an 11 March 1986 interview with Barry V. Johnston. Homans's account was also supported in an 11 April 1990 interview between George W. Goethals and Barry Johnston. Ezra F. Vogel recalls Homans's making a similar statement to Parsons and the audience at the celebration of the founding of the Department of Social Relations. See Ezra T. Vogel "Obituary for George Caspar Homans (1910–1990)," *Footnotes*, December 1990, 14.

30. Parsons, "First Decade," 12.

31. Patrick Schmidt, *Towards a History*, 23. In discussing the earlier meetings of this group Schmidt observed, "The inability to pursue this common interest [Freud and psychoanalysis] without inhibition in their own departments added an emotional dimension to the intellectual bond and lent an air of conspiracy to their meetings" (21). Hence the term "conspirators" in the earlier passage.

32. Announcement from Dean W. S. Ferguson to Chairmen of Departments, 3 June 1941, HUA, Records of the Sociology Department 1930–44.

33. Ibid., 3.

34. Letter from Pitirim A. Sorokin to W. S. Ferguson, 3 June 1941, HUA, Records of the Sociology Department 1930–44.

35. Letter from W. S. Ferguson to Pitirim A. Sorokin, 10 June 1941, HUA, Records of the Sociology Department 1930–44.

36. Letter from Paul H. Buck to Pitirim A. Sorokin, 16 April 1942, HUA, Records of the Sociology Department 1930–44.

37. Letter from L. J. Henderson to A. Lawrence Lowell, 28 February 1940, HUA, Baker Library, L. J. Henderson Papers. It is unlikely that Sorokin had any knowledge of Henderson's recommendation. However, it is plausible to surmise that he would have been pleased to be selected over his adversary.

38. Letter from A. Lawrence Lowell to Pitirim A. Sorokin, 22 March 1940, USSA, "L" general file.

39. Sorokin, Long Journey, 263.

40. Pitirim A. Sorokin, "Declaration of Independence of the Social Sciences," Social Science 16 (July 1941): 221–229.

41. Ibid., 223.

42. Ibid., 224.

43. Ibid.

44. Ibid., 225.

45. Ibid., 226.

46. Ibid., 227.

47. Letter from Read Bain to Pitirim A. Sorokin, 23 January 1941, USSA, American Sociological Review file.

48. Letter from Pitirim A. Sorokin to Read Bain, 3 March 1941, USSA, American Sociological Review file.

49. Letter from Read Bain to Pitirim A. Sorokin, 5 March 1941, USSA, American Sociological Review file.

50. The specifics of this exchange are found in Sorokin to Bain, 10 March 1941, and in Bain to Sorokin, 15 March 1941, USSA, American Sociological Review file.

51. Letter from Read Bain to Pitirim A. Sorokin, 24 December 1941, USSA, American Sociological Review file. There is no correspondence in the collection that suggests why Bain wrote this letter or what he was reacting to. However, the general charge that people could not disagree with Sorokin without becoming personal enemies is not entirely true. Many warm, long-standing relations existed between Sorokin and his critics. However, this confrontation did become personal and was not reconciled until December 1952. See letter from Pitirim A. Sorokin to Read Bain, 9 December 1952, USSA, Read Bain file. It appears that Sorokin warmly responded to an invitation made by Bain, and they put the breech behind them. There is a series of friendly letters that stretch to 6 May 1963, when the file ends.

52. Pitirim A. Sorokin, Social and Cultural Dynamics, vol. 4 (New York: Bedminster Press, 1941), vi.

53. Ibid., 762.

54. Ibid., 763.

55. Ibid., 763–764.

56. Ibid., 746–761.

57. Ibid., v.

58. Sorokin, Crisis, 321.

59. Ibid., 317.

60. Pitirim A. Sorokin, "Integralism Is My Philosophy," in *This Is My Philosophy*, ed. Whit Burnett (New York: Harper and Brothers, 1957), 184.

61. Sorokin, *Crisis*, 320.

62. Nicholas S. Timasheff, "Review of *The Crisis of our Age*," *Thought* 16 (December 1941): 610–612.

63. Rubin Gotesky, "Sociology and the Crisis," *Saturday Review*, 20 December 1941, 20–22.

64. Ibid., 21.

65. Ibid., 22.

66. Joseph S. Roucek, "Review of *The Crisis of our Age*," USSA, Newspaper clipping file. Roucek has even higher praise for the last volume of *Dynamics*. He writes Sorokin: "On return from California, I found your fourth volume of *Social and Cultural Dynamics*. It is a marvelous book—just as all your contributions. You certainly will go through the history of sociology as the outstanding world sociologist. I say that not to please you, but rather to satisfy my sense of admiration for a Slav brother." Letter from J. S. Roucek to Pitirim A. Sorokin, 14 September 1941, HUA, Sorokin Correspondence.

67. Robert M. MacIver, "Review of *Social and Cultural Dynamics, Volume 4*." *American Sociological Review* 6 (December 1941): 904–905.

68. Ibid., 905.

69. Ibid.

70. Wilbert E. Moore, "Review of *Social and Cultural Dynamics*, Volume 4," *Social Forces* 20 (March 1942): 400. For more balanced and certainly less polemical reviews, see Floyd N. House, "Review of *Social and Cultural Dynamics*, Volume 4," *American Journal of Sociology* 47 (May 1942): 994–996; and George Devereux, "Review of *Social and Cultural Dynamics*, Volume 4," *American Anthropologist* 44 (June 1942): 507–510.

71. Harry Elmer Barnes, "Review of *The Crisis of Our Age*," *American Journal of Sociology* 47 (May 1942): 996–997.

72. Read Bain, "Review of *The Crisis of Our Age*," *American Sociological Review* 6 (December 1941): 907.

73. Ibid., 908–909.

74. Ibid., 908.

75. Sidney Hook, "Review of *The Crisis of Our Age*," *Books*, 11 January 1942, 10.

76. Letter from Gordon Allport, Clyde Kluckhohn, Hobart Mowrer, Henry Murray, and Talcott Parsons to Paul S. Buck, 10 June, 1943, HUA, Parsons Papers 1930–59, Allport Committee file.

77. Letter from Paul S. Buck to Professors Allport, Kluckhohn, Mowrer, Murray, and Parsons, 11 June 1943, HUA, Parsons Papers 1930–59, Allport Committee file.

78. Letter from Gordon Allport to Paul Buck, 1 October 1943, HUA, Parsons Papers 1930–59, Allport Committee file.

79. To the Dean of the Faculty of Arts and Sciences from the informal committee appointed by your letter of 11 June 1943, HUA, Parsons Papers 1930–59, Allport Committee file.

80. Ibid., 1.

81. Ibid., 2. It is unclear what would happen to Professor Zimmerman. Would he be a part of the new department, go to economics, or stay with Sorokin? His omission from the list and memo is curious.

82. Alexander Leighton, *Human Relations in a Changing World* (New York: Dutton, 1949), 43.

83. Letter from Talcott Parsons to Edwin F. Gay, 14 July 1944, HUA, Parsons Papers.

84. Letter from Talcott Parsons to Paul S. Buck, 3 April 1944, HUA, Parsons Papers.

85. Ibid., 2–6.

86. Parsons reported in an interview with Patrick Schmidt in 1977 "that there was a great deal of evidence that Paul Buck was very much dissatisfied with the Sorokin situation." See the tapes for the Schmidt thesis, Interview with Talcott Parsons, Tape 2, Side 1, HUA, Pusey Archive. George Homans, in an interview with Barry Johnston on 11 March 1986, stated, "Buck did not think much of Sorokin. He preferred Parsons because he was a better administrator and kept his emotions and ego under control."

87. Letter from Parsons to Gay, 14 July 1944, HUA, Parsons Papers, 2.

88. Letter from Paul S. Buck to Pitirim A. Sorokin, 5 April 1944, HUA, Records of the Sociology Department 1930–44.

89. Letter from Paul S. Buck to Pitirim A. Sorokin, 10 April 1944, HUA, Records of the Sociology Department 1930–44.

90. Letter from Pitirim A. Sorokin to Paul S. Buck, 10 April 1944, HUA, Records of the Sociology Department 1930–44. In *Long Journey* Sorokin reports three out of the four requests for release from the obligations of chairman, once in 1933 at the end of the Lowell administration and twice under Conant, ca. 1938–42. While Conant may have granted the 1942 request, it was not implemented until 1944. Sorokin reports, ". . . I was anxious to be rid of the chairmanship, [as] some other members of the department were very eager to attain this position." *Long Journey,* 250–251. The quote is from p. 251.

91. Letter from Pitirim A. Sorokin to Paul S. Buck, 11 April 1944, HUA, Records of the Sociology Department 1930–44.

92. Letter from Paul S. Buck to Pitirim A. Sorokin, 26 April 1944, HUA, Records of the Sociology Department 1930–44.

93. George Homans in interview with Barry V. Johnston, 11 March 1986.

94. Letter from Pitirim A. Sorokin to Paul S. Buck, 12 May 1944, HUA, Records of the Sociology Department 1930–44.

95. Ibid., 2. Sorokin closed this letter by advising Buck that this appeal was his idea and was done without the knowledge or approval of Mrs. Nobel.

96. Letter from Talcott Parsons to Mrs. Nobel, 12 May 1944, HUA, Records of the Sociology Department 1930–44.

97. Letter from Marjorie Nobel to Talcott Parsons, 13 May 1944, HUA, Records of the Sociology Department 1930–44.

98. Letter from Talcott Parsons to E. Y. Hartshorne, 19 July 1944, HUA, Parsons Papers 1930–59.

99. Ibid., 2.

100. James Ford died on 12 May 1944, about six weeks before Parsons became chairman. The faculty discussed what to do with his position from August 1944 to September 1945. HUA. See Minutes of the Sociology Department 1931–45.

101. Letter from Paul S. Buck to Talcott Parsons, 18 August 1945, HUA, Parsons Papers.

102. Taped interview with Edwin B. Newman by Patrick Schmidt, 11 April 1977, HUA. Newman stated, "I think another important reason why sociology did not remain independent in the 1940s was Robert Merton saying no about coming to Harvard. It was not so much the quality of the faculty that kept him away, but the fact that Harvard was not very supportive, with money, of the social sciences." Newman's speculation, while plausible, misses the mark. In a letter dated "The Authentic Columbus Day, 1994," Professor Merton wrote this author:

> True, I didn't accept the Harvard offer in 1945, but not for the reasons given by Edwin Newman. . . . The actual reason: It had become clear to Paul Lazarsfeld and me that we had grown into a complementary intellectual partnership in both teaching and research. As our graduate students seemed to see was the case. Paul and I had agreed that we would probably never decide to move from Columbia and in any case neither of us would do so alone.

Interestingly, Sorokin and Zimmerman opposed Merton's appointment. They reasoned that while his quality could not be disputed, the department was already rich in theorists and should look to cultivate more breadth. Consequently, Sorokin argued that an expert in empirical research or statistics might be better for the department. "Minutes of the Sociology Department 1931–1945," HUA, Records of the Sociology Department; see, particularly, 2 August 1944 and 10 September 1945.

103. Parsons, *First Decade*, 14. The decision to visit those programs followed up on a brief report that Parsons prepared on "Related Plans at Other Universities." In that document he concludes that the interdisciplinary and corporate research strategy is being followed more by the endowed rather than state universities; that Harvard is trailing behind these institutions; there is a growing faith in programs aimed toward the "unity of science"; and nothing like the proposed Harvard plan has been tried elsewhere. Talcott Parsons, "Related Plans at Other Universities," n.d., HUA, Parsons Papers.

104. Parsons, *First Decade*, 14.

105. Ibid., 15.

106. Ibid.

107. HUA. Minutes of the Department of Sociology 1931–45, 8 December 1945.

108. Patrick Schmidt, "Towards a History of Social Relations," 44–45.

109. Parsons, *First Decade*, 23.

110. Gordon Allport and Edwin G. Boring, "Psychology and Social Relations at Harvard University," *American Psychologist* 1 (April 1946): 119–120.

111. The account of this important historical transition is excerpted from Barry V. Johnston, "Sorokin and Parsons at Harvard: Institutional Conflict and the Origin of a Hegemonic Tradition," *Journal of the History of the Behavioral Sciences* 22 (April 1986): 107–127.

112. Edward A. Tiryakian, "The Significance of Schools in the Development of Sociology," in *Contemporary Issues in Theory and Research,* ed. William E. Snizek et al. (Westport, Conn.: Greenwood Press, 1979), 211–234; Edward A. Tiryakian, "Post-Parsonsian Sociology," *Humboldt Journal of Social Relations* 7 (1979/1980): 17–33.

113. Imre Lakatos, "Falsification and the Methodology of Scientific Research Programs," in *Criticism and the Growth of Knowledge,* ed. Imre Lakatos and Alan Musgrave (London: Cambridge University Press, 1970), 91–196.

114. Tiryakian, "Significance of Schools," 220.

115. Edward A. Tiryakian, "Hegemonic Schools and the Development of Sociology," in *Structures of Knowing: Current Studies in the Sociology of Schools,* ed. Richard Monk (Lanham, Md.: University Press of America, 1986), 417–441. Tiryakian, "Post-Parsonsian."

116. Heeren, *Functional and Critical Sociology,* 172–175. Observations on Sorokin as a teacher can be found in Robin Williams's essay, "Pitirim A. Sorokin: Master and Prophet," in *Sociological Traditions from Generation to Generation,* ed. R. K. Merton and M. W. Riley (Norwood, N.J.: Abex, 1980), 93–108. See also Robert Bierstedt, *Power and Progress* (New York: McGraw-Hill, 1974), 2–3. While Bierstedt's best discussion of Sorokin's background and ideas is found in *American,* 299–348, he best describes Sorokin as a teacher in the earlier work.

117. Heeren, *Functional and Critical Sociology,* 178.

118. Ibid.

119. Sorokin, *Long Journey,* 229.

120. See Nichols, "Deviance," 345.

121. Alvin W. Gouldner, *The Coming Crisis of Western Sociology* (New York: Basic Books, 1970), 167–177.

122. Ibid., 173.

123. Alan Kraut observed: One Harvard professor expressed the objections of numerous others when he complained that too many students were coming from outside the element from which the college had been chiefly recruited for three hundred years. In response, Harvard mounted a restrictive quota system in 1922 that especially affected the increasing number of East European Jews seeking admission. Revised admission questionnaires were designed to flag newcomers by asking, "What change, if any, has been made since birth in your name or that of your father? . . ."

After objections from the American Jewish Committee, a special Faculty Committee investigated admission policies and reported in April 1923, that it recommended that Harvard repudiate such changes and retain a policy of "equal opportunity for all; regardless of race or religion" using "no novel process of scrutiny" to screen applicants. However, covert discrimination at Harvard and elsewhere continued, despite public declarations to the contrary. Alan M. Kraut, *The Huddled*

Masses: The Immigrant in American Society (Arlington Heights, Ill.: Harlan Davidson, 1982), 168.

Sorokin, in a letter to E. A. Ross, noted that foreign scholars had some difficulty at Harvard and suggested the existence of an unofficial quota norm:

> Our experience with visiting foreign professors has shown that they do not do justice to themselves or to the students. By the time they have adapted themselves somewhat to the conditions, their time has expired. For these reasons, and the fact that Harvard has the largest quota of foreign students, Russian, Italian, French, and others, the Administration is not favorably inclined at the present time to further extensions of the quota. (Sorokin to E. A. Ross, 18 January 1937. HUA, Records of the Sociology Department 1930–44)

Also see Marcia G. Synnott, *The Half-Opened Door: Discrimination and Admissions at Harvard, Yale, and Princeton, 1900–1970* (Westport, Conn.: Greenwood Press, 1979), 85–125.

124. Heeren, *Functional and Critical Sociology*, 165.

125. Ibid. 176. See also Robert K. Merton in an interview with Di Lellio, "Le aspettative sociali du durata," 15. A related point was raised by Merton in a discussion with Barry Johnston in Ghent, Belgium, on 16 November 1984. Interestingly, this was not touched on in the Di Lellio text and addresses why students turned to Sorokin. Merton's interest was stimulated by the likelihood that Sorokin would provide in-depth study of European social theory, ideas not readily available at the time in other major graduate departments. Sorokin's history, education, and work on *Contemporary Sociological Theories* prepared him for the role of master explicator of the European heritage. Merton's comment suggests that Parsons, who in the 1930s was largely unknown in the community of sociologists, came to the attention of graduate students because he taught the courses in which many of them were primarily interested. Parsons's style of teaching was also attractive. See also Merton, "Remembering," 70.

126. In addition to the Adams House group, Parsons was tied to other significant discussion groups within the university. Through L. J. Henderson he participated in the Pareto Circle and became occasionally involved with the Society of Fellows and to a lesser extent the Saturday Club. Henderson and Lowell were founding forces behind the Society of Fellows, and both, along with Crane Brinton, participated in the Saturday Club. Parsons's association with these groups added to his prestige and scholarly image within the Harvard community. His acceptance within them (although he was not a member of either the Society of Fellows or the Saturday Club) established him as one who had the ear of many Harvard notables. For an extended discussion of these associations, see Crane C. Brinton's *Society of Fellows* and Barbara Heyl's essay "The Harvard Pareto Circle."

It is also curious that while Sorokin spent much time in *Long Journey* recalling his activities (both personal and intellectual) with students at the University of Minnesota, there is very little discussion about such relations with his Harvard students. Perhaps these differences, in combination with the theoretical ones, made Sorokin less likely to be a candidate for the founder-leader role.

127. Nicholas C. Mullins, *Theory and Theory Groups in Contemporary American Sociology* (New York: Harper and Row, 1973), 40; Harry M. Johnson, *Sociology: A Systematic Introduction* (New York: Harcourt, Brace, and World, 1960). In the Department of Social Relations, Parsons later surrounded himself with a network of contemporaries who helped develop, elaborate, and refine his theoretical system. He had a full cadre of lieutenants who worked within this paradigm, spread his message, and often sent their students back to Harvard for professional development.

128. Patricia Madoo Lengerman, "The Founding of the American Sociological Review: The Anatomy of a Rebellion," *American Sociological Review* 44 (1979): 185–198.

129. Henrika Kuklick, "A Scientific Revolution: Sociological Theory in the United States 1930–1945," *Sociological Inquiry* 43 (1973): 3–22. Further discussion of the period is found in Kuklick, "Boundary Maintenance in American Sociology," *Journal of the History of the Behavioral Sciences* 16 (1980): 201–219; Mark Oromaner, "The Sociological Community and the Works of Talcott Parsons: 1936–1950," *Journal of the History of Sociology* 1 (1979): 76–92; Norbert Wiley, "The Rise and Fall of Dominating Theories in American Sociology," in *Contemporary Issues in Theory and Research*, ed. W. E. Shizek et al. (Westport, Conn.: Greenwood Press, 1979), 47–80.

130. It is not my intent to argue that Parsons's successful replacement of Sorokin gave him disciplinary hegemony. Rather, it gave him the foundation from which to compete successfully for that position. There were certainly other perspectives and theorists with whom Parsons had to vie to lead the discipline. However, as Mullins observes, "By 1951 Parsons was a major figure in American sociology; by 1965 he was *the* major figure. He was central to the Harvard department, to the profession of sociology and to the intellectual specialty of social theory" (*Theory*, 46).

131. Wiley, "Rise and Fall," 48.

132. Don Martindale, "Pitirim A. Sorokin: Soldier of Fortune," in *Sorokin and Sociology: Essays in Honour of Professor Pitirim A. Sorokin*, ed. C. C. Hallen and R. Prasad (Agra, India: Satish Book Enterprise, 1974), 3–24.

133. Sorokin, *Long Journey*, 274.

SOCIAL RECONSTRUCTION

1. James H. Madison, *Eli Lilly: A Life, 1885–1977* (Indianapolis: Indiana Historical Society, 1989), 189–204. In this section Madison discusses Lilly's philanthropy and his support for character development studies, particularly those of Sorokin and Ernest Ligon.

2. Letter from Eli Lilly to Pitirim A. Sorokin, 20 April 1942, USSA, Lilly Endowment file.

3. Letter from Pitirim A. Sorokin to Eli Lilly, 23 April 1942, USSA, Lilly Endowment file.

4. Pitirim A. Sorokin, "A Neglected Factor of War," *American Sociological Review* 3, no. 4 (August 1938): 475–486.

5. Ibid., 478.

6. The data set covered Greece from the fifth century B.C. to the fifth century A.D. and Europe from the twelfth to the twentieth century.

7. Ibid., 485.

8. Pitirim A. Sorokin, "The Conditions and Prospects of a World Without War," *American Journal of Sociology* 49 (March 1944): 441–449.

9. Ibid., 445.

10. Ibid., 448.

11. Sorokin, *Long Journey*, 271–273.

12. Read Bain, "Review of *Man and Society in Calamity*," *American Sociological Review* 8 (February 1943): 91–93.

13. Ibid., 91.

14. Ibid., 92–93.

15. J. L. Gillian, "Review of *Man and Society in Calamity*," *Annals of the American Academy of Political and Social Science* 225 (January 1943): 232.

16. Orville Prescott, "Review of *Man and Society in Calamity*," *New York Times*, 26 October 1942.

17. H. A. Reingold, "The Four Horsemen: Review of *Man and Society in Calamity*," *Commonwealth*, 30 October 1942, 45–46.

18. Floyd N. House, "Review of *Man and Society in Calamity*," *American Journal of Sociology* 49 (July 1943): 85.

19. Ibid., 85. House also argued that as a large-scale study in comparative history and macrosociology the work is out of step with the main lines of inquiry that has made sociology "The American Science."

20. Sorokin, *Dynamics*, 4:vii and note.

21. Pitirim A. Sorokin, *Society, Culture, and Personality: Their Structure and Dynamics: A System of General Sociology* (New York: Harper and Brothers, 1947), 714–723.

22. Ibid., 517–522.

23. Floyd N. House, "Review of *Society, Culture, and Personality: Their Structure and Dynamics: A System of General Sociology.*" *American Journal of Sociology* 53 (November 1947): 225–226. House found the style of the book ponderous, repetitious, and frequently dogmatic.

24. Nicholas S. Timasheff, "Review of *Society, Culture, and Personality: Their Structure and Dynamics: A System of General Sociology.*" *Thought* (1947): 610–611.

25. Sidney Hook, "Man's Destiny: A Scientific View," *New York Times*, 17 August 1947, 4.

26. Ibid., 27.

27. Ibid.

28. Floyd N. House, "Review of *Sociocultural Causality, Space, Time*," *Social Forces* 49 (October 1943): 110.

29. Kurt H. Wolff, "Review of *Sociocultural Causality, Space, Time*," *American Journal of Sociology* 49 (March 1944): 481–484. Sorokin begins the book with his controversial 1940 essay, "Declaration of Independence of the Social Sciences."

30. Anonymous, "Note on *Sociocultural Causality, Space, Time*," *American Sociological Review* 8 (August 1943): 497.

31. Rushton Coulborn, "Social Sciences and the Atomic Age." *Phylon* 9, no. 2 (1948): 166–170.

32. Ibid., 168.

33. Ibid., 169.

34. Ibid., 168.

35. Compare this with Wolff's "Review of *Sociocultural*," 482–483. See specifically his discussions of building a consistent system at the expense of clarity and scientific validity, as well as his comments on misplaced concreteness.

36. Sorokin, *Long Journey*, 267–268.

37. Letter from Pitirim A. Sorokin to Eli Lilly, 11 April 1946, Lilly Foundation Archives (hereafter referred to as LFA).

38. Letter from Eli Lilly to Pitirim A. Sorokin, 17 April 1946, LFA. Sorokin's recollection of this event in *Long Journey* is blurred and imprecise. He reports receiving an unsolicited letter in the winter of 1946 which offered him a considerable sum of money to advance the altruism project. The letter was signed by a man unknown to him—Eli Lilly (see p. 276). Sorokin may be confusing the 1942 and 1946 contacts. There were two letters from Lilly in 1942; only one is in the Sorokin Collection at Saskatoon and none in the Lilly Foundation Archive at Indianapolis. Existing archival records do show that Lilly was the first to contact Sorokin, but that Sorokin raised the question of research support.

39. Sorokin, *Long Journey*, 277.

40. Ibid., 273.

41. Letter from Pitirim A. Sorokin to Eli Lilly, 1 May 1946, LFA. Koussevitzky is widely known for his contributions to American and Russian music. As noted earlier, he was a close friend of the Sorokin family and the namesake of their youngest son. There is little correspondence between him and Sorokin because from 1924 to 1949 he was the conductor of the Boston Symphony and thus most of their contacts were personal and face-to-face. Koussevitzky, like Sorokin, was an emotionally intense and dramatic person whose colorful and unidiomatic English lent additional power to his presence. His finely developed aesthetic sense and sensitivity to human emotion and suffering predisposed him toward the goals and concerns of his friend. More can be learned about Koussevitzky from Arthur Laurie's, *Sergei Koussevitzky and His Epoch* (Freeport, N.Y.: Books for Libraries Press, 1969) and Moses Smith's *Koussevitzky* (New York: Allen, Towne and Heath, 1947).

Igor Ivan Sikorsky was equally distinguished as a pioneer in aircraft design and for the successful development of the modern helicopter. Sikorsky's designs include the first four-engine airplane, the S-40 and S-41 American Clipper for Pan American World Airways, and the record-making VS-300 helicopter. Sikorsky was founder of Sikorsky Aircraft, which became a division of United Aircraft Corporation. He was also an accomplished pilot (holding International Pilot's License number 64) who during his entire career insisted on piloting the first trial flights of all his new designs.

Less well known are Sikorsky's deep religious commitments and his altruistic concern for others. A glimpse into this aspect of the aviator is seen in his books *The Mysterious Encounter* and *The Message of the Lord's Prayer.* As a public lecturer he frequently spoke on topics ranging from "Engineering Education" to the "Evolution of the Soul." He was deeply attracted to Sorokin's works beginning with *The Crisis of Our Age.* The two men became good friends, and exchanged frequent letters and occasional visits. More can be learned of Sikorsky from his autobiographical *Story of the Winged S.* Information for the preceding pastiche was taken from Stanly Sadie, ed., "Koussevitzky, Sergey Alexandrovich," *The New Grove Dictionary of Music and Musicians* (Chicago: University of Chicago Press, 1988), 10:801–802. See also I. I. Sikorsky correspondence with Pitirim A. Sorokin 1943–52, USSA, Dr. Igor I. Sikorsky file.

42. Letter from Pitirim A. Sorokin to Eli Lilly, 1 May 1946, LFA.

43. Letter from Pitirim A. Sorokin to Eli Lilly, 14 June 1946, LFA.

44. Letter from Eli Lilly to Pitirim A. Sorokin, 17 June 1946, LFA.

45. Pitirim A. Sorokin, *The Reconstruction of Humanity* (Boston: Beacon Press, 1948), 7–54.

46. Ibid., 57–60.

47. Ibid., 61–62.

48. Ibid., 64–65.

49. Pitirim A. Sorokin, *The Ways and Power of Love* (Boston: Beacon Press, 1954), 141.

50. Sorokin, *Reconstruction*, 62–64.

51. Ibid., 231–236.

52. Ibid., 101–126.

53. Ibid., 144–149.

54. Ibid., 153.

55. Ibid., 149–154.

56. Ibid., 154–158. Quote is on 158.

57. Ibid., 158.

58. Ibid., 165–178.

59. Ibid.

60. Ibid., 231–236.

61. Eli Lilly, "The Nemesis of Materialism," *Super Vision* 1 (October 1946), cited in Madison, *Lilly,* 305. This essay, according to Madison (305), was probably written for a speech. Lilly also summarized some of Sorokin's writings in his "President's Column," *Super Vision* 1 (October 1946): 1.

62. Lilly, "Nemesis," quoted in Madison, *Lilly,* 149.

63. Sorokin, *Long Journey,* 278, puts the meeting in April 1948. Madison, *Lilly,* 195, sets this meeting in late 1949. A meeting did take place in late August 1949 but was between J. K. Lilly III, his father, and others with Pitirim and Elena. The setting was West Falmouth, for lunch on August 27. Eli Lilly was not there. See the correspondence between Pitirim Sorokin and J. K. Lilly III dated 8 June 1949 to 8 September 1949, USSA, Sorokin Papers, Lilly Endowment file, and letter from Eli

Lilly to Pitirim Sorokin 16 September 1949, LFA. These documents show who attended the lunch and that Madison has the wrong date.

64. Letter from Eli Lilly to Pitirim A. Sorokin, 10 December 1948, LFA.

65. Letter from Pitirim A. Sorokin to Eli Lilly, 14 December 1948, LFA.

66. Eli Lilly, Note to Advisors for the endowment, 15 December 1948, LFA.

67. Letter from Eli Lilly to Pitirim A. Sorokin, 28 December 1948, LFA.

68. Ibid.

69. Letter from Pitirim A. Sorokin to Eli Lilly, 31 December 1948, LFA.

70. Madison, *Lilly*, 190–191.

71. Quoted in Madison, *Lilly*, 204.

72. Madison, *Lilly*, 308. Here Madison repeats part of an interview with J. K. Lilly III conducted on 4 September 1986.

73. Letter from Eli Lilly to Pitirim A. Sorokin, 5 January 1949; letter from Eli Lilly to Paul Buck, 17 January 1949; letter from Pitirim A. Sorokin to Eli Lilly, 5 February 1949. All are found in LFA.

74. The Center was actually established as the Harvard Research Center in Altruistic Integration and Creativity. However, Sorokin refers to it as the Harvard Research Center in Creative Altruism in *Long Journey*. Given that most of the Center's publications and correspondence used the latter title, it is the one used here.

75. Pitirim A. Sorokin, *Altruistic Love: A Study of American Good Neighbors and Christian Saints* (Boston: Beacon Press, 1950), 17.

76. The study of these saints makes up the bulk of the analysis. Additionally, Sorokin examined 415 cases of Russian Orthodox saints. The results of the inquiry conform with the findings for Roman saints and are discussed in *Altruistic*, 240–247.

77. Ibid., 138–150. For an excellent discussion of the history of canonization see Kenneth L. Woodward, *Making Saints: How the Catholic Church Determines Who Becomes a Saint, Who Doesn't, and Why* (New York: Simon and Schuster, 1990). Woodward discusses processes similar to Sorokin's "roads" on pp. 50–127.

78. Sorokin, *Altruistic*, 180.

79. For additional details see Woodward, *Saints*, 15–19, 87–121.

80. Pitirim A. Sorokin, *Explorations in Altruistic Love and Behavior: Symposium* (Boston: Beacon Press, 1950), 3–24.

81. However, he does conceptualize each as a continuum going from 0 to 100. The extraordinary/perfect altruist would have a score of 500 and the pure beast zero. In practice the scales are really more nominal than refined measuring instruments capable of exact scoring.

82. Sorokin, *Explorations*, 59.

83. Ibid., 71.

84. E. K. Francis, "Review of *The Reconstruction of Humanity*," *American Journal of Sociology* 54 (November 1948): 271.

85. Harry Elmer Barnes "Review of *The Reconstruction of Humanity* and Arnold J. Toynbee *Civilization on Trial*," *American Sociological Review* 13 (August 1948): 492–494.

86. Robert Rockafellow, "Review of *The Reconstruction of Humanity*," *Annals of the American Academy of Political and Social Science* 260 (September 1948): 165–166.

87. Harry E. Moore "Review of *The Reconstruction of Humanity*," *Social Forces* 27 (October 1948) 92–94.

88. William L. Kolb, "Review of *Social Philosophies of an Age of Crisis*," *American Sociological Review* 16 (April 1951): 267–268; quote on 267.

89. Ibid., 267.

90. Ibid., 268.

91. Ibid.

92. Pitirim A. Sorokin, *S.O.S.: The Meaning of Our Crisis* (Boston: Beacon Press, 1951), x.

93. Ibid., 16–82.

94. Ibid., 43–46.

95. Ibid., 49.

96. Letter from Pitirim A. Sorokin to Eli Lilly, 19 December 1953, LFA.

97. Pitirim A. Sorokin, "Amitology as an Applied Science of Amity and Unselfish Love," in *Soziologische Forschung In Unserer Zeit*, ed. Karl G. Specht (Cologne: West Deutscher Verlag, 1951), 277–279.

98. Pitirim A. Sorokin, "Harvard Research Center in Creative Altruism," privately duplicated, n.d.

99. Letter from Pitirim A. Sorokin to Charles Dollard, 3 November 1950. USSA, "D" general file. In this letter Sorokin explicitly mentions the enclosed brochure on the Harvard Research Center in Creative Altruism, so it was likely first done in 1950. That is also the year in which the released publications stop and he begins to discuss future works of the Center. Similar brochures were prepared for some years. The last one was Pitirim A. Sorokin, "Studies of the Harvard Research Center in Creative Altruism" 3d ed. (Cambridge, Mass.: Harvard University Press, 1959).

100. Letter from Charles Dollard to Pitirim A. Sorokin, 10 November 1950. USSA, "D" general file.

101. Pitirim A. Sorokin, ed., *Forms and Techniques of Altruistic and Spiritual Growth: A Symposium* (Boston: Beacon Press, 1954), v.

102. Roger Godel, "The Contemporary Sciences and the Liberative Experience of Yoga," in *Forms and Techniques of Altruistic and Spiritual Growth*, ed. Pitirim A. Sorokin (Boston: Beacon Press, 1954), 3–12.

103. Godel, "Yoga," 11.

104. Ibid., 12.

105. Anthony Bloom, "Yoga and Christian Spiritual Techniques: Somatopsychic Techniques in Orthodox Christianity," in *Forms and Techniques of Altruistic and Spiritual Growth*, ed. Pitirim A. Sorokin (Boston: Beacon Press, 1954), 93–108.

106. Ibid., 95.

107. Ibid., 96.

108. Ibid., 106.

109. Pierre Marinier, "Reflections on Prayer: Its Causes and Psychophysiological Effects," in *Forms and Techniques of Altruistic and Spiritual Growth*, ed. Pitirim A. Sorokin (Boston: Beacon Press, 1954), 145–164.

110. Sorokin, *Forms*, 1.

111. Cornelius Krahn, J. Wenfield Fretz, and Robert Kreider, "Altruism in Mennonite Life," in *Forms and Techniques of Altruistic and Spiritual Growth*, ed. Pitirim A. Sorokin (Boston: Beacon Press, 1954), 309–328.

112. Ibid., 325.

113. Eberhard C. H. Arnold, "Education for Altruism in the Society of Brothers in Paraguay," in *Forms and Techniques of Altruistic and Spiritual Growth*, ed. Pitirim A. Sorokin (Boston: Beacon Press, 1954), 293–307.

114. Gordon Allport, "Techniques for Reducing Group Prejudice," in *Forms and Techniques of Altruistic and Spiritual Growth*, ed. Pitirim A. Sorokin (Boston: Beacon Press, 1954), 367–385.

115. But how much change can we realistically expect in prejudice due to these efforts? Sadly, in Allport's estimation, not too much. Prejudice is institutionalized in American society, and "A mounting array of evidence tells us that . . . habits of categorizing, projecting and scapegoating, may be too ingrained to be disturbed. To change the attitudes would require a recentering of the whole personality" (ibid., 368).

116. Ibid., 373.

117. Ibid., 377–379.

118. Ibid., 381.

119. Ibid., 385.

120. J. Mark Thompson, "Experimentation with the Technique of Good Deeds in Transformation of Inimical into Amicable Relationships," in *Forms and Techniques of Altruistic and Spiritual Growth*, ed. Pitirim A. Sorokin (Boston: Beacon Press, 1954), 401–417.

121. Robert W. Hyde and Harriet M. Kandler, "Altruism in Psychiatric Nursing," in *Forms and Techniques of Altruistic and Spiritual Growth*, ed. Pitirim A. Sorokin (Boston: Beacon Press, 1954), 387–399.

122. The international level of involvement is suggested not only by the reach of certain groups' altruism but by the global organization of major religions that institutionalize altruism in their liturgies, codes of conduct, and prescriptions for responsible social action. Problems related to the quest for a corpus of international law are also explored by F. S. C. Northrop in his essay "Philosophical Anthropology and World Law," in *Forms and Techniques of Altruistic and Spiritual Growth*, ed. Pitirim A. Sorokin (Boston: Beacon Press, 1954), 357–363.

123. Pitirim A. Sorokin and Walter A. Lunden, *Power and Morality: Who Shall Guard the Guardians?* (Boston: Porter Sargent, 1959).

124. Ibid., 34.

125. Ibid., 104.

126. Ibid., 160.

127. Ibid., 164. Perhaps even new rules specifying scientific qualifications for public office and restricting voting to the scientifically competent may emerge.

128. Ibid., 165–169.

129. Ibid., 169.

130. Ibid., 174.

131. Ibid., 175.

132. Ibid., 175–180.

133. Ibid., 184–193.

134. Luke Ebersole, "Review of *S.O.S.: The Meaning of Our Crisis*," *Crozier Quarterly* 29 (April 1952), 231.

135. Rudolf Allers, "Review of *S.O.S.: The Meaning of Our Crisis*," *Commonwealth*, 21 December 1951, 282–283. What Sorokin foresaw earlier likely refers to comments in volume 4 of *Dynamics* and *Crisis of Our Age*.

136. Theodore Abel, "Review of *S.O.S.: The Meaning of Our Crisis*," *Annals of the American Academy of Political and Social Science* 281 (May 1952): 220.

137. Ibid., 221.

138. Richard L. Simpson, "Review of *The Ways and Power of Love* and *Forms and Techniques of Altruistic and Spiritual Growth*," *Social Forces* 33 (March 1955): 296–297; quote on p. 297. Another review of *Forms* was written by Joseph Bram, "Review of *Forms and Techniques of Altruistic and Spiritual Growth*," *Library Journal*, 15 June 1954, 1227.

139. Simpson, "Review of *The Ways and Power of Love*," 297.

140. Arnold W. Green, "Review of *The Ways and Power of Love*," *American Journal of Sociology* 60 (May 1955): 600.

141. Oliver R. Reiser, "Review of *The Ways and Power of Love*," *Annals of the American Academy of Political and Social Science* 297 (January 1955): 153–154.

142. Pitirim A. Sorokin, *Fads and Foibles in Modern Sociology and Related Sciences* (Chicago: Henry Regnery, 1956), v.

143. Ibid., 18. Here Sorokin is referring to Parsons's *Social System* (Glencoe, Ill.: Free Press, 1951) and Parsons and Shils's *Toward a General Theory of Action*, (Cambridge, Mass.: Harvard University Press, 1951).

144. Ellsworth Faris, "Review of *The Social System*," *American Sociological Review* 18 (February 1953): 106.

145. The following account is taken from Barry V. Johnston, "Persistent Dilemmas in Sociological Theory," *Free Inquiry in Creative Sociology* 14 (May 1986): 17–20.

146. Ibid.

147. Gary Zukav, *The Dancing Wu Li Masters: An Overview of the New Physics* (New York, Bantam, 1979), 94.

148. See Edmund Husserl, *Ideas: General Introduction to Pure Phenomenology* (New York: Humanities Press, 1931), and also his *Cartesian Meditations* (The Hague: Martinus Nijhoff, 1965).

149. Ronald M. Clark, *Einstein: The Life and Times* (New York: Avon Press, 1972), 413.

150. Gary Zukav, *The Dancing Wu Li Masters: An Overview of the New Physics* (New York: Bantam, 1979); Aaron D. Leener, *Einstein and Newton* (Minneapolis, Minn.: Lerner Publications, 1973).

151. Zukav, *Dancing Wu Li Masters*, 112.

152. Werner Heisenberg, *Physics and Beyond: Encounters and Conversations* (New York: Harper and Row, 1972), 27.

153. Robert K. Merton, *Social Theory and Social Structure*, revised and enlarged ed. (Glencoe, Ill.: Free Press, 1957), 6.

154. Sorokin, *Fads*, 287.

155. Ibid.

156. Ibid., 317.

157. Gresham Sykes, "Review of *Fads and Foibles in Modern Sociology and Related Sciences*," *American Sociological Review* 21 (October 1956): 633–634; quote is on p. 633.

158. Jean Floud, "Review of *Fads and Foibles in Modern Sociology and Related Sciences*," *British Journal of Educational Studies* 1 (November 1957): 85.

159. Ibid.

160. Richard McLaughlin, "Review of *Fads and Foibles of Modern Sociology and Related Sciences*," *Times Literary Supplement*, 2 November 1956, 651. See also John Pfeiffer, "A Manner of Speaking: Review of *Fads and Foibles of Modern Sociology and Related Sciences*," *New York Times*, 21 November 1956, 36.

161. Donald Horton, "Review of *Fads and Foibles of Modern Sociology and Related Sciences*," *American Journal of Sociology* 62 (November 1956): 338.

162. Ibid.

163. Ibid.

164. Pitirim A. Sorokin, "Letter to the Editor: *Fads and Foibles in Modern Sociology*," *American Journal of Sociology* 62 (March 1957): 515.

165. Letter from Pitirim A. Sorokin to Eli Lilly, 22 September 1955, LFA.

166. Letter from Eli Lilly to Pitirim A. Sorokin, 29 September, 1955, LFA.

167. Madison, *Lilly*, 207–208; quote is on p. 208.

168. Memo from G. Harold Duling to Mr. J. K. Lilly, Mr. Eli Lilly, and Mr. J. K. Lilly III, 28 February 1951, LFA.

169. Memo from J. K. Lilly Jr. to E. Beck, 6 March 1951, LFA.

170. Memo to Mr. J. K. Lilly Jr. from E. Beck, 20 March 1951, LFA. Among the organizations listed were the American Peace Crusade, the Civil Rights Congress, and the American Committee for Protection of Foreign Born.

171. Memo from J. K. Lilly Jr. to Eli Lilly, 29 March 1951, LFA.

172. Letter from Eli Lilly to G. Harold Duling, 29 December 1951, LFA.

173. Madison, *Lilly*, 196. It is very likely that Lilly had read many of Sorokin's earlier works along with those associated with the Center. In several of these, Sorokin's condemning opinions of Communism and Communists are clear.

174. Manning M. Pattillo, "Office Memo Re: Boston trip," 13–16 September 1956, LFA. This event is also reported in Madison, *Lilly*, 196.

175. Letter from G. Harold Duling to Nathan M. Pusey, 12 October 1955, LFA.

176. Letter from Nathan M. Pusey, to G. Harold Duling, 20 October, 1955, LFA.

177. Letter from Pitirim A. Sorokin to G. Harold Duling, 3 November 1955, LFA; letter from Pitirim A. Sorokin to Eli Lilly, 18 December 1955, LFA.

178. Pitirim A. Sorokin, *The American Sex Revolution* (Boston: Porter Sargent, 1957).

179. Ibid., 41–42.

180. Ibid., 57–76.

181. Ibid., 57.

182. Pitirim A. Sorokin, "Tentative Plan of Long and Short Range Research of the Research Society of Creative Altruism," 1 March 1956, LFA.

183. Letter from Manning M. Pattillo to Pitirim A. Sorokin, 22 February 1957, LFA.

184. Letter from Manning M. Pattillo to Pitirim A. Sorokin, 21 November 1957, LFA.

185. Letter from Pitirim A. Sorokin to Eli Lilly, 18 October 1957, LFA reports on conference attendance. The book was Abraham Maslow, ed., *New Knowledge in Human Values* (New York: Harper and Brothers, 1959). Sorokin wrote the "Forword for the Society," which gave a brief statement of its history and goals.

FROM OUTCAST TO ELDER STATESMAN

1. Sorokin, *Long Journey,* 294.

2. Ibid., 251. Sorokin may be suggesting that there were changes beginning in 1942 of which he disapproved, but the Department of Social Relations was not established until 1946. Furthermore, Sorokin's chairmanship of the sociology department officially ended on 30 June 1944.

3. Letter from Pitirim A. Sorokin to Roy E. Larsen, 4 May 1954, USSA, "Ti–Ty" general file.

4. Letter from Pitirim A. Sorokin to Roy E. Larsen, 5 May 1954, 1, USSA, "Ti–Ty" general file.

5. Ibid., 3.

6. Ibid., 3–4.

7. Talcott Parsons and Edward Shils, eds., *Toward a General Theory of Action,* vii–viii.

8. Ibid., 3–4.

9. Homans, *Coming to My Senses,* 302–303.

10. Schmidt, "Towards a History of the Department of Social Relations," 61.

11. Three appointments of established scholars with strong interdisciplinary reputations in the late 1950s were not enough to turn the tide. The arrival of David Reisman, Erik Erikson, and Lawrence Wylie was a step in the right direction. However, it was not enough to overcome faculty frustration with the program and its inability to deliver an advance in theoretical integration.

12. Schmidt, *History,* 61.

13. Sorokin, *Fads,* 343 n. 40.

14. Pitirim A. Sorokin, "Similarities and Dissimilarities Between Two Sociological Systems" (notes on Parsons and Shils, *Toward a General Theory of Action;* and T. Parsons, *The Social System,* unpublished memorandum, 1.

15. Ibid., 9–10.

16. Ibid., 10.

17. Robert E. L. Faris, "Recollections of a Half Century of Life in the ASA," *American Sociologist* 16 (1981): 51–52.

18. See *Fads*, 13–15, and *Sociological Theories of Today* (New York, Harper and Row, 1966), 420–431.

19. It is interesting that Parsons sent Sorokin a note in November 1951 expressing his personal delight over the similarities in their theories. Sorokin refers to this note in a letter to Rollin Chambliss, 29 November 1951, USSA, Rollin Chambliss file. I have read the note referred to in the Chambliss letter. It is brief, polite, and without any trace of anger. Unfortunately, I cannot locate my copy to cite for attribution.

20. Sorokin, *Long Journey*, 295.

21. Letter from Rollin Chambliss to Pitirim A. Sorokin, 9 November 1960, USSA, Rollin Chambliss file.

22. Letter from Pitirim A. Sorokin to Rollin Chambliss, 7 November 1960, USSA, Rollin Chambliss file.

23. Letter from Pitirim A. Sorokin to Harry Alpert, 7 November 1960, USSA, *American Sociological Review* file.

24. Sorokin, *Long Journey*, 304.

25. Charles Page, *Fifty Years in the Sociological Enterprise: A Lucky Journey* (Amherst: University of Massachusetts Press, 1982), 21.

26. Ibid., 20.

27. More on Alpert can be found in Richard J. Hill and Walter T. Morton, "In Memoriam Harry Alpert 1912–1977," *Public Opinion Quarterly* 42 (spring 1978): 141–142.

28. Letter from Eli Lilly to Pitirim A. Sorokin, 17 January 1962, LFA.

29. Letter from Robert K. Merton to Pitirim A. Sorokin, 11 January 1962, USSA, Robert K. Merton file. Merton may mean thirty-five years ago, which would put the time closer to 1928 or 1929.

30. Letter from Philip J. Allen to Pitirim A. Sorokin, 28 November 1958, USSA, Philip J. Allen file.

31. Letter from Philip J. Allen to Pitirim A. Sorokin, 22 December 1959, USSA, Philip J. Allen file.

32. Pitirim A. Sorokin, "Sociology of My Mental Life," in *Pitirim A. Sorokin in Review*, ed. Philip J. Allen (Durham N.C.: Duke University Press, 1963), 3–36; quote on p. 4.

33. Ibid., 31–34.

34. Ibid., 35.

35. Anonymous, "Review of *Pitirim A. Sorokin in Review* manuscript," No date, USSA, Philip J. Allen file.

36. Arnold J. Toynbee, "Sorokin's Philosophy of History," in *Pitirim A. Sorokin in Review*, ed. Philip J. Allen (Durham, N.C.: Duke University Press, 1963), 70–71.

37. Sorokin, *Dynamics*, 11:21–22; quoted in Toynbee, "Sorokin's Philosophy of History," 71.

38. Toynbee, "Sorokin's Philosophy of History," 86–87.

39. Ibid., 68–69.

40. Pitirim A. Sorokin, "Reply to My Critics," in *Pitirim A. Sorokin in Review*, ed. Philip J. Allen (Durham, N.C.: Duke University Press, 1963), 414–426.

41. Nicholas S. Timasheff, "Sorokin on Law, Revolution, War, and Social Calamities," in *Pitirim A. Sorokin in Review*, ed. Philip J. Allen (Durham, N.C.: Duke University Press, 1963), 247–275; see p. 259.

42. Alexandre Vexliard, "Sorokin's Psychological Theories," in *Pitirim A. Sorokin in Review*, ed. Philip J. Allen (Durham, N.C.: Duke University Press, 1963), 160–187.

43. Ibid., 168–173.

44. Ibid., 174.

45. Joseph Ford, "Sorokin as Philosopher," in *Pitirim A. Sorokin in Review*, ed. Philip J. Allen (Durham, N.C.: Duke University Press, 1963), 39–66.

46. Sorokin, "Reply to My Critics," in 371–382.

47. Ford, "Philosopher," 52.

48. Ibid., 53.

49. Robert K. Merton and Bernard Barber, "Sorokin's Formulations in the Sociology of Science," in *Pitirim A. Sorokin in Review*, ed. Philip J. Allen (Durham, N.C.: Duke University Press, 1963), 332–368. Originally Merton was to write on Sorokin's sociology of knowledge and Barber on his sociology of science. Barber had assured Allen that there would be no overlap with the Merton essay. Somewhere in the process, a decision was made to collaborate on this article. Letter from Philip J. Allen to Pitirim A. Sorokin, 22 December 1959, USSA, Philip J. Allen file.

50. Park, "Review of *Dynamics*," and quoted by Merton and Barber, "Sorokin's Formulations," 352.

51. Merton and Barber, "Sorokin's Formulations," 353.

52. Ibid.

53. Quoted in Merton and Barber, "Sorokin's Formulations," 355.

54. Ibid., 356–357.

55. Ibid., 357.

56. Ibid., 366–368.

57. Matilda White Riley and Mary E. Moore, "Sorokin's Use of Sociological Measurement," in *Pitirim A. Sorokin in Review*, ed. Philip J. Allen (Durham, N.C.: Duke University Press, 1963), 206–224.

58. Sorokin, "Reply to My Critics," 446.

59. See ibid., 449–454, 495–496.

60. Edward A. Tiryakian, ed., *Sociological Theory, Values, and Sociocultural Change: Essays in Honor of Pitirim A. Sorokin* (New York: Free Press of Glencoe, 1963).

61. Talcott Parsons, "Christianity and the Modern Industrial Society," in *Sociological Theory, Values, and Sociocultural Change: Essays in Honor of Pitirim A. Sorokin*, ed. Edward A. Tiryakian (New York: Free Press of Glencoe, 1963), 33–70.

62. Wilbert E. Moore, "Review of *A Long Journey: The Autobiography of Pitirim A. Sorokin*," *American Journal of Sociology* 70 (November 1964): 387.

63. For a more personable and private glimpse into Sorokin see Elena Sorokin, "My Life with Pitirim Sorokin," *International Journal of Contemporary Sociology* 42 (January–April 1975): 1–27.

64. Edward A. Tiryakian, "Review of *A Long Journey: The Autobiography of Pitirim A. Sorokin,*" *American Sociological Review* 29 (August 1964): 604.

65. Letter from O. D. Duncan to G. S. Basran, 15 December 1977, USSA, G. S. Basran file. O. D. Duncan, telephone interview with Barry V. Johnston, 8 October 1985. The Basran file contains the records of the committee to nominate Sorokin. It was donated by Duncan to the archive, and Professor Basran arranged for the cataloging and inclusion in the Sorokin collection. The records remain listed under his name. The account of this then-unique write-in campaign is excerpted from Barry V. Johnston, "Pitirim Sorokin and the American Sociological Association: The Politics of a Professional Society," *Journal of the History of the Behavioral Sciences* 23 (April 1987): 103–122.

The fact that Sorokin was not renominated is more surprising when one considers the narrow outcome of the 1952 election. As Duncan observed in a 13 March 1963 letter to Talcott Parsons, USSA, G. S. Basran file:

> Sorokin was nominated only once, some ten years ago. If one studies the pattern of nominations after the mail voting procedure was introduced, it is apparent that nominating committees ordinarily have given strong consideration to the advisability of giving the defeated man a second chance. Some of our most eminent presidents have been elected as a consequence. Yet Sorokin was never mentioned again. What is not on the records may also be significant. I have been given to understand that the race between Sorokin and Znaniecki was exceedingly close, so close in fact that the final outcome had to be decided by an arbitrary device. If that information is correct, then it is all the more inexplicable why Sorokin was not subsequently nominated.

Duncan's reference to an "arbitrary device" refers to a then-established practice of the Committee on Nominations and Elections that reads, "In case of a tie for an office, the Chairman decides by lot, in a presence of tellers, between tied candidates." This is a bylaw requirement in the ASA's "Notes on Procedures for the Committee on Nominations and Elections," October 1962, p. 4.

A similar account is found in a 17 April 1963 letter from Joseph B. Ford to Otis Dudley Duncan, USSA, G. S. Basran file. Ford observed, "It has been reported that Sorokin was defeated before by a very narrow margin (one story was that it was only one vote, and that a questionable one)."

It is clear that there was a tendency to renominate unsuccessful candidates who made a decent show. For example, Wilbert Moore was renominated in 1964 and Arnold Rose in 1967.

66. Letter from O. D. Duncan to G. S. Basran, 15 December 1977, USSA, G. S. Basran file.

67. Letter from Robert K. Merton to Otis Dudley Duncan, 25 January 1963, USSA, G. S. Basran file.

68. O. D. Duncan, letter to Herbert Blumer, 4 February 1963, USSA, G. S. Basran file.

69. Herbert Blumer, letter to O. D. Duncan, 6 February 1963, USSA, G. S. Basran file.

70. O. D. Duncan, letter to the Committee of Eight, 4 February 1963, USSA, G. S. Basran file.

71. Anderson wrote 25, T. Lynn Smith 48, O. D. Duncan 25, Robert Merton 30, Herbert Blumer 25, Walter Firey 26, William Sewell 48, and Charles Loomis, with the help of Edgar Schuler, C. Hoffer, and Lee Haak, contacted over 450. Records of the Committee of Eight, January to April 1963, USSA, G. S. Basran file.

72. Ibid. Other participants in the second wave were Thomas Coffee, Werner Cahman, Melville Dalton, Richard Du Wors, Dean Eplay, Mike Hakeem, John Kelly, Richard Laskin, Surindor Mehta, Charles Perrow, William Reeder, Julian Samora, Louis Schneider, Harold Smith, Rupert Vance, M. C. Van Arsdol Jr. This list likely underestimates the number of appeals. Some Committee of Correspondence members did not return lists to Duncan. Others, for example, Timasheff, did large-scale organizing. Timasheff was instrumental in seeing that all members of the American Catholic Sociological Society were reached. Letter from Nicholas S. Timasheff to O. D. Duncan, 7 March 1963, USSA, G. S. Basran file. William V. D'Antonio and Julian Samora were also active in turning out the Catholic vote.

73. Johnston, "Pitirim Sorokin and the American Sociological Association," 112.

74. Anonymous, "Member List, 1963 ASA Committee on Nominations and Elections" (no date), Alice's Files, "1963–1965 Nominations." These are the files of Alice F. Myers, Administration Officer of the American Sociological Association from 1966 to 1979; they contain not only records from her tenure but those from earlier periods as well. American Sociological Association Collection, Library of Congress (hereafter referred to as LC), Washington, D.C.

75. Anonymous, "1963 Nominations and Elections: Ballot Instructions and *Notes on Procedures for the Committee on Nominations and Elections*," October 1962, Alice's Files, American Sociological Association Collection, LC.

76. Roy G. Francis, "Third Ballot," 11 December 1962, Alice's Files, "Nominations and Elections: Ballots: President-Elect" folder, American Sociological Association Collection, LC. It should be noted that the *Notes on Procedures for the Committee on Nominations and Elections*, October 1962, clearly state: "The President-Elect must serve as administrative head of the Society for the period of his tenure; thus the office is in no sense purely honorific" (1). This statement is, of course, at odds with Professor Francis's assessment. *Procedures* also require that all three ballots for the office of president-elect be carried out (2).

77. Talcott Parsons served as ASA secretary from 1961 to 1965. Given the antipathy between Sorokin and Parsons, it is ironic that they were again thrown together so soon after Sorokin retired from Harvard.

78. Otis Dudley Duncan, letter to Wilbert E. Moore, 28 January 1963, USSA, G. S. Basran file.

79. Wilbert E. Moore, letter to Otis Dudley Duncan, 31 January 1963, USSA, G. S. Basran file.

80. Otis Dudley Duncan, letter to Arnold M. Rose, 4 February 1963, USSA, G. S. Basran file.

81. Arnold M. Rose, letter to Otis Dudley Duncan, 9 February 1963, USSA, G. S. Basran file.

82. Ibid.

83. Otis Dudley Duncan, letter to Arnold M. Rose, 11 February 1963, USSA, G. S. Basran file.

84. Wilbert E. Moore, letter to Harold Wilensky, 2 April 1963, USSA, G. S. Basran file.

85. Janice H. Hooper, letter to Pitirim A. Sorokin, 3 April 1963, American Sociological Association Collection, LC.

86. Otis Dudley Duncan, letter to Nicholas S. Timasheff, 11 March 1963, USSA, G. S. Basran file.

87. At the time of this election it was not the policy of the association to report vote totals or to indicate the magnitude of a victory. Given that Arnold M. Rose died on 3 January 1968 (he was then president-elect of the association), I decided to phone Wilbert E. Moore and see how he felt about the results being reported. I explained that because the write-in campaign was a move to honor Sorokin it was important that readers know the magnitude of membership's response. Professor Moore's reply on hearing the tallies was that, for his part, they should indeed be published. He seemed pleased by the response of his fellow sociologists. Wilbert E. Moore, telephone conversation with Barry V. Johnston, 25 February 1986.

88. Letter from George C. Homans to Pitirim A. Sorokin, 12 June 1963, LC.

89. Letter from Pitirim A. Sorokin to George C. Homans, 15 June 1963, LC.

90. Homans, *Coming to My Senses*, 130–131. Homans incorrectly recounts that he was to succeed Sorokin as president (131). Homans was president in 1964 and Sorokin's predecessor. On a more personal note Homans states:

> I became fond of Sorokin and even more of his wife, a distinguished chemist in her own right and, on the side, a talented seamstress. Sorokin once fingered the lapel of a sturdy and stylish coat he was wearing and exclaimed, "See! Made by wife!" The Sorokins gave splendid parties, besides raising a garden full of prize-winning azaleas, at their house in Winchester. . . . Though Sorokin was a charming man socially, he could become less so when one fell under his authority. . . . I attribute his behavior in part to what cultural anthropologists would call his Russian authoritarianism. (130)

91. Letter from Pitirim A. Sorokin to Otis Dudley Duncan, 8 January 1965, USSA, G. S. Basran file.

92. A major restructuring of the procedure for nominating candidates occurred after the Sorokin episode. The old 10 percent rule was changed. The new rule requires only the signatures of a hundred members to nominate a candidate for the

offices of president-elect, vice president–elect, and secretary-elect. Outside nominees for the council become candidates with the signatures of fifty members. These changes have resulted in more outside nominees running and in more being elected to office. For example, James F. Short (president, 1984) Peter H. Rossi (president, 1980), and Alfred McClung Lee (president, 1976) all won office as a result of write-in votes. The presidential race in 1986 had four write-in candidates: Amitai Etzioni, Albert J. Reiss Jr., Edgar F. Borgatta, and Neil J. Smelser. They ran against the candidates selected by the Committee of Nominations and Elections, Herbert J. Gans and Immanuel Wallerstein.

Today the nomination and election procedures are much more open. The nominations committee is no longer appointed by the president and is instead an elected body. The committee is chaired by the vice president, and members are elected by district in order to foster a geographical balance. New voting procedures maximize the expressed will of the electorate and remove any chance that close or tied elections will be decided by arbitrary device. As can be expected in an association with 11,481 members (as of November 1985), some fragmentation has resulted from the new rules. However, the presidency was in 1963 and is today the highest recognition that sociologists can bestow upon a colleague. Whether it is given out of purely honorific motives, because of a candidate's administrative skill, or as an acknowledgment of valued scholarship, the decision now rests more fully in the hands of the membership.

93. Pitirim A. Sorokin, "Sociology of Yesterday, Today and Tomorrow," *American Sociological Review* 30 (December 1965): 833–843.

94. Ibid., 835.

95. Ibid., 834.

96. Ibid., 837. Sorokin rightly observes:

If sociology, or any science, cannot pass from one of these states into the other, it is bound to become stagnant and increasingly sterile because a mere increase of the known specks of the total sociocultural reality cannot give us an adequate knowledge of the whole. On the other hand, without increasing knowledge of these specks and their empirical realities, few if any fruitful syntheses, broad generalizations, and valid uniformities can be formulated: without new and relevant empirical material, the synthesizing and generalizing theories are bound to turn increasingly into empty abstractions, ascetically detached from empirical realities and adding little to our understanding of their what, how, and why. (837)

97. Pitirim A. Sorokin, *Sociological Theories of Today* (New York: Harper and Row, 1966), x.

98. Sorokin, *Contemporary Sociological Theories*, xvi.

99. Sorokin, *Sociological Theories of Today*, 42.

100. Ibid., 37–129, and Sorokin, *Fads*, 21–248. The language of *Fads* is sharper for the most part than that used in *Today*, but the criticisms are nearly identical.

101. Sorokin, *Today*, 45.

102. Ibid., 128.

103. Ibid., 129.

104. Ibid.

105. Ibid., 400–401.

106. Ibid., 411.

107. Ibid., 418–419.

108. Ibid., 419.

109. Ibid., 420–431.

110. Ibid., 447–456.

111. Ibid., 455.

112. Ibid., 528.

113. Sorokin, *Society, Culture, and Personality*, 159–180.

114. Sorokin, *Today*, 585.

115. According to Roscoe Hinkle, "Review of *Sociological Theories of Today*," *American Journal of Sociology* 72 (January 1967): 413–414, Parsons gets thirty-six pages, compared with thirty for Gurvitch. However, twelve of those given to Parsons are filled by the "Similarities" memo and are hardly an exploration of his ideas.

116. Sorokin, *Today*, 485–487.

117. Ibid., 495–496.

118. Ibid., 499.

119. Ibid., 524–525.

120. Ibid., 596.

121. See p. 596–597 for a list of studies that Sorokin considers the most significant.

122. Ibid., 598.

123. Ibid., 625–633.

124. Ibid., 177.

125. This book was republished in 1963 as *Modern Historical and Social Philosophies* (New York: Dover, 1963). It is under this title that Sorokin refers to it in *Sociological Theories of Today*. There were no reviews of the newly titled volume found and portions of Sorokin's descriptions and analysis in *Sociological Theories of Today* appear in *Philosophies*.

126. This body of work is also discussed in *Social Philosophies of an Age of Crisis*, 10–48.

127. Sorokin, *Today*, 378–382.

128. Ibid., 382–383.

129. Ibid., 635–646.

130. Ibid., 647–648.

131. Ibid., 649.

132. Ibid.

133. Sorokin, "Sociology of Yesterday, Today and Tomorrow," 843.

134. Don Martindale, "Review of *Sociological Theories of Today*," *Annals of the American Academy of Political and Social Science* 370 (March 1967): 176–177.

135. Ibid., 176.

136. Werner Stark, "In Search of Tradition," *Trans-Action* 4 (March 1967): 54–55.

137. Ibid., 55.

138. Ibid.

139. Roscoe Hinkle, "Review of *Sociological Theories of Today*," *American Journal of Sociology* 74 (January 1967): 414.

140. Letter from Ruth Lilly and Eli Lilly to Pitirim A. Sorokin, 22 August 1967, LFA. They warmly inform Sorokin that they would be delighted to have the honor of establishing the Sorokin Award and Lectureship, and enclose a personal check for ten thousand dollars. Letter from E. H. Volkart to Mr. and Mrs. Eli Lilly, 17 September 1967, LC, informing them that the award had been established and the first recipient would be named at the August 1968 meeting. Since 1968 the Sorokin Award and Lectureship has gone through two name changes. The last original award was given in 1979, and the ASA Award for a Distinguished Contribution to Scholarship, accompanied by a Sorokin Lectureship, was established in 1980. The name was again changed by the ASA council in September 1986 to the Distinguished Scholarly Publication Award. The winner gives a Sorokin Lecture at a selected regional or state sociological association/society meeting.

141. For a discussion of this episode and insights into Sorokin's character see Edward A. Tiryakian, "Sociology's Dostoyevski: Pitirim A. Sorokin," *The World & I* 3 (September 1988): 569–581.

142. Anonymous, handwritten note, concerning the fate of Sorokin, n.d., LFA. When I found this note, it was in a section of records belonging to Eli Lilly (file 5, no. 1); an archivist experienced with these records believed the writing was Eli Lilly's. However, this is not certain.

143. Don Martindale argued that Sorokin may be the most productive and translated sociologist ever. Martindale, "Pitirim A. Sorokin: Soldier of Fortune," 4.

144. Letter from Pitirim A. Sorokin to Mr. and Mrs. Eli Lilly, 26 June 1967, LFA.

145. Letter from Pitirim A. Sorokin to Mr. and Mrs. Eli Lilly, 17 December 1967, LFA.

146. Letter from Pitirim A. Sorokin to My Wonderful Friends (Mr. and Mrs. Eli Lilly), 2 February 1968, LFA.

147. Letter from Robert F. Bales to Talcott Parsons, n.d., HUA, Parsons Papers. This statement was sent to Parsons, who had been asked by Dean Franklin Ford to chair the committee for preparing the Sorokin Commemorative Minute to be read at the 3 December 1968 meeting of the Harvard faculty.

148. See Letters of Sympathy, USSA. This is a large file of personal letters from Sorokin's friends and admirers around the world.

149. Letter from Pitirim A. Sorokin to Otis Dudley Duncan, 21 January 1960, USSA, Otis D. Duncan file.

150. Sorokin, *Long Journey*, 249. The list is on pp. 248–249. Of those noted, there are letters from nineteen of them in various files at USSA and HUA. This is a significant portion of those alive at the time of Sorokin's death.

151. Letter from Conrad Taeuber to Talcott Parsons, 3 May 1968, HUA, Parsons Papers. This was in response to Parsons's letter seeking information for the Sorokin Minute.

152. Letter from Otis Durant Duncan to Mrs. Sorokin and Sons, 12 March 1968, USSA, Letters of Sympathy file.

Bibliography

For the correspondence listed in this bibliography the archives are designated by the following abbreviations:

HUA   Harvard University Archives, Pusey Library, Cambridge, Massachusetts

LC   Library of Congress, American Sociological Association Collection, Washington, D.C.

LFA   Lilly Foundation Archives, Harvard Center for the Study of Creative Altruism and Pitirim A. Sorokin Papers, Indianapolis, Indiana

USSA   University of Saskatchewan–Saskatoon Archives, Sorokin Collection

VCA   Vassar College Archives, MacCracken Papers, Poughkeepsie, New York

Abbott, Wilbur C. "The Working of Revolution." *Saturday Review of Literature*, 11 April 1925, 664.

Abel, Theodore. "Review of *S. O. S.: The Meaning of Our Crisis*." *Annals of the American Academy of Political and Social Sciences* 281 (May 1952): 220–221.

Allen, Philip J. Letter to Pitirim A. Sorokin, 28 November 1958. USSA, Philip J. Allen file.

——. Letter to Pitirim A. Sorokin, 22 December 1959. USSA, Philip J. Allen file.

——, ed. *Pitirim A. Sorokin in Review*. Durham, N.C.: Duke University Press, 1963.

Allers, Rudolf. "Review of *S. O. S.: The Meaning of Our Crisis*." *Commonwealth*, 21 December 1951, 282–283.

Allport, Gordon W. Letter to Elizabeth Gilboy, 31 March 1938. HUA, Records of the Harvard Committee for Research in the Social Sciences.

——. Letter to Paul Buck, 1 October 1943. HUA, Parsons Papers 1930–59, Allport Committee file.

——. "Techniques for Reducing Group Prejudice." In *Forms and Techniques of Altruistic and Spiritual Growth*, edited by Pitirim A. Sorokin. Boston: Beacon Press, 1954.

——. *Waiting for the Lord: 33 Meditations on God and Man*. New York: Macmillan, 1978.

Allport, Gordon, and Edwin G. Boring. "Psychology and Social Relations at Harvard University." *American Psychologist* 1 (April 1946): 119–120.

Allport, Gordon, Clyde Kluckhohn, Hobart Mowrer, Henry Murray, and Talcott Parsons. Letter to Paul S. Buck, 10 June 1943. HUA, Parsons Papers 1930–59, Allport Committee file.

Allport Committee. Letter to the Dean of the Faculty of Arts and Sciences. HUA, Parsons Papers 1930–59, Allport Committee file.

American Sociological Association. "Notes on Procedures for the Committee on Nominations and Elections." October 1962.

Anderson, C. Arnold. Interview with Barry V. Johnston, 14 June 1985. Chicago.

Anderson, Nels. *The Hobo*. Chicago: University of Chicago Press, 1923.

——. "Review of *Principles of Rural-Urban Sociology.*" *New Republic* 60 (1929): 328.

——. Letter to Pitirim A. Sorokin, 23 August 1929. USSA, "A" general file.

Anonymous. "Review of *Principles of Rural-Urban Sociology.*" *Commonweal*, 7 May 1930, 17–18.

——. Letter to James B. Conant, 6 April 1935. HUA, President Conant's Papers.

——. Letter to James B. Conant, 23 July 1935. HUA, President Conant's Papers.

——. "Note on *Sociocultural Causality, Space, Time.*" *American Sociological Review* 8 (August 1943): 497.

——. "Member list, 1963 ASA Committee on Nominations and Elections." Files of Alice F. Myers. American Sociological Association Collection, LC.

——. "1963 Nominations and Elections: Ballot Instructions and *Notes on the Procedures for the Committee on Nominations and Elections.*" Files of Alice B. Myers. American Sociological Association Collection, LC.

——. "Koussevitzky, Sergey Alexandrovich," *The New Grove Dictionary of Music and Musicians*, Stanley Sadie, ed. New York: Macmillan, 1980, 10:219–220.

——. "Handwritten Note Concerning the fate of Sorokin," n.d. LFA.

——. "Review of *Pitirim A. Sorokin in Review* manuscript," n.d. USSA, Philip J. Allen file.

Arnold, Eberhard C. H. "Education for Altruism in the Society of Brothers in Paraguay." In *Forms and Techniques of Altruistic and Spiritual Growth*, edited by Pitirim A. Sorokin. Boston: Beacon Press, 1954.

Aronson, Moses J. Letter to Pitirim A. Sorokin, 10 May 1938. USSA, Moses J. Arsonson file.

Ashley Montagu, M. F. "Letter to the Editor." *American Journal of Sociology* 44 (September 1938): 282–284.

Ausubel, Herman. *Historians and Their Craft: A Study of the Presidential Addresses of the American Historical Association, 1884–1945*. New York: Russell and Russell, 1965.

Bain, Read. Letter to Pitirim A. Sorokin, 23 January 1941. USSA, *American Sociological Review* file.

——. Letter to Pitirim A. Sorokin, 5 March 1941. USSA, *American Sociological Review* file.

——. Letter to Pitirim A. Sorokin, 15 March 1941. USSA, *American Sociological Review* file.

——. "Review of *The Crisis of Our Age.*" *American Sociological Review* 6 (December 1941): 907–909.

——. Letter to Pitirim A. Sorokin, 24 December 1941. USSA, *American Sociological Review* file.

——. "Review of *Man and Society in Calamity*." *American Sociological Review* 8 (February 1943): 91–93.

Bales, Robert F. Letter to Talcott Parsons, n.d. HUA, Parsons Papers.

Bannister, Robert C. *Sociology and Scientism: The American Quest for Objectivity, 1880–1940*. Chapel Hill: University of North Carolina Press, 1987.

Barber, Bernard L. *J. Henderson on the Social System*. Chicago: University of Chicago Press, 1970.

Barnes, Harry Elmer. "Review of *The Sociology of Revolution*." *The Nation*, 10 June 1925, 668–669.

——. "Review of *The Crisis of Our Age*." *American Journal of Sociology* 47 (May 1942): 996–997.

——. "Review of *The Reconstruction of Humanity* and Arnold J. Toynbee, *Civilization on Trial*." *American Sociological Review* 13 (August 1948): 492–494.

——. Comment on *Contemporary Sociological Theories*, n.d. USSA, folder on *Contemporary Sociological Theories*.

Bates, Ernest Sutherland. "Charting the Coming New Age of Faith—An Erudite Russian Scholar Views the Past History of Mankind and Predicts the Future." *New York Herald Tribune*, Book Review Section, 30 May 1937.

Beck, E. Memo to Mr. J. K. Lilly Jr., 20 March 1951. LFA.

Becker, Howard. *Through Values to Social Interpretation*. Durham, N.C.: Duke University Press, 1950.

Bendix, Reinhard. "The Images of Man in the Social Sciences: The Basic Assumptions of Present Day Research." *Commentary* 11 (1951): 187–192.

Berger, Clarence Q. *Fiftieth Anniversary Report*. Cambridge, Mass.: Crimson Printing, 1983.

Bierstedt, Robert. "Nicholas S. Timasheff (1886–1970)." *American Sociologist* 5 (August 1970): 290–291.

——. *Power and Progress: Essays on Sociological Theory*. New York: McGraw-Hill, 1974.

——. *American Sociological Theory: A Critical History*. New York: Academic Press, 1981.

Bigelow, Karl. Letter to Pitirim A. Sorokin, 23 October 1929. USSA, "B" general file.

——. Letter to Pitirim A. Sorokin, 28 April 1930. HUA, Records of the Committee on Sociology and Social Ethics.

——. Letter to R. B. Perry, 4 June 1930. HUA, Records of the Committee on Sociology and Social Ethics.

Black, John D. Letter to Pitirim A. Sorokin, 23 October 1929. USSA, "B" general file.

——. Letter to Pitirim A. Sorokin, n.d. USSA, "B" general file.

——. Letter to L. J. Henderson, 9 February 1937. HUA, Records of the Harvard Committee for Research in the Social Sciences.

——. Letter to Pitirim A. Sorokin, 9 May 1938. HUA, Records of the Harvard Committee for Research in the Social Sciences.

——. Letter to Dumas Malone, 21 July 1938. HUA, Records of the Harvard Committee on Research in the Social Sciences.

Bloom, Anthony. "Yoga and Christian Spiritual Techniques: Somatopsychic Techniques in Orthodox Christianity." In *Forms and Techniques of Altruistic and Spiritual Growth*, edited by Pitirim A. Sorokin. Boston: Beacon Press, 1954.

Blumer, Herbert. "Science Without Concepts." *American Journal of Sociology* 36 (1931): 515–533.

——. Letter to Otis Dudley Duncan, 6 February 1963. USSA, G. S. Basran file.

Bonn, Dorothy. Letter to Talcott Parsons, 2 October 1939. HUA, Parsons Papers 1930–59.

Bram, Joseph. "Review of *Forms and Techniques of Altruistic and Spiritual Growth.*" *Library Journal*, 15 June 1954, 1227.

Brinton, Crane. "Socio-Astrology." *Southern Review* 3 (autumn 1937): 243–266.

——. *The Society of Fellows.* Cambridge, Mass.: Harvard University Press, 1959.

Brown, J. F. "The Position of Psychoanalysis in the Science of Psychology." *Journal of Abnormal and Social Psychology* 35 (1940): 30–43.

Buck, Paul H. Letter to Pitirim A. Sorokin, 16 April 1942. HUA, Records of the Sociology Department 1930–44.

——. Letter to Professors Allport, Kluckhohn, Mowrer, Murray, and Parsons, 11 June 1943. HUA, Parsons Papers 1930–59, Allport Committee file.

——. Letter to Pitirim A. Sorokin, 5 April 1944. HUA, Records of the Sociology Department 1930–44.

——. Letter to Pitirim A. Sorokin, 10 April 1944. HUA, Records of the Sociology Department 1930–44.

——. Letter to Pitirim A. Sorokin, 26 April 1944. HUA, Records of the Sociology Department 1930–44.

——. Letter to Talcott Parsons, 18 August 1945. HUA, Parsons Papers.

——, ed. *Social Sciences at Harvard 1860–1920: From Inculcation to the Open Mind.* Cambridge, Mass.: Harvard University Press, 1965.

Buckley, Walter. "Social Stratification and the Functional Theory of Social Differentiation." *American Sociological Review* 23 (August 1958): 369–375.

——. "A Rejoinder to Functionalist Dr. Davis and Dr. Levy." *American Sociological Review* 24 (February 1959): 84–86.

Buxton, William. *Talcott Parsons and the Capitalist Nation-State.* Toronto: University of Toronto Press, 1985.

Caplovitz, David. "Robert K. Merton as Editor: Review Essay." *Contemporary Sociology* 6 (1977): 142–150.

Carlsson, Gosta. "Sorokin's Theory of Social Mobility." In *Pitirim A. Sorokin in Review,* edited by Philip J. Allen. Durham, N.C.: Duke University Press, 1963.

Carver, Thomas N. *Recollections of an Unplanned Life*. Los Angeles: Ward Ritchie Press, 1949.

Chamberlin, William Henry. *The Russian Revolution*. Vol. 1. New York: Universal Library, 1965.

Chambliss, Rollin. Letter to Pitirim A. Sorokin, 9 November 1960. USSA, Rollin Chambliss file.

Church, Robert L. "The Economists Study Society: Sociology at Harvard 1891–1902." In *Social Sciences at Harvard 1860–1920: From Inculcation to the Open Mind*, edited by Paul Buck. Cambridge, Mass.: Harvard University Press, 1965.

Clark, Ronald M. *Einstein: The Life and Times*. New York: Avon Press, 1972.

Coffey, W. C. Letter to Carle C. Zimmerman, 26 June 1931. USSA, Zimmerman file.

Cohen, I. Bernard. "George Sarton." *ISIS* 48, no. 3 (1957): 286–299.

Committe of Eight. "Records: Initial Mailings by Members of the Committee." January–April 1963. USSA, G. S. Basran file.

——. "Records: Second Wave of Letters and Personal Appeals by the Committee of Correspondence." January–April 1963. USSA, G. S. Basran file.

Conant, James B. Letter to Pitirim A. Sorokin, 20 December 1934. HUA, Records of the Sociology Department 1930–44.

——. Letter to Anonymous, 12 April 1935. HUA, President Conant's Papers.

——. *My Several Lives: Memoirs of a Social Inventor*. New York: Harper and Row, 1970.

Coser, Lewis A. *Masters of Sociological Thought: Ideas in Historical and Social Context*. 2d ed. New York: Harcourt Brace Jovanovich, 1977.

——, ed. *The Idea of Social Structure: Papers in Honor of Robert K. Merton*. New York: Harcourt Brace Jovanovich, 1975.

Coulborn, Rushton. "Social Sciences and the Atomic Age." *Phylon* 9, no. 2 (1948): 166–170.

Cram, George W. Letter to Ralph Barton Perry, 5 October 1927. HUA, Records of the Committee on Concentration in Sociology and Social Ethics.

Crothers, Charles. *Robert K. Merton*. New York: Tavistock, 1987.

Davis, Jerome K. *The Russian Immigrant*. New York: Macmillan, 1922.

Davis, Kingsley. "A Conceptual Analysis of Stratification." *American Sociological Review* 7 (June 1942): 309–321.

——. "Reply." *American Sociological Review* 18 (August 1953): 394–397.

——. "The Abominable Heresy: A Reply to Dr. Buckley." *American Sociological Review* 24 (February 1959): 82–83.

Davis, Kingsley, and Wilbert E. Moore. "Some Principles of Stratification." *American Sociological Review* 10 (1945): 242–249.

Debus, Allen S., ed. *World Who's Who in Science from Antiquity to the Present*. Chicago: Marquis Publishing, 1968.

Devereux, George. "Letter to the Editor." *American Journal of Sociology* 43 (May 1938): 967–969.

——. "Review of *Social and Cultural Dynamics,* Volume 4." *American Anthropologist* 44 (June 1942): 507–510.

Di Lellio, Anna. "Le aspettative sociali di durata: Intervista a Robert K. Merton." *Rassegna Italiana di sociologia* 26 (1985): 3–26.

Dollard, Charles. Letter to Pitirim A. Sorokin, 10 November 1950. USSA, "D" general file.

"Dr. Sorokine Gives Lectures." *Poughkeepsie Evening Star,* 15 January 1924.

"Dr. Sorokine of Russia Gives Talk to Vassar Girls." *Poughkeepsie Evening Star,* 12 January 1924.

"Dr. Sorokine Talks to Vassar Students; Discusses Revolutions." *Poughkeepsie Eagle News,* 9 January 1924.

Duling, G. Harold. Memo to Mr. J. K. Lilly, Mr. Eli Lilly, and Mr. J. K. Lilly III, 28 February 1951. LFA.

——. Letter to Nathan M. Pusey, 12 October 1955. LFA.

Duncan, Beverly, and Otis Dudley Duncan. "Minorities and the Process of Stratification." *American Sociological Review* 33 (1968): 356–364.

Duncan, Otis Dudley. Letter to Wilbert E. Moore, 28 January 1963. USSA, G. S. Basran file.

——. Letter to Herbert Blumer, 4 February 1963. USSA, G. S. Basran file.

——. Letter to the Committee of Eight, 4 February 1963. USSA, G. S. Basran file.

——. Letter to Arnold M. Rose, 4 February 1963. USSA, G. S. Basran file.

——. Letter to Arnold M. Rose, 11 February 1963. USSA, G. S. Basran file.

——. Letter to Nicholas S. Timasheff, 11 March 1963. USSA, G. S. Basran file.

——. Letter to Talcott Parsons, 13 March 1963. USSA, G. S. Basran file.

——. Letter to G. S. Basran, 15 December 1977. USSA, G. S. Basran file.

——. Letter to Barry V. Johnston, 26 September 1984.

——. Telephone interview with Barry V. Johnston, 8 October 1985.

Duncan, Otis Durant. Letter to Pitirim A. Sorokin, 14 June 1967. USSA, Letters of Sympathy file.

——. Letter to Mrs. Sorokin and Sons, 12 March 1968. USSA, Letters of Sympathy file.

Ebersole, Luke. "Review of *S. O.S.: The Meaning of Our Crisis.*" *Crozier Quarterly* 29 (April 1952): 231.

Elkhadem, Hosam. "George Sarton's Correspondence: Sarton and Irenee van der Ghinst." *ISIS* 75 (1975): 36.

Elliott, William Yandell. "Review of Fluctuations of Social Relationships, War and Revolutions." *Harvard Guardian* 2 (November 1937): 13–16.

Emmet, Dorothy. "Alfred North Whitehead." In *International Encyclopedia of the Social Sciences,* edited by David L. Sills. New York: Free Press, 1968.

Eubank, Nancy. *The Russians in America.* Minneapolis, Minn.: Lerner, 1976.

Evans, Mary Alice, and Howard Ensign Evans. *William Morton Wheeler, Biologist.* Cambridge, Mass.: Harvard University Press, 1970.

Faris, Ellsworth. "Review of *The Social System.*" *American Sociological Review* 18 (February 1953): 103–106.

Faris, Robert E. L. "Recollections of a Half Century of Life in the ASA." *American Sociologist* (1981): 51–52.

Ferguson, W. S. Announcement to Chairmen of Departments, 3 June 1941. HUA, Records of the Sociology Department 1930–44.

——. Letter to Pitirim A. Sorokin, 10 June 1941. HUA, Records of the Sociology Department 1930–44.

Fermi, Laura. *Illustrious Immigrants.* Chicago: University of Chicago Press, 1968.

Fine, Gary Alan, and Janet S. Severance. "Great Men and Hard Times: Sociology at the University of Minnesota." *Sociological Quarterly* 26 (spring 1985): 117–134.

Fitch, Robert E. "The Scientist as Priest and Savior." *Christian Century* 75 (26 March 1958): 368–370.

Floud, Jean. "Review of *Fads and Foibles in Modern Sociology and Related Sciences.*" *British Journal of Educational Studies* 1 (November 1957): 84–86.

Ford, James. "Social Ethics 1905–1929." In *The Development of Harvard University Since the Inauguration of President Eliot 1869–1929,* edited by Samuel Eliot Morison. Cambridge, Mass.: Harvard University Press, 1930.

Ford, Joseph. "Sorokin as Philosopher." In *Pitirim A. Sorokin in Review,* edited by Philip J. Allen. Durham, N.C.: Duke University Press, 1963.

——. Letter to Otis Dudley Duncan, 17 April 1963. USSA, G. S. Basran file.

——. "Life and Works of Pitirim Alexandrovich Sorokin (1889–1968)." *International Review of Sociology* 7 (1971): 820–837.

Frances, E. K. "Review of *The Reconstruction of Humanity.*" *American Journal of Sociology* 54 (November 1948): 271–272.

Francis, Roy G. "Third Ballot." Files of Alice F. Myers. American Sociological Association Collection, LC.

Friedricks, Robert W. *A Sociology of Sociology.* New York: Free Press, 1970.

Galpin, Charles J. "The Story of My Drift into Rural Sociology." *Rural Sociology* 2 (December 1937): 416–428.

——. *My Drift into Rural Sociology.* Baton Rouge: Louisiana State University Press, 1938.

——. Letter to Carle C. Zimmerman, 17 January 1938. USSA, Zimmerman file.

——. Letter to Carle C. Zimmerman, 19 January 1938. USSA, Zimmerman file.

Garvey, George. "Kondratieff, N. D." In *The International Encyclopedia of the Social Sciences,* edited by David L. Sills, New York: Macmillan, 1968, 8:443–444.

Giddings, Franklin. "Sociology à la Carte." *Saturday Review of Literature,* 7 August 1927, 21.

Gieryn, Thomas F. *Science and Social Structure: A Festschift for Robert K. Merton.* New York: New York Academy of Sciences, 1980.

Gillian, J. L. "Review of *Man and Society in Calamity*." *Annals of the American Academy of Political and Social Science* 225 (January 1943): 231–232.

Godel, Roger. "The Contemporary Sciences and the Liberative Experience of Yoga." In *Forms and Techniques of Altruistic and Spiritual Growth*, edited by Pitirim A. Sorokin. Boston: Beacon Press, 1954.

Goethals, George W. Interview with Barry V. Johnston, 11 April 1990.

Goldenweiser, Alexander. "Sociologus: A Platonic Dialogue." *Journal of Social Philosophy* 3 (winter 1938): 350–358.

Gordon, Milton. *Social Class in American Sociology*. New York: McGraw-Hill, 1963.

Gotesky, Rubin. "Sociology and the Crisis." *Saturday Review*, 20 December 1941, 20–22.

Gouch, G. P. *History and Historians in the Nineteenth Century*. Boston: Beacon Press, 1959.

Goul, Roman. "N. S. Timasheff (1886–1970)." *Russian Review* 29 (July 1970): 363–365.

Gouldner, Alvin. *The Coming Crisis of Western Sociology*. New York: Basic Books, 1970.

Green, Arnold W. "Review of *The Ways and Power of Love*." *American Journal of Sociology* 60 (May 1955): 600.

Grierson, J. "Review of *The Sociology of Revolution*." *American Journal of Sociology* 7 (1926): 399.

Gurvitch, Georges. "Petrazhitsky, Lev Iosifovich." In *The Encyclopedia of the Social Sciences*, edited by E. R. A. Seligman and A. Johnson. New York: Macmillan, 1932, 12:103–104.

Harris, Marvin. *The Rise of Anthropological Theory*. New York: Thomas Cardwell, 1968.

Hart, Hornell. "Sorokin's Data Versus His Conclusions." *American Sociological Review* 4 (October 1939): 635–646.

Hartshorne, Edward Y. Letter to Talcott Parsons, 30 April n.y. HUA, Parsons Papers 1930–59, E. Y. Hartshorne file.

——. "Report on Sociology A." HUA, Parsons Papers 1930–59, E. Y. Hartshorne file.

Heberle, Rudolf. "Review of *Social Mobility*." *American Journal of Sociology* 34 (July 1928): 219–225.

Hecker, Julius F. *Russian Sociology: A Contribution to the History of Sociological Thought and Theory*. London: Chapman and Hall, 1934.

Heeren, John. "Functional and Critical Sociology: A Study of Two Groups of Contemporary Sociologists." Ph.D. diss., Duke University, 1975.

Henderson, Lawrence J. Letter to John D. Black, 4 January 1937. HUA, Records of the Harvard Committee on Research in the Social Sciences.

——. Letter to A. Lawrence Lowell, 28 February 1940. HUA, Baker Library, L. J. Henderson Papers.

Heyl, Barbara. "The Harvard Pareto Circle." *Journal of the History of the Behavioral Sciences* 4 (1968): 316–334.

Hill, Richard J., and Walter T. Morton. "In Memoriam Harry Alpert 1912–1977." *Public Opinion Quarterly* 42 (spring 1978): 141–142.

Hinkle, Roscoe. "Review of *Sociological Theories of Today.*" *American Journal of Sociology* 72 (January 1967): 413–414.

Hinkle, Roscoe C., and Gisela J. Hinkle. *The Development of Modern Sociology.* New York: Random House, 1954.

The Historical Register of Harvard University 1636–1936. Cambridge, Mass.: Harvard University Press, 1937.

Homans, George C. Letter to Pitirim A. Sorokin, 12 June 1963. LC.

———. "Lawrence J. Henderson." In *International Encyclopedia of the Social Sciences,* edited by David L. Sills. New York: Free Press, 1968.

———. Interview with Patrick Schmidt, 20 October 1977. HUA.

———. *Coming to My Senses: The Autobiography of a Sociologist.* New Brunswick, N.J.: Transaction Books, 1985.

———. Interview with Barry V. Johnston, 11 March 1986.

Hook, Sidney. "History in Swing Rhythm." *The Nation* 145 (July 1937): 48–49.

———. "Review of *The Crisis of Our Age.*" *Books,* 11 January 1942, 10.

———. "Man's Destiny: A Scientific View." *New York Times,* 17 August 1947, 4.

Hooper, Janice H. Letter to Pitirim A. Sorokin, 3 April 1963. LC.

Hoover, Dwight W. "Schlesinger." In *McGraw-Hill Encyclopedia of World Biography,* edited by David I. Eggenberger. New York: McGraw-Hill, 1973.

Horton, Donald. "Review of *Fads and Foibles of Modern Sociology and Related Sciences.*" *American Journal of Sociology* 62 (November 1956): 338–339.

House, Floyd N. "Review of *Social and Cultural Dynamics,* Volume 4." *American Journal of Sociology* 47 (May 1942): 994–996.

———. "Review of *Man and Society in Calamity.*" *American Journal of Sociology* 49 (July 1943): 85.

———. "Review of *Sociocultural Causality, Space, Time.*" *Social Forces* 49 (October 1943): 108–110.

———. "Review of *Society, Culture, and Personality: Their Structure and Dynamics: A System of General Sociology.*" *American Journal of Sociology* 53 (November 1947): 225–226.

———. Comment on *Contemporary Sociological Theories,* n.d. USSA, folder on *Contemporary Sociological Theories.*

———. "Review of *Principles of Rural-Urban Sociology,*" n.d. USSA.

Hunt, Morton. "How Does It Come to Be So?" *New Yorker,* 25 January 1964, 54–55.

Huntington, Ellsworth. "The Social Pyramid." *Saturday Review of Literature,* 3 December 1927, 370.

Hutchinson, E. P. *Immigrants and Their Children 1850–1950.* New York: Russell and Russell, 1976.

Hyde, Robert W., and Harriet M. Kandler. "Altruism in Psychiatric Nursing." In *Forms and Techniques of Altruistic and Spiritual Growth*, edited by Pitirim A. Sorokin. Boston: Beacon Press, 1954.

Jenness, Arthur. "Gordon W. Allport." In *International Encyclopedia of the Social Sciences: Biographical Supplement*, edited by David L. Sills. New York: Free Press, 1979.

Johnson, Harry M. *Sociology: A Systematic Introduction*. New York: Harcourt, Brace, and World, 1960.

Johnston, Barry V. *Russian American Social Mobility: An Analysis of the Achievement Syndrome*. Saratoga, Calif.: Century Twenty One Publishing 1981.

——. "Sorokin and Parsons at Harvard: Institutional Conflict and the Origin of a Hegemonic Tradition." *Journal of the History of the Behavioral Sciences* 22 (April 1986): 107–127.

——. "Persistent Dilemmas in Sociological Theory." *Free Inquiry in Creative Sociology* 14 (May 1986): 17–20.

——. "Pitirim Sorokin and the American Sociological Association: The Politics of a Professional Society." *Journal of the History of the Behavioral Sciences* 23 (April 1987): 103–122.

Johnston, Barry V., Natalia Y. Mandelbaum, and Nikita E. Pokrovsky. "Commentary on Some of the Russian Writings of Pitirim A. Sorokin." *Journal of the History of the Behavioral Sciences* 30 (January 1994): 28–42.

Johnston, S. Paul. "Sikorsky, Igor (Ivan)." In *The Encyclopaedia Britannica*, edited by Daphne Daune and Louise Watson. Chicago: University of Chicago Press, 1988, 10:801–802.

Joslyn, Carl S. "Review of *Social Mobility*." *Quarterly Journal of Economics* 42 (1927–28): 130–139.

——. Letter to Pitirim A. Sorokin, 11 May 1928. USSA, "J" general file.

Kantor, J. R. "Bekhterev, Vladimir." *International Encyclopedia of the Social Sciences* (1922): 2:498–499.

Keller, Robert T. "The Harvard Pareto Circle and the Historical Development of Organization Theory." *Journal of Management* 10 (1984): 193–203.

Kerensky, Alexander. *Russia and History's Turning Point*. New York: Duell, Sloan and Pierce, 1965.

Kirchner, Walter. *A History of Russia*. 6th ed. New York: Barnes and Noble, 1976.

Knight, Frank H. Letter to Pitirim A. Sorokin, 25 May 1937. USSA, *Social and Cultural Dynamics* file.

——. "Interpreting History." *Saturday Review*, 29 May 1937, 5–6.

Kohn, Melvin L. "Cross-National Research as an Analytic Strategy." *American Sociological Review* 52 (February 1988): 713–732.

Kolb, William L. "Review of *Social Philosophies of an Age of Crisis*." *American Sociological Review* 16 (April 1951): 267–268.

Kolegar, Ferdinand. "T. G. Masaryk's Contributions to Sociology." *Journal of the History of the Behavioral Sciences* 3 (January 1967): 27–37.

Krahn, Cornelius, J. Wenfield Fretz, and Robert Kreider. "Altruism in Mennonite Life." In *Forms and Techniques of Altruistic and Spiritual Growth,* edited by Pitirim A. Sorokin. Boston: Beacon Press, 1954.

Kraut, Alan M. *The Huddled Masses: The Immigrant in American Society.* Arlington Heights, Ill.: Harlan Davidson, 1982.

Kuklick, Henrika. "A Scientific Revolution: Sociological Theory in the United States 1930–1945." *Sociological Inquiry* 43 (1973): 3–22.

——. "Boundary Maintenance in American Sociology." *Journal of the History of the Behavioral Sciences* 16 (1980): 201–219.

Lakatos, Imre. "Falsification and the Methodology of Scientific Research Programs." In *Criticism and the Growth of Knowledge,* edited by Imre Lakatos and Alan Musgrave. London: Cambridge University Press, 1970.

Land, W. G. *Harvard University Handbook: An Official Guide.* Cambridge, Mass.: Harvard University Press, 1936.

Landis, Paul H. *Rural Life in Process.* New York: McGraw-Hill, 1948.

Laurie, Arthur. *Sergei Koussevitzky and His Epoch.* Freeport, N.Y.: Books for Libraries Press, 1969.

Lee, Joseph. Letter to the Harvard Corporation, 29 November 1929. HUA, Lowell Papers.

——. Letter to the Harvard Corporation, 9 January 1930. HUA, Lowell Papers.

Leighton, Alexander. *Human Relations in a Changing World.* New York: Dutton, 1949.

Lengerman, Patricia Madoo. "The Founding of the *American Sociological Review:* The Anatomy of a Rebellion." *American Sociological Review* 44 (1979): 185–198.

Lenin, V. I. "Speech at a Rally in Lenin's Honor, November 20, 1918." In *Collected Works of V. I. Lenin,* edited by Jim Riordin. Moscow: Progress Publishers, 1965.

Lerner, Aaron D. "The Valuable Admission of Pitirim Sorokin." In *Collected Works of V. I. Lenin,* edited by Jim Riordin. Moscow: Progress Publishers, 1965.

Levinger, L. J. *A History of Jews in the United States.* Cincinnati: Union of American Hebrew Congregations, 1949.

Levy, Marion. "Functionalism: A Reply to Dr. Buckley." *American Sociological Review* 24 (February 1959): 83–84.

Lilly, Eli. Letter to Pitirim A. Sorokin, 20 April 1942. USSA, Lilly Endowment file.

——. Letter to Pitirim A. Sorokin, 17 April 1946. LFA.

——. Letter to Pitirim A. Sorokin, 17 June 1946. LFA.

——. "The Nemesis of Materialism." *Super Vision* 1 (October 1946): 1.

——. Letter to Pitirim A. Sorokin, 10 December 1948. LFA.

——. Note to Advisors for the Endowment. 15 December 1948, LFA.

——. Letter to Pitirim A. Sorokin, 28 December 1948. LFA.

——. Letter to Pitirim A. Sorokin, 5 January 1949. LFA.

——. Letter to Paul Buck, 17 January 1949. LFA.

——. Letter to Pitirim A. Sorokin, 16 September 1949. LFA.

——. Memo to G. Harold Duling, 29 December 1951. LFA.

——. Letter to Pitirim A. Sorokin, 29 September 1955. LFA.

——. Letter to Pitirim A. Sorokin, 17 January 1962. LFA.

Lilly, J. K., Jr. Memo to E. Beck, 6 March 1951. LFA.

——. Memo to Eli Lilly, 29 March 1951. LFA.

Lilly, Ruth, and Eli Lilly. Letter to Pitirim A. Sorokin, 22 August 1967. LFA.

Lind, Andrew W. "Review of *Social Mobility.*" *American Journal of Sociology* 33 (March 1928): 847.

Lindzey, Gardner. "Henry A. Murray." In *The International Encyclopedia of the Social Sciences: Biographical Supplement,* edited by David L. Sills. New York: Free Press, 1979.

Livingston, Arthur. "Toward Another Civilization: Sorokin Predicts the Replacement of Ours by a Better Order." *New York Times Book Review,* 20 June 1937, 1.

Loomis, Charles P., and J. Allen Beegle. *Rural Social Systems.* New York: Prentice-Hall, 1950.

——. *Rural Sociology: The Strategy of Change.* Englewood Cliffs, N.J.: Prentice-Hall, 1957.

Lowell, A. Lawrence. Letter to Richard C. Cabot, 9 February 1926. HUA, Records of the Committee on Sociology and Social Ethics.

——. Letter to R. C. Cabot, 20 June 1927. HUA, Lowell Papers.

——. Letter to Pitirim A. Sorokin, 25 September 1929. HUA, Lowell Papers.

——. Letter to Pitirim A. Sorokin, 2 October 1929. HUA, Lowell Papers.

——. Letter to Pitirim A. Sorokin, 11 October 1929. HUA, Lowell Papers.

——. Letter to Pitirim A. Sorokin, 22 March 1940. USSA, "L" general file.

Lynd, Robert. *Knowledge for What?* Princeton, N.J.: Princeton University Press, 1939.

MacCracken, Henry Noble. Letter to Pitirim A. Sorokin, 8 November 1923. VCA.

——. Letter to Pitirim A. Sorokin, 2 August 1924. VCA.

——. Letter to Pitirim A. Sorokin, 22 October 1929. USSA, Henry Noble Mac-Cracken file.

——. Letter to Pitirim A. Sorokin, 26 October 1929. USSA, Henry Noble Mac-Cracken file.

——. Letter to Pitirim A. Sorokin, n.d. USSA, Henry Noble MacCracken file.

MacIver, Robert M. *Labor in a Changing World.* New York: Dutton, 1919.

——. *Community.* London: Macmillan, 1920.

——. "Review of *Contemporary Sociological Theories.*" *Annals of the American Academy of Arts and Sciences* 139 (1929): 216.

——. *The Elements of a Social Science.* 1921; London: Methuen, 1949.

——. *Society: Its Structure and Change.* New York: Ray Long and Richard Smith, 1932.

——. "Review of *Social and Cultural Dynamics*, Volume 4." *American Sociological Review* 6 (December 1941): 904–907.

——. *As a Tale That Is Told: The Autobiography of R. M. MacIver*. Chicago: University of Chicago Press, 1968.

Madison, James H. *Eli Lilly: A Life, 1885–1977*. Indianapolis: Indiana Historical Society, 1989.

Marinier, Pierre. "Reflections on Prayer: Its Causes and Psychophysiological Effects." In *Forms and Techniques of Altruistic and Spiritual Growth*, edited by Pitirim A. Sorokin. Boston: Beacon Press, 1954.

Marquis, Albert N., ed. *Who's Who in America 1938–1939*. Chicago: Marquis Publishing, 1939.

Martel, Martin V. "Talcott Parsons." In *The International Encyclopedia of the Social Sciences: Biographical Supplement*, edited by David Sills. New York: Free Press, 1979.

Martindale, Don. "Review of *Sociological Theories of Today*." *Annals of the American Academy of Political and Social Science* 370 (March 1967): 176–177.

——. "Pitirim A. Sorokin: Soldier of Fortune." In *Sorokin and Sociology: Essays in Honour of Pitirim A. Sorokin*, edited by C. C. Hallen and R. Prasad. Agra, India: Satish Book Enterprise, 1972.

——. *The Romance of a Profession: A Case History in the Sociology of Sociology*. St. Paul, Minn.: Wildflower Publishing, 1976.

Masaryk, Thomas G. *Thomas G. Masaryk: Suicide and the Meaning of Civilization*. Translated by William B. Weist and Robert G. Batson. Chicago: University of Chicago Press, 1970.

Maslow, Abraham, ed. *New Knowledge in Human Values*. New York: Harper and Brothers, 1959.

Massie, Robert K. *Nicholas and Alexandra*. New York: Atheneum, 1967.

Matter, Joseph A. *Love, Altruism and the World Crisis: The Challenge of Pitirim Sorokin*. Chicago: Nelson-Hall, 1974.

McCord, William, and Joan McCord. *Origins of Crime: A New Evaluation of the Cambridge-Somerville Youth Study*. New York: Columbia University Press, 1959.

McKenzie, R. D. *The Neighborhood: A Study of Local Life in the City of Columbus, Ohio*. Chicago: University of Chicago Press, 1923.

——. "Review of *Principles of Rural-Urban Sociology*." *American Journal of Sociology* 36 (July 1930): 135–137.

McLaughlin, Richard. "Review of *Fads and Foibles of Modern Sociology and Related Sciences*." *Times Literary Supplement*, 2 November 1956, 651.

Merton, Robert K. *Social Theory and Social Structure*. Revised and enlarged edition. Glencoe, Ill.: Free Press, 1957.

——. Letter to Pitirim A. Sorokin, 11 January 1962. USSA, Robert K. Merton file.

——. Letter to Otis Dudley Duncan, 25 January 1963. USSA, G. S. Basran file.

——. *Social Theory and Social Structure*. Enl. ed. New York: Free Press, 1968.

——. *The Sociology of Science in Europe*. Carbondale: Southern Illinois University Press, 1977.

——. "Remembering the Young Talcott Parsons." 15 *American Sociologist* (1980): 69.

——. Interview with Barry Johnston, 16 November 1984.

——. "George Sarton: Episodic Recollections of an Unruly Apprentice." *ISIS* 76 (December 1985): 470–486.

——. Letter to Barry V. Johnston, 13 February 1987.

——. Letter to Barry V. Johnston, The Authentic Columbus Day, 1994.

Merton, Robert K., and Bernard Barber. "Sorokin's Formulations in the Sociology of Science." In *Pitirim A. Sorokin in Review*, edited by Philip J. Allen. Durham, N.C.: Duke University Press, 1963.

"Minutes of the Sociology Department," 8 December 1945. HUA, Records of the Sociology Department.

"Minutes of the Sociology Department 1931–1945." HUA, Records of the Sociology Department 1930–45.

Mitchell, Wesley C. "A Review of the Findings by the President's Committee on Social Trends." In *Recent Social Trends in the United States*. New York: McGraw-Hill, 1933, 1:xi–lxxv.

Moore, Clifford. Letter to Carl Joslyn, 24 September 1930. HUA, Records of the Sociology Department 1930–44.

——. Letter to A. Lawrence Lowell, 29 May 1931. HUA, Records of the Sociology Department 1930–44.

Moore, Harry E. "Review of *The Reconstruction of Humanity*." *Social Forces* 27 (October 1948): 92–94.

——. "Review of *Social and Cultural Dynamics*, Volume 4." *Social Forces* 20 (March 1942): 400–403.

Moore, Wilbert E. "Comment." *American Sociological Review* 18 (August 1953): 397.

——. Letter to Otis Dudley Duncan, 31 January 1963. USSA, G. S. Basran file.

——. Letter to Harold Wilensky, 2 April 1963. USSA, G. S. Basran file.

——. "Review of *A Long Journey: The Autobiography of Pitirim A. Sorokin*." *American Journal of Sociology* 70 (November 1964): 387.

——. Interview with Barry V. Johnston, 15 November 1985.

——. Telephone conversation with Barry V. Johnston, 25 February 1986.

Morison, Samuel Eliot. *Three Centuries of Harvard 1636–1936*. Cambridge, Mass.: Harvard University Press, 1936.

——, ed. *The Development of Harvard University Since the Inauguration of President Eliot 1869–1929*. Cambridge, Mass.: Harvard University Press, 1930.

Mullins, Nicholas C. *Theory and Theory Groups in Contemporary American Sociology*. New York: Harper and Row, 1973.

Mumford, Lewis. "Insensate Idealogue." *New Republic* 41 (14 July 1937): 283–284.

Murdock, Kenneth B. Letter to Pitirim A. Sorokin, 16 December 1931. HUA, Records of the Sociology Department 1930–44.

——. Letter to Pitirim A. Sorokin, 17 May 1933. HUA, Records of the Sociology Department 1930–44.

——. Letter to Pitirim A. Sorokin, 23 May 1933. HUA, Records of the Sociology Department 1930–44.

——. Letter to Pitirim A. Sorokin, 14 October 1936. HUA, Records of the Sociology Department 1930–44.

Myers, Alice F. "Alice's Files, 1966–1979." American Sociological Association Collection, LC.

National Cyclopedia of American Biography. Clifton, N.J.: James T. White, 1973.

Nelson, Lowry. *Rural Sociology: Its Origins and Growth in the United States.* Minneapolis: University of Minnesota Press, 1969.

——. Letter to Don Martindale, 28 April 1975. Quoted in Martindale, *Romance,* 219.

Newman, Edwin B. Taped interview with Patrick Schmidt, 11 April 1977. HUA.

Nichols, Lawrence T. "Deviance and Social Science: The Instructive Historical Case of Pitirim Sorokin". *Journal of the History of the Behavioral Sciences* 25 (October 1989): 335–355.

——. "The Establishment of Sociology at Harvard: A Case of Organizational Ambivalence and Scientific Vulnerability." In *Science at Harvard University: Historical Perspectives,* edited by Clark A. Elliott and Margaret W. Rossiter, 191–222. Bethlehem, Pa.: Lehigh University Press, 1992.

Nikolaieff, A. N. "Russia from Within." *New York Evening Post,* 3 January 1925.

Nobel, Marjorie. Letter to Talcott Parsons, 13 May 1944. HUA, Records of the Sociology Department 1930–44.

Norman, Charles. *E. E. Cummings: The Magic Maker.* New York: Bobbs-Merrill, 1972.

Northrop, F. S. C. "Philosophical Anthropology and World Law." In *Forms and Techniques of Altruistic and Spiritual Growth,* edited by Pitirim A. Sorokin. Boston: Beacon Press, 1954.

Novak, Michael. *The Rise of the Unmeltable Ethnics.* New York: Macmillan, 1973.

Oberschall, Anthony. "The Institutionalization of American Sociology." In *The Establishment of American Sociology,* edited by Anthony Obershall. New York: Harper and Row, 1972.

Odum, Howard W. Letter to Pitirim A. Sorokin, 5 October 1929. USSA, Howard W. Odum file.

Ogburn, William F. "A Reply." *Journal of Political Economy* 41 (1933): 210–221.

Oromaner, Mark. "The Sociological Community and the Works of Talcott Parsons: 1936–1950." *Journal of the History of Sociology* 1 (1979): 76–92.

Page, Charles. *Fifty Years in the Sociological Enterprise: A Lucky Journey.* Amherst: University of Massachusetts Press, 1982.

Park, Robert E. "Review of *The Sociology of Revolution.*" *Annals of the American Academy of Arts and Sciences* 123 (1926): 230–231.

——. Letter to Pitirim A. Sorokin, 14 October 1936. HUA, Records of the Sociology Department 1930–44, "P" general file.

——. "Review of *Social and Cultural Dynamics.*" *American Journal of Sociology* 43 (March 1938): 824–832.

Parsons, Talcott, trans. *The Protestant Ethic and the Spirit of Capitalism,* by Max Weber. New York: Scribner, 1930.

——. "Wants and Activities in Marshall." *Quarterly Journal of Economics* 46 (1931): 101–140.

——. "Economics and Sociology: Marshall in Relation to the Thought of His Time." *Quarterly Journal of Economics* 46 (1932): 316–347.

——. "Jean Calvin." In *The Encyclopedia of the Social Sciences,* edited by E. R. A. Seligman and A. Johnson. New York: Macmillan, 1933, 3:151–153.

——. "Malthus." In *The Encyclopedia of the Social Sciences,* edited by E. R. A. Seligman and A. Johnson. New York: Macmillan, 1933, 10:68–69.

——. "Pareto." In *The Encyclopedia of the Social Sciences,* edited by E. R. A. Seligman and A. Johnson. New York: Macmillan, 1933, 11:576–578.

——. "Samuel Smiles." In *The Encyclopedia of the Social Sciences,* edited by E. R. A. Seligman and A. Johnson. New York: Macmillan, 1933, 14:111–112.

——. "Service." In *The Encyclopedia of the Social Sciences,* edited by E. R. A. Seligman and A. Johnson. New York: Macmillan, 1933, 13:672–674.

——. "Society." In *The Encyclopedia of the Social Sciences,* edited by E. R. A. Seligman and A. Johnson. New York: Macmillan, 1933, 14:225–232.

——. "Thrift." In *The Encyclopedia of the Social Sciences,* edited by E. R. A. Seligman and A. Johnson. New York: Macmillan, 1933, 14:623–626.

——. "Some Reflections on the Nature and Significance of Economics." *Quarterly Journal of Economics* 48 (1934): 225–231.

——. "H. M. Robertson on Max Weber and His School." *Journal of Political Economy* 43 (1935): 688–696.

——. "The Place of Ultimate Values in Sociological Theory." *International Journal of Ethics* 45 (1935): 282–316.

——. "Sociological Elements in Economic Thought, I." *Quarterly Journal of Economics* 49 (1935): 414–453.

——. "Sociological Elements in Economic Thought, II." *Quarterly Journal of Economics* 49 (1935): 645–667.

——. Letter to Pitirim A. Sorokin, 4 October 1935. HUA, Parsons Papers.

——. Letter to James B. Conant, 28 September 1939. HUA, Parsons Papers.

——. Letter to Robert K. Merton, 23 October 1940. HUA, Parsons Papers 1923–40.

——. Letter to Robert K. Merton, 20 December 1940. HUA, Parsons Papers 1923–40.

——. Letter to Paul S. Buck, 3 April 1944. HUA, Parsons Papers.

——. Letter to Mrs. Nobel, 12 May 1944. HUA, Records of the Sociology Department 1930–44.

——. Letter to Edwin F. Gay, 14 July 1944. HUA, Parsons Papers.

——. Letter to E. Y. Hartshorne, 19 July 1944. HUA, Parsons Papers 1930–59.

——. *The Structure of Social Action.* New York: Free Press, 1949.

——. *The Social System.* Glencoe, Ill.: Free Press, 1951.

——. *The Department of Social Relations at Harvard: Report of the Chairman on the First Decade: 1946–1956.* Cambridge, Mass.: Harvard University Press, 1956.

——. "A Short Account of My Intellectual Development." *Alpha Kappa Deltan* 29 (winter 1959): 3–12.

——. "Christianity and the Modern Industrial Society." In *Sociological Theory, Values and Sociocultural Chance: Essays in Honor of Pitirim A. Sorokin,* edited by Edward A. Tiryakian. New York: Free Press of Glencoe, 1963.

——. "On Building Social Systems Theory: A Personal History." *Daedalus* 99 (1970): 826–881.

Parsons, Talcott, and Edward Shils, eds. *Toward a General Theory of Action.* Cambridge, Mass.: Harvard University Press, 1951.

——. "Related Plans at Other Universities," n.d. HUA, Parsons Papers.

Pattillo, Manning M. "Office Memo Re: Boston Trip," 13–16 September 1956. LFA.

——. Letter to Pitirim A. Sorokin, 22 February 1957. LFA.

——. Letter to Pitirim A. Sorokin, 21 November 1957. LFA.

Perry, Ralph Barton. "Sociology and Social Ethics." Records of the Committee on Sociology and Social Ethics, n.d., p. 3. HUA.

Persell, Caroline Hodges. "An Interview with Robert K. Merton." *Teaching Sociology* 4 (1984): 470–486.

Petrazhitsky, Leon. *Law and Morality.* Translated by Hugh W. Babb. Cambridge, Mass.: Harvard University Press, 1955.

Pfeiffer, John. "A Manner of Speaking: Review of *Fads and Foibles of Modern Sociology and Related Sciences.*" *New York Times,* 21 November 1956, 36.

Powers, Edwin, and Helen Witmer. *An Experiment in the Prevention of Delinquency: The Cambridge-Somerville Youth Study.* New York: Columbia University Press, 1951.

Prall, D. W. "Review of Fluctuations of Forms of Art." *Harvard Guardian,* 2 November 1937, 8–13.

Prescott, Orville. "Review of *Man and Society in Calamity.*" *New York Times,* 26 October 1942.

The President's Research Committee on Recent Social Trends. *Recent Social Trends in the United States:* New York: McGraw-Hill, 1933.

Pusey, Nathan M. Letter to G. Harold Duling, 20 October 1955. LFA.

Randall, John H., Jr. "Fluctuations of the Systems of Truth, Ethics and Law." *American Sociological Review* 2 (December 1937): 921–924.

Records on the Committee on Research in the Social Sciences, HUA.

Reingold, H. A. "The Four Horsemen: Review of *Man and Society in Calamity.*" *Commonwealth*, 30 October 1942, 45–46.

Reiser, Oliver R. "Review of *The Ways and Power of Love.*" *Annals of the American Academy of Political and Social Science* 297 (January 1955): 153–154.

"Report of the Committee on Sociology and Social Ethics on the Organization of a Division and Department of Sociology at Harvard University." 10 February 1931. HUA.

"Report of the Sociology Department." November 1932. HUA, Records of the Sociology Department 1930–44.

Reuter, Edward B. "Review of *Contemporary Sociological Theories.*" *American Journal of Sociology* 34 (1929): 382.

"Review of *Principles of Rural-Urban Sociology.*" *Commonwealth*, 7 May 1930, USSA.

"Review of *Principles of Rural-Urban Sociology.*" *Information Service* 9 (4 January 1930): 1–2. Published by the Federal Council of Churches of Christ in America.

Riley, Matilda White, and Mary E. Moore. "Sorokin's Use of Sociological Measurement." In *Pitirim A. Sorokin in Review*, edited by Philip J. Allen. Durham, N.C.: Duke University Press, 1963.

Riordin, Jim, ed. *Collected Works of V. I. Lenin*. Moscow: Progress Publishers, 1965.

Rischin, Moses. *The Promised City*. Cambridge, Mass.: Harvard University Press, 1967.

Rockafellow, Robert. "Review of *The Reconstruction of Humanity.*" *Annals of the American Academy of Political and Social Science* 260 (September 1948): 165–166.

Rogers, M. R. "Fluctuations of Forms of Art." *American Sociological Review* 2 (December 1937): 919–921.

Rose, Arnold M. Letter to Otis Dudley Duncan, 9 February 1963. USSA, G. S. Basran file.

Rosenquist, Carl M. "Review of *A Systematic Source Book in Rural Sociology.*" *American Economic Review* 22 (March 1932): 175–176.

Ross, Edward A. Letter to Pitirim Sorokin, 16 May 1927. USSA, Mrs. E. A. Ross file.

——. Letter to Pitirim A. Sorokin: 21 October 1929, USSA, Mrs. E. A. Ross file.

——. Comment on *Contemporary Sociological Theories*, n.d. USSA, folder on *Contemporary Sociological Theories*.

——. *Seventy Years of It*. New York: Appleton-Century, 1936.

Roucek, Joseph S. "Masaryk as Sociologist." *Sociology and Social Research* 22 (May–June 1938): 412–420.

Roucek, Joseph S. "Review of *The Crisis of Our Age*, n.d. USSA, Newspaper clipping file.

Roucek, Joseph S. Letter to Pitirim A. Sorokin, 14 September 1941. HUA, Sorokin Correspondence.

Rubinow, I. M. "Are Revolutions Worthwhile?" *New Leader,* 6 June 1925.

Russett, Cynthia E. *The Concept of Equilibrium in American Social Thought.* New Haven, Conn.: Yale University Press, 1966.

"Russian Professor Is Guest at Vassar." *Poughkeepsie Evening Star,* 28 November 1923. VCA.

"Russian Revolutionist Now Is Guest at Vassar College." *Poughkeepsie Evening Star,* 15 December 1923. VCA.

"Russian Speaker Will Be Vassar's Guest Six Weeks." *Poughkeepsie Evening Star,* 12 November 1923. VCA.

"Russia's Famous Cultural and Political Leader to Remain in Poughkeepsie— Watchful Waiting." *Poughkeepsie Evening Star,* 18 January 1924. VCA.

Sadie, Stanley, ed. "Koussevitzky, Sergey Alexandrovich." In *The New Grove Dictionary of Music and Musicians.* Vol. 10. Chicago: University of Chicago Press, 1988.

Sanderson, Dwight. "Review of *A Systematic Source Book in Rural Sociology,* Volume I." *Annals of the American Academy of Political and Social Sciences* 155 (May 1931): 245.

Sarton, May. *I Knew a Phoenix: Sketches for an Autobiography.* New York: Norton, 1954.

———. "An Informal Portrait of George Sarton." *Texas Quarterly* 16 (autumn 1962): 101–112.

Schmidt, Patrick. Interview with Talcott Parsons. Tape 2, Side 1, HUA.

———. "Towards a History of the Department of Social Relations Harvard University, 1946–1972." Honors thesis, Harvard College, 1978.

Schuler, Edgar. Interview with Barry V. Johnston, 3 July 1985.

Schumpeter, Joseph A. Letter to the Harvard Committee on Research in the Social Sciences, 23 December 1936. HUA, Records of the Committee.

———. *Business Cycles: A Theoretical, Historical and Statistical Analysis of the Capitalistic Process.* 2 vols. New York: McGraw-Hill, 1939.

Schwartz, Richard D. "Functional Alternatives to Inequality." *American Sociological Review* 20 (August 1955): 424–430.

Sheperd, H. "Fads for the Dads." *The Hour Glass,* 3 May 1929, 2.

Sikorsky, I. I. Correspondence with Pitirim A. Sorokin 1943–52. USSA, Igor I. Sikorsky file.

Simerenko, Alex. "Social Origin, Revolution and Sociology: The Work of Timasheff, Sorokin and Gurvitch." *British Journal of Sociology* 24 (March 1973): 84–92.

Simpson, Richard L. "Review of *The Ways and Power of Love* and *Forms and Techniques of Altruistic and Spiritual Growth.*" *Social Forces* 33 (March 1955): 296–297.

———. "A Modification of the Functional Theory of Social Stratification." *Social Forces* 35 (December 1956): 132–137.

Smertenko, Johan J. "Review of *Leaves from a Russian Diary.*" *New York Herald Tribune,* 14 March 1925.

Smith, Moses. *Koussevitzky.* New York: Allen, Towne and Heath, 1947.

Smith, Richard Norton. *The Harvard Century: The Making of a University to a Nation.* New York: Simon and Schuster, 1986.

Smith, T. Lynn. *The Sociology of Rural Life.* New York: Harper and Brothers, 1953.

——. "Sorokin's Rural-Urban Principles." In *Pitirim A. Sorokin in Review,* edited by Philip J. Allen. Durham N.C.: Duke University Press, 1963.

Sorokin, Elena. "My Life with Pitirim Sorokin." *International Journal of Contemporary Sociology* 42 (January–April 1975): 1–27.

Sorokin, Pitirim A. Letter to Henry Noble MacCracken, 9 November 1923. VCA.

——. Letter to Henry Noble MacCracken, 17 August 1924. VCA.

——. Letter to Henry Noble MacCracken, 20 October 1924, VCA.

——. "The New Soviet Codes and Soviet Justice." *Michigan Law Review* 29 (November 1924): 38–52.

——. Letter to Henry Noble MacCracken, 28 November 1924. VCA.

——. *The Sociology of Revolution.* Philadelphia: Lippincott, 1925.

——. Letter to Henry Noble MacCracken, 31 January 1925. VCA.

——. "American Millionaires and Multimillionaires." *Social Forces* 4 (May 1925): 627–640.

——. Letter to Henry Noble MacCracken, 16 July 1925. VCA.

——. "Monarchs and Rulers: A Comparative Historical Study." *Social Forces* 4 (September 1925): 22–35.

——. "Russian Sociology in the Twentieth Century." *Publication of the American Sociological Society* 31 (1927): 57–69.

——. *Social Mobility.* New York: Harper and Brothers, 1927.

——. *Contemporary Sociological Theories: Through the First Quarter of the Twentieth Century.* New York: Harper and Row, 1928.

——. "Experimente zur Soziologie." *Zeitschrift für Volkerpsychologie und Soziologie* (March 1928): 1–10.

——. Letter to A. Lawrence Lowell, 28 September 1929. HUA, Lowell Papers.

——. Letter to A. Lawrence Lowell, 7 October 1929. HUA, Lowell Papers.

——. Letter to A. Lawrence Lowell, 16 October 1929. HUA, Lowell Papers.

——. Letter to Karl Bigelow, 13 May 1930. HUA, Records of the Committee on Sociology and Social Ethics.

——. Letter to Carle C. Zimmerman, 8 December 1930. HUA, Records of the Committee on Sociology and Social Ethics.

——. Letter to Carle C. Zimmerman, 19 February 1931. HUA, Records of the Committee on Sociology and Social Ethics.

——. "Sociology as a Science." *Social Forces* 10 (October 1931): 20–27.

——. Letter to President A. Lawrence Lowell, 14 December 1931. HUA, Records of the Sociology Department 1930–44.

——. Letter to Dean Kenneth B. Murdock, 14 December 1931. HUA, Records of the Sociology Department 1930–44.

———. Letter to Dean Kenneth B. Murdock, 17 December 1931. HUA, Records of the Sociology Department 1930–44.

———. "Metabolism of the Different Strata of Social Institutions and Institutional Continuity." *Metron* 1 and 2 (1932): 319–347.

———. "An Experimental Study of the Influence of Suggestion on the Discrimination and Valuation of People." *American Journal of Sociology* 37 (March 1932): 720–737.

———. Letter to A. Lawrence Lowell, 18 June 1932. HUA, Records of the Sociology Department 1930–44.

———. "Rejoinder to Professor Ogburn's Reply." *Journal of Political Economy* 41 (1933): 400–404.

———. "Studien zur Soziologie der Kunst." *Sociologus* (March 1933).

———. *"Recent Social Trends:* A Criticism." *Journal of Political Economy* 41 (April 1933): 194–210.

———. Letter to Dean Kenneth B. Murdock, 22 May 1933. HUA, Records of the Sociology Department 1930–44.

———. Letter to Kenneth B. Murdock, 8 November 1933. HUA, Records of the Sociology Department 1930–44.

———. Letter to Dean Kenneth B. Murdock, 30 January 1934. HUA, Records of the Sociology Department 1930–44.

———. Letter to James B. Conant, 20 March 1934. HUA, Records of the Sociology Department 1930–44.

———. Letter to James B. Conant, 10 October 1934. HUA, Records of the Sociology Department 1930–44.

———. "Annual Reports on the Condition and Activities of the Department of Sociology of Harvard University, 1934–45." HUA, Records of the Sociology Department 1930–44.

———. Letter to Dean Kenneth B. Murdock, 11 January 1935. HUA, Records of the Sociology Department 1930–44.

———. Letter to Otis Durant Duncan, 18 June 1935. USSA, Otis D. Duncan file.

———. Letter to Talcott Parsons, 21 November 1935. HUA, Parsons Papers.

———. "Department of Sociology: Brief Commentaries on Recommendations for 1936–1937," 3 December 1935. HUA, Records of the Sociology Department 1930–44.

———. "The Fluctuations of Idealism and Materialism, from 600 B.C. to 1920 A.D." In *Reine und Angewandte Soziologie*, Eine Festgabe F. Toennies. Leipzig: H. Buske-Verlage, 1936.

———. Letter to Nicholas S. Timasheff, 17 January 1936. HUA, Records of the Sociology Department 1930–44.

———. Letter to Dean George D. Birkhoff, 24 January 1936. HUA, Records of the Sociology Department 1930–44.

———. "Sociology Department 1931–1936." A report sent to President James B. Conant, 30 March 1936. HUA, Records of the Sociology Department 1930–44.

——. Letter to Dean George D. Birkhoff, 17 April 1936. HUA, Records of the Sociology Department 1930–44.

——. Letter to Nicholas S. Timasheff, 20 July 1936. HUA, Records of the Sociology Department 1930–44.

——. Letter to Nicholas S. Timasheff, 10 August 1936. HUA, Records of the Sociology Department 1930–44.

——. "Form and Problems of Culture Integration and Methods of Their Study." *Rural Sociology* (September 1936): 121–141.

——. Letter to James B. Conant, 17 November 1936. HUA, Records of the Sociology Department 1930–44.

——. "Le Concept d'equilibre est-il necessaire aux sciences sociales?" *Revue international de sociologie* 44 (1937).

——. *Social and Cultural Dynamics.* 3 vols. New York: American Book Co., 1937.

——. Letter to E. A. Ross, 18 January 1937. HUA, Records of the Sociology Department 1930–44.

——. Letter to James B. Conant, 25 May 1937. HUA, Records of the Sociology Department 1930–44.

——. Letter to Dean Kenneth B. Murdock, 26 October 1937. HUA, Records of the Sociology Department 1930–44.

——. "Rejoinder to Devereux." *American Journal of Sociology* 43 (May 1938): 969–970.

——. Letter to John D. Black, 8 May 1938. HUA, Records of the Harvard Committee for Research in the Social Sciences.

——. Letter to John D. Black, 11 May 1938. HUA, Records of the Harvard Committee for Research in the Social Sciences.

——. Letter to Moses J. Aronson, 20 May 1938. USSA, Moses J. Aronson file.

——. "A Neglected Factor of War." *American Sociological Review* 3 (August 1938): 475–486.

——. "Histrionics." *Southern Review* 4 (winter 1938): 555–564.

——. "Pseudo-Sociologus: A Reply to Professor Goldenweiser." *Journal of Social Philosophy* 3 (winter 1938): 359–364.

——. Letter to Dean George D. Birkhoff, 15 May 1939. HUA, Records of the Sociology Department 1930–44.

——. "Comments on Professor Hart's Paper." *American Sociological Review* 4 (October 1939): 646–651.

——. Letter to Dean of the Faculty, 14 February 1940. HUA, Sociology Department Annual Reports file.

——. Letter to W. S. Ferguson, 28 February 1940. HUA, Sociology Department Annual Report file.

——. *Crisis of Our Age.* New York: Dutton, 1941.

——. *Social and Cultural Dynamics.* Vol. 4. New York: Bedminster Press, 1941.

——. Letter to Read Bain, 3 March 1941. USSA, *American Sociological Review* file.

——. Letter to Read Bain, 10 March 1941. USSA, *American Sociological Review* file.

——. Letter to W. S. Ferguson, 3 June 1941. HUA, Records of the Sociology Department 1930–44.

——. "Declaration of Independence of the Social Sciences." *Social Science* 16 (July 1941): 221–229.

——. *Man and Society in Calamity.* New York: Dutton, 1942.

——. Letter to Eli Lilly, 23 April 1942. USSA, Lilly Endowment file.

——. *Sociocultural Causality Space, Time.* Durham, N.C.: Duke University Press, 1943.

——. "The Conditions and Prospects of a World Without War." *American Journal of Sociology* 49 (March 1944): 441–449.

——. Letter to Paul S. Buck, 10 April 1944. HUA, Records of the Sociology Department 1930–44.

——. Letter to Paul S. Buck, 11 April 1944. HUA, Records of the Sociology Department 1930–44.

——. Letter to Paul S. Buck, 12 May 1944. HUA, Records of the Sociology Department 1930–44.

——. Letter to Eli Lilly, 11 April 1946. LFA.

——. Letter to Eli Lilly, 1 May 1946. LFA.

——. Letter to Eli Lilly, 14 June 1946. LFA.

——. *Society, Culture, and Personality: Their Structure and Dynamics: A System of General Sociology.* New York: Harper and Brothers, 1947.

——. *The Reconstruction of Humanity.* Boston: Beacon Press, 1948.

——. Letter to Eli Lilly, 14 December 1948. LFA.

——. Letter to Eli Lilly, 31 December 1948. LFA.

——. Letter to Eli Lilly, 5 February 1949. LFA.

——. *Altruistic Love: A Study of American Good Neighbors and Christian Saints.* Boston: Beacon Press, 1950.

——, ed. *Explorations in Altruistic Love and Behavior: Symposium.* Boston: Beacon Press, 1950.

——. *Leaves from a Russian Diary and Thirty Years After.* Enlarged edition. Boston: Beacon Press, 1950.

——. *Social Philosophies of an Age of Crisis.* Boston: Beacon Press, 1950.

——. "Your Family–The Key to Happiness." *American Magazine,* November 1950, 21.

——. Letter to Charles Dollard, 3 November 1950. USSA, "D" general file.

——. "Amitology as an Applied Science of Amity and Unselfish Love." In *Soziologische Forschung In Unserer Zeit,* edited by Karl G. Specht, 277–279. Cologne: West Deutscher Verlag, 1951.

——. "Similarities and Dissimilarities Between Two Sociological Systems," 1951. Unpublished memorandum.

——. *S.O.S.: The Meaning of Our Crisis.* Boston: Beacon Press, 1951.

——. Letter to Rollin Chambliss, 29 November 1951. USSA, Rollin Chambliss file.

——. Letter to Read Bain, 9 December 1952. USSA, Read Bain file.

——. Letter to Eli Lilly, 19 December 1953. LFA.

——, ed. *Forms and Techniques of Altruistic and Spiritual Growth: A Symposium.* Boston: Beacon Press, 1954.

——. *The Ways and Power of Love.* Boston: Beacon Press, 1954.

——. "A Case Against Sexual Freedom." *This Week,* 3 January 1954.

——. Letter to Roy E. Larsen, 4 May 1954. USSA, "Ti–Ty" general file.

——. Letter to Roy E. Larsen, 5 May 1954. USSA, "Ti–Ty" general file.

——. Letter to Eli Lilly, 22 September 1955. LFA.

——. Letter to G. Harold Duling, 3 November 1955. LFA.

——. Letter to Eli Lilly, 18 December 1955. LFA.

——. *Fads and Foibles in Modern Sociology and Related Sciences.* Chicago: Henry Regnery, 1956.

——. "Review of *Introduction to the Study of Law and Morality,*" by Leon Petrazhitsky and translated by Hugh W. Babb. *Harvard Law Review* 69 (1956): 1150–1157.

——. "Tentative Plan of Long and Short Range Research of the Research Society of Creative Altruism," 1 March 1956, LFA.

——. *The American Sex Revolution.* Boston: Porter Sargent, 1957.

——. "Integralism Is My Philosophy." In *This Is My Philosophy,* edited by Whit Burnett. New York: Harper and Brothers, 1957.

——. "Letter to the Editor: *Fads and Foibles in Modern Sociology.*" *American Journal of Sociology* 62 (March 1957): 515.

——. Letter to Eli Lilly, 18 October 1957, LFA.

——. "Studies of the Harvard Research Center in Creative Altruism." Cambridge, Mass.: Harvard University Press, 1959.

——. Letter to Otis Dudley Duncan, 21 January 1960. USSA, Otis D. Duncan file.

——. Letter to Harry Alpert, 7 November 1960. USSA, *American Sociological Review* file.

——. Letter to Rollin Chambliss, 7 November 1960. USSA, Rollin Chambliss file.

——. *A Long Journey: The Autobiography of Pitirim A. Sorokin.* New Haven, Conn.: College and University Press, 1963.

——. *Modern Historical and Social Philosophies.* New York: Dover, 1963.

——. "Reply to My Critics." In *Pitirim A. Sorokin in Review,* edited by Philip J. Allen. Durham, N.C.: Duke University Press, 1963.

——. "Sociology of My Mental Life." In *Pitirim A. Sorokin in Review,* edited by Philip J. Allen. Durham, N.C.: Duke University Press, 1963.

——. Letter to George C. Homans, 15 June 1963. LC.

——. *The Basic Trends of Our Times.* New Haven, Conn.: College and University Press, 1964.

——. Letter to Otis Dudley Duncan, 8 January 1965. USSA, G. S. Basran file.

——. Letter to Otis Dudley Duncan, 21 January 1965. LC.

———. "Sociology of Yesterday, Today and Tomorrow." *American Sociological Review* 30 (December 1965): 833–843.

———. *Sociological Theories of Today.* New York: Harper and Row, 1966.

———. *Social and Cultural Dynamics.* Vol. 4. New York: Bedminster Press, 1967.

———. Letter to Mr. and Mrs. Eli Lilly, 26 June 1967. USSA.

———. Letter to Mr. and Mrs. Eli Lilly, 17 December 1967. LFA.

———. Letter to My Wonderful Friends (Mr. and Mrs. Eli Lilly), 2 February 1968. LFA.

———. "Rejoinder." In *Power and Progress,* edited by Robert Bierstedt. New York: McGraw-Hill, 1974.

———. *Hunger as a Factor in Human Affairs.* Gainesville: University of Florida Press, 1975.

———. "Harvard Research Center in Creative Altruism," n.d. Privately duplicated.

———. "Life-Span, Age-Composition, and Mortality of Social Organizations." *Mensch en Maatschappij* 9e, Jaargang, nos. 1 and 2 (n.d.).

———. "Soziale Bewehungsvorgange." *Kolner Vierteljahrshefte f. Soziologie.* Jahrgang VII (n.d.): Heft 2.

Sorokin, Pitirim A., Sheldon S. Glueck, and Gordon W. Allport. "James Ford." *Harvard University Gazette* 40 (30 December 1944): 95–96.

Sorokin, Pitirim A., and Walter A. Lunden. *Power and Morality: Who Shall Guard the Guardians?* Boston: Porter Sargent, 1959.

Sorokin, Pitirim S., and Robert K. Merton. "The Course of Arabian Intellectual Development 700–1300 A.D. A Study in Method." *ISIS,* February 1935, 516–524.

Sorokin, Pitirim A., and Robert K. Merton. "Social Time: Methodological and Functional Analysis." *American Journal of Sociology* 42 (March 1937): 615–629.

Sorokin, Pitirim A., Mamie Tanquist, Mildred Parten, and Mrs. C. C. Zimmerman. "An Experimental Study of the Efficiency of Work in Various Specified Conditions." *American Journal of Sociology* 35 (March 1930): 765–782.

Sorokin, Pitirim A., and Carle C. Zimmerman. *Principles of Rural-Urban Sociology.* New York: Henry Holt, 1929.

Sorokin, Pitirim A., Carle C. Zimmerman, and Charles J. Galpin. *A Systematic Source Book in Rural Sociology.* 3 Vols. Minneapolis: University of Minnesota Press, 1930, 1931, 1932.

"Sorokin's Views of Russia's Fate." *Poughkeepsie Courier,* 28 December 1923.

"Soviet Russia Will Continue Under Present Rulers, Belief of Professor Sorokin: Life of Government, However, Will End Within Three Years, Noted Sociologist Says; Addresses Rotary Club." *Poughkeepsie Eagle News,* 24 January 1924.

Speier, Hans. "Fluctuations of Social Relationships, War and Revolutions." *American Sociological Review* 2 (December 1937): 924–929.

Spektorski, E. "Maksim Maksimovich Kovalevsky." In *The Encyclopedia of the Social Sciences,* edited by E. R. A. Seligman and A. Johnson, New York: Macmillan, 1932, 8:595–596.

Stark, Rodney. *Social Problems.* New York: Random House, 1975.

Stark, Werner. "In Search of Tradition." *Trans-Action* 4 March 1967): 54–55.

Stone, Lawrence. "Prosopography." *Daedalus* 100 (1971): 46–79.

Storer, Norman W. "Introduction." In *Robert K. Merton: The Sociology of Science: Theoretical and Emprical Investigations,* edited by Norman W. Storer. Chicago: University of Chicago Press, 1973.

Sutherland, E. H. Letter to Pitirim A. Sorokin, 26 October 1929. USSA, "Su–Sz" general file.

Suzuki, Eitaro. "Review of *A Systematic Source Book in Rural Sociology.*" *Proceedings of the Japanese Sociological Society* 2 (November 1931): 124–146.

Sykes, Gresham. "Review of *Fads and Foibles in Modern Sociology and Related Sciences.*" *American Sociological Review* 21 (October 1956): 633–634.

Synnott, Marcia G. *The Half-Opened Door: Discrimination and Admissions at Harvard, Yale, and Princeton, 1900–1970.* Westport, Conn.: Greenwood Press, 1979.

Sztompka, Piotr. *Robert K. Merton: An Intellectual Profile.* New York: St. Martin's Press, 1986.

Taeuber, Conrad. Letter to Talcott Parsons, 3 May 1968. HUA, Parsons Papers.

Taussig, Frank W. Letter to Pitirim A. Sorokin, 4 February 1928. USSA, "Ta–Th" general file.

——. Letter to Pitirim A. Sorokin, 12 July 1929. USSA, "Ta–Th" general file.

——. "Economics at Harvard 1871–1929." In *The Development of Harvard University Since the Inauguration of President Eliot 1869–1929,* edited by Samuel Eliot Morison. Cambridge, Mass.: Harvard University Press, 1930.

Taylor, Carl C. "Review of *A Systematic Source Book in Rural Sociology.*" *American Journal of Sociology* 37 (January 1932): 657–660.

Taylor, O. H. Letter to John D. Black, n.d. HUA, Records of the Harvard Committee on Research in the Social Sciences.

Thackray, Arnold, and Robert K. Merton. "On Discipline Building: The Paradoxes of George Sarton." *ISIS* 63 (1972): 473–495.

Thompson, J. Mark. "Experimentation with the Technique of Good Deeds in Transformation of Inimical into Amicable Relationships." In *Forms and Techniques of Altruistic and Spiritual Growth,* edited by Pitirim A. Sorokin. Boston: Beacon Press, 1954.

Tibbs, A. E. "Book Reviews of *Social and Cultural Dynamics:* A Study in Wissenssoziologie." *Social Forces* 21 (May 1943): 473–480.

Timasheff, Nicholas S. Letter to Carle C. Zimmerman, 4 March 1936. HUA, Records of the Sociology Department 1930–44.

——. Letter to Pitirim A. Sorokin, 31 July 1936. HUA, Records of the Sociology Department 1930–44.

——. "Review of *The Crisis of Our Age.*" *Thought* 16 (December 1941): 610–612.

——. "Review of *Society, Culture, and Personality: Their Structure and Dynamics: A System of General Sociology.*" *Thought* (1947): 610–611.

——. *Sociological Theory: Its Nature and Growth.* New York: Random House, 1955.

——. "Sorokin on Law, Revolution, War, and Social Calamities." In *Pitirim A. Sorokin in Review,* edited by Philip J. Allen. Durham, N.C.: Duke University Press, 1963.

——. Letter to Otis Dudley Duncan, 7 March 1963. USSA, G. S. Basran file.

——. *An Introduction to the Sociology of Law.* Westport, Conn.: Greenwood Press, 1974.

Tiryakian, Edward A. "Review of *A Long Journey: The Autobiography of Pitirim A. Sorokin.*" *American Sociological Review* 29 (August 1964): 603–604

——. "Hegemonic Schools and the Development of Sociology." In *Structures of Knowing: Current Studies in the Sociology of Schools,* edited by Richard C. Monk, 417–441. Lanham, Md.: University Press of America, 1986.

——. "The Significance of Schools in the Development of Sociology." In *Contemporary Issues in Theory and Research,* edited by William E. Snizek et al. Westport, Conn.: Greenwood Press, 1979.

——. "Post-Parsonian Sociology." *Humboldt Journal of Social Relations* 7 (1979/1980): 17–33.

——. "Sociology's Dostoyevski: Pitirim A. Sorokin." *The World & I* 3 (September 1988): 569–581.

——, ed. *Sociological Theory, Values, and Sociocultural Change: Essays in Honor of Pitirim A. Sorokin.* New York: Free Press of Glencoe, 1963.

Toynbee, Arnold J. "Sorokin's Philosophy of History." In *Pitirim A. Sorokin in Review,* edited by Philip J. Allen. Durham, N.C.: Duke University Press, 1963.

Tumin, Melvin. "Some Principles of Stratification: A Critical Analysis." *American Sociological Review* 18 (August 1953): 387–394.

——. "Reply to Kingsley Davis." *American Sociological Review* 18 (December 1953): 672–673.

——. "Rewards and Task Orientations." *American Sociological Review* 20 (August 1955): 419–423.

U.S. Department of Commerce/Bureau of the Census. *Historical Statistics of the United States: From Colonial Times to 1957.* Washington, D.C.: U. S. Government Printing Office, 1960.

Usher, Abbot Payson. "Review of *Fluctuations of Systems of Truths, Ethics and Law.*" *Harvard Guardian* 2 (November 1937): 5–8.

Utechin, S. V. *A Concise Encyclopedia of Russia.* New York: Dutton, 1964.

Veber, B. G. "Kovalevsky, Maksim Maksimovitch." In *The Great Soviet Encyclopedia,* edited by A. M. Prokhorov. New York: Macmillan, 1973, 12:620–621.

Vexliard, Alexandre. "Sorokin's Psychological Theories." In *Pitirim A. Sorokin in Review,* edited by Philip J. Allen. Durham, N.C.: Duke University Press, 1963.

Vidich, Arthur K., and Stanford M. Lyman. *American Sociology: Worldly Rejections of Religion and Their Directions.* New Haven, Conn.: Yale University Press, 1985.

Vogel, Ezra F. "Obituary for George Caspar Homans (1910–1990)." *Footnotes,* December 1990, 14.

Volkart, E. H. Letter to Mr. and Mrs. Eli Lilly, 17 September 1967. LC.

Wertsman, Vladimir. *The Russians in America: A Chronology and Factbook.* New York: Oceania Publications, 1977.

Wetmore, Louis H. "Review of *Leaves from a Russian Diary.*" *Commonwealth,* 4 March 1925, 469–470.

Wiley, Norbert. "The Rise and Fall of Dominating Theories in American Sociology." In *Contemporary Issues in Theory and Research,* edited by W. E. Shizek et al. Westport, Conn.: Greenwood Press, 1979.

Williams, Robin, Jr. "Pitirim A. Sorokin: Master and Prophet." In *Sociological Traditions from Generation to Generation,* edited by R. K. Merton and M. W. Riley. Norwood, N.J.: Abex, 1980.

——. Interview with Barry V. Johnston, summer 1985.

Wilson, E. B. Letter to James B. Conant, 8 December 1934. HUA, President Conant's Papers.

——. Letter to Elizabeth Gilboy, 31 March 1938. HUA, Records of the Harvard Committee for Research in the Social Sciences.

Wineberg, Julius. *Edward Alsworth Ross.* Madison: State Historical Society of Wisconsin, 1972.

Wirth, Louis. *The Ghetto.* Chicago: University of Chicago Press, 1928.

Wolfe, A. B. "Review of *Contemporary Sociological Theories.*" *American Economic Review* 15 (1929): 715.

Wolfe, Bertram D. *Three Who Made a Revolution.* New York: Dell, 1964.

Wolff, Kurt H. "Review of *Sociocultural Causality, Space, Time.*" *American Journal of Sociology* 49 (March 1944): 481–484.

Woodward, Kenneth L. *Making Saints: How the Catholic Church Determines Who Becomes a Saint, Who Doesn't, and Why.* New York: Simon and Schuster, 1990.

Zimmerman, Carle C. Letter to Charles J. Galpin, 3 January 1938. USSA.

——. Letter to Charles J. Galpin, 28 January 1938. USSA.

——. "My Sociological Career." *Revue internationale de sociologie* 9 (April–August 1973): 89–117.

Zorbaugh, Harvey W. *The Gold Coast and the Slum.* Chicago: University of Chicago Press, 1929.

Zukav, Gary. *The Dancing Wu Li Masters: An Overview of the New Physics.* New York: Bantam, 1979.

Index

Abbott, Wilbur C., 35
Abel, Theodore, 202, 203
Abolition of Poverty (Ford), 89
Adams House Group (Harvard), 95,
    96–97, 161
AEA (American Economic Association),
    50
Agricultural Academy (Czarskoe Selo), 18
Agriculture, Department of, 41, 45,
    292(n22)
Alberle, David, 160
"Alleged Liberal Myth of Harvard"
    (Cambridge Teachers' Union), 91
Allen, Philip J., 232–233
Allers, Rudolf, 203
Allport, Gordon W., 65, 71, 130, 135,
    136, 137, 150, 157, 158, 186,
    197–198, 220, 223, 312(n24)
Alpert, Harry, 230–231
Altruism, 10, 22, 167, 168, 175, 176–180,
    190, 192, 195–196, 204, 219, 271
    defined, 177
    ego-centered, 194, 199
    integration levels, 198
    sociologists' interest in, 214, 220
    See also Harvard Research Center in
        Creative Altruism
Altruistic Love: A Study of American Good
    Neighbors and Christian Saints
    (Sorokin), 183–185
American Economic Association (AEA),
    50
American Economic Review, 39, 47
American Journal of Sociology, 35, 39, 43,
    51–52, 73, 204, 212, 213, 246
    and University of Chicago, 164–165
    See also *American Sociological Review*
American Occupational Structure, The
    (Blau, Duncan, and Tyree), 268
American Sex Revolution, The (Sorokin),
    217, 218–219, 245

American Society (Williams), 164
American Sociological Association (ASA),
    86, 229–230, 231, 246–254, 268,
    332(n65)
"American Sociological Forum, The,"
    series proposal, 232–234
American Sociological Review, 28, 118, 120,
    142, 149, 165, 173, 228, 230, 246,
    265
American Sociological Society, 49–50,
    53, 60, 61, 86, 140, 149
    and University of Chicago, 28, 164–165
Amherst College, 93
Amitology, 191, 192, 202
Anderle, Othmar, 223, 235, 237–238,
    262
Anderson, C. Arnold, 31, 32, 45, 79, 91,
    247, 270
Anderson, Nels, 43
Annals of the American Academy of Arts and
    Sciences, 39
Annals of the American Academy of Political
    and Social Science, 187
Anthropology, 10, 222. See also Harvard,
    Department of Anthropology
Arabian intellectual development, 85
Arnold, C. H. Eberhard, 196
Arnold, Melvin, 217
Aronson, Moses, 116
Asch, Soloman, 73
Ashley Montagu, M. F., 147, 186
Ayers, Clarence, 94

Bain, Read, 142–143, 149, 169, 232
Bakhemetiev, B. A., 23
Bakke, E. Wright, 88–89
Bales, Robert Freed, 139, 228, 270
Barbar, Elinor, 245
Barber, Bernard, 160, 226, 233,
    241–244, 245, 261
Barnes, Harry Elmer, 35, 38, 148, 187
Barnes, Irene, 31

367